SUNBEAM TIGER AND ALPINE
Gold Portfolio
1959~1967

Compiled by
R.M. Clarke

ISBN 1 870642 49X

Distributed by
Brooklands Book Distribution Ltd.
'Holmerise', Seven Hills Road,
Cobham, Surrey, England
Printed in Hong Kong

BROOKLANDS BOOKS

BROOKLANDS BOOKS SERIES
AC Ace & Aceca 1953-1983
AC Cobra 1962-1969
Alfa Romeo Alfasud 1972-1984
Alfa Romeo Alfetta Coupes GT.GTV.GTV6 1974-1987
Alfa Romeo Giulia Berlinas 1962-1976
Alfa Romeo Giulia Coupés 1963-1976
Alfa Romeo Spider 1966-1987
Allard Gold Portfolio 1937-1958
Alvis Gold Portfolio 1919-1967
Aston Martin Gold Portfolio 1972-1985
Austin Seven 1922-1982
Austin A30 & A35 1951-1962
Austin Healey 3000 1959-1967
Austin Healey 100 & 3000 Collection No. 1
Austin Healey 'Frogeye' Sprite Collection No. 1
Austin Healey Sprite 1958-1971
Avanti 1962-1983
BMW Six Cylinder Coupés 1969-1975
BMW 1600 Collection No. 1
BMW 2002 1968-1976
Bristol Cars Gold Portfolio 1946-1985
Buick Automobiles 1947-1960
Buick Riviera 1963-1978
Cadillac Automobiles 1949-1959
Cadillac Automobiles 1960-1969
Cadillac Eldorado 1967-1978
Camaro 1966-1970
Chevrolet Camaro & Z-28 1973-1981
High Performance Camaros 1982-1988
Chevrolet Camaro Collection No. 1
Chevrolet 1955-1957
Chevrolet Impala & SS 1958-1971
Chevelle & SS 1964-1972
Chevy II Nova & SS 1962-1973
High Performance Corvettes 1983-1989
Chrysler 300 1955-1970
Citroen Traction Avant 1934-1957
Citroen DS & ID 1955-1975
Citroen 2CV 1948-1988
Cobras & Replicas 1962-1983
Cortina 1600E & GT 1967-1970
Corvair 1959-1968
Daimler Dart & V-8 250 1959-1969
Datsun 240Z 1970-1973
Datsun 280Z & ZX 1975-1983
De Tomaso Collection No. 1
Dodge Charger 1966-1974
Excalibur Collection No. 1
Ferrari Cars 1946-1956
Ferrari Dino 1965-1974
Ferrari Dino 308 1974-1979
Ferrari 308 & Mondial 1980-1984
Ferrari Collection No. 1
Fiat-Bertone X1/9 1973-1988
Fiat Pininfarina 124+2000 Spider 1968-1985
Ford Automobiles 1944-1959
Ford Fairlane 1955-1970
Ford Falcon 1960-1970
Ford RS Escort 1968-1980
Honda CRX 1983-1987
High Performance Escorts MkI 1968-1974
High Performance Escorts MkII 1975-1980
High Performance Mustangs 1982-1988
Hudson & Railton Cars 1936-1940
Jaguar Cars 1957-1961
Jaguar Cars 1961-1964
Jaguar XK120 XK140 XK150 Gold Portfolio 1948-1960
Jaguar MK2 1959-1969
Jaguar E-Type Gold Portfolio 1961-1971
Jaguar E-Type 1966-1971
Jaguar E-Type V12 1971-1975
Jaguar XJ6 1968-1972
Jaguar XJ6 Series II 1973-1979
Jaguar XJ6 & XJ12 Series III 1979-1985
Jaguar XJ12 1972-1980
Jaguar XJS Gold Portfolio 1975-1988
Jensen Cars 1946-1967
Jensen Cars 1967-1979
Jensen Interceptor Gold Portfolio 1966-1986
Jensen Healey 1972-1976
Lamborghini Cars 1964-1970
Lamborghini Cars 1970-1975
Lamborghini Countach Collection No. 1
Lamborghini Countach & Urraco 1974-1980
Lamborghini Countach & Jalpa 1980-1985
Lancia Stratos 1972-1985
Land Rover 1948-1973
Land Rover Series II & IIa 1958-1971
Land Rover Series III 1971-1985
Land Rover 90 & 110 1983-1989
Land Rover 90 & 110 1983-1989
Lotus Cortina 1963-1970
Lotus Elan Gold Portfolio 1962-1974
Lotus Elan Collection No. 2
Lotus Elite 1957-1964
Lotus Elite & Eclat 1974-1981
Lotus Turbo Esprit 1980-1986
Lotus Europa 1966-1975
Lotus Europa Collection No. 1
Lotus Seven 1957-1980
Lotus Seven Collection No. 1
Marcos Cars 1960-1988
Maserati 1965-1970
Maserati 1970-1975
Marcos Cars 1960-1988
Mazda RX-7 Collection No. 1
Mercedes 190 & 300SL 1954-1963
Mercedes 230/250/280SL 1963-1971
Mercedes 350/450SL & SLC 1971-1980
Mercedes Benz Cars 1949-1954
Mercedes Benz Cars 1954-1957
Mercedes Benz Cars 1957-1961
Mercedes Benz Competition Cars 1950-1957
Metropolitan 1954-1962
MG TC 1945-1949
MG TD 1949-1953
MG TF 1953-1955
MG Cars 1957-1959
MG Cars 1959-1962
MG Midget 1961-1980
MGA Collection No. 1
MGA Roadsters 1955-1962
MGB Roadsters 1962-1980
MGB GT 1965-1980
Mini Cooper 1961-1971
Morgan Cars 1960-1970
The Morgan 3-Weeeler Gold Portfolio 1910-1952
Morgan Cars Gold Portfolio 1968-1989
Morris Minor Collection No. 1
Olosmobile Automobiles 1955-1963
Old's Cutlass & 4-4-2 1964-1972
Oldsmobile Toronado 1966-1978
Opel GT 1968-1973
Packard Gold Portfolio 1946-1958
Pantera 1970-1973
Pantera & Mangusta 1969-1974
Plymouth Barracuda 1964-1974
Pontiac Fiero 1984-1988
Pontiac GTO 1964-1970
Pontiac Firebird 1967-1973
Pontiac Firebird and Trans-Am 1973-1981
High Performance Firebirds 1982-1988
Pontiac Tempest & GTO 1961-1965
Porsche Cars 1960-1964
Porsche Cars 1964-1968
Porsche Cars 1968-1972
Porsche Cars in the Sixties
Porsche Cars 1972-1975
Porsche 911 1965-1969
Porsche 911 1970-1972
Porsche 911 1973-1977
Porsche 911 Carrera 1973-1977
Porsche 911 SC 1978-1983
Porsche 911 Turbo 1975-1984
Porsche 914 Gold Portfolio 1969-1976
Porsche 914 Collection No. 1
Porsche 924 Gold Portfolio 1975-1988
Porsche 928 1977-1989
Porsche 944 1981-1985
Reliant Scimitar 1964-1986
Riley 1½ & 2½ Litre Gold Portfolio 1945-1955
Rolls Royce Silver Cloud 1955-1965
Rolls Royce Silver Shadow 1965-1980
Range Rover Gold Portfolio 1970-1988
Rover 3 & 3.5 Litre 1958-1973
Rover P4 1949-1959
Rover P4 1955-1964
Rover 2000 + 2200 1963-1977
Rover 3500 1968-1976
Rover 3500 & Vitesse 1976-1986
Saab Sonett Collection No. 1
Saab Turbo 1976-1983
Studebaker Hawks & Larks 1956-1963
Sunbeam Tiger and Alpine Gold Portfolio 1959-1967
Thunderbird 1955-1957
Thunderbird 1958-1963
Thunderbird 1964-1976
Toyota MR2 1984-1988
Triumph 2000-2.5-2500 1963-1977
Triumph Spitfire 1962-1980
Triumph Spitfire Collection No. 1
Triumph Stag 1970-1980
Triumph Stag Collection No. 1
Triumph TR2 & TR3 1952-1960
Triumph TR4.TR5.TR250 1961-1968
Triumph TR6 1969-1976
Triumph TR6 Collection No. 1
Triumph TR7 & TR8 1975-1982
Triumph GT6 1966-1974
Triumph Vitesse & Herald 1959-1971
TVR Gold Portfolio 1959-1988
Volkswagen Cars 1936-1956
VW Beetle 1956-1977
VW Beetle Collection No. 1
VW Golf GTi 1976-1986
VW Karmann Ghia 1955-1982
VW Scirocco 1974-1981
VW Bus-Camper-Van 1954-1967
VW Bus-Camper-Van 1968-1979
VW Bus-Camper-Van 1979-1989
Volvo 1800 1960-1973
Volvo 120 Series 1956-1970

BROOKLANDS MUSCLE CARS SERIES
American Motors Muscle Cars 1966-1970
Buick Muscle Cars 1965-1970
Camaro Muscle Cars 1966-1972
Capri Muscle Cars 1969-1983
Chevrolet Muscle Cars 1966-1972
Dodge Muscle Cars 1967-1970
Mercury Muscle Cars 1966-1971
Mini Muscle Cars 1961-1979
Mopar Muscle Cars 1964-1967
Mopar Muscle Cars 1968-1971
Mustang Muscle Cars 1967-1971
Shelby Mustang Muscle Cars 1965-1970
Oldsmobile Muscle Cars 1964-1970
Plymouth Muscle Cars 1966-1971
Pontiac Muscle Cars 1966-1972
Muscle Cars Compared Book 2 1965-1971

BROOKLANDS ROAD & TRACK SERIES
Road & Track on Alfa Romeo 1949-1963
Road & Track on Alfa Romeo 1964-1970
Road & Track on Alfa Romeo 1971-1976
Road & Track on Alfa Romeo 1977-1989
Road & Track on Aston Martin 1962-1984
Road & Track on Auburn Cord & Duesenberg 1952-1984
Road & Track on Audi 1952-1980
Road & Track on Audi 1980-1986
Road & Track on Austin Healey 1953-1970
Road & Track on BMW Cars 1966-1974
Road & Track on BMW Cars 1975-1978
Road & Track on BMW Cars 1979-1983
Road & Track on Cobra, Shelby & Ford GT40 1962-1983
Road & Track on Corvette 1953-1967
Road & Track on Corvette 1968-1982
Road & Track on Corvette 1982-1986
Road & Track on Datsun Z 1970-1983
Road & Track on Ferrari 1950-1968
Road & Track on Ferrari 1968-1974
Road & Track on Ferrari 1975-1981
Road & Track on Ferrari 1981-1984
Road & Track on Fiat Sports Cars 1968-1987
Road & Track on Jaguar 1950-1960
Road & Track on Jaguar 1961-1968
Road & Track on Jaguar 1968-1974
Road & Track on Jaguar 1974-1982
Road & Track on Jaguar 1983-1989
Road & Track on Lamborghini 1964-1985
Road & Track on Lotus 1972-1981
Road & Track on Maserati 1952-1974
Road & Track on Maserati 1975-1983
Road & Track on Mazda RX7 1978-1986
Road & Track on Mercedes 1952-1962
Road & Track on Mercedes 1963-1970
Road & Track on Mercedes 1971-1979
Road & Track on Mercedes 1980-1987
Road & Track on MG Sports Cars 1949-1961
Road & Track on MG Sports Cars 1962-1980
Road & Track on Mustang 1964-1977
Road & Track on Peugeot 1955-1986
Road & Track on Pontiac 1960-1983
Road & Track on Porsche 1951-1967
Road & Track on Porsche 1968-1971
Road & Track on Porsche 1972-1975
Road & Track on Porsche 1975-1978
Road & Track on Porsche 1979-1982
Road & Track on Porsche 1982-1985
Road & Track on Porsche 1985-1988
Road & Track on Rolls Royce & Bentley 1950-1965
Road & Track on Rolls Royce & Bentley 1966-1984
Road & Track on Saab 1955-1985
Road & Track on Toyota Sports & GT Cars 1966-1986
Road & Track on Triumph Sports Cars 1953-1967
Road & Track on Triumph Sports Cars 1967-1974
Road & Track on Triumph Sports Cars 1974-1982
Road & Track on Volkswagen 1951-1968
Road & Track on Volkswagen 1968-1978
Road & Track on Volkswagen 1978-1985
Road & Track on Volvo 1957-1974
Road & Track on Volvo 1975-1985
Road & Track Henry Manney at Large & Abroad

BROOKLANDS CAR AND DRIVER SERIES
Car and Driver on BMW 1955-1977
Car and Driver on BMW 1977-1985
Car and Driver on Cobra, Shelby & Ford GT40 1963-1984
Car and Driver on Datsun Z 1600 & 2000 1966-1984
Car and Driver on Corvette 1956-1967
Car and Driver on Corvette 1968-1977
Car and Driver on Corvette 1978-1982
Car and Driver on Corvette 1983-1988
Car and Driver on Ferrari 1955-1962
Car and Driver on Ferrari 1963-1975
Car and Driver on Ferrari 1976-1983
Car and Driver on Mopar 1956-1967
Car and Driver on Mopar 1968-1975
Car and Driver on Mustang 1964-1972
Car and Driver on Pontiac 1961-1975
Car and Driver on Porsche 1955-1962
Car and Driver on Porsche 1963-1970
Car and Driver on Porsche 1970-1976
Car and Driver on Porsche 1977-1981
Car and Driver on Porsche 1982-1986
Car and Driver on Saab 1956-1985
Car and Driver on Volvo 1955-1986

BROOKLANDS MOTOR & THOROUGHBRED & CLASSIC CAR SERIES
Motor & T & CC on Ferrari 1966-1976
Motor & T & CC on Ferrari 1976-1984
Motor & T & CC on Lotus 1979-1983

BROOKLANDS PRACTICAL CLASSICS SERIES
Practical Classics on Austin A 40 Restoration
Practical Classics on Land Rover Restoration
Practical Classics on Metalworking in Restoration
Practical Classics on Midget/Sprite Restoration
Practical Classics on Mini Cooper Restoration
Practical Classics on MGB Restoration
Practical Classics on Morris Minor Restoration
Practical Classics on Triumph Herald/Vitesse
Practical Classics on Triumph Spitfire Restoration
Practical Classics on VW Beetle Restoration
Practical Classics on 1930S Car Restoration

BROOKLANDS MILITARY VEHICLES SERIES
Allied Military Vehicles Collection No. 1
Allied Military Vehicles Collection No. 2
Dodge Military Vehicles Collection No. 1
Military Jeeps 1941-1945
Off Road Jeeps 1944-1971
V W Kubelwagen 1940-1975

BROOKLANDS BOOKS

CONTENTS

Page	Title	Publication	Date	Year
5	The New Sunbeam Alpine	Autosport	July 24	1959
7	Sunbeam Alpine	Sports Car Graphic	May	1960
8	Sunbeam Alpine	Autocar	Aug. 21	1959
12	Sleek and Snug	Motor Trend	Sept.	1959
14	The Sunbeam Alpine (with Overdrive) Road Test	Motor	Nov. 18	1959
18	Sunbeam Alpine Road Test	Road & Track	May	1960
22	Alpine Plus	Motor	Oct. 9	1960
23	Sunbeam Alpine Series II Road Test	Autocar	Dec. 2	1960
28	The Harrington Alpine (Stage III)	Autosport	April 21	1961
30	Alpine 1600 Road Test	Canada Track & Traffic	May	1961
32	Alpine Grand Tourer	Autocar	June 23	1961
34	Sunbeam Alpine Road Test	Road & Track	Oct.	1961
38	Sunbeam Harrington Le Mans Road Test	Car and Driver	April	1962
41	Race Tuning the Sunbeam Alpine	Car and Driver	May	1962
43	Sunbeam Alpine GT Series III Road Test	Autocar	Sept. 20	1963
48	Sunbeam Alpine Series III Road Test	Road & Track	Sept.	1963
52	Sunbeam Alpine Series IV	Autocar	Jan. 17	1964
53	Sunbeam Alpine GT Series IV Road Test	Cars Illustrated	March	1964
56	Sunbeam Tiger 260 New Model Report	Autocar	April 10	1964
60	Sunbeam Alpine IV Automatic Road Test	Motor	Oct. 10	1964
65	Sunbeam Tiger Road Research Report	Car and Driver	Nov.	1964
72	Sunbeam Alpine IV Road Test	Road & Track	Nov.	1964
74	Sunbeam Tiger Road Test	Sports Car Graphic	Nov.	1964
78	Red Hot Sunbeam Tiger Road Test	Sports Car Graphic	Nov.	1964
80	Sunbeam Tiger Road Test	Road & Track	Nov.	1964
84	Tiger Tiger Burning Bright	Hot Rod	Jan.	1965
88	Ford Makes a Tiger of the Sunbeam Road Test	Motor Trend	Feb.	1965
92	Sunbeam Tiger: Right-Hand Drive	Autocar	March 5	1965
93	Sunbeam Tiger 260 Road Test	Autocar	April 30	1965
99	The Sunbeam Tiger	Motor Sport	April	1965
100	A Tiger for Rallying	Road & Track	May	1965
102	Sunbeam Tiger Road Test	Motor	May 1	1965
108	Sunbeam Tiger	Popular Imported Cars	June	1965
112	Sunbeam Tiger	Autosport	July 30	1965
114	Tigers Can be Tamed	Modern Motor	June	1965
117	Sunbeam Tiger Road Test	Car and Car Conversions	Sept.	1965
121	Sunbeam Tiger	Auto Topics	Aug.	1965
124	The 4.2 Litre V8 Sunbeam Tiger	Motor Sport	Oct.	1965
127	Now up to 1725cc	Car and Car Conversions	Jan.	1966
129	Sunbeam Alpine Series V Road Test	Sports Car Graphic	Feb.	1966
131	1725cc Sunbeam Alpine Road Test	Road & Track	March	1966
134	10,000 Miles in a Tiger	Autosport	April 15	1966
136	Sunbeam Alpine Series V Road Test	Autocar	May 13	1966
142	Alpine Series V Sports Tourer	World Car Catalogue		1966
143	Civilized Sports Car Road Test	Motor	July 23	1966
149	Chris Amon's Sunbeam Tiger	Autocar	Dec. 9	1966
151	Sunbeam Tiger with Teeth Road Test	Car and Car Conversions	Dec.	1966
154	Shoehorn Jobs	Autocar	May 11	1967
157	Sunbeam Tiger II Road Test	Road & Track	Sept.	1967
160	Sunbeam Tiger II	Popular Imported Cars	Nov.	1967
163	The Beefy Sunbeam Tiger	Sports Car World	Nov.	1969
166	Tale of a Tiger Two Long Term Assessment	Autocar	June 26	1969
169	Buying an Alpine ... or perhaps a Tiger	Practical Classics	Jan.	1983
174	Soft Options Profile	Classic and Sportscar	March	1985
178	Alpine Owners View	Classic and Sportscar	March	1985
179	They're Grrreat! Profile	Classic and Sportscar	Sept.	1986

BROOKLANDS BOOKS

ACKNOWLEDGEMENTS

It has become customary in our books for us to write a short introduction to the cars that we are dealing with. We have decided however, that it would be superfluous in this instance as we have included in the body of the book two comprehensive Profiles from Classic and Sportscar on both the Alpine and the Tiger.

The first covering the Alpine written by Mike Taylor and Richard Sutton can be found on page 174 and the second on the Tiger by Mick Walsh and Martin Buckley starts on page 179.

Brooklands books are a reference series for owners of interesting cars. They currently cover over 200 makes and models and within their pages will be found some 6,000 historical motoring stories and road tests going back to the early twenties.

Our mentors are the worlds leading publishers, motoring writers and photographers, who have unstintingly supported us for over 30 years by allowing us to include their informative copyright articles. We are indebted in this instance to the management of Autocar, Autosport, Auto Topics, Canada Track & Traffic, Car and Car Conversions, Car and Driver, Cars Illustrated, Classic and Sportscar, Hot Rod, Modern Motor, Motor, Motor Sport, Motor Trend, Popular Imported Cars, Practical Classics, Road & Track, Sports Car Graphic, Sports Car World and the World Car Catalogue for their ongoing help.

R.M. Clarke

The New Sunbeam Alpine

A 1½ litre Sports Car of completely new design

BEARING NO RESEMBLANCE to any of the existing Rootes models, the Alpine has very pleasing and distinctive lines. This model (left) has the detachable hardtop in place and also has the optional wire wheels. Disc brakes are standard on the front wheels.

FOR some time now it has been known that the Rootes group were working on a new sports car to fit into the "under £1000" price range. This car, known as the Alpine, was introduced to the motoring world on Wednesday and it would seem certain that this little car is destined for a very warm reception.

The car is powered by a four cylinder, 1½-litre O.H.V. engine (79.0 x 76.2 m.m., 1494 c.c.) which produces 83.5 b.h.p. at 5,300 r.p.m. An aluminium cylinder head is used which gives excellent cooling characteristics. This allows a high compression ratio of 9.2:1 to be used. Two Zenith 36 W.I.P.2 downdraught carburetters are used and the exhaust system is streamlined to ensure maximum performance and fuel economy.

A close ratio four-speed gearbox is employed, with syncromesh on second,

ALL THERE and nicely placed. The facia panel of the Alpine has been well thought out. Instruments include rev. counter, speedometer, clock, fuel gauge, screen washer, ammeter and temperature gauge.

THE OCCASIONAL SEAT behind the two front seats can be used for small children, additional luggage or one adult passenger if required. As can be seen the front seats hinge forward to give easy access to the back.

THE LUGGAGE COMPARTMENT is seen here, showing the stowage of the hood and spare wheel. As can be seen, with careful packing, a fair amount of luggage can be carried.

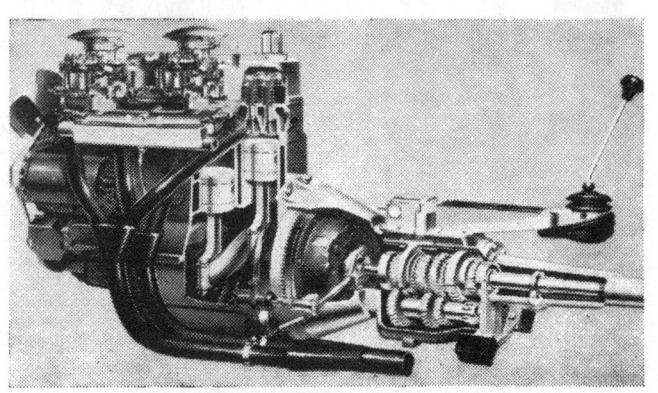

POWER UNIT. The four-cylinder engine develops 83.5 b.h.p. at 5,300 r.p.m. An aluminium cylinder head gives excellent cooling characteristics allowing a compression ratio of 9.2:1.

THE SUNBEAM ALPINE

An Exclusive Autosport Cutaway Drawing
by Theo Page

third and top gears. newly designed Laycock de Normanville overdrive, operating on third and fourth gears can be had for £60 4s. 2d. (inc. p.t.) if desired.

The brakes are Girling manufacture, being discs on the front and drum at the rear.

Sunbeam's considerable rally experience in rallies has been put to good use in the production of this car and the interior is comfortable and well appointed. A completely concealed fold-away hood and wind down side windows give the car good all-weather comfort. A detachable hard top is available. Both front seats are of deep foam rubber and are designed to hold driver and passenger firmly when cornering. There is generous leg and elbow room, and there is an occasional seat behind the front seats. Between the front seats is a padded arm rest, concealing a lockable glove box. There is also a cubby box in the facia panel.

Optional extras include the hard top, tonneau cover (£10), centre locking wire wheels (£38 5s.) and Road Speed tyres (£11 13s. 9d.). All prices include purchase tax.

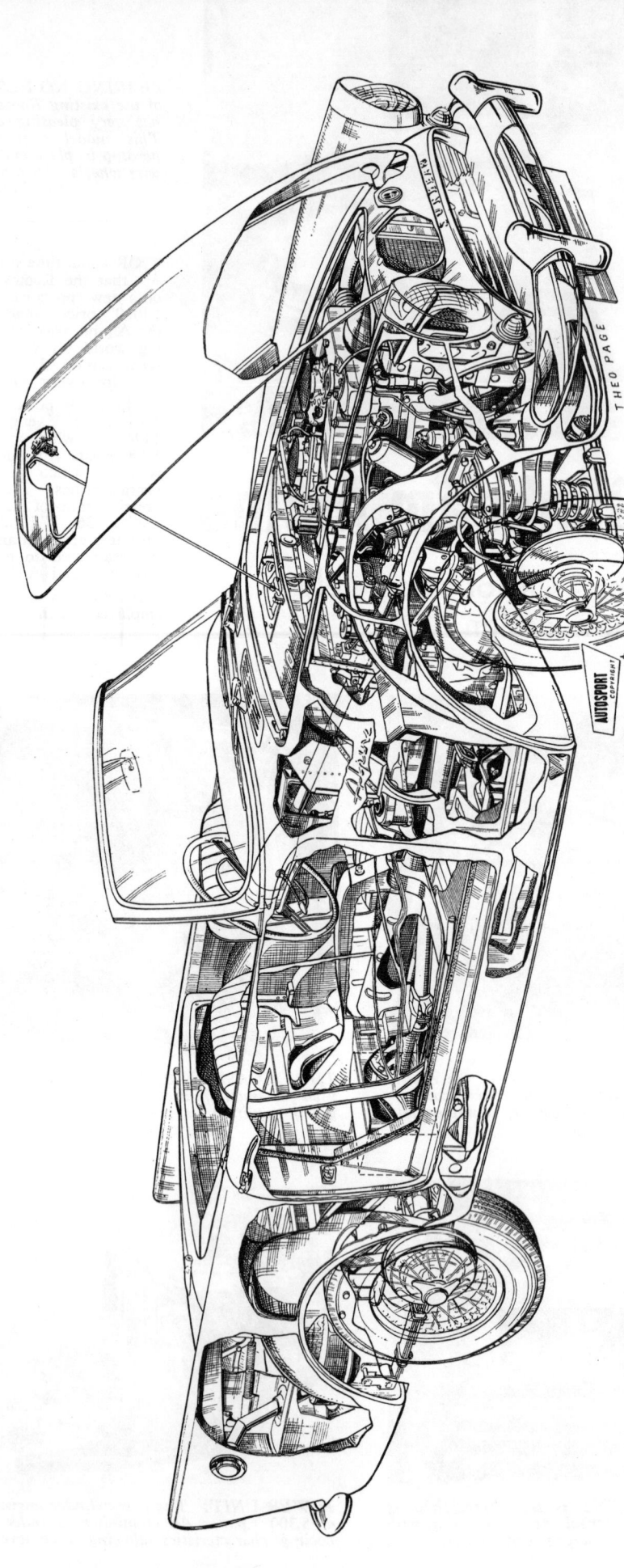

SPECIFICATION DATA

Sunbeam Alpine. Price £685 plus £286 10s. purchase tax. Total £971 10s. Extra: Laycock de Normanville overdrive £60 4s. 2d. including purchase tax.

Engine: 4 cylinders 79.0 x 76.2 mm. (1,494 c.c.). Pushrod and rocker operated overhead valves. Compression ratio: 9.2 to 1. 83.5 b.h.p. at 3,500 r.p.m. Twin Zenith carburetters.

Transmission: Borg and Beck single dry plate clutch. Four speed gearbox with syncromesh on 2nd, 3rd and 4th gears. Ratios: 1.0, 1.392, 2.141 and 3.346. Hardy Spicer open propeller shaft. Semi-floating hypoid rear axle.

Chassis. Front suspension. Independent coil spring with Torsional anti-roll bar. Burman recirculating ball steering. Rear axle on semi-elliptic springs. Armstrong telescopic shock absorbers at front, Armstrong lever arm at rear. Girling hydraulic disc brakes at front and leading and trailing shoe drums at rear. Total brake swept area: 295 sq. ins. 5.60 x 13 ins. tyres with pressed steel disc wheels. (Centre lock wire wheels optional extra.)

Electrical Equipment. Lucas 12-volt battery.

Sunbeam Alpine revived a famous name in British cars but this one has not been designed for serious rally competing.

Removable hardtop is an Alpine option as are the center-lock wire wheels. Small wheel size tends to make the car unsuitable for racing.

SUNBEAM ALPINE

Rootes Motors' relatively new Sunbeam Alpine proves that a sportscar doesn't have to be expensive to be among the very best available. This car has been designed as a personal sportscar rather than a dual-purpose sports-race machine and viewed in that context it serves very well.

Looking somewhat like a scaled-down two-passenger Thunderbird, the unit-bodied Alpine seats a pair of adults plus a child on what is termed a rear bench seat measuring 38½ by 16 inches. There is good useful luggage space in the trunk as well. All mechanical parts are based on the Sunbeam Rapier but the engine is extensively modified to raise the power to a reliable 83.5 bhp from its 1494cc (91.2 cubic inches). Creature comfort was the first consideration in designing the Alpine. Wind-up side windows make the car weathertight with either the folding top or the smart detachable hard top. A further appearance option is either knock-off wire or bolt-on disc wheels. Following current sportscar practice, the Alpine has included 9½-inch-diameter Girling disc brakes on the front wheels in conjunction with nine-inch drum brakes on the rear wheels.

The Alpine's performance is good but not startling; it's just a nice well-made fun car at a reasonable ($2595 p.o.e.) price.

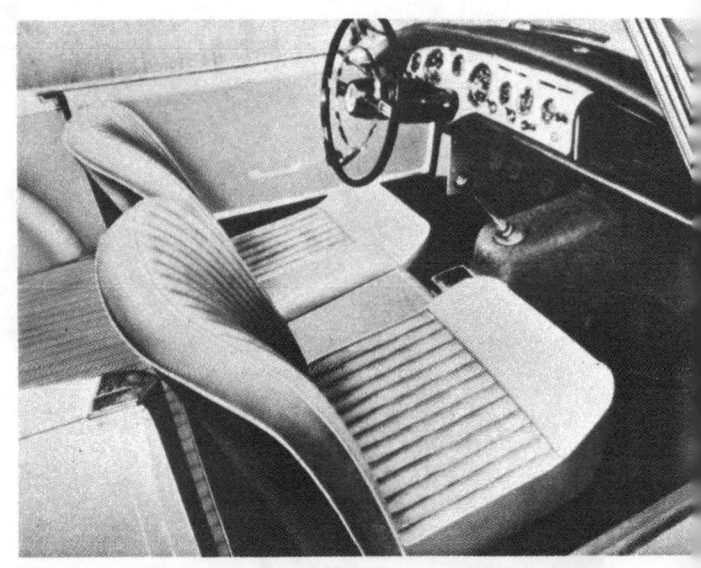

Interior layout is carefully planned; instruments and switches show strong Italian influence. The occasional rear seat is strictly for children and the glove box is open.

SUNBEAM *Alpine*

1960 MODELS

1½-litre sports-tourer with 78 b.h.p. engine and front disc brakes

ALTHOUGH, of course, the Sunbeam Rapier is a car of sporting character, there has not been an open two-seater in the Rootes range since the previous Alpine—a version of the earlier Mark III Sunbeam—went out of production in 1955.

The new model bearing this name must be classed as a sports-tourer rather than as an out-and-out sports car, though its performance, including a maximum speed in the region of 100 m.p.h., should satisfy most owners. The basic price is £685, so that on the home market, when British purchase tax is added, the total is under £1,000 —actually £971 10s 10d.

Accent is on appearance and comfort, the body having simple, tasteful lines, with a low, sloping bonnet and elongated rear wing

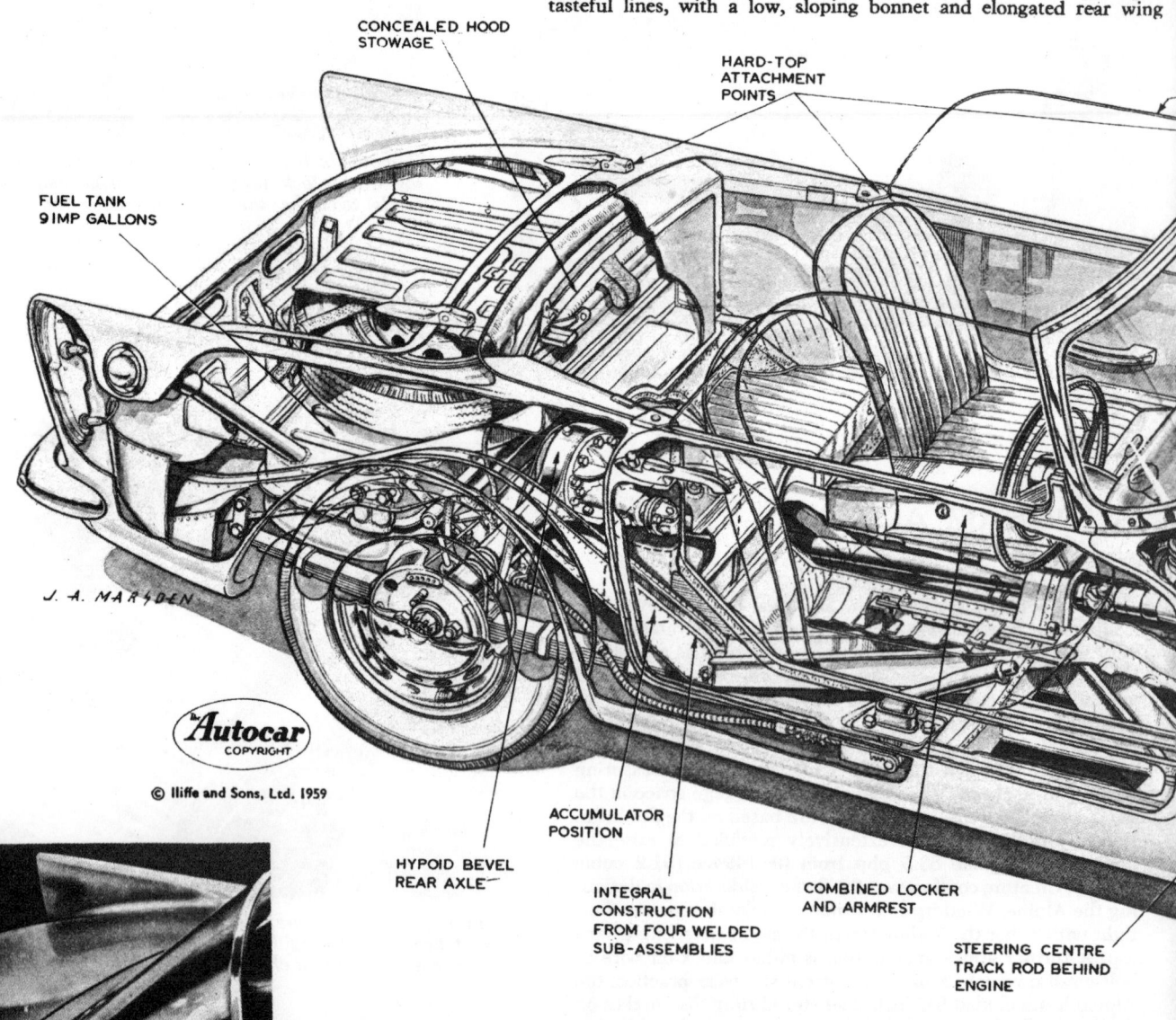

Cutaway illustration labels:
- FUEL TANK 9 IMP GALLONS
- CONCEALED HOOD STOWAGE
- HARD-TOP ATTACHMENT POINTS
- HYPOID BEVEL REAR AXLE
- ACCUMULATOR POSITION
- INTEGRAL CONSTRUCTION FROM FOUR WELDED SUB-ASSEMBLIES
- COMBINED LOCKER AND ARMREST
- STEERING CENTRE TRACK ROD BEHIND ENGINE

J. A. MARSDEN

The Autocar COPYRIGHT
© Iliffe and Sons, Ltd. 1959

One of the two spring-loaded plungers which secure the hardtop to the rear decking

8

Left: The Alpine with the metal hardtop in position. This is an extra item of equipment, as are the centre-lock wire wheels and whitewalled tyres.
Right: There is a fully equipped and well laid out facia with padded rolls above and below it; a rev counter is standard equipment

pressings which give the impression of fins. A rising line from nose to tail produces a pleasing wedge shape. Comfortable, well-shaped bucket seats give good support to driver and passenger, and behind them is a large space, additional to that provided by the boot, which can be used for luggage or to accommodate children—it is not large enough for an adult, since head and leg room are restricted.

In fine weather, good protection is afforded by the fixed wrap-round screen and frameless side windows, which may be wound down fully into the doors. For complete enclosure a soft folding hood can be erected in about one minute, and it is designed to remain taut and rigid up to maximum speed. When folded away it is hidden below the body surface beneath three hinged flaps in the decking. An aluminium hardtop, with full-width rear window, is available at a cost of £60 including purchase tax. Doors of exceptional width make it particularly easy to enter or leave the car. As is customary with Rootes products, the finish and the attention to detail, both externally and internally, are of a high standard.

A number of mechanical components common to other Rootes cars is used. Engine, clutch and gear box are basically the same as in the current Rapier, but a new cylinder head and other changes have brought about an increase of 10 b.h.p. Front suspension, too, is also Rapier-derived, with modifications for fitting Girling disc brakes.

Of integral construction in welded steel, the body shell is new, but is based on the Hillman Husky underbody, including the front and rear wheel arches, upon which are assembled and welded three other sub-assemblies. Together with the doors, these make up the complete body-chassis structure. They comprise a unit incorporating the bulkhead and bonnet sides, with two tubular ties from bulkhead to wheel arches, which can be unbolted to facilitate engine removal. To this unit is welded a shell which forms the front wings, nose and scuttle. At the rear, a single spot-welded assembly embraces rear wing pressings and boot. Open bodies of unit construction often lack the rigidity afforded by the roof of a saloon or coupé, and, as compensation, additional cross-bracing channels have been welded beneath the Husky underbody unit.

Use of this latter assembly has dictated the wheel-base, which is 7ft 2in—10in less than that of the Rapier—but the front track at 4ft 3in is 2in greater on this new model. Rear track remains the same as for the Rapier—4ft 0½in.

Basically, the engine of the Alpine is the 1,494 c.c. four-cylinder unit used for the Rapier with the over-square cylinder dimensions of 79 × 76.2mm bore and stroke. To provide an increase in power, however, an entirely new cylinder head has been developed. The material — aluminium alloy in place of cast iron— gives improved heat conductivity as well as a substantial reduction in weight. Push rod and rocker operation is retained for the valves, these being in line in the head, and inclined at a small angle to the vertical to increase the size of water passages between valve seats and manifold joint face. Inserts in the head for valve seats are in Brimol cast iron, shrunk in position. These changes have made possible an increase in compression ratio from 8.5 to 9.2 to 1. All ports are separate and on the same side of the casting (opposite to the push rods and sparking plugs) and inlet and exhaust ports are arranged alternately, to give a better thermal gradient along the head.

An aluminium alloy cast manifold distributes mixture to the inlet ports from two down-draught Zenith carburettors, with small separate air cleaners. In the interest of low-speed tractability, a water jacket partially surrounds the longitudinal passage connecting the four branches with the carburettors; pipes connect the jacket with the rear of the cylinder head and the water pump. Circulation can be blanked off readily for competition work, when an increase of 1 to 1½ b.h.p. is obtained.

Free exit for the gases is ensured by a well-swept

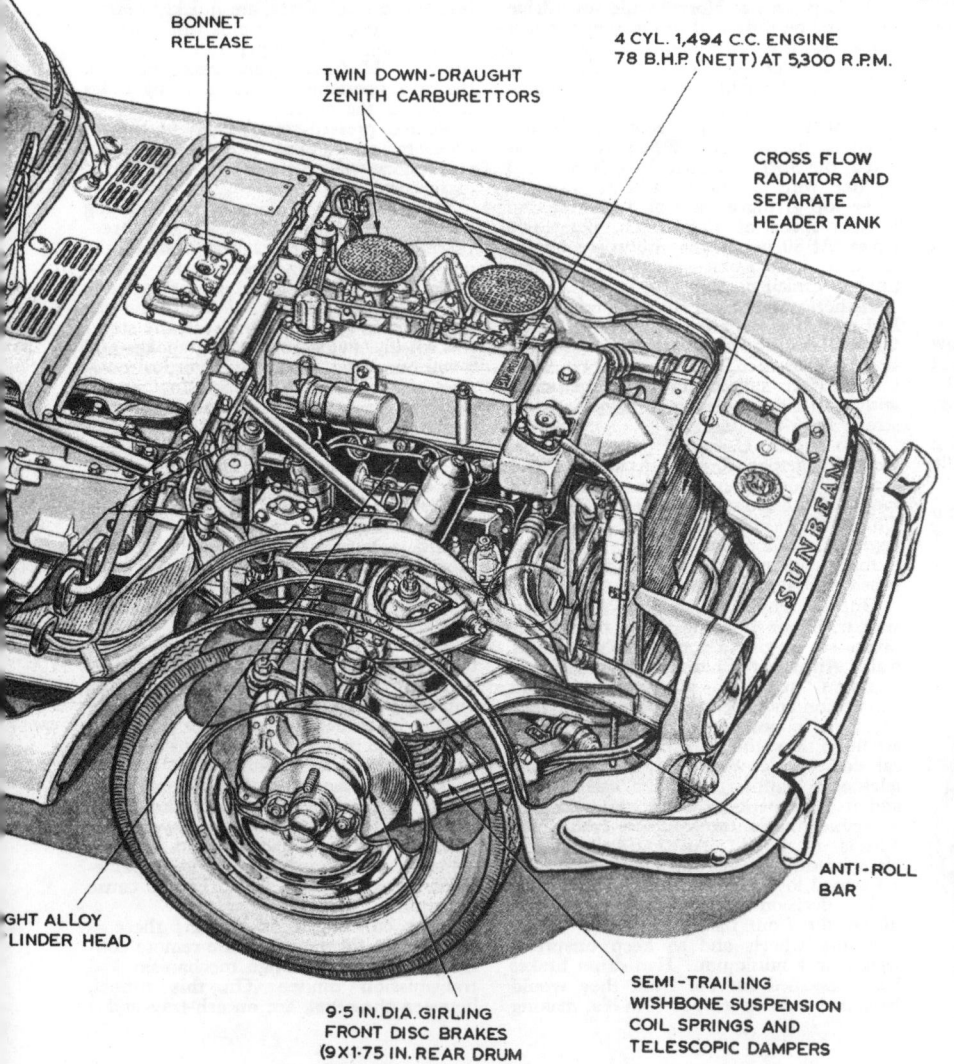

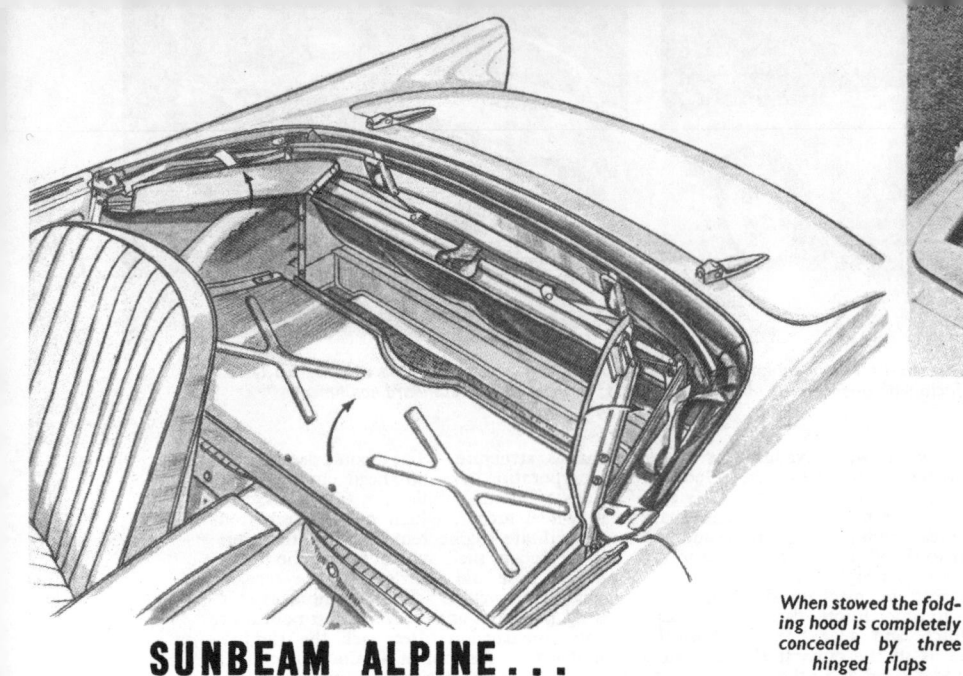

Wide doors give particularly easy access. Between the seats is a lockable compartment which also forms an arm rest. The driver's seat is at the centre of its fore and aft adjustment and the passenger seat is fully forward

SUNBEAM ALPINE...

When stowed the folding hood is completely concealed by three hinged flaps

exhaust manifold fabricated from tube. It is in two parts, with separate paired branches for Nos. 1 and 4 and 2 and 3 cylinders, the two outlet pipes merging immediately before entering the silencer.

Currently the Rapier engine develops 68 b.h.p. net at 5,200 r.p.m. and the modifications embodied in the Alpine engine have increased this to 78 b.h.p. net at 5,300 r.p.m.. Maximum b.m.e.p. has been raised from 134 lb sq in at 3,000 r.p.m. to 148 lb sq in at 3,400 r.p.m. As the kerb weight of the Alpine is 19.1cwt—approximately 1.5cwt less than that of the Rapier—power-weight ratio is 82 b.h.p. per ton, sufficient to ensure very lively acceleration.

Alterations to the oil sump baffles which ensure more thorough circulation of the oil have made it unnecessary to increase the capacity. However, for competition work an oil cooler is available; this is not required for normal fast motoring.

To reduce bonnet height and allow a distinct fall-away of the nose, the radiator is mounted low. It is of the cross-flow type with a separate header tank—a light alloy casting—mounted in front of the rocker cover (also an aluminium casting) immediately above the six-bladed fan. A measure of ducting is provided by shaping the passage behind the shallow inlet grille

Girling front disc brakes have a shroud on the inner face of each disc to protect it from grit thrown up by the tyres

DISC SHROUD

PAD RETAINING PINS

in the nose to lead air towards the radiator. Air enters also through slots beneath the bumper.

In recent months the Rapier four-speed gear box has had the ratios re-arranged to reduce the wide gap that existed between second and third. This unit, also used on the Alpine, has synchromesh for the three upper closely spaced ratios.

A Laycock-de Normanville overdrive operating on third and top may be fitted at extra cost; it is controlled by a lever on the right of the steering column. Overdrive ratio is 0.803 to 1, giving 24.6 per cent engine speed reduction, compared with the ratio of 0.756 to 1 (32.2 per cent) of the unit fitted to the Rapier. When overdrive is fitted, the 3.90 to 1 final drive is replaced by one with a ratio of 4.22 to 1, overdrive top giving a ratio of 3.38 to 1 and a road speed of 19.9 m.p.h. per 1,000 r.p.m. At 80 m.p.h. the equivalent engine speed is 4,020 r.p.m.—safe revs for continuous cruising.

Hitherto the smaller Rootes models have had rear axles with spiral bevel final drive. On the Alpine, however, a new hypoid bevel unit is used, manufactured by Salisbury. Rear suspension is conventional, with semi-elliptic springs damped by Armstrong lever-arm units.

Two similar U-shaped pressings, spot-welded together, form a detachable box-section cross member on which are mounted the front suspension assemblies. This cross member is shaped to provide engine clearance, and brackets welded to it form engine front bearers, with interposed semi-shear rubber mountings.

Unequal length top and bottom suspension wishbone pressings have their inner pivots set to give a considerable angle of trail. An upper spherical joint and lower trunnion assembly accommodate both suspension and steering movements. Metal bearings, in preference to rubber bushes, are fitted throughout the suspension. Helical coil springs are used, with co-axial telescopic dampers; between each spring and its abutments is a thick rubber pad to reduce noise transmission from road wheels to body. An anti-roll bar is clamped directly in rubber at each end to a forward lower wishbone.

The decision to fit disc brakes of 9.5in dia at the front made it possible to use 13in dia wheels and so keep unsprung weight to a minimum. Had drum brakes been specified for the front they would have had to be at least of 10in dia, making a larger wheel necessary; in addition, they would have raised the problem of restriction of cooling air circulation. Girling hydraulic equipment is employed, the rear drum brakes being of 9in dia, and incorporating the usual mechanical linkage between shoe expanders and hand brake lever which is on the floor beside the driver's seat. A single enclosed cable, kept as short as possible to ease lubrication difficulties, links up with the bell-crank and transverse rods carried on the axle.

Front brake discs are provided with a sheet steel shroud close to the inner face of each, to prevent scoring by grit thrown up from the tyres; the gap between disc and shroud is sufficient for cooling air to reach the braking surface. In the two-piece caliper, segmental friction pads, bonded to steel plates, are quickly renewable after two retaining pins which bridge the opening in the caliper have been withdrawn. Hydraulic connection between the two operating cylinders is by holes drilled in the castings.

Vented pressed-steel wheels with rim-finishers are standard equipment, but centre-lock wire wheels are available at extra cost.

Steering is by a Burman recirculating ball box, idler lever assembly and three-piece ball-jointed track rod system, the centre rod passing behind the engine cylinder block. With the steering box set fairly high on the bulkhead, and the low position of the driving seat, the steering wheel, having two sprung spokes and a full horn ring, is in a near vertical position. Instruments, comprising speedometer, rev counter, oil pressure gauge, water thermometer and fuel gauge, have black circular faces with white figures, including metric calibrations. Ammeter and clock are extras. Below the instruments, in a line, are the ignition-start switch and choke, and tumbler switches for lights, wipers and panel light. Above them, in horizontal quadrants, are controls for cockpit ventilation and heating—a heater is among the extra equipment available.

Air for ventilation or heating enters through grilles in the scuttle immediately ahead of the screen, and passes to a box built into the body structure behind the facia, with outlets which direct air to the driver's and passenger's feet, and upwards to screen de-misting ducts.

In front of the passenger is a large open locker in the facia, and both the flared edge of the scuttle and the lower edge of the facia are padded with sponge rubber and trimmed. There is no paintwork between screen and driver to cause reflections.

Floor covering is in rubber; there is carpet over the gear box, the remote control central gear-change mechanism and transmission tunnel. On this tunnel, between the seats, are an ash-tray and a

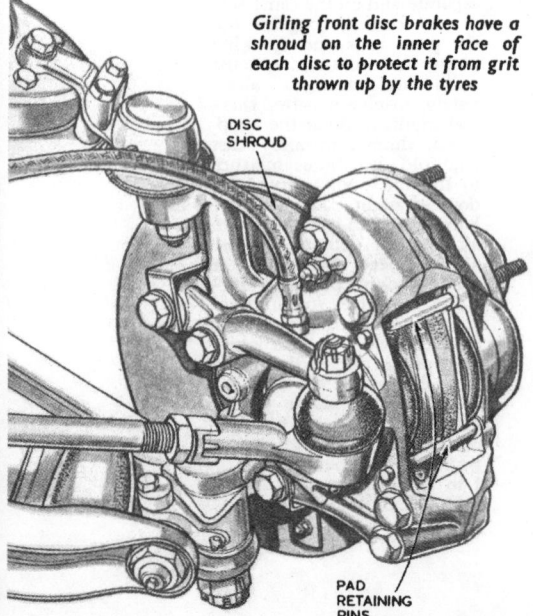

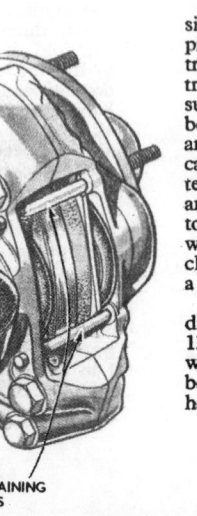

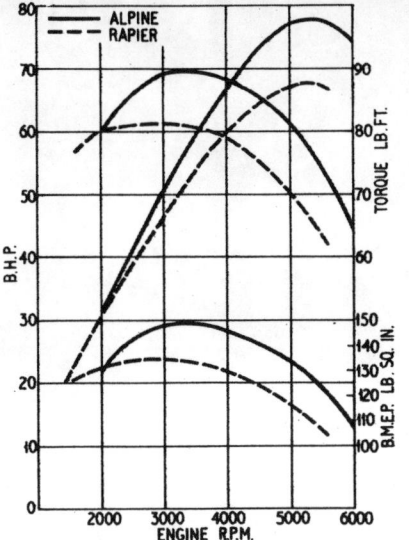

Net performance curves for the new engine compared with those for the Rapier Mark II

SUNBEAM ALPINE...

Induction system for the new light alloy cylinder head has twin downdraught Zenith carburettors and a water heated jacket. All induction and exhaust ports are separate

doors, and at the corners of the screen.

A lockable, push-button catch secures the boot lid, which has two struts with over-centre hinges to hold it open. Some of the boot space is occupied by the spare wheel, which lies horizontally above the fuel tank, secured by a webbing strap. A platform over the wheel, with hinged flap for access to the wheel, provides a flat surface for luggage. Tools and jack are stowed in a recess below the level of the boot opening.

Hinged at the front for safety reasons, the bonnet lid is held by a catch on top of the engine bulkhead, with a release handle beneath the lower edge of the facia.

lockable compartment for maps and other equipment, with its hinged lid padded to form an arm-rest. Bucket seats have curved back-rests, and the cushion is a deep, cellular sponge rubber moulding that requires no supporting springs and fits directly into the seat pan. Seats are trimmed in pleated Vynide with edge piping, and there is a similar covering for the space behind the seats. Cushions to fit beneath this covering are extras.

There are six mounting points for the hardtop—at forward extensions of the external hinges for the boot lid, on the decking behind the rear edge of the

In addition to items already mentioned, optional extras for the Alpine are a laminated windscreen in place of toughened glass, a tonneau cockpit cover, larger capacity battery, and a micro-element air cleaner for the carburettor intakes. There is a choice of two makes of radio, and reversing lights can be fitted, among a large list of other Rootes accessories for this model.

In the production of the Alpine there is, perhaps, a unique example of co-operation between two motor manufacturers. Assembly takes place entirely at the Coventry works of Bristol-Siddeley Engines, Ltd., where production capacity is available. This arrangement breaks fresh ground for that company, which for so long has been engaged solely in the production of large quality cars in limited numbers. Components for the combined body-chassis are supplied by the Pressed Steel Company and Joseph Sankey, while most of the mechanical components, such as engine, gear box and suspension are made by Humber at their Stoke works.

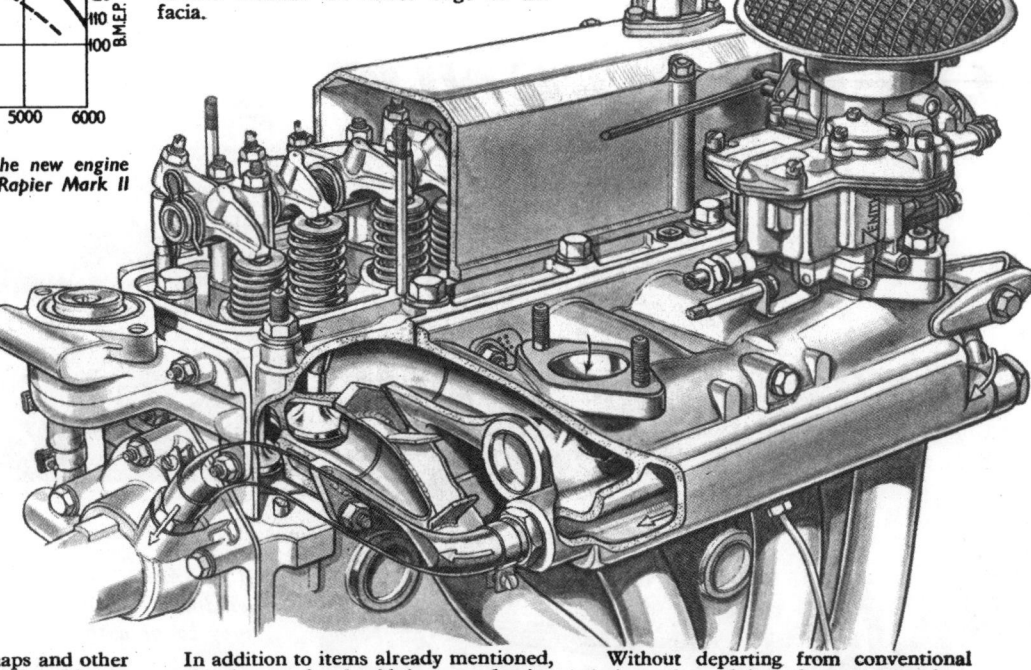

Without departing from conventional design, the Alpine demonstrates how successfully groups of well-tried components can be combined to produce something a little different. The bodywork is both elegant and practical, the cockpit being spacious and comfortable, and evidently planned with considerable thought. There is ample luggage space for two on a Continental tour, or, alternatively, children can be carried. Although it is not designed specifically for competition work, it is very probable, nevertheless, that the Alpine will be seen frequently in rallies.

SPECIFICATION

ENGINE
No. of cylinders	4 in line
Bore and stroke	79 x 76.2mm (3.11 x 3.0in)
Displacement	1,494 c.c. (91.13 cu in).
Valve position	o.h.v., pushrods
Compression ratio	9.2 to 1
Max. b.h.p. (net)	78 at 5,300 r.p.m.
Max. b.h.p. (gross)	83.5 at 5,300 r.p.m.
Max. b.m.e.p. (gross)	148 lb sq. in at 3,400 r.p.m.
Max. torque (gross)	89.5 lb ft at 3,400 r.p.m.
Carburettor	Two Zenith 36 W.I.P.2
Fuel pump	Engine-driven A.C. diaphragm type
Tank capacity	9 Imp. gallons (30.28 litres)
Sump capacity	8 pints (4.54 litres) (incl. oil filter)
Oil filter	Full flow
Cooling system	Pump, fan and thermostat
Battery	12 volt, 38 amp hr.

TRANSMISSION
Clutch	Single dry plate, 8in dia.
Gear box	Four speeds, synchromesh on 2nd, 3rd and top; central floor change
Overall gear ratios	Top 3.90; 3rd 5.41; 2nd 8.32; 1st 13.01; reverse 16.48
	With Laycock overdrive: O/D Top 3.38; Top 4.22; O/D 3rd 4.72; 3rd 5.88; 2nd 9.04; 1st 14.13; reverse 17.90
Final drive	Hypoid, ratio 3.90 to 1 (4.22 to 1 with overdrive)

CHASSIS
Brakes	Girling hydraulic; discs front, L and T shoes rear
Disc dia.	9.5in
Drum dia., shoe width	9 x 1.75in
Suspension: front	Independent, wishbones and coil springs, anti-roll bar
rear	Live axle, semi-elliptic leaf springs
Dampers: front	Telescopic direct-acting hydraulic
rear	Hydraulic lever-arm type
Wheels	Steel disc (centre-lock wire wheels optional)
Tyre size	5.60—13in
Steering	Recirculating ball
Steering wheel	Sprung two-spoke, 16.5in dia.
No. of turns lock to lock	Three

DIMENSIONS (Manufacturer's figures)
Wheelbase	7ft 2in (218.4cm)
Track	F, 4ft 3in (129.5cm); R, 4ft 0.5in (123.2cm)
Overall length	12ft 11.25in (394.3cm)
Overall width	5ft 0.5in (153.7cm)
Overall height	4ft 3.5in (130.8cm)
Ground clearance	5.12in (13.0cm)
Turning circle	34ft (10.36m)
Kerb weight	2,136lb—19.1 cwt (967.6 kg)

PERFORMANCE DATA
Top gear m.p.h. per 1,000 r.p.m.	17.22 (overdrive 19.9)
Torque lb ft per cu. in engine capacity	0.982
Brake surface area swept by linings	295 sq. in.
Weight distribution (dry)	F, 50.2 per cent
	R, 49.8 per cent

SLEEK AND SNUG

A two-seater roadster with wind-up windows, the Alpine converts into a snug coupe with an extra-cost detachable hard top. Space behind front bucket seats is limited for small packages, and trunk space is sparse. A lockable glove compartment fills gap between seats and acts as a folding armrest. The dash carries a full complement of instruments. Two Zenith down-draft carburetors and dual exhaust system, plus a higher compression ratio and a new aluminum head, increase 1494cc engine output to 83.5 hp without reducing reliability.

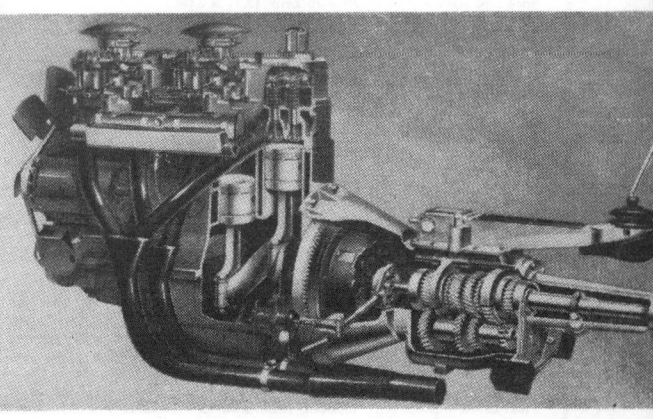

Rootes' new sportscar—the Sunbeam Alpine—has disc brakes, steel unit body and clean lines...all for a popular price

ROOTES ARE ENTERING the sportscar market with a popular-priced two-seater which has smooth style, unusual weather protection and disc brakes. Introduction of the new model is scheduled for the early fall; p.o.e. price (not yet announced) will probably be around $2500.

Mechanical parts are based on those of the Sunbeam Rapier, but the engine is extensively modified to raise the power output to a reliable 83.5 hp, and the car has an entirely new all-steel unit structure. Basic model is a two-seater roadster with wrap-around windshield and wind-up side windows, but a detachable hard top is available. There is a small luggage trunk and additional space for baggage or parcels behind the seats on a platform 38½ x 16 ins., which can also seat two children.

Power of the four-cylinder ohv pushrod engine (1494cc) has been raised nearly 10 per cent, chiefly by the use of a new aluminum cylinder head with inclined valves in line and a compression ratio of 9.2 to 1. There are four intake and four exhaust ports and this has permitted valves to be arranged alternately —intake/exhaust, intake/exhaust, etc.— right down the head, simplifying cooling and allowing better breathing for higher specific output. The three bearings of the crankshaft are white metal; the big ends are copper lead with indium lining. There is a new camshaft, also in three bearings. To strengthen the block for the higher power output, stiffening webs now run down inside the crankcase wall. The crankshaft itself is made of steel with higher tensile strength than that used for the Rapier coupe and convertible. Carburetors are two down-draft Zeniths and there is a four-branch exhaust system merging into twin down-pipes.

Transmission is through a single-plate Borg and Beck clutch of 8-in. diameter with hydraulic control, and four-speed gearbox with synchromesh on top three, controlled by a central lever, to a hypoid rear axle. In the gearbox, top, third and second gears are more closely grouped than on the Rapier, which is a welcome improvement, but bottom gear is lower than ever, so that the gap between first and second is much wider. However, as the axle ratio is 3.89 to 1 against 4.55 to 1 on the Rapier coupe, the overall first gear is still higher.

Front suspension is the same as on the coupe—wishbones, coil springs, anti-roll bar and telescopic shocks. Rear suspension is conventional, with rigid axle, semi-elliptic springs, and piston-type, double-acting shocks. Girling disc brakes of 9½-in. diameter are used at front, with pads giving 20.6 sq. ins. of friction area. Drum brakes are used at the rear with nine-inch drums and 60 sq. ins. of lining area. Wheels are perforated bolt-on discs, but center-lock wire wheels with triple-eared knock-offs are an optional extra.

Interesting feature of the interior is a central armrest forming a locker for gloves, sun glasses or camera; it has a lockable lid. Instruments include speedometer, tachometer, oil pressure gauge, fuel gauge, thermometer, ammeter.

The Alpine's combination of sensible design features and styling motif (resembling the popular two-seater T-Bird) should help make it a bright ray in the Sunbeam line.

by Gordon Wilkins European Editor

Cutaway of Alpine shows wishbone and coil spring front suspension with Girling disc brakes and ball joint steering. Rear brakes are drum type.

The Motor Road Test No. 29/59 (Continental)

Make: Sunbeam **Type:** Alpine (with overdrive)
Makers: Sunbeam-Talbot Ltd., Ryton-on-Dunsmore, Coventry

Test Data

World copyright reserved; no unauthorized reproduction in whole or in part.

CONDITIONS: Weather: Hot and dry with light breeze. (Temperature 67°-77°F., Barometer 29.9–30.0 in. Hg.) Surface: Dry tarred macadam and concrete. Fuel: Premium grade pump petrol (approx. 96 Research Method Octane Rating).

INSTRUMENTS
Speedometer at 30 m.p.h.	2% fast
Speedometer at 60 m.p.h.	4% fast
Speedometer at 90 m.p.h.	6% fast
Distance recorder	Accurate

WEIGHT
Kerb weight (unladen, but with oil, coolant and fuel for approx. 50 miles) .. 19½ cwt.
Front/rear distribution of kerb weight .. 51/49
Weight laden as tested .. 23¼ cwt.

MAXIMUM SPEEDS
Flying Quarter Mile. (Overdrive top gear)
Mean of four opposite runs .. 99.5 m.p.h.
Best one-way time equals .. 100.6 m.p.h.
"Maximile" Speed (Timed quarter mile after one mile accelerating from rest).
Mean of opposite runs .. 95.1 m.p.h.
Best one-way time equals .. 95.7 m.p.h.
Speed in gears (at 5,600 r.p.m.)
Max. speed in direct top gear .. 91 m.p.h.
Max. speed in overdrive 3rd gear .. 81 m.p.h.
Max. speed in direct 3rd gear .. 65 m.p.h.
Max. speed in 2nd gear .. 42 m.p.h.
Max. speed in 1st gear .. 27 m.p.h.

FUEL CONSUMPTION
(Overdrive top gear)
46.0 m.p.g. at constant 30 m.p.h. on level.
45.0 m.p.g. at constant 40 m.p.h. on level.
39.5 m.p.g. at constant 50 m.p.h. on level.
35.0 m.p.g. at constant 60 m.p.h. on level.
31.0 m.p.g. at constant 70 m.p.h. on level.
27.5 m.p.g. at constant 80 m.p.h. on level.
24.5 m.p.g. at constant 90 m.p.h. on level.
(Direct top gear)
41.5 m.p.g. at constant 30 m.p.h. on level.
40.0 m.p.g. at constant 40 m.p.h. on level.
35.0 m.p.g. at constant 50 m.p.h. on level.
31.0 m.p.g. at constant 60 m.p.h. on level.
28.0 m.p.g. at constant 70 m.p.h. on level.
25.0 m.p.g. at constant 80 m.p.h. on level.

Overall Fuel Consumption for 2,721 miles, 99.4 gallons, equals 27.4 m.p.g. (10.3 litres/100 km.).
Touring Fuel Consumption (m.p.g. at steady speed midway between 30 m.p.h. and maximum, less 5% allowance for acceleration). 31.4 m.p.g.
Fuel tank capacity (maker's figure) 9 gallons.

STEERING
Turning circle between kerbs:
Left .. 33¼ feet
Right .. 34¾ feet
Turns of steering wheel from lock to lock 3¼

BRAKES from 30 m.p.h.
0.91g retardation (equivalent to 33 ft. stopping distance) with 70 lb. pedal pressure
0.60g retardation (equivalent to 50 ft. stopping distance) with 50 lb. pedal pressure
0.30g retardation (equivalent to 100 ft. stopping distance) with 25 lb. pedal pressure

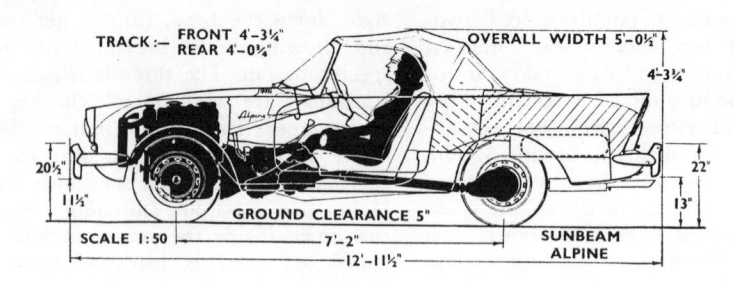

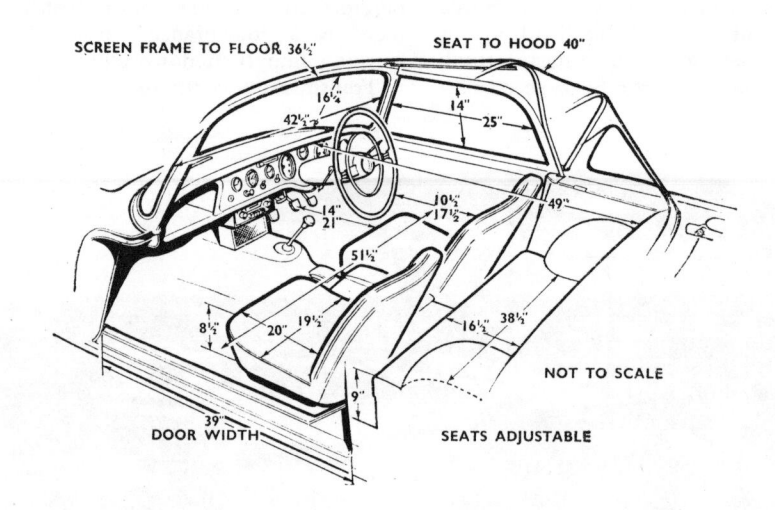

ACCELERATION TIMES from standstill
0-30 m.p.h.	4.9 sec.
0-40 m.p.h.	7.0 sec.
0-50 m.p.h.	10.2 sec.
0-60 m.p.h.	13.6 sec.
0-70 m.p.h.	17.9 sec.
0-80 m.p.h.	24.7 sec.
0-90 m.p.h.	35.0 sec.
Standing ¼-mile.	19.7 sec.

ACCELERATION TIMES on upper ratios
	Overdrive top gear	Direct top gear	Overdrive 3rd gear	Direct 3rd gear
10-30 m.p.h.	—	10.8 sec.	9.6 sec.	7.7 sec.
20-40 m.p.h.	14.6 sec.	10.2 sec.	9.6 sec.	6.8 sec.
30-50 m.p.h.	14.9 sec.	9.9 sec.	8.3 sec.	6.2 sec.
40-60 m.p.h.	15.8 sec.	10.3 sec.	8.6 sec.	6.9 sec.
50-70 m.p.h.	17.3 sec.	10.9 sec.	9.5 sec.	8.8 sec.
60-80 m.p.h.	21.0 sec.	13.5 sec.	12.2 sec.	11.8 sec.
70-90 m.p.h.	29.5 sec.	17.1 sec.	—	—

HILL CLIMBING at sustained steady speeds
Max. gradient on Overdrive top gear .. 1 in 13.5 (Tapley 165 lb./ton)
Max. gradient on Direct top gear .. 1 in 9.5 (Tapley 235 lb./ton)
Max. gradient on Overdrive 3rd gear .. 1 in 8.7 (Tapley 255 lb./ton)
Max. gradient on Direct 3rd gear .. 1 in 6.4 (Tapley 345 lb./ton)
Max. gradient on 2nd gear .. 1 in 4.1 (Tapley 535 lb./ton)

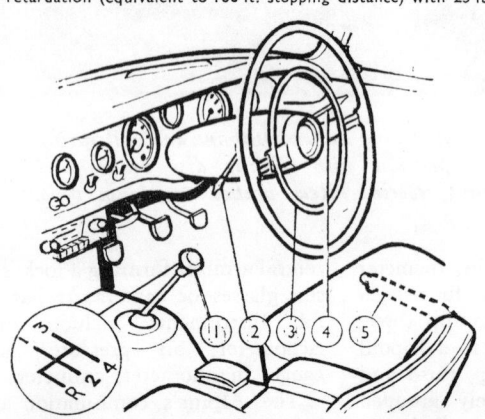

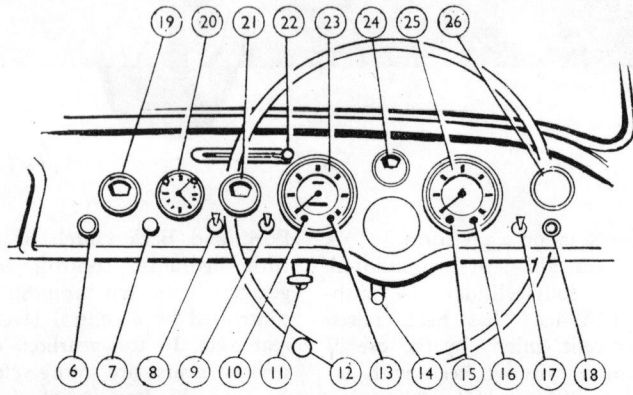

1, Gear lever. 2, Direction indicator switch. 3, Horn ring. 4, Overdrive switch. 5, Handbrake. 6, Ignition and starter switch. 7, Choke control. 8, Panel light switch. 9, Lights switch. 10, 16, Direction indicator warning lights. 11, Bonnet catch release. 12, Headlamp dip switch. 13, Dynamo charge warning light. 14, Trip re-setting knob. 15, Main beam indicator. 16,—see 10. 17, Windscreen wipers switch. 18, Windscreen washer button. 19, Fuel contents gauge. 20, Clock. 21, Water thermometer. 22, Ventilator control. 23, Speedometer and distance recorder. 24, Oil pressure gauge. 25, Blank (for optional ammeter).

Sports-car Fun in Armchair Comfort

AT HOME in the mountains, the Sunbeam Alpine corners on a Swiss pass during our five-country test.

INTRODUCED during the summer as a completely new model, the Sunbeam Alpine which we have been able to test in England, Belgium, France, Germany and Switzerland, combines in a single competitively-priced car some of the best of two worlds. Eye-catching sports car lines are matched by the brisk acceleration, the maximum speed of virtually 100 m.p.h., highly responsive steering and reassuringly powerful disc brakes. But, if this is a sports car, it belongs to the new generation of sports cars which is not merely weatherproof when required, but offers two people greater comfort than they would enjoy in many quite expensive touring cars.

It is no secret that the competitive price of this model (including purchase tax, it only exceeds £1,000 when extras such as the overdrive are added to its basic specification) is possible because the design takes advantage of tooling which has been laid down for other Rootes Group models: the power unit has a basic similarity to Hillman and Singer units, and the chassis uses some Husky estate car pressings in its make-up. Consequently, it is pleasing to be able to record at the end of an extended trial that certain characteristics which have recently been noted almost as "family failings" seem to have been eradicated. Oil consumption on this car was so small, for example, that the Alpine ran nearly 2,000 miles in our hands before any excuse could be found for topping up the engine sump with a single pint. Gearbox ratios which used to earn almost automatic criticism have given place to ratios whose spacing should please anyone who is not actually allergic to gear levers. Handling qualities far more sensitive and responsive than might have been expected have been built into this model. Despite a higher compression ratio than has been used on any former Rootes engine, this car with its new aluminium cylinder head (in which no two exhaust valves adjoin one another) is happy even on the not-very-good petrol of France.

Scaling not very far short of one ton in convertible form (it is easy to add a rigid "hardtop" without removing the folded hood) this 1½-litre car has too much strength and comfort built into it to offer "racing" acceleration, but it will perform well for two different kinds of driver. In sporting mood, and using the overdrive and the four gearbox ratios freely to let the engine get up to and beyond 5,000 r.p.m. quite frequently, a keen driver gets over the ground very fast indeed to the tune of a hearty bark from the exhaust. More sedately driven and perhaps with the overdrive switch used as a lazy-man's substitute for the gear lever, the Alpine still gets over the ground quite quickly and with a lot less exhaust noise, the engine being perfectly willing to pull away from 1,000 r.p.m. in one of the higher gears, but its torque rising gradually over much of the speed range at a rate which in top gear roughly matches the car's rise in air resistance, so that top gear acceleration remains remarkably constant in rate from 10 m.p.h. right up to 70 m.p.h.

With such a versatile engine, there were naturally wide variations in fuel consumption according to where and how the Alpine was driven, our worst figure over a substantial distance being 19.4 m.p.g. when hard-driving members of the staff sampled the car in and near to London, our best reading 32.2 m.p.g. during fairly leisurely exploration of Black Forest mountain roads. The fuel tank capacity of this model is nominally 9 gallons, but a gauge which indicated an emphatic zero when 7 gallons had been used out of a brim-full tank discouraged long drives without refuelling.

Our test car had the Laycock-de Normanville switch-controlled overdrive as a very welcome supplement to the four-speed gearbox, operative in conjunction with top or third gears, and smooth in engagement yet free from slip at all times; in conjunction with the overdrive a 4.222 axle ratio gives livelier top gear acceleration than the 3.889 ratio otherwise specified. For sheer maximum speed, the combination used for our test may not be ideal, 5,600 r.p.m. (the red mark on the tachometer dial, and a speed beyond which the valvegear becomes suddenly very noisy)

In Brief
Price (including overdrive, as tested) £727 10s., plus purchase tax £304 5s., equals £1,031 15s. 0d.
Price without overdrive (including purchase tax), £971 10s. 10d.
Capacity ... ... 1,494 c.c.
Unladen kerb weight ... 19½ cwt.
Acceleration:
  20-40 m.p.h. in top gear ... 10.2 sec.
  0-50 m.p.h. through gears 10.2 sec.
Maximum direct top gear gradient ... ... 1 in 9.5
Maximum speed ... ... 99.5 m.p.h.
"Maximile" speed ... ... 95.1 m.p.h.
Touring fuel consumption ... 31.4 m.p.g.
Gearing (with 5.90—13 tyres): 16.2 m.p.h. in top gear at 1,000 r.p.m. (overdrive, 20.2 m.p.h.); 32.4 m.p.h. at 1,000 ft./min. piston speed (overdrive, 40.4 m.p.h.)

WEATHER PROTECTION which does not destroy vision is provided by a folding hood with broad three-piece rear window, and by winding glass windows which are firmly braced to the curved glass windscreen.

TWIN downdraught carburetters on a water-jacketed inlet manifold, a divided exhaust system and a new light-alloy cylinder head allow the 1½-litre engine to provide a maximum speed of around 100 m.p.h.

representing 91 m.p.h. in direct top gear but the timed maximum of 99.5 m.p.h. in overdrive top gear being short of the 5,300 r.p.m. at which maximum power is developed. For anything other than level-road maximum speed, however, the overdrive obviously much improves the car, there being a "right" ratio available for acceleration over any possible speed range, and a sustained 80 m.p.h. on day-long Autobahn drives seeming effortless and quite economical at only 4,000 r.p.m.

An extremely pleasant central remote control is provided for this model's silent new four-speed gearbox, which has quite good synchromesh on gears other than 1st. Overdrive 3rd is a ratio only slightly lower than direct top gear (at 5,000 r.p.m. one gives 72 m.p.h. and the other 81 m.p.h.) and is used very frequently, in town for quiet progress at 30 m.p.h. or on the open road when regaining cruising speed.

X-braced amidships and with the scuttle structure linked to the i.f.s. anchorages by tubular struts, the Alpine's integral body-chassis structure appears notably rigid, cobbled Flanders by-ways causing no evident distortion—something which it is rarely possible to say about an open car with wide doors. The springing is soft enough for *pavé* to cause no discomfort whatever, even with the Dunlop "Road Speed" tyres at the higher inflation pressures advised for fast motorway cruising, and some buyers might actually prefer rather firmer damping of the springs.

It is low build and reasonable track width which let this car corner quickly with very little body roll, and not the use of harsh springs. Really pushed towards the limit on a bumpy corner, the Alpine's rear axle can begin to hop somewhat under its semi-elliptic springs, but general standards of road holding are high.

In respect of steering this car invites judgment by far higher standards than any other recent Rootes car, a driver soon learning that he can relax physically and guide the car with finger pressures on the wheel rim at most times. There is feel in the steering but not any tiring amount of reaction from bumpy roads, the further improvement which might be welcome being closer harmony between fairly strong castor and understeer when the car is cornering and an almost excessive degree of steering sensitivity during fast driving along a straight road. Despite the vestigial tail fins formed by the rear wings, the car yields noticeably to wind rather than "weathercocking" towards it, but with correctly matched front and rear tyre pressures this is

LOCK-UP accommodation for a certain amount of luggage is provided on this flat shelf above the spare wheel. When the hood is raised, bulky loads can extend forwards into the body interior, thanks to use of a flexible container for its fabric.

a car which makes fast progress along reasonably traffic-free roads a real joy.

In making notes about the Alpine, it was afterwards realised that all reference to the brakes had been completely omitted, which for a rapid and hard-driven car is a silent testimony to their excellence. Disc brakes behind the bolt-on front wheels work with the drum-type rear brakes to give all the braking which is required or which road adhesion permits, quietly and in response to a comfortably moderate pedal pressure, whilst the handbrake can hold the car on a 1 in 3 gradient.

Amenities for the driver and passenger in the Alpine are centred on two bucket seats; their upholstery is reasonably firm but the standard of comfort provided on a long journey is far higher than on the superficially soft cushions (providing little or no lateral support) of most family saloons. Since the first batch of Alpines went into showrooms, the steering column has been raised to bring the steering wheel rim clear of a driver's thighs, and the driving position of our test model made people of very varied shapes and sizes comfortable. At first acquaintance, headroom when the hood is erect seems limited and a piece of hood-frame is rather near to a tall driver's head, but the car is so sprung that proximity never becomes contact.

Whereas most sporting cars which can

TWO seats which are thoroughly comfortable are divided by a central armrest, which serves also as a locked glovebox. The space behind these seats can accommodate a good deal of luggage or if necessary an adult passenger or two small children.

be compared in price with the Alpine use removable sidescreens, and can gain elbow width by having hollowed-out or cutaway doors, this model has wind-down glass windows. In respect of weatherproofness, clear vision and general convenience this is obviously an advantageous arrangement. At first acquaintance, a bulky driver is conscious that his shoulder readily contacts the door, but tumblehome on the body sides provides extra width at elbow level, even more width at floor level so that a very convenient pull-up handbrake lever can be accommodated on the driver's off side. Erect, the side windows seal against rubber strips on the windscreen frame, and lowered they disappear completely from view, but a tendency for the hood sides to suck outwards at speeds over 60 m.p.h. can interfere with the complete closing of an opened window.

FALLING bonnet line to provide good driving vision, full-width bumpers, and doors wide enough to make entry to a low-built car easy, are practical details shown in this view of the Alpine.

Separate from the spare wheel stowage, the lockable rear luggage compartment has a flat floor which will not harm cases, but is too shallow to be very capacious. A large well behind the front seats provides a great deal more carrying capacity, and a passenger sitting sideways can travel here. Extra accommodation under lock and key is provided inside what appears to be only an armrest (and a very useful one) between the front seats.

As an open car, the Alpine has no visible trace of any hood, three hinged metal covers painted to match the rest of the coachwork concealing both fabric and framework. As a closed car, there is full protection against draughts and rain, but a fair amount of "wind whistle" which builds up as the cruising speed goes beyond 70 m.p.h. and, on a motorway, demands rather a high volume from the loud speaker if a radio programme is to be enjoyed. As always, practice allows the job to be done more quickly and more neatly, but neither erection of the hood nor its neat stowage in the wells provided are particularly rapid though both jobs are entirely practicable single-handed. A further nuisance for well-laden holidaymakers is that the hood covers will not hinge open fully unless the rear "seat" is cleared of luggage. A parcel compartment of substantial size on the facia, with a lip which holds maps and guide-books in position, helps tourists to keep their car reasonably tidy.

Equipment on this car lets both the sporting motorist and the sybarite enjoy it. The former has a neat and legible set of instruments, including oil pressure gauge, coolant thermometer, trip speedometer, rev. counter and provision for an ammeter if desired; a good all-round view kept clear by windscreen washing sprays, and convenient controls which include a horn ring. The latter can have a heater to supplement the fresh-air ventilation system, will appreciate doors wide enough to make this amongst the easiest of low-built cars to enter, and can relax thanks to the vibration-free engine and shock-free springing.

A dual appeal is, in fact, the essence of the Alpine. For young people who want a sports car but need accommodation for one or two small children, it can satisfy both the wish and the need at reasonable cost. Anyone of an older generation whose family have grown up and bought their own cars, and who is getting bored with driving on crowded roads, should consider whether perhaps a comfortable yet nimble car such as the Alpine is not perhaps the "prescription" for putting pleasure back into motoring.

Specification

Engine

Cylinders	4
Bore	79 mm.
Stroke	76.2 mm.
Cubic capacity	1,494 c.c.
Piston area	30.4 sq. in.
Valves	Pushrod o.h.v.
Compression ratio	9.2/1
Carburetter	Two Zenith W.I.P. 36 downdraught
Fuel pump	AC mechanical
Ignition timing control	Centrifugal and vacuum
Oil filter	Fram or Tecalemit full-flow
Max. power (gross)	83.5 b.h.p. (net, 78 b.h.p.)
at	5,300 r.p.m.
Piston speed at max. b.h.p.	2,650 ft./min.

Transmission

Clutch	Borg & Beck 8 in. s.d.p.
Top gear (s/m)	4.22 (overdrive, 3.39)
3rd gear (s/m)	5.88 (overdrive, 4.72)
2nd gear (s/m)	9.04
1st gear	14.13
Reverse	17.9
Overdrive	Laycock-de Normanville
Propeller shaft	Hardy Spicer open
Final drive	Hypoid bevel
Top gear m.p.h. at 1,000 r.p.m.	16.2 (overdrive, 20.2)
Top gear m.p.h. at 1,000 ft./min. piston speed	32.4 (overdrive, 40.4)

Chassis

Brakes	Girling hydraulic, disc front and drum rear
Brake disc diameter	9½ in.
Brake drum internal diameter	9 in.
Friction lining area	80.6 sq. in.

Suspension:
Front: Independent by coil springs, transverse wishbones and anti-roll torsion bar.
Rear: Semi-elliptic springs and rigid axle.

Shock absorbers:

Front	Armstrong telescopic
Rear	Armstrong lever arm
Steering gear	Burman re-circulating ball
Tyres	Dunlop 5.90—13 Road Speed on test car (or Dunlop 5.60—13 tubeless)

Coachwork and Equipment

Starting handle	Yes
Battery mounting	Under occasional rear seat
Jack	Pillar type
Jacking points	Four external on bumper brackets

Standard tool kit: Jack, wheelbrace, tool roll, sparking plug spanner and tommy bar, adjustable spanner, pliers, screwdriver, distributor key, tyre valve key, nave plate removal key, four open-ended spanners, grease gun.

Exterior lights: 2 headlamps, 2 sidelamps/flashers, 2 stop/tail lamps, number plate lamp.

Number of electrical fuses	Two
Direction indicators	Self-cancelling flashers (white front, amber rear)
Windscreen wipers	Electrical two-blade, self-parking
Windscreen washers	Optional extra
Sun visors	None

Instruments: Speedometer with decimal-trip and total distance recorder, rev. counter, oil pressure gauge, coolant thermometer, fuel contents gauge.

Warning lights: Dynamo charge, headlamp main beam, direction indicators.

Locks:

With ignition key	Ignition/starter switch and either door
With other key	Glove locker and luggage locker

Glove lockers: Open cubbyhole on facia and lockable compartment in central arm-rest.

Map pockets	None
Parcel shelves	None
Ashtrays	None
Cigar lighters	None
Interior lights	None
Interior heater	Optional extra fresh-air heater and screen de-mister
Car radio	Optional extra, Radiomobile orEkco

Extras available: Centre lock wire wheels, Road Speed or white-wall tyres, laminated glass windscreen, tonneau cover, oversize battery, oil cooler, air filter radio, heater, removable hard top, reversing lights, etc.

Upholstery material	Vynide
Floor covering	Rubber mats
Exterior colours standardized	Five colours
Alternative body styles	None (Removable hard-top optional on open body)

Maintenance

Sump (10° F. to 90° F.)	7 pints, S.A.E. 20 or 10W/30
Gearbox	2¾ pints plus 1¼ pints in overdrive S.A.E. 30
Rear axle	1¾ pints S.A.E. 90 E.P.
Steering gear lubricant	S.A.E. 160 gear oil
Cooling system capacity	14 pints (2 drain taps)
Chassis lubrication	By oil gun every 1,000 miles to 23 points
Ignition timing	5°-7° before t.d.c. static
Contact-breaker gap	0-014-0.016 in.
Sparking plug type	14 mm. Champion N5
Sparking plug gap	0.025 in.

Valve timing: Inlet opens 14° before t.d.c. and closes 52° after b.d.c.; exhaust opens 56° before b.d.c. and closes 10° after t.d.c.

Tappet clearances (cold):

Inlet	0.012 in.
Exhaust	0.014 in.
Front wheel toe-in	⅛ in. at tyres
Camber angle	½°-1°
Castor angle	4° 41′
Steering swivel pin inclination	5°-5½°

Tyre pressures:

Front	22-25 lb.
Rear	23-27 lb. according to speed
Brake fluid	Lockheed or Girling to S.A.E. specification 70 R.3
Battery type and capacity	Lucas BT.7A 12 volt 38 amp./hr.

road test

The name is old, but the car is all new

MANY OF OUR READERS will recall that the English Sunbeam company introduced an Alpine model back in 1953. Widely advertised as a sports car, it turned out to be a rather tame 2-seater version of the company's 4-passenger convertible. It was not a great success, and at that time our road test was actually blamed for its early demise. In retrospect, the early Alpine was probably a few years ahead of its time, for many of the latest sports cars are now built along similar lines; a personal car with wind-up windows and other luxury details not always favored by the true sports car enthusiasts, but indicative of our expanding market.

In 1958 we began to hear rumors from England that there was a new Alpine in the works. Rootes' European competition experience with the hearty new 1494-cc engine stimulated some thought along sports car lines,

A very comfortable interior aids the driver's control.

Horsepower is 83 @ 5300 rpm from 1500-cc displacement.

since the latest version of the Rapier handled well and was quite a spirited performer. Obviously, it was logical further to exploit the good engine and chassis, come up with an attractive body design and introduce a new sports car, again named the Alpine. This is a name the manufacturer has earned from the outstanding success throughout the years in the rally of the same name, as well as many others.

Our testing procedure for this car was even more thorough than usual, in that we put many miles on two different cars, obtained from different sources. The quality level of panel fit and finish varied considerably between the two. On the one, a soft top model from a dealer, the general finish was quite poor and the hood popped open whenever the car was driven hard on winding roads. The door fit could have been improved and there was a lot of resonance in the body panels. The other car, a hardtop model obtained direct from Rootes' Los Angeles branch office, was a much different car. All panels were well fitted and the finish, inside and out, was excellent. The removable hardtop seemed to eliminate the body panel resonance, but it amplified the engine noise. This, however, should be no detriment, since a good healthy sound is extremely pleasant, even stimulating, to the sports car buyer.

On first jumping into the car one notices several things almost simultaneously. The seats are very comfortable, our only criticism being that they seem a little too vertical; more rake would be desirable for traveling great distances.

Next, the steering wheel seemed a bit low. In order to sit comfortably, one had to sit with the knees far apart to avoid rubbing on the bottom of the steering wheel. Ladies on our staff found it a bit awkward, since they could not get their legs under the wheel, maintain their dignity, and still depress the clutch satisfactorily. Our conclusion was that the steering wheel should be raised about an inch and the rear portion of the seat lowered about half that amount, which would also increase the back rake. When this was mentioned to the local Rootes office, we were told these changes are being made and it would be easy to make the change on early production

Limited trunk space is augmented by room behind the seats.

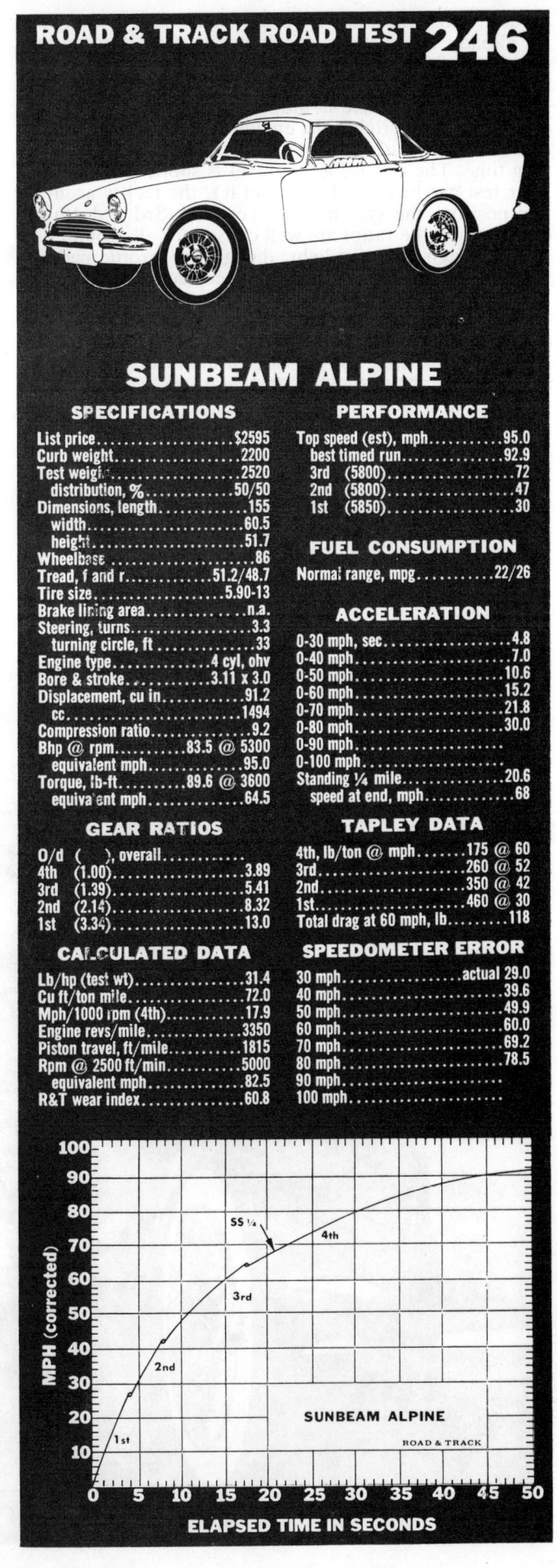

ROAD & TRACK ROAD TEST 246

SUNBEAM ALPINE

SPECIFICATIONS
List price	$2595
Curb weight	2200
Test weight	2520
distribution, %	50/50
Dimensions, length	155
width	60.5
height	51.7
Wheelbase	86
Tread, f and r	51.2/48.7
Tire size	5.90-13
Brake lining area	n.a.
Steering, turns	3.3
turning circle, ft	33
Engine type	4 cyl, ohv
Bore & stroke	3.11 x 3.0
Displacement, cu in	91.2
cc	1494
Compression ratio	9.2
Bhp @ rpm	83.5 @ 5300
equivalent mph	95.0
Torque, lb-ft	89.6 @ 3600
equivalent mph	64.5

GEAR RATIOS
O/d ( ), overall	
4th (1.00)	3.89
3rd (1.39)	5.41
2nd (2.14)	8.32
1st (3.34)	13.0

CALCULATED DATA
Lb/hp (test wt)	31.4
Cu ft/ton mile	72.0
Mph/1000 rpm (4th)	17.9
Engine revs/mile	3350
Piston travel, ft/mile	1815
Rpm @ 2500 ft/min	5000
equivalent mph	82.5
R&T wear index	60.8

PERFORMANCE
Top speed (est), mph	95.0
best timed run	92.9
3rd (5800)	72
2nd (5800)	47
1st (5850)	30

FUEL CONSUMPTION
Normal range, mpg	22/26

ACCELERATION
0-30 mph, sec	4.8
0-40 mph	7.0
0-50 mph	10.6
0-60 mph	15.2
0-70 mph	21.8
0-80 mph	30.0
0-90 mph	
0-100 mph	
Standing ¼ mile	20.6
speed at end, mph	68

TAPLEY DATA
4th, lb/ton @ mph	175 @ 60
3rd	260 @ 52
2nd	350 @ 42
1st	460 @ 30
Total drag at 60 mph, lb	118

SPEEDOMETER ERROR
30 mph	actual 29.0
40 mph	39.6
50 mph	49.9
60 mph	60.0
70 mph	69.2
80 mph	78.5
90 mph	
100 mph	

models. This will make a world of difference and change an already comfortable car into one that is very near to being faultless.

Driving the car is great fun for anyone who likes the sports car feel. There is ample room for your feet and everything seems right. The engine has a solid healthy note and the transmission is one of the best we've used in a long time. The control lever travel is short, if a little stiff (our test car had 1300 miles on it), the feel is accurate and positive, the synchromesh (on 2nd, 3rd and 4th) is effective and the ratios are well chosen for all-around use.

The clutch action is light, though the throttle pedal is not. On moving off, the throttle needs considerable pressure, due to its stiff spring, to avoid stumbling, and 2nd gear starts are not possible. This is fine as far as we are concerned, since we believe everyone should have the experience of learning the use of a properly spaced 4-speed transmission. The Alpine's 3rd and 4th gears may be treated like a dual high gear: one for zip and one for economical cruising at low engine speeds.

During the performance tests we were bothered somewhat by the strange sensation of engine sluggishness. Actually, most of this feeling was due to the very stiff accelerator spring and the stopwatch figures proved this to be correct; the actual times recorded are very acceptable, with no need for apology. Nevertheless, our own preference would be a more drastic clutch bite and perhaps a lighter flywheel. Such a modification would particularly facilitate downward changes of gear where at present the usual stab on the accelerator fails to produce a sufficient number of revs. However, not everyone would like this more sporting type of control, and the Alpine is undoubtedly more tractable and docile the way it is, and therefore will appeal to a larger market.

In the ride and handling departments, we would rate the former as being extraordinarily good for a car of this size and category. It also strikes an excellent compromise between boulevard softness and high speed stability, all accomplished most creditably with very little roll in fast corners. The pitch and bounce are exceptionally well controlled, so well that it is impossible to detect the ride handicaps usually inherent in a car with a wheelbase as short as 86 in. The steering, at 3.3 turns lock to lock, gives good control at high speeds without being overly sensitive and is quick enough for good maneuverability, though the sports car enthusiast might like it to be a little quicker. Small changes in direction at speed seem to require too much wheel movement, immediately to either side of center, but this can be obviated by carrying 28 psi in the front tires. There is understeer, and vigorous cornering requires a rather heavy pull at the wheel rim to counteract caster and self-aligning

Low angle was used by the photographer to emphasize rear fender treatment.

The Sunbeam Alpine has been compared to the Thunderbird, so we posed the two cars together to show the remarkable similarity between them. If the cars had similar hoods and front bumpers they would be almost indistinguishable at a distance. The T-Bird,

a 1957, has a nonstandard straight-bar grille replacing its original stamped counterpart, which adds further to the confusion and loss of identity between the two. If the Alpine gives its buyer as much pleasure and resale value as the T-Bird has, it is a good buy.

torque. When cornered beyond the limit of wheel adhesion, all four wheels break loose in a friendly sort of way (not at all frightening) and if you have chosen the proper gear, the Alpine can be taken through turns with professional elán.

With respect to steering (and subsequent handling), the Alpine is regarded by this staff as being far better than other products of the Rootes Group. This is not a criticism of other Rootes cars (Sunbeam Rapier, Hillman, Singer and Humber), but is meant as praise for the Alpine. Credit for this superiority must be attributed to chassis refinements, as some chassis components are actually "borrowed" from the Hillman Estate wagon and the power unit is quite similar to those of the Hillman and Singer. We can't overlook the advantage of the seating position which, being far superior to the family line, allows the driver to devote his entire attention to the controls while riding in a comfortable, form-fitting seat.

The brakes are excellent and exhibited no fade or any tendency to lock up. Even under hardest braking there was no yaw or wheel judder, which helps bear out our contention that this car's good manners make it a good vehicle for the tyro enthusiast.

Normal fuel consumption varies a great deal of course, but the lowest figure we obtained during vigorous driving was 21 mpg, and the average was 24 mpg. The above figures do not include the performance testing, and under careful, steady highway driving a consumption of 26 mpg should be obtainable. An overdrive is also available, but this does not necessarily mean any better fuel consumption under hard driving, though steady cruising should produce 2 to 3 more miles per gallon.

The optional overdrive is the Laycock-de Normanville type with a ratio of 0.802. When this unit is ordered, an axle ratio of 4.22 is included, rather than the standard 3.89 axle as found in our test car. Thus, an overdrive model will give considerably better acceleration figures; we estimate a 0 to 60 time of under 14 sec. In addition, the overdrive produces an effective ratio of 3.39, which will not only give better cruising with lower fuel consumption, but will also add about 5 mph to the top speed. Under favorable circumstances the overdrive model will just touch 100 mph. While we are ordinarily not strong proponents of the overdrive (and we like this car better without the addition), it must be admitted that anyone seeking the maximum possible performance in terms of acceleration, speed and economy should certainly order overdrive.

A word of explanation might be in order here regarding the overdrive and other extras. The basic price of the car, as quoted in the data panel at $2645, obviously doesn't include the overdrive, which retails at $160. Our test car was equipped with white sidewall tires (Dunlop Gold Seal) at $35, fresh air heater at $60, wire wheels at $105, tonneau cover at $39 and the hardtop at $260. Rootes Motors, Inc., makes no charge for inland freight, if any, and this is paid for by the selling dealer. The car as tested, then, will go "out the door" for $3144, plus tax and license in the Los Angeles area.

The Alpine weighs 200 lb less than the Rapier, a creditable and worthwhile saving, which has been accomplished without any apparent sacrifice in torsional rigidity—a difficult problem in view of the unitized construction. The transmission of road noise, a perennial problem with unitized bodies, is completely absent, as are squeaks and rattles.

Ostensibly, the jump seats provided are supposed to be "for kids or extra luggage" but don't for one minute assume that this is a family car for more than a very short distance. Look at other cars in the Rootes line before you try to telescope your children into shapes you wouldn't recognize after a long trip.

The Sunbeam Alpine is a happy compromise for the buyer who wants the sports car feel and a few creature comforts too (for two). In a country such as this, already pre-conditioned to the "personal car," it should find many a happy home.

ALPINE PLUS

Improved Series II Sunbeam has 1·6-litre Engine

Shields, resembling backplates, are now fitted to the front disc brakes to avoid road splashes affecting their efficiency in bad weather.

One of the new hood cant rails, added to give better rain sealing round the windows, is seen here partly detached.

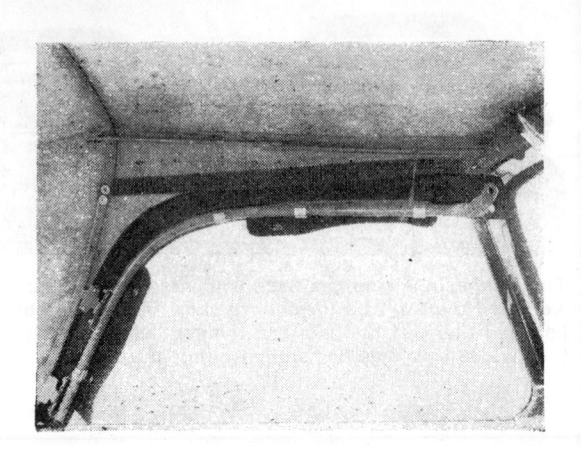

MANY improvements are to be found in the new Series II version of the Sunbeam Alpine which makes its first appearance today. Most notable is an increase of approximately 100 c.c. in engine size to 1,592 c.c., but various changes have also been made to the transmission, brakes and suspension, whilst the body has been improved in detail.

The engine changes have been planned more with a view to increased torque than increased power, although the latter is also slightly greater. Thus, the maximum output of 85.5 b.h.p. gross at 5,000 r.p.m. represents a 2½% gain over the former 83.5 b.h.p. at 5,300 r.p.m. compared with a 5% increase in maximum torque; the latter now stands at 94 lb. ft. at 3,800 r.p.m. in place of the former 89.5 lb. ft. The higher torque, moreover, is given over a considerably greater range, the Series II engine maintaining a figure above 90 lb. ft. between 2,600 r.p.m. and 4,600 r.p.m.—from all of which a greatly improved top-gear performance is to be expected.

The new characteristics result from an increase in cylinder bore from 79 mm. to 81.5 mm. in conjunction with a slight reduction in compression ratio, although the latter, at 9.1 : 1, remains high for a production engine. For overseas territories where high octane fuels are not available, a lower-compression version (8.5 : 1) remains available.

To deal with the increased output, a stiffer crankshaft with increased overlap and larger-diameter connecting-rod bearings is now used. The big-end diameter has gone up from 1⅞ in. to 1¹⁵⁄₁₆ in. In addition, the sizes of both the water pump and the oil pump have been increased to provide greater capacity, and a new silencer is fitted. The two carburetters (Zenith 36 WIP 2) remain as before, but the choke size has been increased from 28 mm. to 30 mm.

For the transmission, a new 8-in. Borg and Beck clutch with strap drive is now fitted to cope with the higher torque and an interesting detail is the use of a hydrostatic slave cylinder arranged to take up play automatically. Apart from minor modifications to the main shaft, the gearbox is basically identical with the Series I, but the top cover and remote-control casing for the centre-floor change is now identical with that used on the Series III Sunbeam Rapier. In addition, the steering-column switch for the Laycock - de Normanville overdrive (an optional extra) is now fitted in a more convenient position. Some of these modifications have, incidentally, already been put into production on the later examples of the Series I.

A very welcome chassis change lies in the elimination of eight greasing points. Two of these are accounted for by the use of a propeller shaft with sealed, pre-packed universals, and the remaining six have been dispensed with by employing new steering joints with nylon inserts for the track-rod joints and upper swivel bearings.

In the rear suspension, greater lateral stability has been achieved by substituting 2¼-in. wide rear-spring blades for the former 1¾-in. size and larger capacity lever-arm shock absorbers improve riding qualities and reduce fade. Other new features are the fitting of dirt shields to the front disc brakes, and a three-lobe petrol filler cap which matches the hub nuts of optional wire wheels.

To turn to coachwork, Series II improvements are confined to small details, but it is worth noting that the seating accommodation of later examples of the Series I models was improved considerably by reducing the steering wheel diameter to 15½ in. and raising the column by 1 in. to give more thigh clearance, whilst the seat itself was repositioned 2 in. rearwards to give more leg room; at the same time two-position adjustable pedals were introduced.

The new body features for 1961 include the addition of an interior light directly above the cubby box, an alteration of the hinging of the lid of the combined centre armrest and glove box to make this receptacle equally accessible to driver or passenger, and improvements to the hood stowage panel which also forms the backrest of the occasional rear seat; this is now more substantial and has a positive locking arrangement. Finally, to give better rain sealing round the wind-up windows, detachable hood cant rails are now provided and chromium-plated window support channels are fitted to the doors.

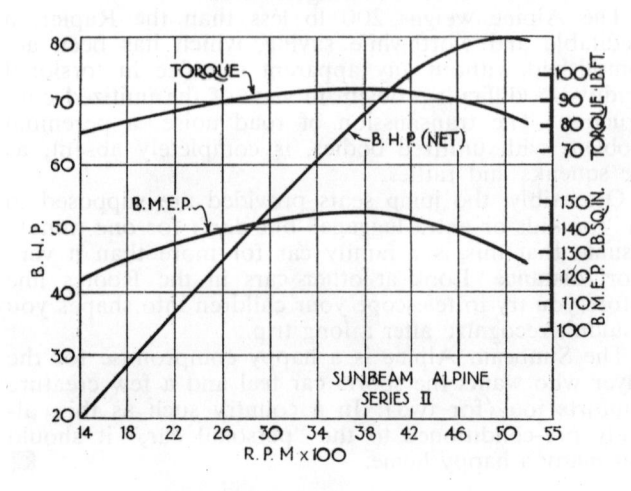

22

The Autocar road tests

SUNBEAM ALPINE Series II

With wire wheels, optional extras in place of the normal disc wheels, the hub nuts are hexagonal, and a large spanner is supplied for them

SINCE the original design was frozen for production, a number of important improvements, based on greater experience, has been incorporated in the Sunbeam Alpine. It is now coming off the line in Series II form; this latest model, the subject of the test, was introduced at the recent London Show. While some aspects of the car may still leave room for improvement, undoubtedly it is now a two-seater of special merit: it offers the essential qualities of a true sports car without the barbarities often associated with this class of vehicle.

One of the most important of the recent changes is the raising of engine capacity from 1,494 c.c. to 1,592 c.c., done by increasing the cylinder bore from 79 to 82mm. It should be remembered, of course, that this represents an increase of only 6½ per cent, and those who make comparisons against our test of the earlier Alpine have no need to be disappointed that the improvements in performance are small. Indeed, some of the acceleration times at high speeds are fractionally slower than they were with the smaller engine, reflecting differences of engine tune and test weather conditions.

More noticeable engine improvements are that the new power unit is smoother, particularly at low revs, and it is less obtrusive than before. There is still considerable exhaust resonance, heard as a harsh snarl when the car is accelerating, but both this and general engine noise are less than on the Series I model. Starting is immediate whether the engine is hot or cold, and after a night in the open in cold November weather the car could be driven off without choke within a few seconds of starting; in fact, the choke was scarcely used at all throughout the test.

Twin Zenith carburettors continue to be fitted, but they differ from those on the Series I models in having 30mm chokes instead of the previous ones of 28mm. With this change, and the increase in engine size, it is not surprising that the new model uses a little more fuel. Even so, the Alpine can be relied upon to return fuel consumptions always on the right side of 20 m.p.g. The overall figure of 20·6 m.p.g. recorded in the data includes frequent hard driving, numerous M1 journeys in which the car sustained 90 m.p.h. without fuss, and, as is our practice, the whole of the performance testing. In more restrained conditions, up to 27 m.p.g. was obtained readily enough.

Peak power output is now developed at 5,000 r.p.m. (previously 5,300 r.p.m.), but the engine gives no impression of beginning to flag at this point; only the red line on the rev. counter suggests that 5,500 r.p.m. is an upper limit to be observed. Acceleration is strong to 80 m.p.h.; thereafter it tails off, but the car will build up speed towards a true maximum around 97 m.p.h. Given favourable conditions, the Alpine is good for 100 m.p.h. At the lower speeds, acceleration is brisk, as indicated by the standing quarter-mile time of 19·7 secs. In this test from standstill, the Alpine was found to reach 70 m.p.h. by the end of a straight quarter-mile.

Accelerator pumps on each of the carburettors are operated by rocking cams which override on nylon rollers after approximately two-thirds of full throttle opening. The

The neat facia is capped by a firmly padded protective roll. The glove locker on the left is supplemented by a useful locker between the seats. Here the rubber mats are still wet from leakage in a shower (see text)

23

SUNBEAM ALPINE...

Front and rear bumpers wrap round sufficiently to protect the corners of the car. The fuel filler, which will not take the full pump delivery without blow-back, has a threaded cap

point at which the accelerator pumps are fully actuated is felt clearly on the accelerator pedal; this gives a somewhat jerky action to the pedal movement, although the linkage is rod-operated, with extensive use of nylon connectors.

Conveniently near to the driver's left hand on the steering wheel is the central remote-control gear change. It was rather stiff to operate, especially across the gate, but there was no free play at the lever when any gear was engaged. The synchromesh is very effective and copes easily with fast changes. Bottom gear does not have synchromesh, but is readily engaged while the car is on the move. In practice this is usually unnecessary, however, because second gear is so low that the car will start from rest, or pick up speed eagerly from walking pace, in this ratio. Third gear is also low, and even with the engine's willingness to rev, it provides the modest maximum of only 68 m.p.h.

These comments apply, of course, to the overdrive model tested on which, in keeping with usual Rootes policy, a back axle of low effective gearing is fitted. The result of this is that overdrive top gives only 19.8 m.p.h. per 1,000 r.p.m., and while the Alpine will, it is true, pull away without snatch from as low as 20 m.p.h. in overdrive top gear, this is a virtue not needed in a sports car. Direct top gear, when overdrive is not fitted, corresponds to 17.3 m.p.h. per 1,000 r.p.m., from which it will be seen that the speed difference at 4,000 r.p.m. is only 10 m.p.h. when the overdrive model is specified.

Clutch operation is light, and the clutch will absorb smoothly full engine power for acceleration from a standing start, or for making a restart on a severe gradient. On our usual 1-in-3 test hill there was no difficulty at all in getting away.

A pleasing mixture of firmness with resilience is achieved by the suspension, and the Alpine is certainly not a car that must be confined to smooth tarred roads. On rough pavé it gives an unusually stable ride without pitching or violent vertical movement, and in colonial conditions ample vertical wheel movement is allowed by the suspension to absorb severe bumps. On normal roads, the car sits down firmly and minor irregularities pass almost unnoticed. Exceptionally stable cornering characteristics are a side-product of the suspension.

A very slight understeering tendency is noticed, but the balance of the car in severe cornering is near enough to neutral for the driver to feel entirely in command. When the Alpine is cornered to the limit of adhesion, breakaway does not occur suddenly and, although on wet roads the car can be made to slide fairly readily, it is again extremely easy and reassuring to correct this.

Much of this simplicity of control results from steering which is undoubtedly the best that Rootes have achieved. Reasonably light at all speeds, the steering is absolutely precise—one can detect no lost movement at all—and the response to small movements of the wheel is immediate. There are now 3½ turns of the steering wheel from lock to lock (previously 3), but this does not imply that the steering is lower-geared than before; the maximum lock-over angle of the front wheels has been increased, and the minimum turning circle between kerbs has been reduced by nearly 2ft to 33ft 4in. At speed on certain surfaces a slight tremor of vibration is fed back through the steering, and a trace of scuttle shake is noticed when rough roads are taken at speed.

Directional stability of the Alpine is first rate, and it is not greatly affected by cross winds, requiring little correction even at high speeds.

Girling disc brakes are fitted for the front wheels, in conjunction with drum rear brakes, and they proved powerful and responsive. Quite powerful braking is available in return for light pedal pressures, and 0.97g deceleration on dry roads was obtained repeatedly and without wheel lock.

Rapid pad wear was experienced on the disc brakes of earlier Alpines, and to limit this the dust shield is now extended to enclose the edge of the disc. This change may be the cause of a new failing experienced on the Alpine

The forward-hinged bonnet does not open wide, yet accessibility and space for engine work are good. All service components are reached easily

A self-cancelling finger-tip control is provided on the left of the steering column for the winking indicators, which have individual tell-tales in the speedometer and rev. counter. There is an ashtray between the seats

Melodious yet penetrating horns are operated by a small ring on the steering wheel. Partial obstruction of the instruments results from this horn ring, and many owners would probably be glad to lose the top segment of it. Instruments comprise a commendably accurate and steady speedometer incorporating a trip mileometer (for which the reset knob is on the other side of the steering column), rev counter, oil pressure and fuel gauges, and a coolant thermometer. The panel is neat and well-planned, and incorporates blanks for extra instruments and accessories. To complete the facia set-up would cost £10 13s 4d for a clock, cigarette lighter, ammeter and screen washer; a fog lamp switch and heater controls would still be needed to fill all the blanks. Fitted to the test car, the fresh air heater (£12 including blower) proved agreeably powerful, but took some time to become effective after a cold start. A rheostat control for the blower would be useful, as in slow traffic the heater is either ineffective or overpowering. Air for the heater is drawn in through vents just forward of the windscreen.

Also available as accessories are rear compartment seats for children (£3 15s), although this space should be regarded primarily as for luggage. With the front seat set well forward, which makes driving difficult, it was found that a child of 10 could not sit with her knees in front of her.

Adequate Lighting Provided

A glove-locker light is now fitted, and the switch for it is incorporated in the panel lamps switch on the facia. This switch, incidentally, is now fitted where the lighting switch used to be, with the result that the lights control is reached more readily. All switches are of positive action tumbler type. The headlamps have good spread coupled with powerful long-range beams which allow high speeds to be used in safety at night. There is no reversing lamp. The number of grease points for attention every 1,000 miles has been reduced to seven.

Still the only British car in its class to be fitted with winding side windows, the Alpine now scores from extra improvements in the weather protection above the waist line. A chrome pillar on the leading edge of both doors extends to the full height of the windscreen, ensuring excellent draught proofing, while around the frameless side windows a sure fit with the hood is obtained by use of detachable fillets. These are extra objects to remove when the hood is lowered, but they ensure that the hood fit is thoroughly snug. The car is as well sealed with the hood up as are most saloons and apart from the gains in appearance and

—temporarily impaired braking on wet roads. This was at its worst at high speed on M1 in the rain, but it was still unpleasantly noticeable on ordinary wet road surfaces at speeds above about 40 m.p.h., when a full second or more would elapse before the brakes would respond to pedal pressures. Recovery was then unsynchronized, so that the car would pull to left or right without warning. The handbrake lever is well shaped and conveniently situated to the right of the driver's seat. It is not quite powerful enough to secure the car on a 1-in-3 gradient.

Wet weather, which unfortunately prevailed throughout most of the test period, revealed a shortcoming on the test car—imperfect sealing at the point where the doors join the scuttle, just below the windscreen. Water dripped in here on both sides in rain, but fortunately moulded rubber mats cover the floor to either side of the carpeted transmission hump, and they did not suffer from the soaking which resulted.

Improved Driving Position

Anyone who knows the Series I Alpine would find that the greatest improvement of the car is in the driving position, which is now superbly comfortable. There is ample legroom, so that even tall drivers can sit with their legs extended and relaxed, and the smaller steering wheel is pleasant to handle. Mounting the wheel a little higher has resulted in ample thigh room below the lower part of the rim, yet the wheel is still low enough at the top not to obstruct forward vision. The curved screen allows a wide view, and the screen pillars are slender and unobtrusive.

To perfect the driving position only one change is needed. The steering wheel should be mounted nearer to the facia, enabling those who wish to do so to hold the steering wheel at arm's length, and allowing lady drivers to take advantage of the generous range of forward seat adjustment. The old pedal position, nearer to the driver, is still available. Larger pedals are now fitted. Passenger accommodation is less comfortable than that for the driver because of the awkward shape of the floor on the left; the passenger can find no part of the toeboard large enough to rest his feet on. The seats are comfortable, extending well under the thighs, and providing sufficient lateral support. Trimming is in Vynide.

Large areas of the windscreen are cleared by the single-speed self-parking wipers, but at above 75 m.p.h. they lift from the screen, leaving runnels of uncleared rainwater on the glass. The wiper motor is mounted below the facia, and is consequently more audible than usual.

Luggage space in the boot itself is rather small. A practical toolkit, including a fine copper hammer, is provided in the spare wheel locker

life of the hood, there is less to be said than usual in favour of specifying a hardtop. The hood is also notably free from drumming or wind flap at speed. When folded, it tucks neatly away behind hinged panels at the rear of the car.

Because of the long wait for satisfactory weather for performance testing, the Alpine was in our hands for longer than are the majority of Road Test cars. Several points required attention in this time: the overdrive became slow to engage and would not disengage without causing a jolt (unless the clutch was used); the gear change became stiff; a rear damper broke loose, and the radio came adrift. Otherwise the car stood up to sustained hard use for over 2,000 miles, and drew praise from all who drove it.

Designed and developed against a formidable background of experience and success in international rallies, the Sunbeam Alpine typifies a size and type of vehicle in which the British industry excels. Even when the numerous items of extra equipment are added to its basic cost, it remains relatively inexpensive, and should enjoy a wide following in world markets.

SUNBEAM ALPINE II

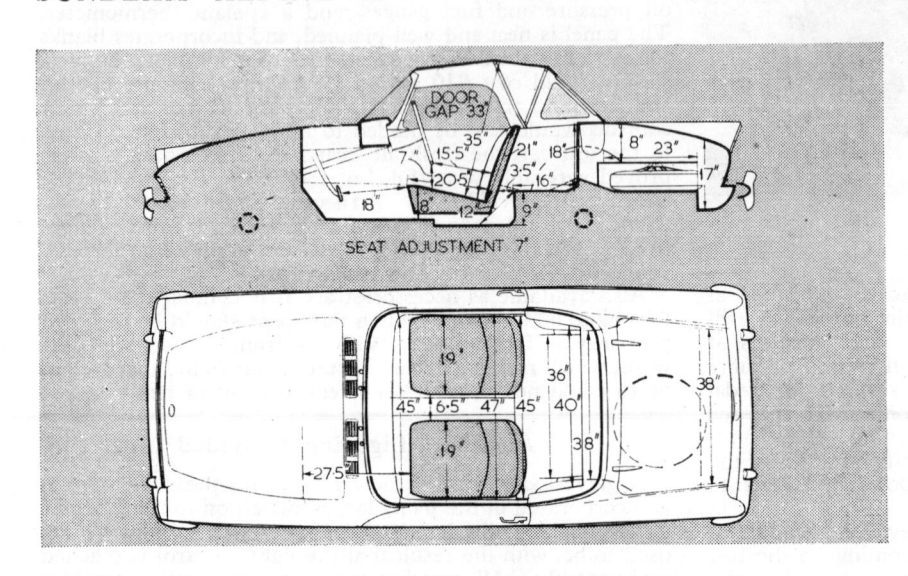

Scale ⅛in to 1ft. Driving seat in central position. Cushions uncompressed

---

PERFORMANCE

ACCELERATION TIMES (mean):
Speed range, Gear Ratios and Time in Sec.

m.p.h.	*3·39 to 1	4·22 to 1	*4·72 to 1	5·88 to 1	9·04 to 1	14·12 to 1
10–30	—	—	—	7·5	4·7	—
20–40	—	10·3	9·3	7·0	4·5	—
30–50	15·1	10·5	9·4	6·8	—	—
40–60	16·5	10·9	10·4	7·4	—	—
50–70	19·0	12·4	12·1	—	—	—
60–80	22·2	15·7	17·5	—	—	—
70–90	35·9	31·5	—	—	—	—

*Overdrive.

From rest through gears to:
- 30 m.p.h. .. 4·5 sec.
- 40 ,, .. 6·6 ,,
- 50 ,, .. 10·3 ,,
- 60 ,, .. 14·8 ,,
- 70 ,, .. 20·3 ,,
- 80 ,, .. 29·8 ,,
- 90 ,, .. 50·2 ,,

Standing quarter mile 19·7 sec.

MAXIMUM SPEEDS ON GEARS:

Gear		m.p.h.	k.p.h.
O.D. Top	(mean)	96·7	155·6
	(best)	98	158
Top	.. ..	94	151
O.D. 3rd	.. ..	87	140
3rd	.. ..	68	119
2nd	.. ..	44	71
1st	.. ..	28	45

TRACTIVE EFFORT (by Tapley meter):

	Pull lb per ton	Equivalent gradient
O.D. Top	135	1 in 16·6
Top	190	1 in 11·7
O.D. 3rd	225	1 in 9·9
Third	310	1 in 7·1
Second	480	1 in 4·6

BRAKES (at 30 m.p.h. in neutral):

Pedal load in lb	Retardation	Equiv. stopping distance in ft
25	0·26g	115
50	0·48g	63
75	0·76g	40
100	0·97g	31

FUEL CONSUMPTION (at steady speeds):

	Direct Top	O.D. Top
30 m.p.h.	45·4 m.p.g.	51·3 m.p.g.
40 ,,	40·0 ,,	46·1 ,,
50 ,,	33·9 ,,	40·0 ,,
60 ,,	30·3 ,,	34·5 ,,
70 ,,	26·3 ,,	29·8 ,,
80 ,,	22·8 ,,	26·5 ,,
90 ,,	19·1 ,,	22·1 ,,

Overall fuel consumption for 1,937 miles, 20·6 m.p.g. (13·7 litres per 100 km.).
Approximate normal range 20–27 m.p.g. (14·1–10·5 litres per 100 km.).
Fuel: Premium grade.

TEST CONDITIONS: Weather: Overcast, showers, 15–25 m.p.h. wind.
Air temperature, 48 deg. F.

STEERING: Turning circle:
Between kerbs, L, 33ft 8in.; R, 33ft 4in.
Between walls, L, 35ft 1in.; R, 34ft 9in.
Turns of steering wheel from lock to lock, 3·5.

DATA

PRICE (basic), with open two-seater body, £695.
British purchase tax, £290 14s 2d.
Total (in Great Britain), £985 14s 2d.
Extras: Radio £22 1s 0d.
  Heater £12 0s 0d.
  Overdrive £60 4s 2d.
  Hardtop £65.
  Road Speed tyres £11 13s 9d.
  Centre-locking wire wheels £38 5s 0d.
  Tonneau cover £10 0s 0d.
(Above prices include purchase tax.)

ENGINE: Capacity, 1,592 c.c. (97·1 cu. in.).
Number of cylinders, 4.
Bore and stroke, 81·5 × 76·2 mm (3·2 × 3·0in.).
Valve gear, overhead, pushrods.
Compression ratio, 9·1 to 1.
B.h.p. 80 (net) 85·5 (gross) at 5,000 r.p.m. (B.h.p. per ton laden, 70).
Torque, 94 lb. ft. at 3,800 r.p.m.
M.p.h. per 1,000 r.p.m. in top gear, 15·9; in overdrive, 19·8.

WEIGHT: (with 5 gal fuel): 19·8cwt (2,219 lb).
Weight distribution (per cent): F, 52; R, 48.
Laden as tested, 22·8 cwt (2,555 lb).
Lb per c.c. (laden), 1·6.

BRAKES: Type, Girling, disc (front), drum (rear).
Method of operation, hydraulic, no servo.
Disc diameter: 9·5in.
Drum dimensions: 9·0in. diameter; 1·75in. wide.
Swept area: F, 196 sq. in.; R, 99 sq. in. (259 sq. in. per ton laden).

TYRES: 5·90—13in. Dunlop Road Speed.
Pressures (p.s.i.): F, 22; R, 23 (normal); F, 24; R, 25 (fast driving); F, 28; R, 31 (prolonged high speeds).

TANK CAPACITY: 9 Imperial gallons.
Oil sump, 8 pints (incl. filter).
Cooling system, 15 pints (including heater).

DIMENSIONS: Wheelbase, 7ft 2in.
Track: F, 4ft 3in.; R, 4ft 0·5in.
Length (overall), 12ft 11·3in.
Width, 5ft 0·5in.
Height, 4ft 3·5in.
Ground clearance, 5·2in.
Frontal area, 16 sq. ft. (approx.).
Capacity of luggage space, 7 cu. ft. (approx.).

ELECTRICAL SYSTEM: 12-volt; 38 ampère-hour battery.
Head lamps, 50–40 watt bulbs.

SUSPENSION: Front, coil springs, semi-trailing wishbones, anti-roll bar.
Rear, live axle, semi-elliptic leaf springs.

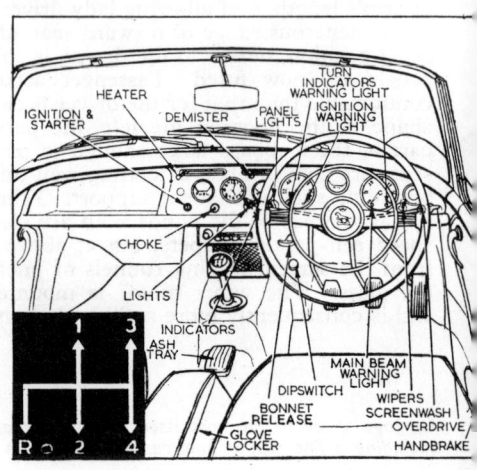

SPEEDOMETER CORRECTION: m.p.h.

Car speedometer	10	20	30	40	50	60	70	80	90	100
True speed ..	14	21	30	40	49	58	69	78	88	99

NEW SUNBEAM ALPINE

SLEEK
SWIFT
SPECTACULAR

Look at the spectacular
New Sunbeam Alpine—
no other sports car offers so
many sparkling new features:

NEW

power-packed 1½-litre engine—
develops 83.5 b.h.p. at
5,300 r.p.m.—vivid acceleration
and road speeds up to
100 m.p.h. with outstanding
economy.

NEW

exclusive styling has exciting
modern flair . . . wrap-around
windscreen . . . retractable hood.
A detachable hard-top
is available as an extra.

NEW

comfort unique to sports cars
. . . wide-opening doors,
wind down windows . . .
occasional seat or luggage space
plus roomy boot.

NEW

safety with front disc brakes . . .
and rock-steady road holding.
Price £685 plus £286.10.10 P.T.
*Wire Wheels, White Wall Tyres,
Overdrive and Hard-Top
as optional extras.*

Bred from success in the world's greatest rally events

A product of
ROOTES MOTORS LIMITED

Sunbeam-Talbot Ltd Coventry · London Showrooms and Export Div: Rootes Ltd Devonshire House Piccadilly London W1

ABOVE: The Grand Touring bodywork enhances still further the good looks of the Alpine and is the result of considerable experimentation.

THE HARRINGTON ALPINE (STAGE III)

A 110 m.p.h. G.T. Version of the Sunbeam with Hartwell-tuned Engine

BY GREGOR GRANT

As the owner of a Sunbeam Alpine hardtop, I was most interested to do a road test of the recently introduced Harrington Alpine with Grand Touring bodywork. This particular edition had a specially tuned Stage III "Hartwellized" engine, with 10.2 to 1 compression ratio, two double-choke 40 mm. Weber carburetters, competition manifolds and clutch, lightened flywheel, high-lift camshaft and other aids to efficiency. Power output is stated to be 100 b.h.p. at 6,200 r.p.m.

Additionally, stiffer suspension is used, and gearbox, steering, and so on, are stripped and rebuilt to full racing specification. Brakes are also modified to cope with the greatly increased performance. The Stage costs £215 extra, and is primarily intended for the competition owner.

As can be judged from George Phillips's photographs, the Harrington

RIGHT: The interior extras include a wood-rimmed steering wheel, Microcell bucket-type seats and an electronic rev. counter.

*

BELOW: The Stage III engine as shown, which has twin double-choke 40 mm. Weber carbs., competition manifolds, high-lift camshaft and lightened flywheel.

G.T. Alpine is extremely well-proportioned, with modern styling. The car is not merely a standard Alpine to which a reinforced plastic roof has been added, but is the result of considerable experimentation entailing many alterations from the Rootes product. Removal of the compartment which houses the fabric top and irons has enabled the designers greatly to increase interior space, including exceptionally good luggage accommodation. The blending of the glass-fibre portion to the steel bodywork has been most cleverly done, and is something more than a conversion.

After all, Thos. Harrington, Ltd., of Hove, is known all over the world for high-quality coachwork on all types of passenger and commercial vehicles, and what the concern's craftsmen do not know about the application of plastic materials is hardly worth considering. The coaches, in particular, are regarded as being the last word in road transport vehicles. It is also worth mentioning that all moulds are produced in the factory at Hove.

MR. NORMAN HARRINGTON and George Hartwell with their Stage III car which is capable of getting from standstill to 60 m.p.h. in 10.6 secs.

The Harrington Alpine—continued

The Harrington Alpine is produced with the full co-operation of the Rootes Group, the company being under the chairmanship of George Hartwell, 500 c.c. racing pioneer and an experienced competitions driver of Sunbeam, Hillman and Singer products.

With a production not exceeding 250 units per year, Harrington's are able to offer "tailor-made" interiors to suit individual tastes. This includes a wide variety of special equipment and seats, practically all of which comes within the list price.

Again, the standard Rootes "extras" can be ordered, such as wire wheels, Dunlop RS5 tyres, Laycock-de Normanville overdrive, fitted luggage, safety harness and suchlike components.

The example tested had no occasional rear seats, but had racing-type bucket seats which Hartwell intends to replace with more comfortable ones. A Leston-Carlotti wood-rim steering wheel replaced the normal Rootes wheel, the conversion necessitating a separate, flick-type horn switch. Sole addition to the instrumentation was a Crypton electronic rev. counter.

On the road, the Harrington was remarkably free from wind-noise at high speeds, and even the use of the rearward-opening quarter lights did not make any appreciable difference. These certainly do provide draught-free ventilation, impossible to obtain on the standard hard-top. On the other hand, reduction in size of the rear window has cut down visibility, and I feel that rear-view mirrors of the Wallpress pattern would be of great advantage.

I thought that the suspension was a trifle too hard, but road-holding is definitely first-class. On wet roads the Dunlop RS5s provide almost uncanny adhesion, and it was so difficult to provoke wheelspin, that I had to confirm that no limited-spin device was fitted. There was a suspicion of front-wheel patter at about 90 m.p.h. cruising, but this may have been due to incorrect wheel-balancing. Braking was good at all times, and there was no squealing whatsoever at low traffic speeds.

The car was fairly sensitive to tyre pressure, and I found that 32 p.s.i., front and rear, seemed to be admirable on M1. For normal road use, 26 p.s.i. would be a useful compromise.

Getaway was aided by a completely spin-free clutch, which does, of course, require considerably more foot pressure than on the standard Alpines. It was impossible to cause clutch-slip, and changes are more rapid than with the normal clutch, without having to do anything in the nature of "straight-through" changes.

No chokes are used with the Webers, but starting is instantaneous, and the engine warms up rapidly at 1,500-2,000 r.p.m. Synchronization was not 100 per cent., which resulted in a certain amount of lumpiness at tick-over speeds, and it was also felt that the pilot jets were about one size too large. However, performance was there in plenty, as a standing quarter-mile in 17.9 secs. proves. Taken by and large, the acceleration of the Stage III car is exceptionally good, although one has to be extremely careful not to get over 6,000 r.p.m. in the intermediate ratios. Actually, 6,200 r.p.m. was reached on direct top, which rather indicates that the car has good inherent aerodynamic characteristics to take advantage of the high power-output from the 1,600 c.c. engine.

The car can achieve 110 m.p.h. in overdrive, as the mean of several two-way runs was 108-109 m.p.h. Best speed recorded, under good conditions, and with a slightly favourable tail-wind, was 111.6 m.p.h., with the tachometer showing 5,700 r.p.m. (o/d). Oil pressure, at the highest r.p.m., showed a constant 50 p.s.i., and never once did the water temperature gauge exceed 170 deg. The cable-driven speedometer was inclined to be optimistic, and went right off the clock (120 m.p.h. plus) during maximum speed tests.

With the Webers, it was not possible to use the fuel consumption test-tank without a great deal of modification.

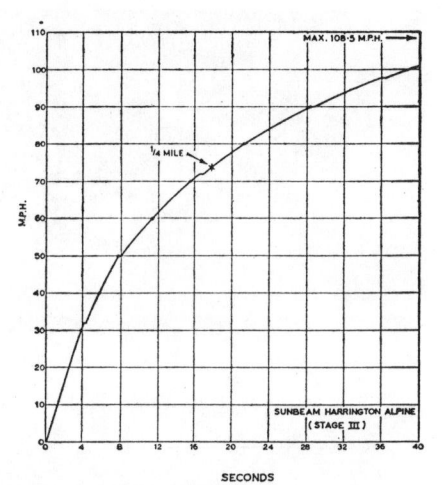

ACCELERATION GRAPH

However, something around 22 m.p.g. could be taken as a hard-driving figure, with the probability of 30 m.p.g. at more gentle cruising gaits, using overdrive.

The noise level is slightly greater than on my own car, the unsilenced carburetters making an audible contribution, and the exhaust-note producing a fair-sized crackle whilst accelerating hard. There is no body-drumming, but the front-windows are inclined to rattle. The overdrive pump was audible at low speeds.

A good point was the fitting of anti-dazzle shields, but I was surprised to take over a vehicle which was neither provided with windscreen washers, nor had provision for their fitting. I should say that these are an essential part of any modern vehicle equipment, as anyone who has driven on M1 on a dirty day will agree.

Summing up, the Stage III car ought to make a good competition car in the 1,600 c.c. GT category, and for people who do not mind the extra mechanical sound and somewhat "beefy" exhaust note which the engine emits, the machine will make a most likeable high-speed cruising vehicle. As is the case with the more normal Alpines, the Harrington appears to be less fatiguing to drive over long distances than many smallish-capacity sporting cars. Also, for what one gets, it cannot be regarded as an expensive proposition.

It is possible that the Stage I version, with 88 b.h.p. at 5,500 r.p.m., will make a wider appeal, and there is also a Stage II with 93 b.h.p. at 5,700 r.p.m. Nevertheless, the thought of having a push-rod engine which gives 100 b.h.p.—and appears to do so with complete reliability,—might turn the scales for the more discriminating 1.6-litre, GT enthusiasts.

SPECIFICATION AND PERFORMANCE DATA

Manufacturers: Thos. Harrington, Ltd., Sackville Works, Hove, Sussex.
Price: £1,225 (incl. P.T.). Extras: Stage III engine, £215; centre-lock wire wheels, £38 5s.; RS5 tyres, £11 13s. 9d.; overdrive, £60 4s. 2d. heater, £12. Total (as tested), £1.562 2s. 11d.
Engine: Four cylinders, o.h.v. (push-rod). light-alloy cylinder head; 81.5 x 76.2 mm. (1,592 c.c.); 10.2 to 1 compression ratio; 100 b.h.p. at 6,200 r.p.m. Two DC40 Weber carburetters. Mechanical fuel pump. Lucas coil ignition.
Transmission: Borg and Beck competition clutch; four-speed gearbox with synchromesh on 2nd, 3rd and 4th. Laycock-de Normanville overdrive. Ratios, 14.12, 9.04, 5.88 (4.72 o/d), 4.22 (3.39 o/d) to 1. Hardy-Spicer open propeller shaft; hypoid bevel rear axle.
Suspension: Independent front by helical springs and semi-trailing wishbones, anti-roll bar. Semi-elliptic rear. Telescopic hydraulic dampers.
General: Girling disc brakes (front), drum (rear); 5.90 x 13 Dunlop RS5 tyres; centre-lock wire wheels; nine-gallon rear petrol tank; 12-volt electrical equipment.
Dimensions, etc: Wheelbase, 7 ft. 2 ins.; length (overall). 12 ft. 11¼ ins.; height, 4 ft. 3¼ ins; track (front), 4 ft. 3 ins., (rear) 4 ft. 0½ in.; ground clearance, 5¼ ins.; turning circle, 33 ft. 8 ins.; weight (unladen), 19 cwt. 18 lb. (as tested) 22 cwt. 54 lb.
Performance: Maximum speed, 108.5 m.p.h. Acceleration: 0-30 m.p.h., 3.9 secs.; 0-40 m.p.h., 5.8 secs.; 0-50 m.p.h., 7.8 secs.; 0-60 m.p.h., 10.6 secs.; 0-70 m.p.h., 15.6 secs.; 0-80 m.p.h., 21.2 secs.; 0-90 m.p.h., 28.4 secs. Standing quarter-mile, 17.9 secs. Speeds in gears: 1st, 32 m.p.h.; 2nd, 50 m.p.h.; 3rd, 72 m.p.h. (90 m.p.h. o/d); top, 98 m.p.h. (108.5 m.p.h. o/d)
Petrol Consumption: Driven hard, 22 m.p.g.

CT&T ROAD TEST
Alpine 1600

The Sunbeam Alpine continues to gain both in popularity and respect in Canada, a happy trend for Rootes which no doubt will be strengthened by an increase in capacity and performance at low speeds in the latest models to reach this country.

The beefier Alpine cannot be told apart from its predecessor by sight alone. The slim, sleek, delicately finned car with the rakish hood line is just as before externally. It was a good design and did not need changing. The latest Alpine is known as the "Series II" or the "1600" the latter name referring to the increase in capacity from 1494 cc to 1592 cc. The extra capacity, accompanied by a fractional drop in compression ratio, does not show up in top speed figures, nor, prospective drivers will be happy to know, in the overall fuel consumption.

The increased capacity of the Alpine's 4-cylinder ohv engine is brought about with a slightly increased bore, 3.21 cc (81.5 mm) as against 3.11 cc (79 mm). The stroke remains the same at 3.00 ins (76.2 mm). The crankshaft and connecting rod assembly has been strengthened and the compression ratio reduced from 9.2:1 to 9.1:1.

The revised engine develops more power and reaches it peak sooner with 85.5 bhp at 5,000 rpm as against 83.5 bhp developed at 5,300 rpm. Maximum torque of 94 ft/lbs is reached at 3,800 rpm, an increase over 89.5 ft/lbs for the same engine speed on the 1494 cc unit.

As might be expected, these changes do not yield great bonuses of speed but do make for a more flexible engine with more beef in the lower speed ranges. The test car loaned to CT&T by Rootes Motors (Canada) Ltd., was fitted with overdrive and a lower axle ratio than the standard Alpines which include the model tested by CT&T in December 1959. Bearing in mind that the final drive was 4.22:1 compared with 3.89:1 in our earlier test, the following acceleration figures make an interesting comparison:

1961 ALPINE

0-30 mph — 4.5 secs.
0-40 mph — 6.6 secs.
0-60 mph — 14.0 secs.
Best timed run: 97.5 mph

1959 ALPINE

0-30 mph — 5.0 secs.
0-40 mph — 7.5 secs.
$-60 mph — 14.5 secs.
Best timed run: 98 mph

Other differences between the two test vehicles include a soft top and 50 lbs more weight on the 1961 car. The 1959 Alpine was fitted with a plastic hardtop. When this was removed it resulted in a drop of 5 mph in the maximum speed.

The gearbox ratios are unchanged. There is a tendency with the 1600 Alpine to feel that first gear (3.346:1) it too low, for the car accelerates away very rapidly with the rapidly rising engine noise telling the driver he is approaching maximum revs faster than he expects on first acquaintance. This first gear, however, is the outcome of a desire to give the car snappy performance in mountainous country (after all, it was named for the great successes its forerunners enjoyed in the Alps in Europe). First gear, therefore, will provide really fast getaways with a rapid shift into second at about 4500 rpm. Carrying the revs higher than this in first in normal driving results in a flood of engine noise. Unfortunately first gear is not included in the synchromesh arrangement. Third gear with a ratio of 1.39 in direct drive was a real workhorse on the test car with the low rear axle.

The Laycock overdrive was fitted to top and third and provided a delightful combination of gears for use at the driver's pleasure, for a simple flick of an arm extending from the steering column will engage or remove the overdrive, even when travelling at considerable speeds. Thus a shift from overdrive top to direct third gives the Alpine a remarkable passing gear which can be used at speeds up to 60 mph. We found that smoother shifts into and out of overdrive can be accomplished by double declutching.

The overdrive also converts this snappy sports car into an economical tourer with judicious use of overdrive

Luggage space is limited . . .

we were able to turn in a fuel consumption range of between 24 and 27 mpg. The tach is readlined at 6,000 equal to 32 mph in second, 68 mph in third and 86 in top. However, with overdrive engaged the engine is loafing at 3,800 rpm, at 80 mph and 60 mph requires only 2,800 rpm in overdrive as against 3500 rpm for the same speed direct.

Overdrive is an optional item costing $150. The test car was equipped also with wire wheels ($95) tonneau cover ($35) all of which brings the basic price of $2695 for the test Alpine 1600 up to $2975. Other options include hardtop $195 and road speed tires $25.

The test car was fitted with 5.60 x 13 Dunlop Gold Seal Tires which proved the equal to all the test requirements. The ride given by the Alpine was a very pleasant compromise between sports and touring stiffness and long journeys can be undertaken in an Alpine with little discomfort. Apart from the engine the most noticeable change in the 1600 Alpine is the improved handling brough about by employing 2¼ inch leafs in the rear semi-elliptic springs as against 1¾ inches in the earlier models. The improvement shows up quickly in the corners where the former tendency of the rear end to hop when the car was pushed hard is now replaced by considerabl tenacity which, when the car finally breaks away, become a gentle, easily controllable four wheel slide which instills great confidence in the car.

The Alpine's braking system is fully equal to it's lively performance, the stopping operation being divided between Girling disc brakes on the front wheels and 9 inch drum brakes at the rear. Since the earlier or "Series I" Alpine a shield has been fitted to each of the discs for protection against dust and wet. It was not entirely successful in keeping water off the discs and the car tended to pull on the first application of the brakes when it was raining. A couple of dabs at the brake pedal were sufficient in every case to clear the discs for hard stopping.

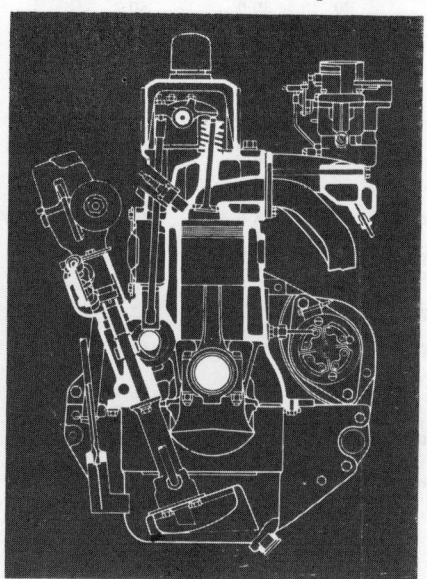

For those who are not acquainted with the Alpine, a brief mention is in order of the interior comforts which greet the driver and passenger. The interior finish is of high quality with two leather upholstered foam rubber seats which give more than adequate support. There is a smaller seat in the rear which would accomodate a child but for short distances only and this car must be considered strictly a two-seater for all practical purposes. The instrument panel is suitably sporting. A small lockable box is situated between the front seats with the top padded for a very useful arm rest. The short gear lever is well positioned but the action is not as smooth as the performance of the car deserves. There is more than one moment of awkwardness for the driver when it comes to making turns, for the turn signal lever and the overdrive lever are identical except for the fact that they sprout from opposite sides of the steering column. A moment's forgetfulness and the car will lurch into overdrive just when the driver is expecting to see his turn signals flashing.

The Alpine hardtop is an excellently fitting piece of equipment and in the opinion of CT&T testers greatly to be desired over the soft top, which while also providing a snug fit, has two large blind spots on both quarters making the fitting of fender mirrors an absolute necessity for safety's sake.

The heater delivers ample warmth which is easily controllable by movement of a chrome lever moving in a horizontal slot at the top of the instrument panel. A similar lever is an identical slot controls flow of air to floor or windshield while a pull on this lever brings the blower into action. The blower, as is the case in most imports, is not up to the job when it comes to normal Canadian winter weather and a second and higher speed is necessary for the Canadian market.

Despite extravagant claims in official literature that "the Alpine offers exceptional luggage accomodation for a sports car, making it eminently suitable for touring," the car falls far short of this claim, except when in direct comparison with other sports cars. In view of the obvious pleasure to be derived from touring in an Alpine, the lack of luggage space is lamentable.

SUNBEAM ALPINE 1600

SPECIFICATIONS

Model Tested:	Sunbeam Alpine 1600
Price of Test Model:	$2975

ENGINE

Cylinders:	4 in line, watercooled
Bore & Stroke:	3.21 ins x 3.00 ins
Displacement:	1592 cc
Torque:	94 ft/lbs @ 3,800 rpm
B.H.P:	85.5 @ 5,000 rpm
Compression Ratio:	9.1:1

DIMENSIONS

Wheelbase:	86 ins.
Track:	
Front:	51 ins.
Rear:	48½ ins.
Length Overall:	155.35 ins.
Width Overall:	60.05 ins.
Heigth Overall:	51.5 ins.
Ground Clearance:	5.125 ins.

DRIVE AND SUSPENSION

Transmission:	Four Speed manual box. 1st: 3.346; 2nd: 2.141; 3rd: 1.39; 4th: 1; Rev. 4.239.
Final Drive:	4.22 (3.89 with standard transmission)
Suspension:	Coil spring and swinging links with telescopic shocks. Semi-elliptic with lever arm shocks.
Steering:	3½ turns lock to lock
Tires:	5.60 x 13
Electrical System:	12 volt

PERFORMANCE

Times:
- 0-30 mph — 4.5 secs.
- 0-40 mph — 6.6 secs.
- 0-50 mph — 10.0 secs
- 0-60 mph — 14.0 secs.
- 0-70 mph — 19.3 secs.
- 0-80 mph — 27.2 secs.

Maximum speed (mean of three one way runs): 96.2 mph

	Indicated	True
30 mph		28.0 mph
40 mph		38.0 mph
50 mph		47.8 mph
60 mph		58 mph

Fuel Consumption:	27 mpg.
Fuel Tank:	9 Imperial gallons
Heater Rating:	Good
Timing Equipment:	S. Smith & Sons

ALPINE GRAND TOURER

EXPERIENCES WITH THE HARRINGTON VERSION, HARTWELL-TUNED

A few laps were put in on the Heysel circuit at Brussels before the grand prix. With a full tank front-rear weight distribution of the Harrington Alpine is about 50-50

A grand touring two-seater with a permanent roof, extra headroom and plenty of luggage space

SUNBEAM'S victory with the Alpine in the Thermal Efficiency Index at Le Mans was all the more praiseworthy because this was the first time they have entered for the race. The successful car, driven by Peter Harper and Peter Proctor, which averaged 90·92 m.p.h. for the 24 hours, was the one with coachwork modifications by Thomas Harrington Ltd. of Hove. Special changes for the race included sinking the headlamps beneath plastic covers and fitting a full undertray, but the permanent glass-fibre roof and modifications to the tail were the same as those on production Harrington Alpines. These were described in *The Autocar* of 31 March this year.

Since that time we have driven nearly 1,000 miles, some on the Continent, in one of these cars, which also had engine modifications by George Hartwell Ltd., of Bournemouth. Harrington Alpines are supplied in standard mechanical form or with one of three stages of engine tune. Ours was a Stage II example described as "... designed for the motorist who wishes to enter competitions with a good chance of success, without loss of smoothness and economy of running when touring." It was claimed that power output of the 1,592 c.c. engine had been increased from 85·5 b.h.p. gross at 5,000 r.p.m. to 93 b.h.p. at 5,700 r.p.m., the cost of the conversion being £75. The total price of the converted car is £1,300, including purchase tax.

Modifications made to the engine are as follows. A lightweight flywheel and competition-type clutch are fitted, the crankshaft, flywheel and clutch being balanced as a unit. Changes to the valve gear consist of a special high-lift camshaft and stronger valve springs. The valve throats and induction ports are reshaped and polished, the exhaust ports are cleaned up and the manifolds are matched to the cylinder head, which is modified to raise the compression ratio to 9·5 to 1 (from 9·1 to 1). Outwardly the engine appears unchanged and the twin 30 m.m. downdraught Zenith carburettors are retained.

A special silencer had been fitted which made the car very noisy. This was worst at 2,500 to 3,000 r.p.m.—a speed range which it was difficult to avoid in towns—and there was a deep bark on the overrun at high revolutions. On subsequent cars the standard Alpine silencer has been used.

In spite of the slightly higher compression ratio of the modified engine, ordinary premium fuels could be used with complete freedom from pinking, although there was super premium in the tank for performance testing. Starting was always immediate, whether the engine was cold or hot, and very little use of the choke was required.

At about 2,500 r.p.m. there is an unmistakable but by no means abrupt increase in engine torque, and from this speed, equivalent to 40 m.p.h. in top gear, there is a substantial increase in pulling power compared with the standard Alpine, as is borne out by the acceleration figures in the table. Other

PERFORMANCE TABLE

Acceleration from rest through gears to:	M.p.h.	Harrington Alpine sec	Sunbeam Alpine II* sec
	30	4·2	4·5
	40	6·4	6·6
	50	9·6	10·3
	60	12·7	14·8
	70	17·3	20·3
	80	24·3	29·8
	90	39·0	50·2
Standing start quarter-mile:		19·3	19·7
10-30 m.p.h. in 2nd		4·4	4·7
10-30 m.p.h. in 3rd		7·3	7·5
20-40 m.p.h. in 2nd		4·1	4·5
20-40 m.p.h. in 3rd		6·3	7·0
20-40 m.p.h. in top		9·5	10·3
30-50 m.p.h. in 3rd		6·0	6·8
30-50 m.p.h. in top		9·1	10·5
40-60 m.p.h. in 3rd		6·6	7·4
40-60 m.p.h. in top		9·2	10·9
50-70 m.p.h. in O.D. 3rd		8·6	12·1
50-70 m.p.h. in top		9·7	12·4
50-70 m.p.h. in O.D. top		13·9	19·0
60-80 m.p.h. in O.D. 3rd		11·7	17·5
60-80 m.p.h. in top		13·1	15·7
60-80 m.p.h. in O.D. top		16·7	22·2
70-90 m.p.h. in top		20·4	31·5
70-90 m.p.h. in O.D. top		23·9	35·9
Maximum speed:			
mean m.p.h.		98·5	96·7
best m.p.h.		99·0	98·0
Overall fuel consumption m.p.g.		24·1	20·6
Kerb weight, lb		2,168	2,219

*The Autocar Road Test, 2 December 1960.

Thomas Harrington Ltd., Sackville Works, Old Shoreham Road, Hove, Sussex.

Alpine Grand Tourer...

The Harper-Proctor Alpine, which won the Thermal Efficiency Index at Le Mans, at the Esses in company with two of the Maseratis

figures show that at lower engine speeds there is also a small increase in torque and the engine does not then become inflexible or "lumpy."

Full throttle acceleration to high speeds showed the car to its best advantage, 90 m.p.h. being reached from rest in 39.0 sec compared with 50.2sec for a standard Alpine II. Wheelspin was not readily provoked when getting away on dry tarmac, as the clutch took up the drive smoothly but rather slowly when engaged at high engine speeds. One of the more impressive acceleration figures was 20.4sec for the interval 70-90 m.p.h. in top—11.1sec quicker than standard.

With the Alpine the choice of gear ratios when an overdrive is fitted is such that overdrive top must be regarded as the normal top gear, overdrive third being much less useful with a ratio close to that of direct top. In overdrive top the natural, most comfortable cruising speed was about 82 m.p.h. (an indicated 90 m.p.h. on the optimistic speedometer). Wind noise at this speed and above was very slight. Opening one of the excellent hinged side windows and setting the heater temperature regulator to cold produced a very strong flow of air inside the car.

As compared with the standard Alpine, the mean maximum speed was increased only fractionally from 96.7 to 98.5 m.p.h., this at 5,000 r.p.m. engine speed. In direct top the best figure observed was 94 m.p.h. at 5,900 r.p.m.

Overall fuel consumption, not including the mileage in Belgium, where the overdrive ceased to operate, was 24.1 m.p.g. for 536 miles. During a distance of 244 miles of very hard driving, high speed cruising and performance testing, a consumption of 22.3 m.p.g. was obtained. These figures are an improvement on those recorded during our road test of the standard Alpine II with soft hood last December, when, admittedly, weather conditions were bad and performance testing accounted for a larger than usual proportion of the total mileage.

Unexpectedly the Harrington Alpine, although carrying an extra 28 lb of bodywork and glass, was lighter than the Alpine road tested by 51 lb. This can be accounted for by the use of heavier wire wheels and the fitting of a radio on that car and, of course, the weight of the soft hood is absent from the Harrington version. Front-rear weight distribution comes very near to 50-50 on this G.T. saloon. There is a noticeable

increase in structural rigidity, as a result of bolting the arched roof to the screen and body and adding a cross member ahead of the abbreviated lid for the boot. The body is entirely free from boom and rattles. In heavy rain water entered above the screen, but this has been rectified on subsequent models.

With the quite large volume enclosed by this roof and the two extra inches of headroom it provides, there is no sense of the restriction or even oppression sometimes experienced under a small hardtop. The large window area, very slim screen pillars and absence of pivoting windows in the doors provide excellent visibility. In the mirror there is a good view through the large moulded plastic rear window. The roof is lined with a light coloured, dotted plastic material and the body is very well finished.

Luggage space is greater than in a standard Alpine, in which room has to be found for the hood, and the compartment is fully carpeted and trimmed. There is limited access to it from the tail through an opening only 4in. deep, so that bulky objects must be loaded through the doors. Fitted luggage can

There is a fully carpeted and trimmed luggage space behind the seats and a deep shelf under the large rear window. Hinged side windows promote thorough ventilation

be supplied. There is an interior lamp under the left rear window.

The small change in weight distribution has scarcely altered the handling characteristics of the car, which is stable and predictable, although when cornering on wet roads with the tyre pressures set for fast driving, the rear wheels can be made to lose their grip quite easily. The excellent brakes (disc front, drums rear) are well up to their task.

Altogether this is a valuable addition to the slender ranks of British grand tourers and one which has a number of points to appeal to the less sporting-minded as well.

SUNBEAM ALPINE

Detail changes make an already desirable car more so

FEW OF THE CARS coming to our shores are as obviously American-oriented as the products from England's Rootes Group, a company that manufactures a line of economy sedans that look for all the world as though their origin was Detroit, rather than Coventry. These cars reflect, if not exactly the average American's tastes, then at least what the Rootes people *think* they are—and they are not too far off-target at that, as their sales record here will show. It was, therefore, hardly surprising that when Rootes made its re-entry into the sports car field, it was with a vehicle quite different from the traditional British sporting machine.

The Sunbeam Alpine, as the new car was designated, was Rootes' answer to the sales-proven concept of the "personal car." Like the personal cars preceding it, it featured a soft ride, proper wind-up side windows and such aids to creature comfort as a real cockpit ventilation system—all of which drew hoots of derision from some of the "old-line" sports car types. But, on the other hand, most people (and you should pardon what follows) didn't give a hoot for tradition; they simply liked the Alpine's tail-finned looks and its dual practical/sporty character, and responded by buying them in batches. That was the Series I Alpine, which we tested at the time of its introduction (R&T, May 1960) and which, like all brand-new designs, had its share of deficiencies but was a success nonetheless. Now, a year later, the accumulation of consumer comment has had its effect and there is a new model, incorporating the changes suggested by experience.

The Sunbeam Alpine Series II is externally unchanged

from the model we tested last year; it still has a bit too much of the "forward-look" to suit our taste—but all the girls here liked the styling, so we must be rather reactionary in this area. The quality of the paint and the general finish of the car's exterior were consistent with its price but we have the feeling that the panels are made of too light-gauge a material. We discovered, for instance, that the channel in the top of the door through which the side window slides could be squeezed completely shut with one hand, the door panel flexing easily under pressure.

Inside the Alpine, there are several points of considerable improvement over the Series I model. The seats, which were and are soft enough to suit anyone, now recline back at a comfortable angle, instead of forcing one into the former bolt-upright driving position. Also, the steering wheel, which our legs had fit around rather than under, has been redone slightly—the wheel itself is smaller in diameter—and though the change is slight the improvement is substantial. Another change that caught our eye, almost literally, was the guide channel for the side window; there have been complaints about the windows rattling and Rootes has extended the channel from its former 4-in. stub into a full length support. This stands menacingly near the area where one's head is likely to pass when getting into the car—but we suppose it might be a purely mental hazard. On the bright side, we *are* of the opinion that a single encounter would annoy one sufficiently to prevent its ever happening again.

The positioning of the controls (excepting the shift lever, which is a long reach into 3rd) is good, and there is now an extension-piece to the side of the throttle for easier heel-and-toe downshifting. Unfortunately, this last item tends to get caught under one's brake foot and could conceivably create some very distressing moments in close traffic.

The Alpine's instrumentation is almost without fault, our only complaint being that all the instruments are not in front of the driver. This is a purely personal thing and the instruments used most often—tach, speedometer and oil pressure—*are* in front of the driver. But, the horn ring always seemed to be right in the way of the tach and speedo—and neatly blotted out the oil-pressure scale. Still, all the instruments were there and the use of those barbarous colored lights was restricted to items like the high-beam warning light. You may have to peer about a moment before finding the gauge appropriate to your mental question, but you can be sure that if it matters, there will be such a gauge.

Undoubtedly, the most improved aspect of the Series II car is the engine. Officially, the changes here have been very minor: a change of cylinder bore (from 79 to 82 mm) gives a trifle less than a 100-cc increase in displacement and the 2 Zenith carburetors have 30 mm instead of the previous 28-mm throats. Power and torque are changed very little from the Series I car and, indeed, the engine feels de-tuned—an impression which is confirmed by the fact that maximum power comes in 300 rpm below the old 83.5-bhp peak at 5300 rpm. The torque is also rated only slightly higher, but we would judge that the engine pulls very near its peak over a wide rpm range. Apart from these considerations, the new model is also much improved in smoothness and, most important, the engine will "blip" up to speed very quickly, whereas it was definitely sluggish in this respect before. The final proof of the effectiveness of these changes is seen in the performance figures; the top speed is not much better, but the standing ¼-mile has been improved by 1.3 sec and the medium-speed-range road performance has been considerably enhanced.

No differences could be found in general road behavior between the Series I and II Alpines; both ride very well and have exceptionally stable handling. We did note that the clutch in the Series II car had a much better bite, but that may have been simply a difference between two individual cars, rather than a real change. At any rate, the clutch took the engine's output so well that our standing starts were marked by considerable wheelspin and some bouncing of the rear axle.

The wheelspin may possibly be due to the tires, as there seemed to be an early loss of adhesion on almost any type of road surface during brisk cornering. While we were somewhat unnerved by the early breakaway, we are forced to admit that plenty of warning is given the driver and, because all four wheels seem to lose adhesion at about the same time, the driver would have to be the greenest novice to get into serious trouble.

Ken Miles, a better-than-average West Coast driver, is preparing a Sunbeam Alpine for racing in the production category and it will be interesting to see the result of his program. Regardless of that outcome, it is still a good car for the money.

ROAD TEST
SUNBEAM ALPINE MK II

SCALE: 10" DIVISIONS

DIMENSIONS

Wheelbase, in	86.0
Tread, f and r	51.2/48.7
Over-all length, in	155.2
width	60.5
height	51.7
equivalent vol, cu ft	282
Frontal area, sq ft	17.4
Ground clearance, in	5.2
Steering ratio, o/a	n.a.
turns, lock to lock	3.3
turning circle, ft	33.5
Hip room, front	2 x 19
Hip room, rear	n.a.
Pedal to seat back	44.0
Floor to ground	11.5

CALCULATED DATA

Lb/hp (test wt)	29.1
Cu ft/ton mile	75.6
Mph/1000 rpm (4th)	17.9
Engine revs/mile	3350
Piston travel, ft/mile	1675
Rpm @ 2500 ft/min	5000
equivalent mph	89.9
R&T wear index	56.1

SPECIFICATIONS

List price	$2595
Curb weight, lb	2150
Test weight	2490
distribution, %	50/50
Tire size	5.90-13
Brake swept area	196
Engine type	4 cyl, ohv
Bore & stroke	3.21 x 3.00
Displacement, cc	1592
cu in	97.1
Compression ratio	9.1
Bhp @ rpm	85.5 @ 5000
equivalent mph	89.9
Torque, lb-ft	94 @ 3800
equivalent mph	68.2

GEAR RATIOS

4th (1.00)	3.89
3rd (1.39)	5.41
2nd (2.14)	8.32
1st (3.34)	13.0

SPEEDOMETER ERROR

30 mph	actual, 29.8
60 mph	56.2

PERFORMANCE

Top speed (mfr), mph	100
best timed run	
3rd (5500)	71
2nd (5500)	46
1st (5600)	30

FUEL CONSUMPTION

Normal range, mpg	19/25

ACCELERATION

0-30 mph, sec	4.9
0-40	6.8
0-50	9.9
0-60	14.0
0-70	19.7
0-80	28.7
0-100	
Standing ¼ mile	19.3
speed at end	69

TAPLEY DATA

4th, lb/ton @ mph	186 @ 60
3rd	275 @ 50
2nd	420 @ 35
Total drag at 60 mph, lb	120

ENGINE SPEED IN GEARS

ACCELERATION & COASTING

37

Road Test:

Sunbeam Harrington Le Mans

Begoggled John Panks corners in his 1921 Sunbeam Grand Prix car as the newest Sunbeam, the Harrington Le Mans, speeds by.

Sunbeam's Le Mans is made for enthusiasts seeking performance and comfort

The cars shown on this month's cover with the proud owner of the dark-green beauty are two of the most notable models made in the 63-year history of the Sunbeam make. One is a 1921 straight-eight twin-overhead-cam grand prix car, while the other is the rebuilt Alpine called the Harrington Le Mans. CAR AND DRIVER had the unique opportunity to test both, the older being the only one of its kind (all the other four originals having been destroyed or modified). Driving both not only pointed out the great advances that have been made in Sunbeam engineering over the past 41 years, but demonstrated why lovers of old-time racing cars find them exhilarating to drive. The '21 was highly exciting. Racing around the snow-covered track in a face-numbing wind was literally breathtaking but we were delighted to climb out of the GP into the warm coupé, with its shift lever inside instead of outside, its soft upholstery instead of hard cushions, and its smooth ride.

The light Le Mans coupé pulls away from its 41-year-old ancestor, although both cars have comparable power and top speed.

The power output of the two cars was comparable. The GP developed 108 bhp at 4,000 rpm, against 104 bhp at 6,000 rpm in the Le Mans. Top speed is surprisingly similar: about 104 for the race car and 108 on the Le Mans. We were able to compare both cars because John T. Panks, managing director of Rootes Motors in New York, was both kind enough to offer his wonderful old Sunbeam and brave enough to drive it all afternoon in below-freezing weather. The '21 GP is his own car and the Le Mans coupé is the one brought over for the April International Automobile Show at the New York Coliseum. In the form we saw it, the '21 was set up with the "sprint back," tail section chopped off just behind the great copper gas tank. For long races, two spare wheels were added.

Despite the coldness of the day, the car fired up quickly after a frozen gas line was remedied. The 2,973-cc engine idled with an alarming clatter, but revved up freely, leaving only traces of Castrol R and the roar of its exhaust in its wake as the car moved off smoothly and swiftly. Riding in the cramped two-seat cockpit emphasized the heroic quality racing had in the old days. Even on smooth asphalt the steering required considerable attention, making clear just how difficult it must have been to drive this or a similar Le Mans car for about five hours at maximum speed. The riding mechanic was kept busy with brake adjustment and engine lubrication to fuss over, while at the same time trying to stay out of the way of the driver. The car's acceleration, if not brisk in the modern sense of the word, has a quality of sheer forcefulness, probably the result of the low engine revs and the total lack of wheelspin as the car moves down the straightaway. Still, the 3.69-to-one rear axle used will propel it well into the 70s in third. By contrast, the Harrington coupé has a fast-revving 1,592-cc engine which produces a sharp, loud exhaust note and can burn rubber easily on a standing start. The Le Mans body was built by Thomas Harrington, Ltd. which carries out the conversion on the standard Alpine (see CAR AND DRIVER, June, 1961, page 56) with a special fiberglass fastback upper half, more luxurious interior appointments and a Hartwell-tuned engine. This engine is identical to that used in the Alpine which averaged 98 mph in the 1961 Le Mans race, and won the Thermal Efficiency Award.

Engine modifications include higher compression, polished ports, stronger valve springs, a special cam, an oil cooler, lightened flywheel and balanced clutch and crank. These modifications seem to offer most of their boost over 70 mph, and the Le Mans can be held at an indicated 100 mph without effort. Perhaps because of its slightly higher center of gravity, the coupé had more roll than the standard Alpine, yet none of the Alpine's roadholding capabilities have been lost. The good manners are supplemented by power-assisted disc brakes on the front wheels for stopping fast with a minimum of effort. The body of the Le Mans is steel up to the beltline, with fiberglass used above.

A chrome strip covers the joint and the over-all finish is good. Primarily a two-seater, the coupé has a jump

The coupé's interior is well laid out with controls placed conveniently. Seat position is low, but visibility is fine.

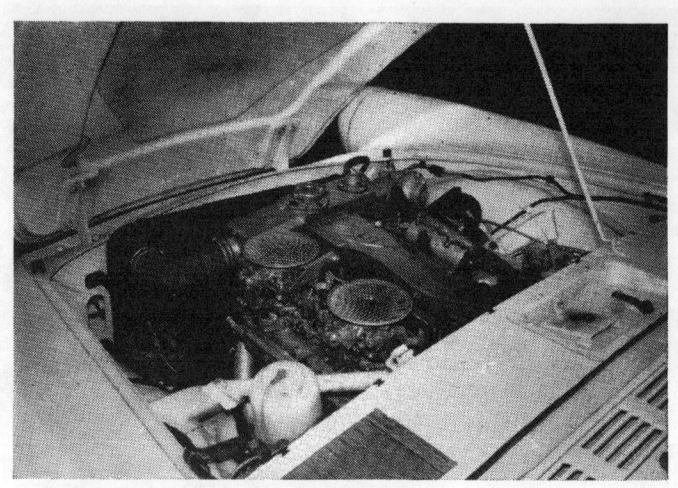

Access to the engine is good with the wide-opening hood, but the simple wire-screen air cleaners cause much noise.

seat for children. It can be folded flat for luggage. The baggage area is reached from the back through a spring-loaded door operated from the cockpit. The limited amount of seat travel and non-adjustable steering wheel may bother some drivers, but those of average size will find it ideal. Its distinctive interior has armrests, a walnut dashboard, wooden shift lever and Carlotti wood-rimmed steering wheel. However, the horn control has moved from a wheel button to a column-mounted lever, so that until one becomes familiar with the layout it's possible to blow the horn when you try to signal a turn or engage overdrive.

For storing small items there is a glove compartment, door pockets and a lockable hinged center armrest. Heating and defrosting are excellent and instrument lighting is glare-free. The ride of the Le Mans is smooth and firm, with some choppiness on rough surfaces. The car seems well suited for long-distance touring, and has a snug feel. Slow running is possible with the modified engine, but it really starts feeling right above the 2,000 rpm mark on the tachometer. Rootes hopes the Le Mans will be able to compete as successfully as the old straight-eight, whose achievements include finishing fifth in the 1921 Indianapolis 500. The old car's main success was at the Isle of Man Tourist Trophy in 1922. There Jean Cassagne won in heavy rain at 55.76 mph, while Sir Henry Segrave drove the Panks car to the fastest lap, 57.7 mph. Plans call for building about 1,000 Harrington Le Mans coupés each year. We'd guess it won't be enough to meet the demand.

SUNBEAM HARRINGTON LE MANS

Price as tested: $3,995
Importer:
Rootes Motors, Inc.
42-32 21st Street
Long Island City 1, New York

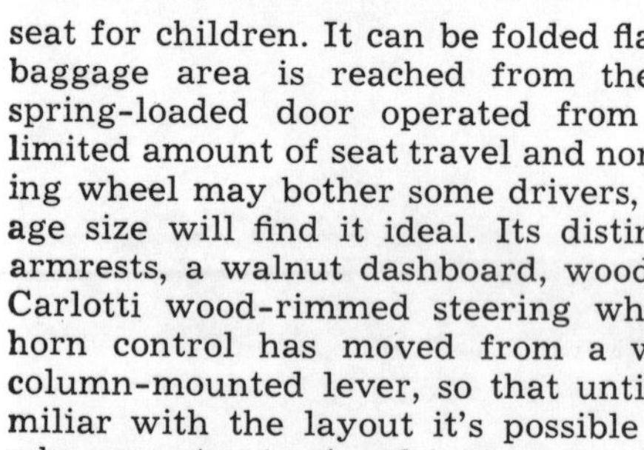

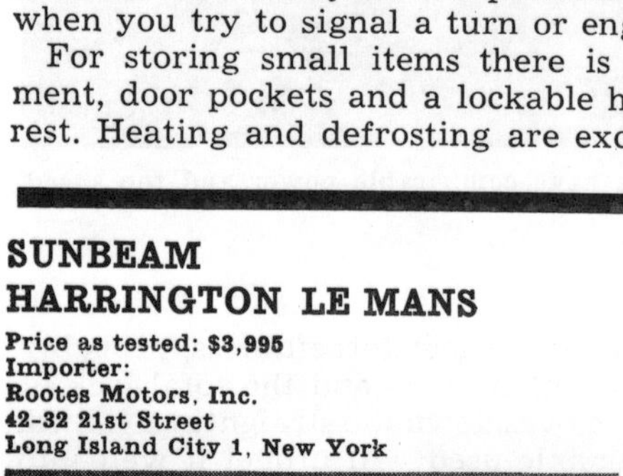

ENGINE:
Displacement.................97.1 cu in, 1,592 cc
Dimensions....4 cyl, 3.21-in bore, 3.00-in stroke
Valve gear: pushrod-operated inclined overhead
Compression ratio..................9.5 to one
Power (SAE)..............104 bhp @ 6,000 rpm
Torque..................105 lb-ft @ 4,500 rpm
Usable range of engine speeds..1,000-6,000 rpm
Corrected piston speed @ 5500 rpm...3,100 fpm
Fuel recommended....................Premium
Mileage..........................18-22 mpg
Range on 10.8-gallon tank........195-240 miles

CHASSIS:
Wheelbase............................86 in
Tread..................F 48½ in, R 50½ in
Length..............................155 in
Ground clearance....................5½ in
Suspension: F, Ind. wishbones and coil springs, telescopic shock absorbers. R, Live axle and semi-elliptic leaf springs, lever arm shocks
Steering....................Recirculating ball.
Turns, lock to lock....................3¼
Turning circle diameter between curbs....34 ft
Tire and rim size..........5.60 x 13, 13 x 4½J
Pressures recommended..........F 24, R 25
Brakes; type, swept area: Girling discs front, 9-in. drums rear, 197 sq. in.
Curb weight (full tank)..............2,268 lbs
Percentage on the driving wheels..........51

DRIVE TRAIN:

Gear	Synchro	Ratio	Step	Overall	Mph per 1000 rpm
Rev	No	4.23	—	17.89	-3.7
1st	No	3.34	—	14.13	4.7
2nd	Yes	2.14	56%	9.04	7.4
2nd OD	Yes	1.72	24%	7.25	9.5
3rd	Yes	1.39	31%	5.87	11.4
3rd OD	Yes	1.12	24%	4.71	14.2
4th	Yes	1.00	12%	4.22	15.9
4th OD	Yes	0.80	25%	3.39	19.7

Final drive ratio: 4.22 to one (3.89 on cars without overdrive).

ACCELERATION:

Zero to	Seconds
30 mph	4.3
40 mph	6.7
50 mph	10.2
60 mph	14.4
70 mph	19.6
80 mph	27.4
Standing ¼-mile	19.8

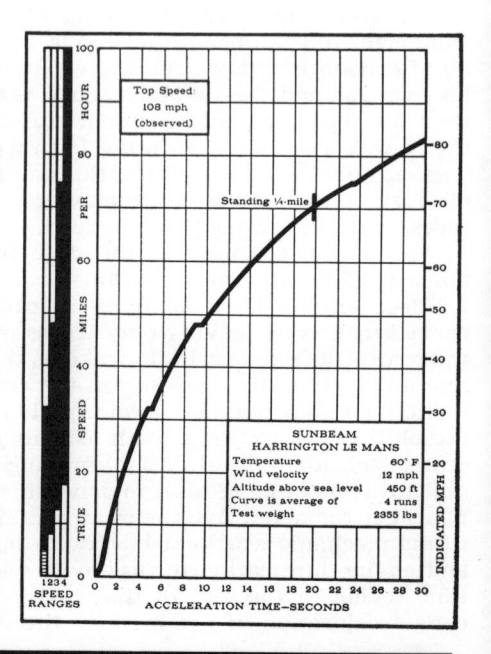

SUNBEAM HARRINGTON LE MANS
Temperature.................60° F
Wind velocity...............12 mph
Altitude above sea level....450 ft
Curve is average of.........4 runs
Test weight................2355 lbs

Top Speed: 108 mph (observed)

40

Race-Tuning the Sunbeam Alpine

By Wayne Thoms

Factory-supplied tuning parts can transform the Alpine into a racing car

Racing sells cars. With that idea firmly in mind, Rootes Motors executives have quietly helped Sunbeam Alpines onto local road racing courses all over the United States for the past year. As the Alpine comes off the showroom floor it is a splendid sports-touring machine but hardly a satisfactory racing car. To get the straight word on racing preparation, CAR AND DRIVER asked Stu Haggart, the Los Angeles mechanic who maintains Lew Spencer's Alpine. For the latest on factory speed options, we went to Ian Garrad, head of Rootes' Los Angeles Branch.

Anyone planning to race an Alpine should get a copy of "Special Tuning," a 32-page manual published by the Service Department of Sunbeam-Talbot Ltd., and available through Sunbeam dealers. The optional equipment, approved for production racing, is divided into kits comprising stages I and II, plus a long list of parts, many of which are standard in the kits, others which are nice if the budget can stand it.

Stage I is an engine kit whose major components include a camshaft, a distributor, Champion N3 spark plugs and larger jets. Stage I tuning, apart from installing these parts, requires cutting off the hot water to the intake manifold, renewing main-bearing bolts and nuts, and cleaning up the very important task of intake and exhaust ports.

Stage II goes a long way farther, with a high-compression cylinder head and pistons. Intermediate stages can be set up, too—the Stage II head with the standard pistons produces about 11-to-one compression; and with the racing pistons the compression ratio is raised to 12 to one. The new pistons with a stock head place compression at 10.1 to one. Decision on the ratio should be made by an experienced racing mechanic. While 12 to one will impress fellow bench racers, it may not be the most practical means of winning —or finishing—races.

The Stage II kit also includes a racing clutch, a balanced, lightweight flywheel assembly, a brake kit with extra-hard front pads and specially lined rear shoes, a rear-axle kit with specially heat-treated axle shafts, keys and hubs (required only with disc wheels) and a suspension kit—⅞-inch-diameter anti-roll bar, stiffer front springs and rear shock absorbers. There is also an oil-cooler kit, for sustained high rpm.

Reinforced throttle-shaft bracket for the front carburetor is held above stock version (installed) for comparison. Bracing prevents the bracket from cracking.

The intake-port sleeve has been removed and the port ground out for better flow.

The combustion chamber shows results of cutting around valves and in both ports.

The dark rocker is stock, the other is polished, as are the crankshaft and rod.

A Good Bet in Sports-Car Road Racing

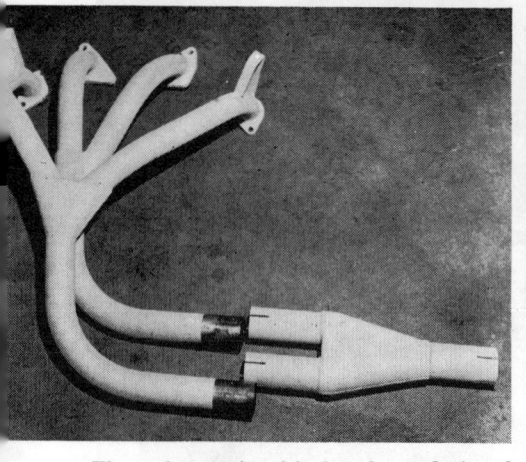

The exhaust-pipe kit has been designed for maximum extraction—but not silence.

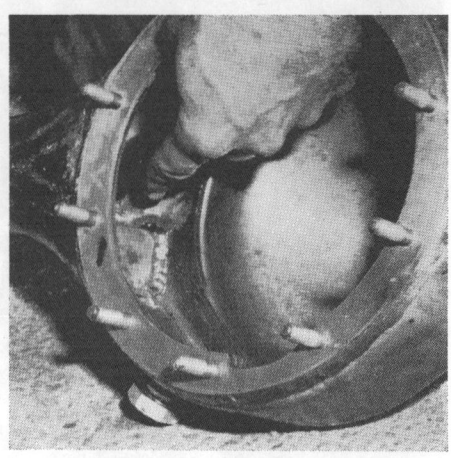

This baffle prevents the oil from being thrown along rear-axle tubes to the hubs.

The useful but not really essential department includes more delightful pieces: overdrive, 25-gallon auxiliary gas tank, Microcel competition seats, close-ratio gears (2.97, 1.90, 1.24 and 1.00), rear-axle ratios of 5.22, 4.55 and 4.78, and a limited-slip differential. The items are largely self-explanatory. Overdrives in racing are a matter of personal preference—I, for one, consider them of limited value. The tank is nice for distance racing, but crowds the trunk rather badly for touring.

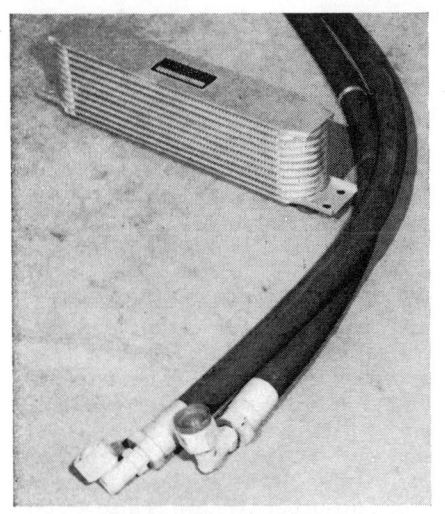

Two camshafts are available. One is made by the factory; the other is an Iskenderian product. The factory racing grind has intake open at 25° BTDC, close at 59° ABDC; exhaust opens at 63° BTDC, closes at 21° ATDC. The Iskenderian SB-2 has 19-60, 54-25 timing and 400-inch lift, a hotter cam. In comparison, the stock cam is 14-52, 56-10. The racing clutch in the factory kit is excellent, but Haggart recommends a substitute clutch disc manufactured by Bid, which has not been nationally sanctioned by the SCCA, though it is legal under West Coast (Cal Club Region) rules.

The seats are lightweight, beautifully contoured and extremely comfortable. Close-ratio transmissions are always handy, while axle ratios are dictated by the course. Finally, the limited-slip differential requires a change in cornering technique that is well worth learning.

The crank and rods in the Spencer Alpine have been polished, balanced and Magnafluxed. Some people feel that polishing is not essential, but it relieves surface stress and can be crucial with a three-bearing crank. Another and highly effective means of relieving stress, and actually strengthening rods and crank, is to have them shot-peened, even though Alpine components are quite strong as designed. Haggart thoroughly endorses grinding and polishing rocker arms. Grinding removes about an ounce of metal, and polishing removes grinding scratches. Only one ounce? Doesn't sound like much but it's in the valve-train so it counts.

Rootes recommends two reinforcements, one of which Haggart followed. The throttle-shaft bracket on the front carburetor should definitely be stiffened to prevent cracking. The step that Stu left out, at least temporarily, is installing an engine stabilizer. This is a kit that restricts engine torque movement via a plate attached rigidly to the block and rubber-bushed to the firewall, the theory being that throttle response

The oil cooler will lower the oil temperature by about 35°F at high speeds.

The husky front anti-roll bar helps keep inside rear wheel from losing its grip.

will be more accurate with less movement in the linkage.

After the budding racing driver has performed all the engine work and installed the suspension options, there are just a few more tips: Haggart recommends filling the shock absorbers with heavy-grade Girling fluid. Also, he says it is a good idea to relocate the coil onto the body so that the bracket doesn't break from vibration. He sets up the front end with one degree negative camber and zero toe-in, to keep understeer at a minimum. With Dunlop RS tires, start off with 45 psi in the front and 40 psi in the rear. Adjust until the handling suits you.

The Bid clutch disc (left) can be used to replace the standard Alpine disc for both street use and racing, combining a smooth action with the necessary bite.

Sunbeam Alpine G.T. Series 3 1,592 c.c.

WHEN the Rootes Group introduced the Sunbeam Alpine in the late summer of 1959, they really set a new trend in sporting motoring in the 1½-litre class. Gone were the flapping sidescreens, cramped cockpits and rather basic suspensions of former years. In their place were wind-up windows, roomy seating and near-saloon car comfort. Other manufacturers were not slow to climb on the bandwagon and now comfort has become a major selling point in sports cars.

In recent months, both the GT and Sports Tourer versions of the Alpine have had changes in their carburation. Last July, the GT went over to using the single, twin-choke Solex carburettor in place of two Zenith instruments. The Sports version followed suit at the beginning of this month. The effect of this and other changes has been to produce a smoother and quieter-running engine and a greatly improved overall fuel consumption.

Mechanically, the GT is very similar to the sports car. The jet sizes in the carburettor are slightly smaller and to reduce noise the exhaust manifold is of cast iron, instead of the free-flow four branch one of welded steel tubes. A lot of attention has been paid also to cutting down induction noise, and there is now a big air cleaner and silencer. Excess engine noise is reduced by thick padding under the bonnet panel.

These mechanical refinements have meant a reduction in power. The GT develops 82·5 b.h.p. (gross) at 5,000 r.p.m., compared with the sports engine's 86 b.h.p. Torque has dropped only slightly to 91 lb. ft. at 3,500 r.p.m. Those people used to the rather noisy Alpine engine will be very pleasantly surprised by the smoothness and quietness of the GT's power unit. Starting is quite quick and straightforward, the choke being needed only for the first start of the day; it can then be pushed home after half a mile or so.

The engine is not at all temperamental and pulls smoothly from 1,500 r.p.m. right up to the red-band limit of 5,500

PRICES		£	s	d
GT coupé		744	0	0
Purchase Tax		155	11	3
	Total (in G.B.)	899	11	3
Extras (including P.T.)				
Overdrive		51	7	1
Wire wheels		32	12	6
Dunlop RS5 tyres		8	5	7
Seat Belts		4	15	0
Heater		10	0	0
Radio		30	11	0

Autocar road test • No. 1941

Make • SUNBEAM Type • Alpine GT
(Front engine, rear-wheel drive)

Manufacturers: Sunbeam-Talbot Ltd., Ryton-on-Dunsmore, Coventry

Test Conditions
Weather .... Bright, with 8-10 m.p.h. wind
Temperature ... 10 deg. C. (50 deg. F.). Barometer 29.5in. Hg.
Dry concrete and tarmac surfaces.

Weight
Kerb weight (with oil, water and half-full fuel tank) 20.4cwt (2,282lb-1,035kg.)
Front-rear distribution, per cent F. 50; R. 50.
Laden as tested 23.4cwt (2,618lb-1,187kg)

Turning Circles
Between kerbs .... L, 33ft 10in.; R, 34ft 6in.
Between walls .... L, 34ft 6in.; R, 35ft 2in.
Turns of steering wheel lock to lock 3.6

Performance Data
Overdrive top gear m.p.h. per 1,000 r.p.m. 21.9
Top gear m.p.h. per 1,000 r.p.m. 17.6
Mean piston speed at max. power ...... 2,500ft/min.
Engine revs. at mean max. speed ...... 5,430 r.p.m.
(in direct top gear)
B.h.p. per ton laden 66

MAXIMUM SPEEDS AND ACCELERATION TIMES

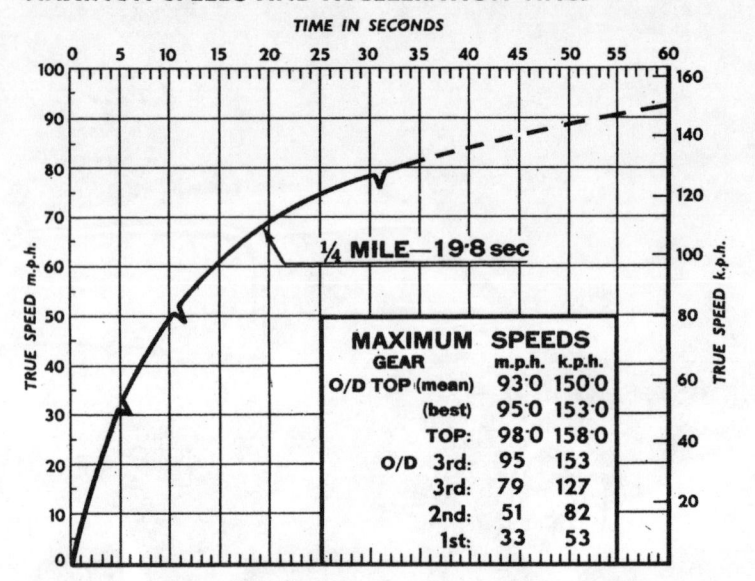

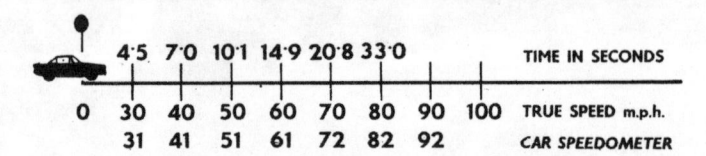

¼ MILE — 19.8 sec

MAXIMUM SPEEDS
GEAR	m.p.h.	k.p.h.
O/D TOP (mean)	93.0	150.0
(best)	95.0	153.0
TOP	98.0	158.0
O/D 3rd	95	153
3rd	79	127
2nd	51	82
1st	33	53

Acceleration from rest:
Time (sec)	4.5	7.0	10.1	14.9	20.8	33.0
True Speed m.p.h.	30	40	50	60	70	80
Car Speedometer	31	41	51	61	72	82

(90 / 92, 100 true/speedo)

Speed range, gear ratios and time in seconds

m.p.h.	O.D. Top 3.12	Top 3.89	O.D. 3rd 3.85	3rd 4.80	2nd 7.38	1st 11.35
10—30	—	—	—	9.6	5.5	3.8
20—40	16.3	11.6	12.3	9.0	5.3	—
30—50	18.2	14.8	13.1	9.0	5.9	—
40—60	19.2	14.6	14.2	9.7	—	—
50—70	24.4	14.5	16.1	11.2	—	—
60—80	36.3	20.1	21.1	—	—	—

FUEL AND OIL CONSUMPTION

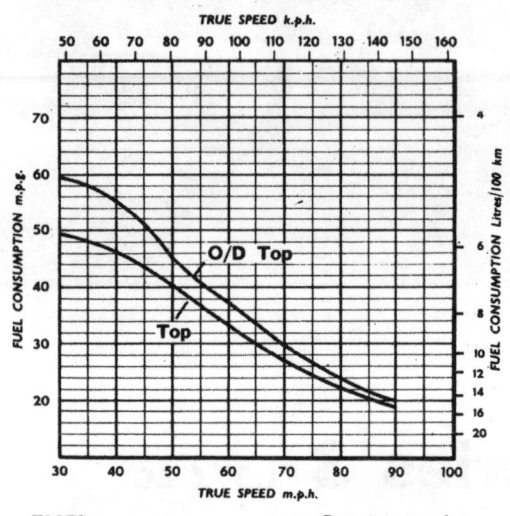

FUEL .... Premium grade (95-97 octane RM)
Test Distance .... 1,250 miles
Overall Consumption .... 24.9 m.p.g. (11.3 litres/100 km.)
Normal Range .... 21-27 m.p.g. (13.4-10.4 litres/100 km.)
OIL: S.A.E. 30 ...... Consumption 3,500 m.p.g.

BRAKES
(from 30 m.p.h. in neutral)

Pedal Load	Retardation	Equiv. distance
25lb	0.17g	177ft
50lb	0.46g	66ft
75lb	0.77g	39ft
100lb	1.0g	30ft
Handbrake	0.40g	75.5ft

CLUTCH Pedal load and travel — 35lb and 4.5in.

HILL CLIMBING AT STEADY SPEEDS

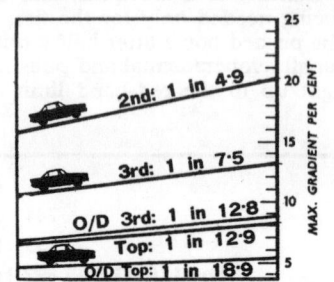

2nd: 1 in 4.9
3rd: 1 in 7.5
O/D 3rd: 1 in 12.8
Top: 1 in 12.9
O/D Top: 1 in 18.9

GEAR	O.D. Top	Top	O.D. 3rd	3rd	2nd
PULL (lb per ton)	125	190	185	295	445
Speed range (m.p.h.)	45-50	44-48	44-48	40-44	28-30

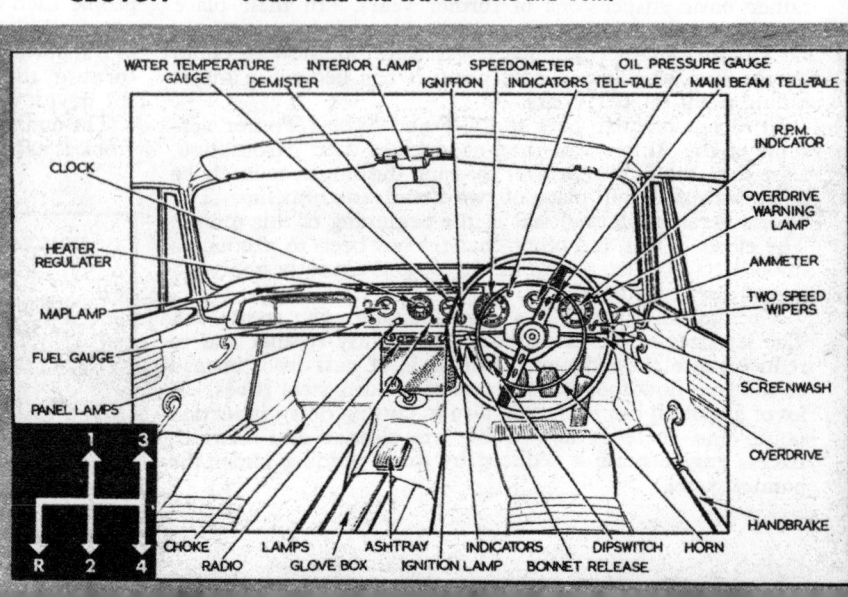

Gear shift pattern: R 1 2 3 4

Dashboard labels: WATER TEMPERATURE GAUGE, INTERIOR LAMP, SPEEDOMETER, OIL PRESSURE GAUGE, DEMISTER, IGNITION, INDICATORS TELL-TALE, MAIN BEAM TELL-TALE, CLOCK, R.P.M. INDICATOR, OVERDRIVE WARNING LAMP, HEATER REGULATOR, AMMETER, MAPLAMP, TWO SPEED WIPERS, FUEL GAUGE, SCREENWASH, PANEL LAMPS, OVERDRIVE, CHOKE, LAMPS, ASHTRAY, INDICATORS, DIPSWITCH, HORN, HANDBRAKE, RADIO, GLOVE BOX, IGNITION LAMP, BONNET RELEASE

A well-positioned radio loudspeaker unit fills the gap between the facia and transmission tunnel. The steering wheel is in its forward position here

Sunbeam Alpine GT Series 3 . . .

r.p.m. While it may lack the ability to give "punch in the back" acceleration, it has a smooth delivery of power.

A four-speed gearbox, with effective synchromesh on the upper three ratios, is supplemented by Laycock-de Normanville overdrive on 3rd and top gears; this is of the latest self-cancelling type which, when a change is made from overdrive 3rd or top into the 1st-2nd gear plane, the drive is automatically returned to direct. Particularly neat is the steering-column-mounted switch, which has a positive movement. In terms of performance, the Alpine GT is very similar to the former Series 2 models. The standing-start quarter-mile took 19·8sec, 0·1sec slower than the earlier car, while 60 m.p.h. was reached in 14·9sec, again just 0·1sec slower. The spacing of the ratios, including those with overdrive, calls for some clarification. Overdrive 3rd has virtually the same ratio as top, while overdrive top is strictly for motorways and other high-speed roads.

However, when pressing on along twisting main roads, the ability to flick in and out of overdrive 3rd is a great help, saving movement of the rather heavy but nevertheless precise gear shift. The need for synchromesh on first gear becomes the more apparent after the nasty noises even experienced drivers occasionally make when changing down into this ratio. Apart from first, which makes a truly Vintage noise, the other gears are quiet.

As the same back axle ratio is now fitted to Alpines whether or not overdrive is fitted, overdrive top is really high, and at 95 m.p.h. the maximum speed in this gear, the rev counter shows only 4,300 r.p.m. The car's maximum one-way speed of 98 m.p.h. was reached in direct top, while overdrive 3rd gave a best one-way speed of 95 m.p.h. The slightly slower speed in this ratio is probably due to churning losses through the overdrive unit.

Derived as it is from a sports car, the GT's suspension is fairly firm. However, with the tyres at their touring pressures of 24 p.s.i. all round, the ride never becomes harsh. Putting the tyres up to their high-speed pressures of 30 p.s.i. all round makes the bumps felt. On fast corners, the stiffness of the rear suspension in conjunction with the rigid axle can be felt when a cat's eye or rough patch is hit. The back wheels are inclined to hop sideways, tweaking the car a little and calling for steering correction. But our special *pavé* and washboard tests were covered remarkably well, the suspension standing up manfully to the hammering it received. The car remained directional stable and the bump stops were only reached on the worst crags. Normal *pavé*, say Guildford High Street, was no embarrassment.

Precise Steering

In the past we have had reason to criticize the heaviness of Rootes steering. On the Alpine they seem to have taken our comments to heart; the mechanism is really light and precise, with almost no lost movement at the wheel. With its 50-50 weight distribution the car does not understeer as much as previous models, and is delightfully balanced. The excellent roadholding never once gave our drivers any qualms that the car might take charge. With the tyres at the high pressures, extra care understandably had to be taken in the wet. Generally the optional extra Dunlop RS5 tyres inspired great confidence.

The disc-front, drum-rear braking system, helped by a vacuum servo, is very good indeed. With 100lb pedal pressure, a retardation of 1·0g was recorded. Nothing would make the brakes fade, and they pulled the car up fair and square every time. Brakes on the previous Alpines have been criticized for one-sided operation after getting wet. Those on the GT have been cured of this behaviour and still worked evenly when drenched with water. The handbrake lever, on the outside of the driving seat, had a rather loose action on the test car, with the release button sticking. It failed to hold the car on the 1-in-3 test hill, and the car would not move away on this gradient.

While fuel consumption may not be of prime importance to the prospective purchaser of a sporting car, the recarburation of the Alpine has helped a great deal in giving better figures. The overall consumption, which included several very fast motorway journeys, was 24·9 m.p.g.; this compares very favourably with the Series 2's 20·6 m.p.g. overall. There can be no doubt that the higher overall gearing contributes towards this better figure. On normal round-the-houses motoring the car returned 26·4 m.p.g.,

Left: With the seats set right back, a back-seat passenger would have to sit sideways; small children would have rather more comfort. The comprehensive instrument array is shown clearly here. Right: Front seats tip forward to give access to the rear, and the backs can be collapsed forward for convenience when loading small objects on the back seat

With the familiar Alpine shape, the GT version is recognisable by the large rear window. The "knock-off" hub caps for the wire wheels are removed by a large spanner

while fast runs on motorways only reduced this to 22·5 m.p.g. During the 1,250-mile test the engine used three pints of oil.

Just a glance inside the Alpine GT's cockpit will confirm the impression that this is a very well planned car. It is typically British—in the nicest sense of the word. Microcell make the seats and they contribute a lot towards the ride comfort. The "suspension" is by dead elastic webbing, which kills any sympathetic shocks immediately. The backs can be adjusted for rake, and the whole seat tilted through a few degrees by means of eccentric rubber blocks. Location is very good, and the proper support is given to the spine.

The driver, having set his seat to the right angle and reach, can then adjust the steering column over 2·5in. Adjustment of the column is by an effective and neat system of Rootes' own design; the central boss of the steering wheel is undone a few turns and then tapped. This unlocks the expanding cone and the wheel can be moved. The pedals are also adjustable for reach by using a spanner. The pendant pedal layout and geometry are excellent; brake and clutch pedals have big oval pads, while the treadle action accelerator has a smooth and progressive action. Heel-toe action comes almost naturally. When the left foot is not working the clutch it rests directly on the rubber-covered pad of the dip switch.

On the highly polished wood facia the driver is faced with a complete battery of instruments. In front of him are the large-dialled rev counter and speedometer which includes a trip distance recorder. Between these is the all-important oil pressure gauge. Across the centre of the facia are the fuel gauge, clock and water temperature gauge, while to the right of the rev counter, and on its own, is an ammeter. Electrical switches are along the lower edge of the facia, under the dials. All the lettering on the dials is in no-nonsense white figures against a black ground, with the pointers finished in red Dayglow paint. With typical Rootes thoughtfulness, metric equivalents are marked on those instruments that need them.

Instrument lighting is controlled by a two-position switch. On bright, the intensity is adequate for town and country driving; the alternative is so dim that the dials can hardly be seen, let alone read. A separate map light is provided for the passenger, tucked away under the facia crash padding. The sealed beam headlamps have a very good range and spread. Between the sun vizors is the interior lamp which comes on when either door is opened; it really does light up the interior of the car, so that maps can be easily read at night.

Stowage space inside the car is limited to a small open parcel shelf in front of the passenger; part of this is cut away to form an unobtrusive grab handle. Between the seats is a lockable glove box to take valuables which some people find so attractive in unattended cars.

Seating for two children is provided behind the main seats, but it would be possible to carry adults there for a short trip. The thinly padded seat lifts off to reveal the battery, which is thus well away from engine heat.

Prospective owners of the Alpine GT must think of the car as having a fixed hardtop which can be removed—if that makes sense. No provision at all is made for a hood, but a tonneau cover can be supplied. So well fitting is the hardtop that it looks as if it cannot be removed. In fact, after undoing four strong clips, it can be lifted off in

Left: With the fuel tanks now in each rear wing, boot space is much larger; the spare wheel can be laid flat on the boot floor if this suits luggage shape better. The lid is held up with over-centre stays. Right: The bonnet has to be propped up with a stay, but access to the engine is very good. The brake servo can just be seen next to the stay. Note the large air cleaner-silencer unit for the carburettor

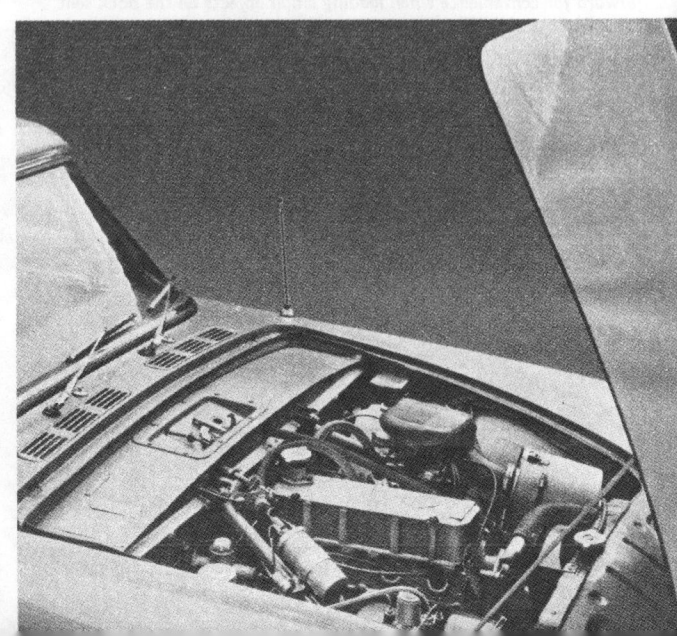

Sunbeam Alpine GT Series 3 . . .

a matter of seconds by two people. Front-hinged quarter-lights are attached to the top; these have rather weak over-centre catches. It is a pity that the small quarter-lights in the front windows do not open. In warm weather, a flow of air through the car can be obtained only by winding down one of the door windows slightly. Although this does not create a draught, it does send the noise level up a great deal at speed. Overall wind noise, even with all the windows closed, is rather high. The frameless door windows close on rubber flap seals which could be a lot stiffer. An effective fresh-air heater, with a single-speed booster fan, is fitted.

Trim inside the Alpine GT has been carried out in the best of taste. Neatly tailored, removable carpets cover the floor, while the doors and body sides are covered in fine-grained leathercloth. The wood-rimmed steering wheel has a very high-gloss finish, while the rather too soft and mellow horns are sounded by pressing a full-circle ring on the steering wheel. For headlamp flashing the direction indicator lever is pulled back. This lever is matched on the other side of the steering column by that for the overdrive; with overdrive in operation, a pale amber lamp glows on the facia, and with the sidelamps on it is dimmed.

In matters of safety, the Alpine GT is well equipped. Thick crash padding of the proper firmness runs right across the upper and lower edges of the facia. The sun-vizors are also flexible, and cover the projecting clips for the hardtop. Rootes-approved Irvin lap and diagonal seat belts are fitted, with the correct angles for hip and shoulder straps. Unfortunately, the glove box gets in the way of the buckles when the belts are being fastened.

The rearrangement of the fuel tankage has nearly doubled the amount of room in the boot. Before, the single fuel tank was in the floor, with the spare wheel above it. Now, two fuel tanks are used, one in each rear wing, and connected with a large-diameter balance pipe. The filler, on the right-hand wing, will take the full flow of a petrol pump, and both tanks fill quickly without any blow-back. The 11-gallon capacity gives a range of about 270 miles—a useful asset when on the Continent. The spare wheel is now stowed vertically against the rear boot bulkhead, with the jack, tool kit and copper hammer for the optional knock-off wire wheels behind and alongside it.

Visibility is good, with slim screen pillars and plenty of glass. In wet weather, the two-speed, twin-squeegee wipers clear a sensible amount of the screen, but the sharp wraparound defeats the blades' ability to stay in contact at the limits of their sweep. For parking, all four corners of the car can be seen from the driving seat. A good point is that the convex mirror is mounted off-centre, so that it can be swung round to suit drivers of differing heights.

Since its introduction, the Alpine has grown up considerably. The Grand Touring version is a sophisticated form of transport, capable of carrying two people and their luggage for long distances with great ease. The attention which has been paid to the seating will be specially appreciated on very long journeys. What the car may lack in punch it makes up for in the relative quietness of its progress; and one must admire its good looks.

Specification

Scale: 0.3in. to 1ft.

Cushions uncompressed.

ENGINE
Cylinders	4
Bore	81.5mm (3.21in.)
Stroke	76.2mm (3.0in.)
Displacement	1,592 c.c. (97.1 cu in.)
Valve gear	Overhead, pushrods and rockers
Compression ratio	9.1 to 1
Carburettor	Solex 32 PAIA
Fuel pump	AC mechanical
Oil filter	Full flow
Max. power	77 b.h.p. (nett) at 5,000 r.p.m.
Max. torque	91 lb. ft. at 3,500 r.p.m.

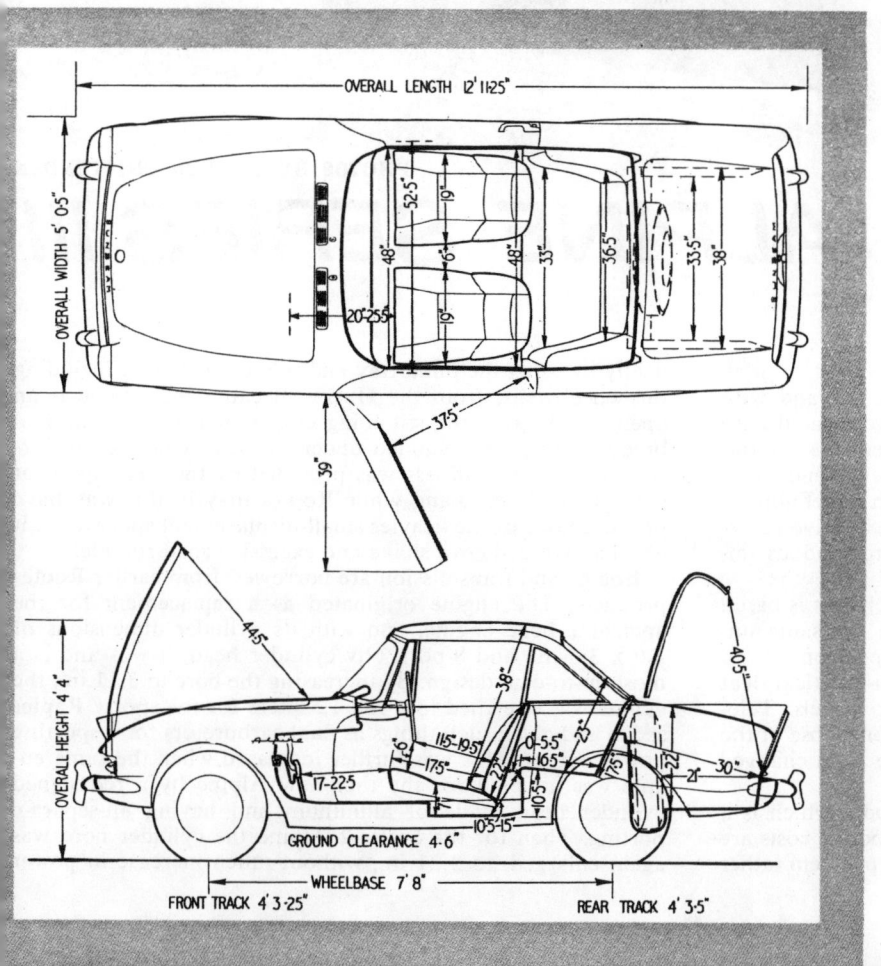

TRANSMISSION
Clutch	Borg and Beck diaphragm spring 8in. dia.
Gearbox	Four speed, synchromesh on upper three ratios, central floor control
Overall ratios	OD Top 3.12, Top 3.89, OD 3rd 3.85, 3rd 4.80, 2nd 7.38, 1st 11.53 Reverse 14.61
Final drive	Hypoid bevel 3.89 to 1

CHASSIS
Construction	Integral, with steel body

SUSPENSION
Front	Independent, wishbones and coil springs, anti-roll bar, telescopic dampers
Rear	Live axle, half elliptic springs, telescopic dampers
Steering	Burman recirculating ball
Wheel dia.	15.5in.

BRAKES
Type	Disc front, drums rear, servo assisted
Dimensions	F, 9.85in. dia.; R, 9.0in. dia., 1.75in. wide shoes
Swept area	F, 196 sq in.; R, 99 sq. in. Total, 295 sq in. (255.2 sq in. per ton laden)

WHEELS
Type	Wire spoked, centre lock 4in. wide rim
Tyres	5.90—13in. Dunlop RS5

EQUIPMENT
Battery	12-volt 38-amp hr.
Headlamps	Sealed beam 60-40-watt
Reversing lamp	None
Electric fuses	2
Screen wipers	Two speed, self parking
Screen washer	Standard, manual plunger
Interior heater	Extra, fresh air
Safety belts	Extra, anchorages provided
Interior trim	Leathercloth
Floor covering	Carpet
Starting handle	Standard
Jack	Screw pillar
Jacking points	4, two on each bumper
Other bodies	Sports Tourer

MAINTENANCE
Fuel tank	11.25 Imp. gallons (no reserve)
Cooling system	12.5 pints (including heater)
Engine sump	8 pints. Change oil every 3,000 miles; change filter element every 6,000 miles
Gearbox and overdrive	4 pints SAE 30. Change oil every 6,000 miles
Final drive	1.75 pints SAE 90EP. Change oil every 6,000 miles
Grease	12 points every 3,000 miles
Tyre pressures	F and R, 24 p.s.i. (normal driving) F and R, 30 p.s.i. (fast driving)

PHOTOS BY GORDON CHITTENDEN

SUNBEAM ALPINE SERIES III

New heights for the Alpine

Sunbeam's Alpine, introduced in mid-1959, is now available in its third edition, the Series 3, and with this new model Rootes Motors has demonstrated once again that it is possible to make radical improvements without radical changes. All major mechanical elements and body paneling remain virtually the same, but a touch of refining of the mechanism here and there, with a rather extensive refurbishing of the interior, has worked a really tremendous improvement.

In its essentials, the Alpine is orthodox. Its chassis is based on the long-established Hillman Husky, with the same unequal-length A-arm and coil spring front suspension, and a conventional live rear axle carried on semi-elliptical leaf springs. An anti-roll member links the front wheels. Telescopic dampers are used on the front suspension; those at the rear were of the lever-acting variety, but have been changed to telescopics.

The chassis structure is in unit with the body, which is a very good method of construction if the high tooling costs are overlooked. Rootes worked its way around this problem rather neatly by using the undertray and related structure, including the wheel-wells, from the Husky. Because the Alpine is an open car, lacking the stiffening effects of a roof, additional bracing had to be included under the Husky-derived understructure. More stiffness was provided by the welding-on of cowl, fenders, etc., and while Rootes may in this way have produced one of the heavier small-displacement sports cars, it also has avoided cowl shake and excessive road-rumble.

Engine and transmission are borrowed from earlier Rootes products. The engine originated as a replacement for the ancient L-head engine, and with its cylinder dimensions of 3.0 x 3.0 in., and 8-port, ohv cylinder head, it was and is a most up-to-date design. By increasing the bore to 3.11 in., the engine was stretched to a full 1.5 liters for the sporty Rapier sedan and given such things as dual carburetors for a sporting power output. This was further increased when the same engine was adopted for the then-new Alpine by a redesigned cylinder head made of aluminum and having all-separate porting. Then for the Series-2 Alpine the cylinder bore was again enlarged, to 3.21 in., without much increase in power but with a great improvement in flexibility.

The Series 3 Alpine is being made in two versions, the Sports Tourer and the GT, and there are minor differences in engine specifications between the pair. The Sports Tourer has Zenith Type 36 WIP3 carburetors, "gravel-strainer" air cleaners and 88 bhp. The GT has 36 WIA3 carburetors that draw air through a big filter-cum-silencer, and has a cast-iron, 2-branch exhaust manifold in place of the welded-up extractor-type system that is supplied on the Sports Tourer's engine, these changes giving it less power (80 bhp) and torque, but making it quieter and smoother.

For the Series 3 model, the transmission has been given close-ratio gears, although nothing has been done about the non-synchro 1st gear—an unfortunate omission in this day. Be that as it may, the new ratio staging is a definite improvement, as it leaves no awkward pauses after shifting while the engine rebuilds lost speed, and 1st gear has been made "tall" enough to allow a fine burst of speed before making the change to 2nd. A Laycock de Normanville overdrive is offered as an optional accessory, and when this is bolted on behind the main transmission, one has an 0.78:1 overdrive on both 3rd and 4th gears. Previously a higher axle ratio was supplied as a companion piece to the overdrive; now the same 3.89:1 gearing is used with or without that accessory.

Changes that really make the difference are all inside the car, in the trunk, and in the people-compartment. Trunk space is never very generously supplied in a sports car, and the earlier Alpine was very scantily endowed in that area, with fuel-tank and spare just about filling the rear section. Now the finned rear fenders have been given something to do besides just splitting the breeze, and each fender houses a 6.75-gal. fuel tank, giving a total capacity of 13.5 gal. The spare wheel, which was previously mounted flat over the fuel tank, now stands vertically at the front of the luggage compartment. The combined effects of these relocations has doubled trunk space—and has provided a useful increase in fuel capacity as well.

Passenger accommodations are all-new. The boundaries of the basic package are essentially the same, but the seats are now heavily side-bolstered, for better support, and have foam-rubber cushions over elastic webbing that offers what seemed to us to be just the right amount of firmness. Also, the makers have shown their awareness that drivers exist in many sizes by providing the seats with a wide range of adjustments. There is about 7 in. of fore-and-aft adjustment, and the seat backs have a wide range of rake—set by a locking-handle on the seat-back hinge. In addition, the entire seat may be moved vertically, albeit only about an inch, and the lower cushion can be tilted to suit the angle of one's legs.

To complement the multitudinous seating adjustments, there is a telescoping steering column to enable the driver to move the wheel for a comfortable reach. The wheel is locked into position by screwing down the steering wheel hub, which has a padded center—the makers claim for crash protection, although that seems a mite far-fetched to us. Yet further provision for adjustment is found at the pendant-type clutch and brake pedals, which have a 2-position arrangement to help in accommodating drivers of the extremely long or short-legged types. This is a car intended to be comfortable for everyone from the Cardiff Giant to J. Fred Muggs.

Our test car was the Series 3 GT, which is a coupe with a removable hardtop. It has no folding soft-top, as does the Sports Tourer, and it is actually intended to be a coupe, though it allows the owner the option of removing the roof if the weather forecast is favorable. The hardtop can, of course, be purchased as an option in addition to the soft-top that is standard on the Sports Tourer. This hardtop is, incidentally, one of the better examples of the type—or would be but for a single, fatal flaw. It is weather tight, does not rattle, is insulated for both warmth and noise dampening, and has very convenient pivoting triangular rear quarter windows that aid ventilation. Moreover, it has a simple and effective latching arrangement that makes it easy to remove, and window area that would be virtually impossible to improve upon. The fine visibility provided by this window area is, unfortunately, not going to last very well. The quarter and rear windows are made of clear plastic, intended, we suppose, to lighten the hardtop and make it easier to lift off, and this soft material was, even on our comparatively new test car, already beginning to develop a network of scratches that bid fair to render it anything but transparent.

The windshield and side windows were of glass, and hard enough to be immune to casual damage. The side windows are divided, with the main portion being retractable into the doors, but there is a small, fixed, wedge-shaped panel extending up to prevent air from spilling off the windshield and pouring directly into the car's interior. The theory, apparently,

The fuel tanks—one in each rear fender—are interconnected and fed from a common filler on the right side.

SUNBEAM ALPINE

is that this will enable one to drive with the windows cranked partially down and enjoy draft-free ventilation. It doesn't work. The only way to get any substantial amount of fresh air is to crank the windows down and ignore all of the buffeting around the ears. We tried swinging out the rear quarter windows (which have latches that double as props) and opening the fresh-air vent leading in through the heater/defroster system, but without much effect.

Most of the Alpine's controls are well situated, and the instrumentation is unusually complete—there being "real" gauges for keeping tabs on the engine's more important functions. We were less impressed with the wood-veneer covering on the instrument panel, but this would seem to be an inevitable consequence when the British set out to build a Luxury Car. The steering wheel is wood-rimmed, too, and while such things do impress many people, they also add to the overall maintenance requirements of the car. Woodwork may not need frequent refinishing in Foggy Old Blighty; our hot American sun tends to create problems with deterioration of the varnish.

There is one control combination in the Alpine that forms an especially neat trap for the unwary. When the handbrake lever (mounted between the driver's seat and the left door) is pulled up, it is placed so that the window-crank swings very near. Then, when the driver tries to crank the window up or down, the back of his hand is swung into sharp contact with the brake handle's release button. This, combined with that same lever's propensity for equally sharp contact with yet another part of one's anatomy (when entering or exiting from the driver's side), is grossly annoying. We respectfully suggest that another location might be better for the handbrake lever.

With regard to performance, the Alpine GT is a retrograde step. The engine changes we mentioned previously have made the engine outstandingly smooth and quiet, by 4-cylinder standards, but the reduction in power output has taken away a lot of the zing possessed by the Series 2 Alpine and, presumably, by the Series 3 Sports Tourer. Insofar as the standing-¼-mile performance is concerned, there has also been a loss caused by the reduction in 1st-gear ratio. The Series 3 Alpine is very definitely slower than earlier models in churning away from the mark, and it is not until the car reaches 15-20 mph in 1st gear that it begins to pull strongly. Our test car was further handicapped by a clutch that refused to bite properly; if it had been possible to bang in the clutch and get the wheels spinning, the engine would not have bogged down quite so badly and the initial rate of acceleration would have been improved.

The Alpine's ride and handling are exceptional. The car will glide along as smoothly as a 2-ton sedan, and yet does not bob and sway. When pressed, the Alpine's springing seems to stiffen, and it suddenly turns into a pure sporting machine, with quite good road adhesion (something it has not always had) and confidence-inspiring stability. It is worth mentioning that the Alpine's steering gear is of the recirculating-ball type, instead of the now almost-universal rack-and-pinion system, and although admittedly more complicated and expensive, it gives all of the lash-free precision of rack-and-pinion steering without that type's tendency toward excessive feed-back of road shocks.

Impressive, too, were the Alpine's brakes. These have been enlarged in the Series 3 model, with slightly greater diameters for the front discs and rear drums, and a manifold-vacuum servo is now standard equipment. Pedal pressure is, consequently, fairly low, with enough pressure required to give adequate "feel" for braking control. And, as is invariably the case when disc brakes are involved, the braking power is of a very high order.

Apart from the Alpine's other worthwhile features, which include such incidentals as window washers, 2-speed wipers, map-light, etc. (wire wheels are optional at extra cost, as is overdrive), there is that great attraction to the family-man: a back seat. True, it is a seat that offers only the most restricted accommodations, particularly in leg room, but it is a useful cubby for carrying children (or extra luggage), and that will be enough to tip the scales for many people out shopping for a sports car.

Effective intake-air silencing for the GT.

Relocation of fuel supply and spare gives deep trunk.

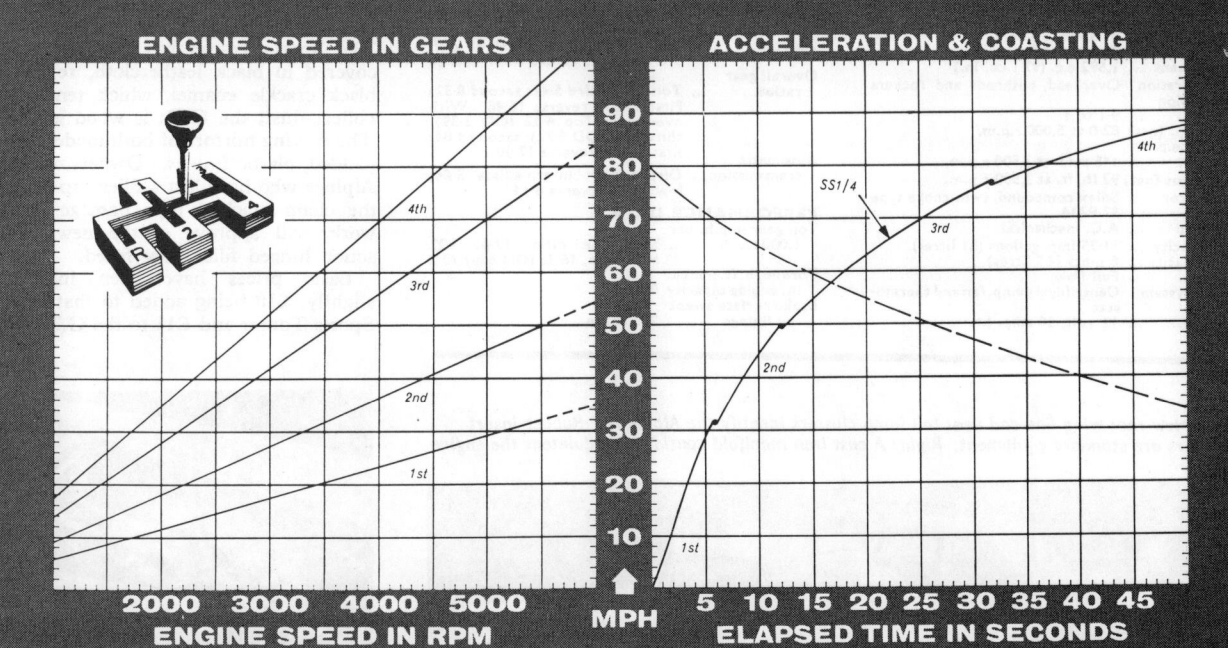

ROAD TEST
SUNBEAM ALPINE SERIES III

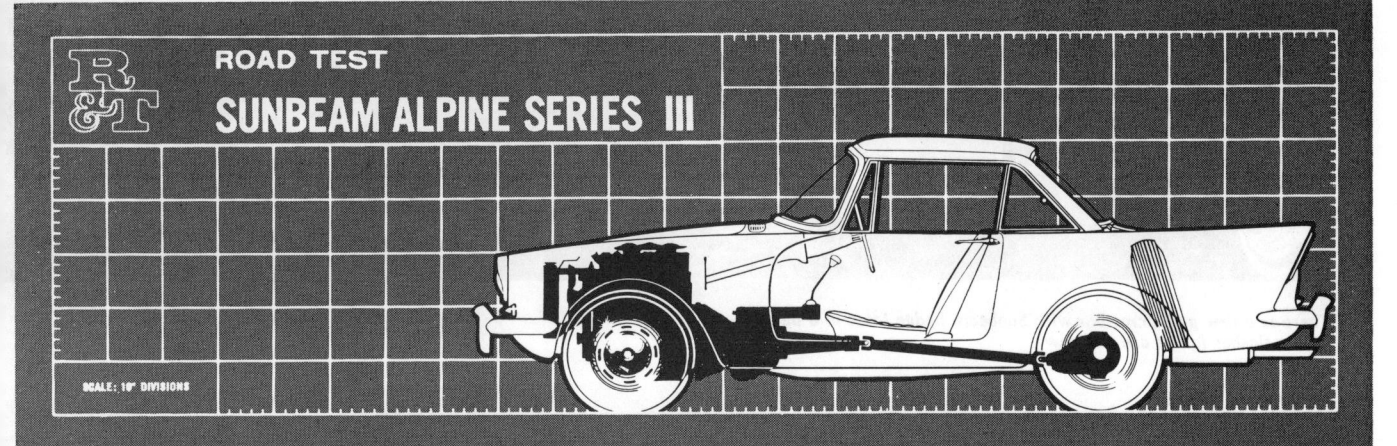

DIMENSIONS

Wheelbase, in............86.0
Tread, f and r......51.2/48.7
Over-all length, in......155.2
    width................60.5
    height...............52.5
    equivalent vol, cu ft....286
Frontal area, sq ft.......17.7
Ground clearance, in......5.2
Steering ratio, o/a........n.a.
    turns, lock to lock.......3.3
    turning circle, ft........34
Hip room, front......2 x 19.5
Hip room, rear..........n.a.
Pedal to seat back, max...42.7
Floor to ground..........11.5

CALCULATED DATA

Lb/hp (test wt)..........31.5
Cu ft/ton mile...........77.0
Mph/1000 rpm (4th)....17.3
Engine revs/mile........3465
Piston travel, ft/mile....1735
Rpm @ 2500 ft/min......5000
    equivalent mph........87
R&T wear index..........60.1

SPECIFICATIONS

List price.............$2749
Curb weight, lb........2185
Test weight............2530
    distribution, %......51/49
Tire size............6.00-13
Brake swept area........295
Engine type......4-cyl, ohv
Bore & stroke....3.21 x 3.00
Displacement, cc.......1592
    cu in................97.1
Compression ratio........9.1
Bhp @ rpm......80.2 @ 5000
    equivalent mph........87
Torque, lb-ft......92 @ 3600
    equivalent mph........62

GEAR RATIOS

4th (1.00)..............3.89
3rd (1.23)..............4.80
2nd (1.90)..............7.38
1st (2.96).............11.5

SPEEDOMETER ERROR

30 mph..........actual, 27.9
60 mph................55.5

PERFORMANCE

Top speed (mfr), mph.....100
  Shifts, rpm-mph
    3rd (5500).............77
    2nd (5500).............50
    1st (5500).............32

FUEL CONSUMPTION

Normal range, mpg.....20-27

ACCELERATION

0-30 mph, sec............5.4
0-40.....................8.6
0-50....................12.0
0-60....................18.1
0-70....................25.0
0-80....................36.9
0-100
Standing ¼ mile........22.2
    speed at end............66

TAPLEY DATA

4th, maximum gradient, %..8.3
3rd....................11.5
2nd....................18.3
Total drag at 60 mph, lb...110

ENGINE SPEED IN GEARS

ACCELERATION & COASTING

51

★ NEW MODEL

SUNBEAM ALPINE SERIES IV

There is a new grille crossbar with Sunbeam badge inset in a bezel; amber flasher lamps are also new

FOR the first time since its introduction in 1959, the Sunbeam Alpine is the subject of major styling changes in Series IV form, and these are exhibited for the first time at the Brussels Show which opened on Wednesday. Closely following the lines of the Alpine displayed at the Turin Show by Touring of Milan, the main styling change has been to lower the tips of the rear fins and to square off the ends, giving the car a more compact, taut look. A new radiator air intake decoration, consisting of a crossbar and central circular badge surround, distinguishes the front.

The main alteration to the 1,592 c.c. four-cylinder engine has been to adopt a cast-iron exhaust manifold, giving the same flow characteristics as that of the welded tubular, "bunch of bananas" manifold previously used only on the Alpine Series III roadster. Resonance due to the poor sound damping properties of sheet metal made these tubular manifolds too noisy for the closed Series III G.T. model, which utilized the less powerful (77 b.h.p.) Rapier engine using cast-iron manifolds. The new manifold is a replica of the sheet metal version. A further improvement to the manifolding is a pair of tubular "steadies" taken from the end of the manifold water jacket and picking up with an engine mounting bolt and a starter mounting bolt respectively.

A Micronic element air filter is used, and a self-consuming crankcase ventilation system is fitted. Output of this revised engine is 82 b.h.p. at 5,000 r.p.m., and it is used in both versions of the Alpine.

The Alpine is best regarded as a tourer rather than an out-and-out sports car, and there is ample justification for a version with automatic transmission. Rootes have chosen the Borg Warner 35 unit which is already available on the Super Minx and Minx V models. In the Alpine it has a floor-mounted, fore-and-aft selector quadrant, which is unusual.

Laycock-de Normanville overdrive is available when the manual gearbox is fitted, and on the Series IV Alpine it will be used with a 4·22 to 1 rear axle; on previous models the axle ratio was unchanged when overdrive was fitted.

PRICES

	Basic	Total (inc. P.T.)
	£	£ s d
Sports Tourer	705	852 8 9
G.T.	755	912 17 1

Extras (including P.T.):
Laycock-de Normanville overdrive £51 7 1
Borg-Warner automatic transmission £90 12 6
Wire wheels £7 11 1
Whitewall tyres £10 11 6
Road Speed tyres £10 11 6
Road Speed Whitewall tyres £15 8 2

To improve the ride at medium speeds, the rates of both front and rear springs have been reduced, with Armstrong GT constant-viscosity dampers adopted to control the greater wheel movement. Front suspension pillars now have pre-packed nylon-insert ball joints, and the wishbones pivot on rubber bushes. The steering idler lever joints and propeller shaft joints have "sealed-for-life" bearings, and the handbrake cable casing has a nylon, grease-impregnated lining.

Minor improvements in the cockpit include warning lights with adjustable lenses to reduce glare at night. The comprehensive instrumentation is the same as that of Series III models, except that the cable-driven rev counter has been replaced by an electronic impulse type. The Sports Tourer has the facia panel covered in black leathercloth, replacing black crackle enamel, which tended to collect dust; the GT's is wood grained. The driving mirrors of both models have padded, plastic frames. Owners of older Alpines who have lost a filler cap or had the chain-attached type damage paintwork, will approve of the new snap-action hinged filler now fitted.

Basic prices have been increased slightly, £10 being added to that of the Sports Tourer and £11 to the G.T.

Specification

ENGINE
No. of cylinders: 4 in-line
Bore: 81·5mm (3·21in.)
Stroke: 76·2mm (3·0in.)
Displacement: 1,592 c.c. (97·1 cu. in.)
Valve operation: Overhead, pushrods and rockers
Compression ratio: 9·1 to 1
Max. b.h.p. (net): 82·0 at 5,000 r.p.m.
Max. b.m.e.p. (net): 145 p.s.i. at 3,500 r.p.m.
Max. torque (net): 93 lb. ft. at 3,500 r.p.m.
Carburettor: Solex compound, twin-choke type 32 PAIA
Fuel pump: A.C. mechanical
Tank capacity: 11·25 Imp. gallons (51 litres)
Sump capacity: 8 pints (4·5 litres)
Oil filter: Full-flow
Cooling system: Centrifugal pump, fan and thermostat
Battery: 12 volt, 38 amp. hr.

TRANSMISSION
Clutch: Borg and Beck diaphragm, strap-drive, 8in. dia.
Gearbox: Four-speed, synchromesh on 2nd, 3rd and top, centre floor change
Overall gear ratios: Top 3·89; third 5·41; second 8·32; First 13·01; reverse 16·48. With overdrive: Top 4·22 (OD 3·39); third 5·88 (OD 4·72); second 9·04; first 14·13; reverse 17·90
Automatic transmission: Direct 3·89; intermediate 5·64; low 9·31; reverse 8·14

PERFORMANCE DATA
Top gear m.p.h. per 1,000 r.p.m.: 3·89 axle ratio, 17·6; 4·22 axle ratio, 16·2; (OD top) 20·2
Torque lb. ft. per cu. in. engine capacity: 0·96
Brake surface swept by linings: 295 sq. in.

Below: New rear wing line and neat tail lamp clusters identify the Alpine IV. Rubber insert overriders are standard equipment. Right: A cast iron manifold considerably quietens the engine

Cars ON TEST

SUNBEAM ALPINE G.T.

SERIES 4

THE SUNBEAM ALPINE has enjoyed a lengthy reputation in 1½-litre form as a comfortable, well-equipped two-seater of which the performance, if not exactly electrifying, is nevertheless of a sporting calibre, and sufficient to permit the maintenance of high average speeds. It is impossible to please everyone, and the earlier Alpines' body styling was the subject of some criticism, particularly with regard to the prominent tail-fin effect at the back. With the Series 4 version, however, this aspect has disappeared, and we must say that we consider the car to be a good deal more handsome without it.

The car supplied for test was the G.T. version, with the attractive, if somewhat angular, hard-top, and with the manual four-speed transmission: the car is now available with Borg-Warner automatic transmission as an option. The hard-top is fairly readily detachable, and further refinements which have been added in the past twelve months or so to the Alpine are the provision of adjustable seat-squabs and an easily-adjustable steering column, one of the biggest improvements to have been effected in the car's interior. Additionally, the pedals have a two-position adjustment.

The power unit is the four-cylinder 1,592 c.c. engine, developing 87.75 b.h.p. net at 5,000 r.p.m. on the G.T. model with good flexibility. Performance in the middle speed range is good, but there is a tendency to "tail off" at higher crankshaft speeds which gives the effect of providing better high speed acceleration in, say, top gear than in third. It is a silent, smooth unit, with a pleasing lack of fuss and a "lazy" quality, while throughout the test it was a ready starter, whether hot or cold. Idling was smooth, silent and reliable.

The transmission fitted to the test car was the Rootes four-speed and reverse gearbox, with synchromesh on the upper three forward ratios only, and with the optional Laycock de Normanville overdrive operating on third and top gears. The gearbox was quiet in operation, and the overdrive control mounted on the steering column, a positive return type switch, was rigid and firm to use. The gearbox itself was rather stiff, but the test car's mileage was small and there is no reason to doubt that this action will improve as further mileage is added to the car. The clutch is rather heavy, but is precise in its take-up of the drive, while the gear ratios are well-spaced for a car of this type. Appropriate use of the overdrive provides a wide range of well-stepped ratios from which a gear to suit the conditions can almost always be found.

Conventional suspension employs wishbones and coil springs at the front, with an anti-roll bar, while at the rear there are the usual longitudinal semi-elliptic leaf springs. The ride is firm, and wheel movement is well controlled by telescopic dampers, but there is noticeable body roll on corners while really hard cornering at the limit of tyre adhesion causes a good deal of lurching. Despite this, driver and passenger travel in comfort, and the car feels solid, breakaway being readily controllable. Road noise is well-insulated on good surfaces, but bad roads produce a steady drumming which is rather insidiously apparent. The test car was fitted with the optional centre-lock wire wheels.

The seating arrangements we have already discussed, together with the adjustable steering wheel and pedals, provide an excellent driving position which is comfortable for long journeys and yet also gives the driver a feeling of full control. The steering itself is reasonably light, if a little low-geared for the class of car, and the pedals are well spaced and arranged for heel-and-toe operation. The interior of the test car was smartly upholstered in black leather and was fully carpeted, with heavy layers of padding over the facia and doors. The seats are comfortable, and provide really good lateral support for both driver and

53

Large areas of glass in the G.T. hard-top provide good all-round visibility, but the effect is rather spoiled by the apparently pointless quarter-light frame on the side-windows: these windows are not provided with opening quarter-lights, although the rear quarter-lights open and ensure adequate ventilation of the interior.

passenger against cornering forces: from this point of view, they must rate among the best seats of their kind we have yet encountered. As indicated earlier, the squabs are adjustable for rake, while generous fore-and-aft adjustment is provided.

The dashboard is neatly arranged and fully-equipped. Immediately in front of the driver are the speedometer and matching rev.-counter, the former incorporating trip and total mileage recorders. Between them, and directly in the driver's natural line of vision, is the all-important oil-pressure gauge, while other instruments, including fuel contents and water temperature gauges and a clock, are grouped in the centre of the facia, and all dials are calibrated in metric equivalents as well as in British markings. Minor controls for lights, screen wipers and washers are well-placed for easy access and are simply identified after dark: instru-

The "tail-fin" effect of earlier Alpine bodies is no longer with us, and the Series 4 rear-end is neat and attractive.

54

ment lighting can be varied from bright to dim by a separate switch. The facia includes a glove compartment, with no lid, on the passenger's side, and the "floor" of this space is ingeniously contrived as a grab-handle. For valuables, a lockable compartment is revealed by raising the centre arm-rest. All-round visibility is excellent. The Alpine's existing slim screen pillars have their advantages summarily—and inexplicably—removed by the fitting of vertical bars, which resemble opening quarter-light frames, to the front of the side windows: as there are, in fact, no opening quarter-lights in these windows the provision of these vision-hampering metal strips is pointless. The hard-top's rear quarter-lights are hinged at the leading edge and remain open in a pleasantly positive fashion even at the car's maximum speed: the ventilation provided is draught-free, while valuable extraction of stale air, cigarette smoke and so on is provided. The rear window is all glass, and rearward vision is virtually without blind spots. A minute occasional seat is provided in the back of the car which, one supposes, could accommodate a child for short journeys. For access, the front seat squab hinges forward and, although this rear seat is endowed with upholstery, no doubt the majority of owners would come to regard it as merely supplementary luggage space. The brakes—9½ in. discs at the front, 9 in. drums at the rear—are more than adequate for the car's performance, and vacuum servo assistance requires only light pedal pressure to stop the Alpine in good order and with noticeable efficiency. No fade or judder was experienced at any time during the test mileage.

Although not an outstandingly fast car, even by 1½-litre standards, the Alpine G.T. is a particularly pleasant machine to drive. In overdrive top, it will cruise comfortably for mile after mile at 80–85 m.p.h., which translates into a reading of well under 4,000 r.p.m. on the tachometer. At this speed the power unit emits a pleasant purr, and there is no unobtrusive mechanical noise from either power unit or transmission. In addition, the engine is running at around the speed at which it develops its maximum torque, and this output is sufficient to enable the car to take main-road hills in its stride, with only fractional loss of speed. This silence, ease of progress and the comfort of the interior make it an outstandingly untiring machine even over long distances while, without any apparent effort, one can be pleasantly surprised at the high average speeds which the car has maintained.

It is not at first apparent that the man who is in a real hurry is equally well satisfied by the Alpine, and a glance at the performance figures does not indicate this either. A maximum speed, taken as the mean of runs in opposite directions, of only just over 93 m.p.h., together with acceleration times from 0–60 m.p.h. of 13.8 seconds, and the standing start quarter-mile of 19.2 seconds, label the car as being nothing out of the ordinary for machines of this type and capacity. However, the car's good handling—which exploration proves to be far better than is at first realised—first-class brakes and general feeling of strength and safety encourage the keen driver to take liberties which turn out not to be liberties at all, but feats well within the car's capabilities. The handling itself is of the type in which initial understeer changes smoothly and predictably to oversteer, which is readily controllable: the power unit now has the same performance as that of the sports tourer Alpine, and there is sufficient power under one's foot to enable oversteer to be promoted deliberately in the process of assisting the tail round tight corners, while on wet surfaces the machine's balance is good enough to allow it to be slid on all fours, although this sort of thing is not something which CARS ILLUSTRATED would encourage on public roads.

If full use of the performance is made, fuel consumption is rather high at around 22 m.p.g., although gentle driving improves this by two or three miles per gallon. An 11-gallon fuel tank provides a useful touring range of nearly 250 miles, even at the worst figure, however. Directional stability is good, and the car can be driven "hands-off" at high speed without wandering, while lights are good and permit high after-dark cruising speeds. A curious point is that the dip-switch requires amazingly heavy pressure, and if one drives the car in light shoes a few miles of night motoring can be extremely painful to the sole of the left foot. The screen-wipers clear a good area of the screen, although a blind spot of unswept glass is left on the off-side edge of the windscreen. Demisting of the screen is effective, but in cold weather the heater seems reluctant to produce anthing more positive than merely warm air, which allows the large areas of glass at the back of the car to grow misty.

Part of the space in the boot is occupied by the spare wheel, but if the car is required as a two-seater—as must be the case for journeys of any length—the space is still adequate for the occupants' luggage.

In short, the Alpine G.T. series 4 is very much a car which grows on one: we handed it back to Rootes Group's Alan Powell with feelings of real regret, liking it a good deal more after nearly 1,000 miles than at the conclusion of the first hundred.

SPECIFICATION AND PERFORMANCE DATA

Sunbeam Alpine G.T. Series 4 two-door, two-seater coupé with detachable hard-top. Price: £755, plus £157 17s. 1d. purchase tax. Total: £912 17s. 1d. Extra on test car: Laycock de Normanville overdrive, price £42 10s. Purchase tax: £8 17s. 1d.; total: £51 7s. 1d.

Engine: Four cylinder, 81.5 mm. × 76.2 mm. (1,592 c.c.). Compression ratio 9 : 1; 87.75 b.h.p. at 5,000 r.p.m. Push-rod operated overhead valves, single Solex 32 PAIA twin-choke carburetter.

Transmission: Four-speed and reverse gearbox with synchromesh on upper three forward ratios. Central floor-mounted remote control lever; overdrive on 3rd and 4th gears on test car.

Suspension: Front, independent with coil springs, wishbones and anti-roll bar. Rear, Semi-elliptic longitudinal leaf springs. Tyres: 6.00 × 13. Centre-lock wire wheels on test car.

Brakes: Front, 9.8 in. discs; rear, 9 in. drums. Vacuum servo assistance.

Equipment on test car: 12-volt lighting and starting. Self-parking, two speed windscreen wipers. Screen washers. Speedometer, rev.-counter, oil pressure, water temperature, fuel contents gauges. Headlamp flasher unit. Flashing direction indicators. Heating and demisting equipment. Adjustable front seat squabs, steering wheel and pedals.

Dimensions: Overall length 12 ft. 11¼ in; overall height 4 ft. 3½ in.; overall width 5 ft. 0½ in.; turning circle 34 ft. 6 in.; dry weight 2,290 lb.

Performance: Maximum speed (mean of opposite runs) 93.1 m.p.h. Best one-way speed: 94.6 m.p.h. Speeds in gears: 1st, 29 m.p.h.; 2nd, 42 m.p.h.; 3rd, 64 m.p.h.; overdrive 3rd, 83 m.p.h.; 4th, 93 m.p.h.; overdrive 4th 93.1 m.p.h. Acceleration: 0–30 m.p.h., 4.4 secs.; 0–40, 6.1 secs.; 0–50, 10.2 secs.; 0–60, 13.8 secs.; 0–70, 19.6 secs.; 0–80, 30.6 secs. Standing quarter-mile: 19.2 secs. Fuel consumption: 22–25 m.p.g.

SUNBEAM TIGER 260

NEW ★ MODEL

ROOTES FIT FORD V8 4·2-LITRE ENGINE TO THE POPULAR ALPINE TWO-SEATER BODY

AMERICAN engines built in huge quantities for a power-hungry public have about the best power-to-cost ratio to be found anywhere. Normally designed to give wheelspinning acceleration to very heavy motor cars, they produce quite startling results when installed in lightweight European chassis, as we have seen with the A.C. Cobra and the Lola G.T., among others. The idea is not new. Railton, Lammas-Graham and Brough proved the point back in the 1930s, but the idea is even more exciting now that power is greater. The engines are lighter and the know-how exists to install them in light chassis with good road-holding and brakes.

It is an especially good formula for sports cars which are to be exported to America, for service facilities for the power section of the car are universally available and a big range of performance improving kits is marketed. Rootes have been quick to appreciate the possibilities of this combination, and their adoption of the 260 cu. in. (4·2-litre) V8 Falcon engine for the newly announced Sunbeam Tiger 260 is a new departure for a major manufacturer.

In its latest Tiger form, the Sunbeam

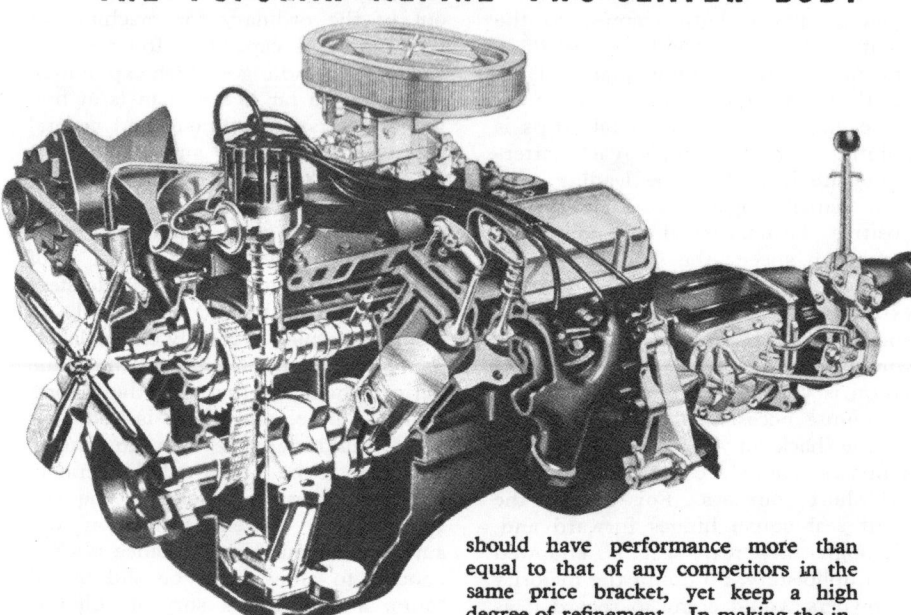

4·2-litre Ford Falcon V8 engine in unit with its all-synchromesh four-speed gearbox

Only the unusual gear lever and the lack of a choke control betray the nature of the beast to the observer. The closed GT model has a wood veneered panel

should have performance more than equal to that of any competitors in the same price bracket, yet keep a high degree of refinement. In making the installation, the appearance has not been changed, nor has the essential character of the Alpine, that of a comfortable touring car, been lost. Those who have driven prototypes of the car are as impressed by its smooth running as they are by its performance. First production will go to America, and the car was announced at the New York Show, but a right-hand drive English version is to follow. No price has been fixed for the latter, but it is likely to be about £300 more than that of the four-cylinder model—that is, around £1,200 total.

The chosen engine for the Beasty, as the project was named, is the 260 cu. in., 4,260 c.c., 96·5×73mm, V8 unit which normally propels Ford Fairlanes and the Falcon Sprints. The cylinder block is a thin-wall iron casting with an overall weight little more than that of an aluminium casting. This foundry technique and the V8 arrangement permits all-round water jacketing of each cylinder, the water space being carried right down to the base of the block. However, because of the compact dimensions of the engine there is insufficient room inside the crankcase for large enough crankshaft balance weights, so extra external counterweights, one on the flywheel and one on an extension of the crankshaft outside the timing case, are used to give 100 per cent balance.

Combustion chambers are wedge-shaped and the inclined valves are aluminized; they are operated by self-adjusting hydraulic tappets, pushrods

In GT guise the Tiger's hardtop is fixed, but a detachable one is optional for the roadster

and pressed steel rockers pivoting on ball joints, in the American manner. The separate inlet ports are fed through a cast-iron manifold from a centrally disposed Ford two-barrel carburettor. Exhaust ports on the outside of each bank of cylinders feed separate, cast-iron manifolds with individual exhaust systems running inside and parallel with the side members and underneath the rear axle. Engine output is quoted as 164 b.h.p. gross at 4,400 r.p.m. There is no official figure for the net output, but the Ford tuning manual mentions a figure of 141 b.h.p., which seems to be a realistic estimate.

Installation of the engine has presented fewer difficulties than might be imagined. The Ford unit is only 3·5in. longer and 2in. deeper than the Alpine unit it replaces, although it is naturally much wider, and the only main structural alterations necessary have been to dish the engine bulkhead to accommodate the larger clutch housing of the American unit, and to give increased clearance between the rocker covers and the bulkhead. The top-hat section inner wheel arch supports have also been reduced in depth to clear the cylinder banks.

Existing mounting points for the Burman steering box on the Alpine IV are fitted with pendant cast-iron brackets to carry standard Ford rubber-in-shear front engine mountings. These pick up with horizontal machined faces on the underside of each bank of cylinders. The rubber waffle-type Ford rear mounting, under the gear box, sits in a fabricated steel box welded to a short crossmember bolted inside the forward vee of the chassis cruciform member. Small heat deflectors on the front engine mountings shield their rubbers from exhaust heat.

Only minor modifications have been necessary to the engine to make it fit into the Sunbeam Tiger. For ease of servicing, the oil filter has been moved from its normal place on the left of the block to a new position high on the right-hand side of the engine where it is more readily accessible; it has a rated life of 36,000 miles. Engines will be supplied with modified pulleys, setting the pulley line back approximately one inch, and a new exhaust manifold has been designed with a vertical outlet matching that of the standard left-hand manifold, in place of the Fairlane and Falcon manifold which has a horizontal outlet.

Because of the width of the engine, it is impossible to fit the standard Alpine Burman steering box in its usual position. An Engineering Products rack-and-pinion layout has been adopted therefore. This is mounted on the forward side of the detachable front suspension cross-member, pockets being cut in the pressing to clear the ends of the rack. A short, universally jointed rod connects the steering pinion with the lower end of the steering column, which is steadied by a bracket welded to the left-hand wing valance.

For extra engine cooling a crossflow radiator is mounted in the normal position, with a separate, cylindrical header tank on the left-hand wing valance. To improve the flow of air to this unit the valance stiffener below the bumper is cut away, the starting handle tube being retained to support the rear edge of the panel. The standard Ford four-bladed fan supplies forced draught.

Power is transmitted through a 10in. Ford clutch with segmental linings and weighted, toggled levers which increase the clamping pressure by centrifugal force at high engine speeds. The Ford four-speed gearbox is synchronized on all speeds, using Warner baulk-ring synchromesh, and is operated by a remote gear change linkage mounted on the left-hand side of the output extension housing. The gear change itself, built up from heavy steel pressings, is extremely robust and effective. It is connected to the selector levers on the side of the gearbox by cranked rods. A lift-up crossbar, on a tube concentric with the gear lever, disengages the reverse lock and is almost the only feature inside the cockpit to distinguish the Tiger from the Alpine IV.

With so much extra power and torque to be transmitted, a stronger axle and higher ratio are called for, and a Salisbury hypoid bevel unit is installed with a 2·88 to 1 final drive ratio. To prevent transverse axle movement and to control

The spare wheel lies flat under a false floor to give more useable boot space. The box on the right is the battery cover

Full of good works. Most of the main services of the 260 engine are readily accessible, but plug changing is not easy

57

SUNBEAM TIGER 260...

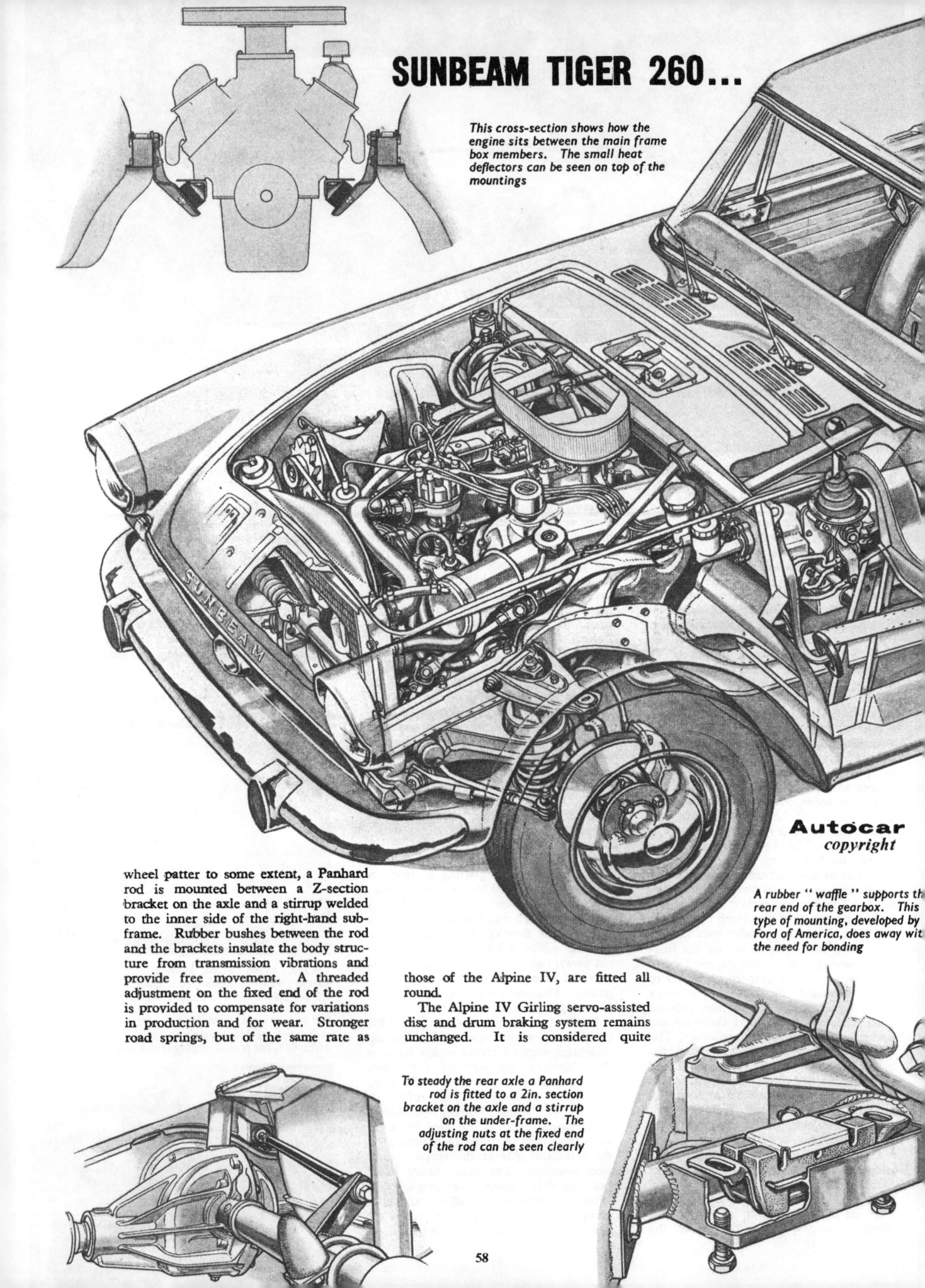

This cross-section shows how the engine sits between the main frame box members. The small heat deflectors can be seen on top of the mountings

A rubber "waffle" supports the rear end of the gearbox. This type of mounting, developed by Ford of America, does away with the need for bonding

Autocar *copyright*

wheel patter to some extent, a Panhard rod is mounted between a Z-section bracket on the axle and a stirrup welded to the inner side of the right-hand subframe. Rubber bushes between the rod and the brackets insulate the body structure from transmission vibrations and provide free movement. A threaded adjustment on the fixed end of the rod is provided to compensate for variations in production and for wear. Stronger road springs, but of the same rate as those of the Alpine IV, are fitted all round.

The Alpine IV Girling servo-assisted disc and drum braking system remains unchanged. It is considered quite

To steady the rear axle a Panhard rod is fitted to a 2in. section bracket on the axle and a stirrup on the under-frame. The adjusting nuts at the fixed end of the rod can be seen clearly

58

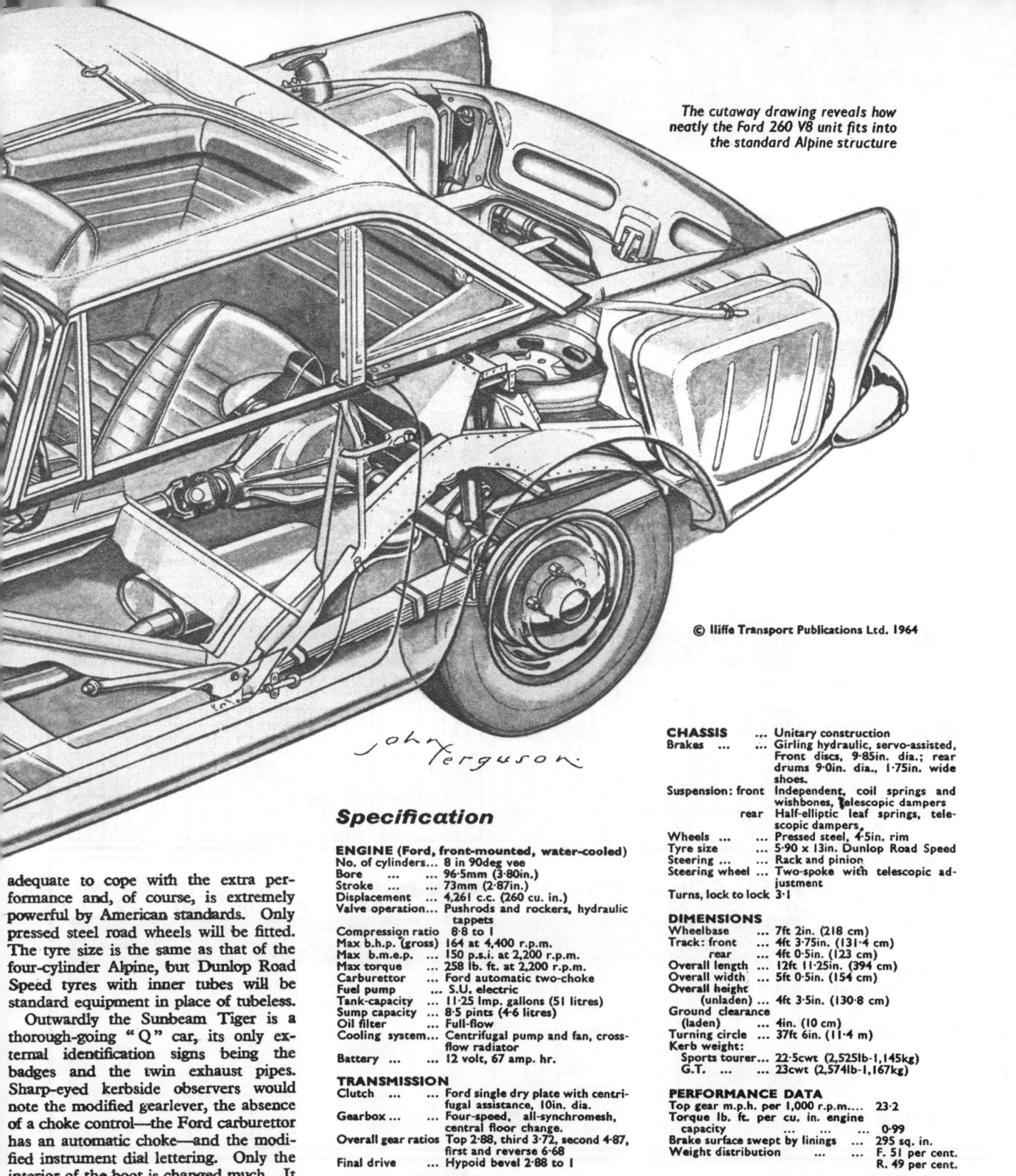

The cutaway drawing reveals how neatly the Ford 260 V8 unit fits into the standard Alpine structure

© Iliffe Transport Publications Ltd. 1964

John Ferguson

adequate to cope with the extra performance and, of course, is extremely powerful by American standards. Only pressed steel road wheels will be fitted. The tyre size is the same as that of the four-cylinder Alpine, but Dunlop Road Speed tyres with inner tubes will be standard equipment in place of tubeless.

Outwardly the Sunbeam Tiger is a thorough-going "Q" car, its only external identification signs being the badges and the twin exhaust pipes. Sharp-eyed kerbside observers would note the modified gearlever, the absence of a choke control—the Ford carburettor has an automatic choke—and the modified instrument dial lettering. Only the interior of the boot is changed much. It has been necessary to move the battery from its usual place beneath the right-hand seat, where it would have fouled one exhaust pipe, to a new home inside the boot. To make the best use of the boot space with this arrangement the spare wheel has been laid flat under a false floor, hinged at the forward end and covered with moulded plastic.

Many of us have driven the latest American cars have developed a distinct yen to install one of their husky powerplants in a really compact European chassis with restrained body styling and good brakes. Rootes have done this for us at what is expected to be modest cost.

Specification

ENGINE (Ford, front-mounted, water-cooled)
No. of cylinders... 8 in 90deg vee
Bore ... 96.5mm (3.80in.)
Stroke ... 73mm (2.87in.)
Displacement ... 4,261 c.c. (260 cu. in.)
Valve operation... Pushrods and rockers, hydraulic tappets
Compression ratio 8.8 to 1
Max b.h.p. (gross) 164 at 4,400 r.p.m.
Max b.m.e.p. ... 150 p.s.i. at 2,200 r.p.m.
Max torque ... 258 lb. ft. at 2,200 r.p.m.
Carburettor ... Ford automatic two-choke
Fuel pump ... S.U. electric
Tank capacity ... 11.25 Imp. gallons (51 litres)
Sump capacity ... 8.5 pints (4.6 litres)
Oil filter ... Full-flow
Cooling system... Centrifugal pump and fan, cross-flow radiator
Battery ... 12 volt, 67 amp. hr.

TRANSMISSION
Clutch ... Ford single dry plate with centrifugal assistance, 10in. dia.
Gearbox ... Four-speed, all-synchromesh, central floor change.
Overall gear ratios Top 2.88, third 3.72, second 4.87, first and reverse 6.68
Final drive ... Hypoid bevel 2.88 to 1

CHASSIS ... Unitary construction
Brakes ... Girling hydraulic, servo-assisted, Front discs, 9.85in. dia.; rear drums 9.0in. dia., 1.75in. wide shoes.
Suspension: front Independent, coil springs and wishbones, telescopic dampers
rear Half-elliptic leaf springs, telescopic dampers
Wheels ... Pressed steel, 4.5in. rim
Tyre size ... 5.90 x 13in. Dunlop Road Speed
Steering ... Rack and pinion
Steering wheel ... Two-spoke with telescopic adjustment
Turns, lock to lock 3.1

DIMENSIONS
Wheelbase ... 7ft 2in. (218 cm)
Track: front ... 4ft 3.75in. (131.4 cm)
rear ... 4ft 0.5in. (123 cm)
Overall length ... 12ft 11.25in. (394 cm)
Overall width ... 5ft 0.5in. (154 cm)
Overall height (unladen) ... 4ft 3.5in. (130.8 cm)
Ground clearance (laden) ... 4in. (10 cm)
Turning circle ... 37ft 6in. (11.4 m)
Kerb weight:
Sports tourer... 22.5cwt (2,525lb-1,145kg)
G.T. ... 23cwt (2,574lb-1,167kg)

PERFORMANCE DATA
Top gear m.p.h. per 1,000 r.p.m.... 23.2
Torque lb. ft. per cu. in. engine capacity ... 0.99
Brake surface swept by linings ... 295 sq. in.
Weight distribution ... F. 51 per cent. R. 49 per cent.

External recognition points are the twin exhausts and the side motifs. Body styles are identical with those of the Alpine IV, a roadster and a GT coupé being available

Number 40 MOTOR TESTED 2250 MILES

"Sporting enthusiasts look upon it as a pleasant tourer for two."

SUNBEAM ALPINE IV automatic

PRICE
£830 plus £174 9s. 7d. purchase tax equals £1,004 9s. 7d. total.

How they run...

MAXIMUM SPEED (m.p.h.)

Car	Speed
Alpine IV (automatic) £1,004	~87
Alpine III (manual) £905	~92
Renault Caravelle £974	~78
MG B £834	~103
Panhard 24CT £1,330	~80

FUEL CONSUMPTION — ■ OVERALL / ☐ TOURING (m.p.g.)

Car	Overall	Touring
Alpine IV (automatic)	~22	~28
Alpine III (manual)	~28	~37
Renault Caravelle	~26	~36
MG B	~22	~27
Panhard 24CT	~30	~44

ACCELERATION — ■ 0-50 / ☐ 20-40 IN TOP (seconds)

Car	0-50	20-40 in top
Alpine IV (automatic)	~14	~11
Alpine III (manual)	~13	~14
Renault Caravelle	~13	~12
MG B	~10	~10
Panhard 24CT	~22	~16

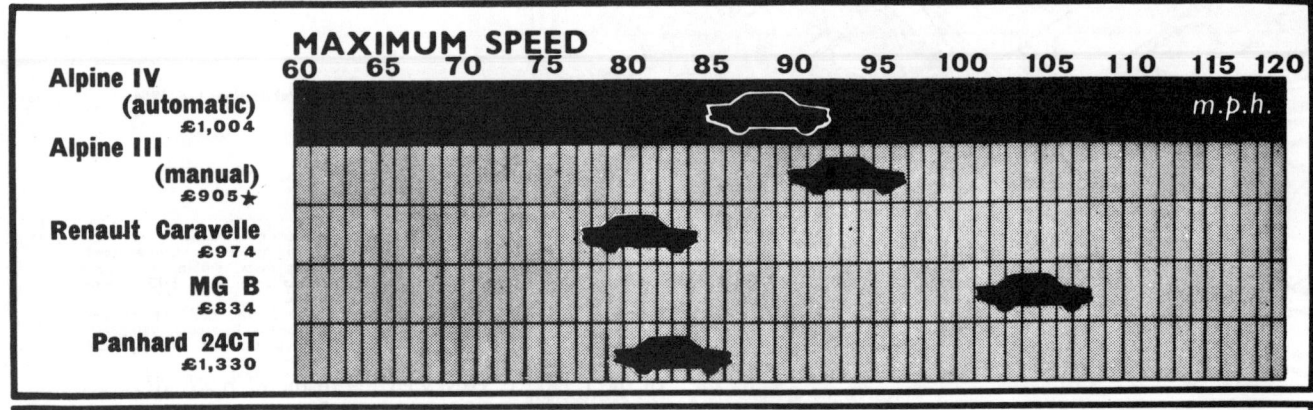

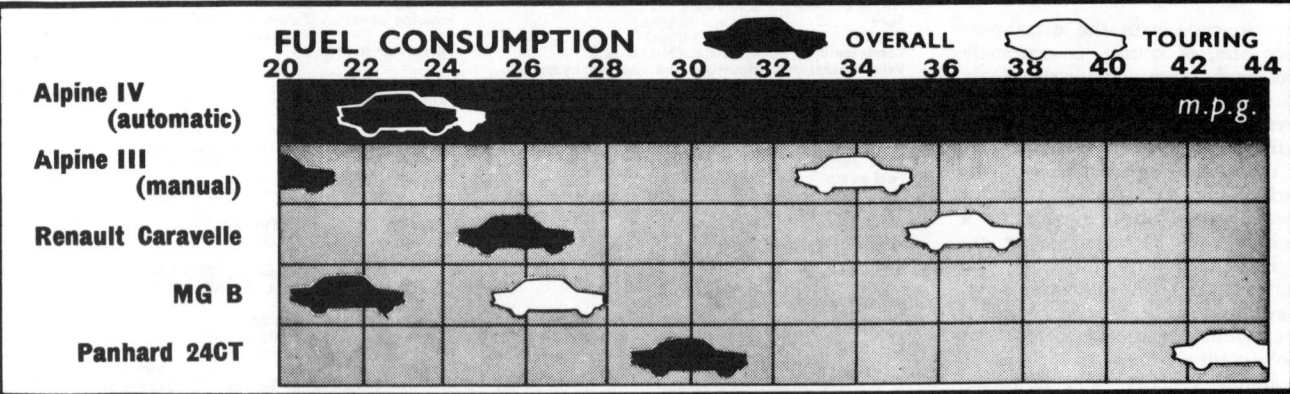

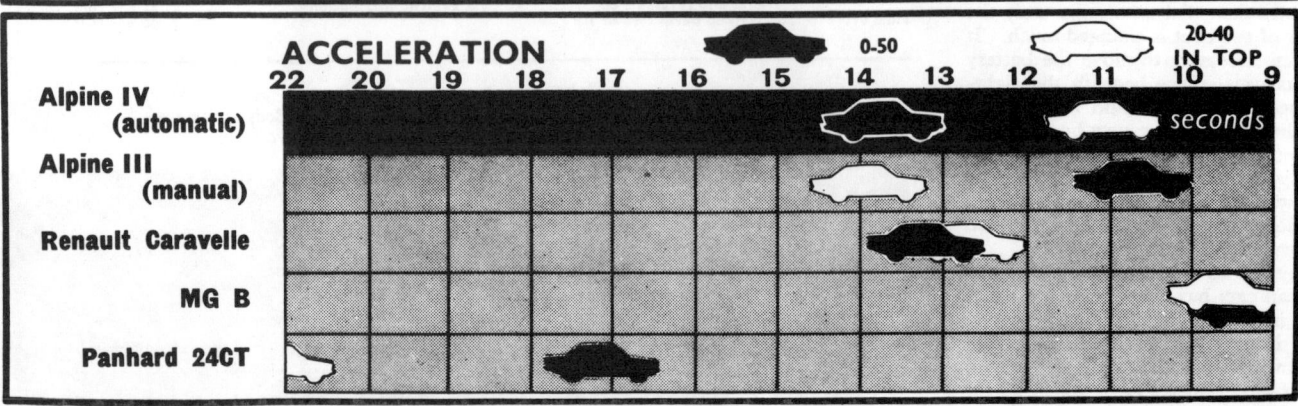

Attractive transport for two with saloon car comfort and amenities. Wire wheels are an optional extra.

PEOPLE accustomed to saloons regard the Sunbeam Alpine as a sports car; sporting enthusiasts look upon it as a pleasant tourer for two. It is thus a car with an enormously wide market spectrum, appealing to a very large cross section of the motoring public. With this in mind, the adoption of automatic transmission as an option to the standard 4-speed manual gearbox is not so irrational as some people seem to think.

The Alpine does not go as fast as its rakish looks might suggest (several 1½-litre saloons can accelerate more quickly) but for comfortable driving in elegant surroundings it has few peers among mass-production two-seaters. The Borg-Warner 35 transmission inevitably impairs performance and economy a little (0–50 in 13·0 sec. compared with 10·0 sec. for the manual car) but it changes gear very smoothly and, for a sporting flavour, is controlled by a neat floor-mounted lever; using low-gear hold and the rev counter, sports car drivers found it a realistic substitute for playing with a manual box. At the same time, there is the same relaxed ease-of-control which an automatic inspires in busy town traffic.

Firm, well-insulated suspension gives good, well-balanced roadholding, the fairly heavy steering with little sensitivity suggesting saloon rather than sports car handling. The comfort of the seats and the very large range of adjustments (reach, rake and steering wheel) are in the best grand touring tradition and models for other manufacturers to copy. Other attractions include sensible luggage accommodation and an easily removed hardtop (supplemented by a soft hood).

Performance and economy

IN VARIOUS forms, the Rootes 1½-litre engine has been with us for years, and even now ranges from the 40 b.h.p. of the 1,390 c.c. Husky engine to the 82 b.h.p. of the Alpine 1,600 c.c. Stretching it this far has not affected the smoothness or reliability of a well-tried four-cylinder engine with pushrod overhead valves.

The engine fires easily when cold with some choke; after less than a mile the choke can be returned and the full performance used. With some power lost in the transmission, acceleration figures of 0–60 m.p.h. in 17 sec. and a standing quarter mile in 21·8 sec. are modest, but the easy availability of maximum power ensures that the Alpine is not left behind after an initial lag from standing starts.

The automatic transmission normally keeps the engine below 4,000 r.p.m., when it is remarkably smooth; beyond that, with kick-down using nearly 5,500 r.p.m., it gets distinctly fussy and mechanically noisy. Maximum speed at 92·2 m.p.h. corresponds to 5,400 r.p.m. but normal cruising up to 80 m.p.h. keeps the noise at an unobtrusive level.

If the kick-down is used often, fuel consumption will be fairly heavy, probably approaching our overall figure of 24·3 m.p.g., but, by restricting speed to 60 m.p.h., 30 m.p.g. is attainable.

Despite a lowest possible overall ratio of 18·1 : 1, (allowing for 2 : 1 torque conversion) the Alpine failed our 1 in 3 start while the gearbox churned away, but 1 in 4 was surmounted.

Transmission

BORG-WARNER's type 35 transmission is now well known on many different vehicles; the three-speed epicyclic gearbox with torque converter has reached such a stage of development that even "stick shift" addicts will find little cause for

SUNBEAM ALPINE IV automatic

complaint. The ability to hold a gear with the kick-down switch (5,500 r.p.m. in bottom and 5,000 in second), or select a lower ratio with an easy lever movement, is all the overriding control that one needs. This is one of the smoothest installations of this gearbox that we have encountered, even the full throttle changes into and out of first gear being substantially jerk-free.

Absence of tail fins (above left) and a neat hard-top (with good head room) distinguish the latest line of Alpines.

At 9·7 cu. ft. luggage capacity (top) is better than in many saloons; the five boxes (above) go in the boot, the other four behind the front seats—at the expense of a third passenger.

The very comfortable bucket front seats (below) are adjustable for reach and rake, and the steering column length can also be changed by releasing the central steering wheel boss. Both front seats tip forward (left) for access to the considerably less roomy rear bench which can be used for two cramped passengers or lots of luggage.

Performance—

Test Data: World copyright reserved: no unauthorized reproduction in whole or in part.

Conditions: Weather: Occasional drizzle, gusty winds 15-35 m.p.h. (Temperature 54°-59°F, Barometer 28·95-28·80 in. Hg.). Surface: Damp tarmacadam. Fuel: 97 octane.

ACCELERATION TIMES

0-30 m.p.h.	6·8 sec.
0-40	9·2
0-50	13·0
0-60	18·0
0-70	27·2
0-80	39·0
Standing quarter mile	21·8

m.p.h.	Top sec.	Kick-down sec.
10-30	—	6·8
20-40	10·4	4·8
30-50	12·4	6·2
40-60	15·5	8·8
50-70	18·2	14·2
60-80	21·0	21·0

1, brake fluid reservoir. 2, oil filler cap. 3, starter solenoid. 4, windscreen washer reservoir. 5, crankcase fume filter. 6, carburetter. 7, coil. 8, distributor. 9, dip stick. 10, brake servo. 11, radiator filler cap.

Using the kick-down in bottom gear, engine noise encourages an early change but if the throttle is eased for too long, second is missed altogether and top comes in. Sometimes the rather light kick-down switch allows bottom to be selected unintentionally but a sensitive toe can avoid this; a heavier spring might be better but the problem of kicking-down to first gear when only intermediate is needed would still remain.

One of the sporting features that has been retained is a floor gearchange; a small light lever moves in a fore-and-aft plane, spring-loaded sideways into notches for each position—P, R, N, D, L,—with extra resisting springs making P and L a more positive effort to engage. Manœuvring thus needs an easy flick from R to D with no fear of engaging P while still slipping forwards.

On paper, the ratios seem very wide, but a torque converter giving a multiplication factor of up to two helps to bridge the gaps between the three speeds.

Handling and brakes

SAFE AND flat describes handling which is good by saloon standards but not outstanding among sports cars. Conventional coil spring and wishbone front, with semi-elliptic live-axle rear suspension is set up to give consistent understeer, and is little affected by accelerator position. The steering feels quite light in a straight line but gets heavier on lock, especially when cornering quickly. Rough roads do not throw the live rear axle off course, and generally seem to affect the car less the faster it goes. The suspension feels well damped and insulated from road shocks and the pleasant ride is perhaps a good compromise for a grand tourer which can still be cornered smoothly and quickly with little roll.

Although it is possible to use engine braking, is it more normal for the gearbox to be in top when slowing down and the brakes can get harsh treatment; they are perfectly capable of standing up to it and servo-assistance keeps the effort down to a reasonable level. The handbrake on the rear drum brakes provides a useful emergency stop and can hold the car on a 1 in 3 hill.

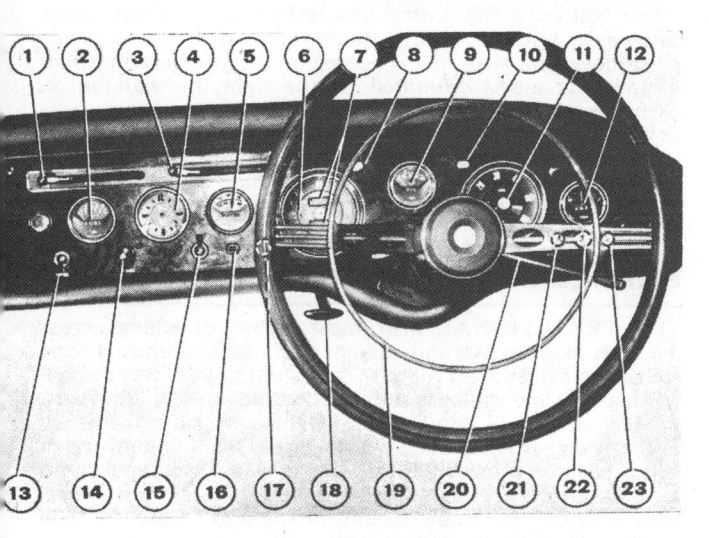

1 and 3, heater controls. 2, fuel gauge. 4, clock. 5, water thermometer. 6, speedometer. 7, trip and mileage recorder. 8, ignition light. 9, oil pressure gauge. 10, main beam warning light. 11, rev. counter. 12, ammeter. 13, panel light. 14, choke. 15, lights. 16, indicator warning light. 17, ignition/starter. 18, bonnet release. 19, horn ring. 20, indicators and flasher. 21, wipers. 22, washers. 23, fog and spot lights. Instruments are set attractively in a polished walnut facia, with padded protection above and below. Roll over lids dim lights 8 and 10.

MAXIMUM SPEEDS

Mean lap speed banked circuit 92.2 m.p.h.
Best one way ¼-mile 98.8
Intermediate 61
Low 41
"Maximile" Speed: (Timed quarter mile after 1 mile accelerating from rest)
Mean 90.8
Best 95.6

BRAKES

Pedal pressure, deceleration and equivalent stopping distance from 30 m.p.h.

lb.	g	ft.
25	0.28	107
50	0.61	49
75	0.86	35
100	0.98	30½
110	1.00	30
Handbrake	0.42	71½

FUEL CONSUMPTION

Touring (consumption midway between maximum and 30 m.p.h. less 5% allowance for acceleration) .. .. 25.0 m.p.g.
Overall .. .. .. 24.3 m.p.g.
(=11.7 litres/100 km)
Total test distance .. .. 2,250 miles

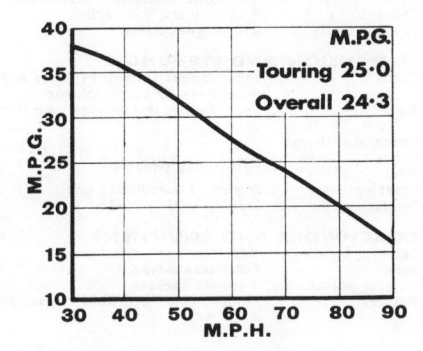

Touring 25.0
Overall 24.3

STEERING

Turning circle between kerbs: ft.
Left 33
Right 32
Turns of steering wheel from lock to lock .. 3¼

SPEEDOMETER

30 m.p.h. .. .. .. 1% fast
60 .. .. .. accurate
90 .. .. .. 1% fast
Distance recorder .. .. 3% slow

WEIGHT

cwt.
Kerb weight (unladen with fuel for approximately 50 miles) 19.8
Front/rear distribution .. 53½/46½
Weight laden as tested 23.5

63

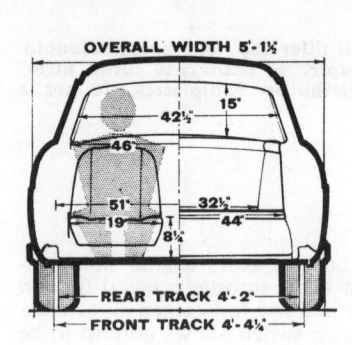

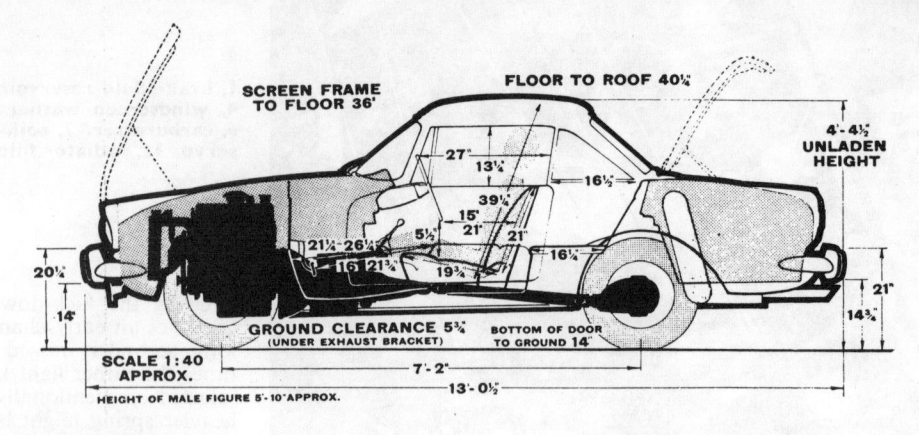

SUNBEAM ALPINE IV automatic

Comfort and control

THE INTERIOR of the Alpine immediately gives an impression of comfort, confirmed after trial; wooden facias can so easily jar with surrounding trim but this one fits well with the black leather-cloth seats and facia top. People of all sizes can fit the driver's seat with plenty of leg room, and an adjustable back-rest takes care of arm positions; in contrast, the emergency rear seat takes no one unless the front one is pushed uncomfortably far forward, but it can be used for children and certainly for portable cots. The front seats give good side support and the steering wheel is adjustable for reach.

On poor surfaces the car tends to follow the undulations at slow speeds which vibrate the mirror, but going faster the road flattens out and the ride becomes not unpleasantly firm. Our test car had a well-trimmed hard top which enhanced the touring car outlook. It is easily removed by undoing four over-centre clips and sliding two spigots out of holes in the boot hinges; the sealing is particularly good except at the rear of the side windows which whistle at over 75 m.p.h. It is completely waterproof.

With the hood on or off, wind noise will not affect conversation or radio volume at normal cruising speeds and engine noise is only noticeable at high revs in the lower gears; in general the noise level is in keeping with comfortable touring.

All controls are within easy reach (even the radio) with a seat belt on. The central arm-rest obstructs direct access to the gear selector, but the motion is so slight that a gentle wrist movement is all that is needed on the rare occasions that the lever is used. Mounted on the right, the handbrake, when on, obstructs the window winder.

With the hardtop's full-width rear window and thin pillars, visibility is very good and there are no blind spots. At night the lights are excellent and give more than sufficient illumination for the car's performance.

Fittings and furniture

THE TRADITIONAL instrument layout stretching across the facia is attractive and easy to read; all instruments have metric equivalents—a handy conversion table for foreign touring—all the switches are labelled and easy to find and the fuel gauge tells you how many gallons (or litres) remain.

The heater is adequate for keeping the small volume warm when the hood is on, but for driving in a cool evening without a roof a greater leg-blast would be welcome. Its two sliding lever controls are simple to understand and to use and one of them controls the fan as well.

Luggage and oddments are well catered for with a boot taking 5.8 cu. ft. of our test cases; a further 3.9 cu. ft. can fit on the rear seat. The arm-rest is a glove locker and there is an open facia pocket whose paper contents get a little disturbed with the hood off.

For safety, the test car was fitted with seat belts, and there is padding along the facia top and on the steering boss.

MAKE Sunbeam • **MODEL** Alpine IV automatic • **MAKERS** Rootes Motors Ltd., Coventry, England

---

ENGINE
Cylinders .. 4
Bore and stroke .. 81.5 mm. × 76.2 mm.
Cubic capacity .. 1,592 c.c.
Valves .. Pushrod o.h.v.
Compression ratio 9.1 : 1
Carburetter .. Solex compound twin choke
Fuel pump .. AC mechanical
Oil filter .. Full flow
Max. power (net) . 82 b.h.p. at 5,000 r.p.m.
Max. torque (net) 93.4 lb. ft. at 3,500 r.p.m.

TRANSMISSION
Borg-Warner 35 automatic with torque convertor, and 3-speed epicyclic gearbox
Top gear .. 1.0
Intermediate .. 1.45
Low .. 2.32
Reverse .. 2.1
Final drive .. Hypoid bevel 3.89 : 1
M.p.h. at 1,000 r.p.m. in:—
Top gear .. 17.2
Intermediate .. 11.9
Low .. 7.4

CHASSIS
Construction .. Unitary

BRAKES
Type .. Girling servo-assisted disc/drum
Dimensions .. 9.85 in. discs, 9 in. drums
Friction areas .. 298 in. swept area

SUSPENSION AND STEERING
Front .. Independent with coil springs and wishbones, and anti-roll bar
Rear .. Semi-elliptic leaf springs with live axle
Shock absorbers:
Front }
Rear } .. Armstrong telescopic
Steering gear .. Burman recirculating ball
Tyres .. Dunlop 6.00—13 RS5

COACHWORK AND EQUIPMENT
Starting handle .. Yes
Jack .. Pillar screw-type
Jacking points .. 4 corner sockets
Battery .. Under rear occasional seat, 38 Amp. hr.
No. of electrical fuses .. 2
Indicators .. Self-cancelling flasher
Screen wipers .. Electrical self-parking two-speed
Screen washers .. Manual plunger
Sun visors .. Two
Locks:
  With ignition key Ignition/starter and doors
  With other keys Boot
Interior heater .. Optional fresh air
Extras .. Clock, radio, heater, wire wheels, soft hood, and range of Rootes accessories
Upholstery .. P.v.c.
Floor covering .. Carpet
Alternative body types .. None

MAINTENANCE
Sump .. 8 pints S.A.E. 20W or multigrade 10W/30
Gearbox .. 11 pints Shell Donax T6
Rear axle .. 1¾ pints S.A.E. 90 EP
Steering gear .. 90 EP
Cooling system .. 12½ pints (2 drain taps)
Chassis lubrication No points
Ignition timing .. 7°–9° b.t.d.c.
Contact breaker gap .. 0.015 in.
Sparking plug type KLG FE75
Sparking plug gap .025 in.
Tappet clearances (hot) .. Inlet .012 in., Exhaust .014 in.
Front wheel toe-in .125 in.
Castor angle .. 4° 40'
Tyre pressures .. 24 lb. front and rear

Road Research Report:

SUNBEAM TIGER

Tigers are all the rage: Rootes is holding a winner by the tail.

They said it couldn't be done; but it was, and results are beyond anyone's expectations. Yes, friends, the rumors are correct: there *is* a Sunbeam sports car Powered-by-Ford (as what isn't these days). Not just a one-off curiosity, nor even a limited production item to be sold at a whopping price; instead, a car that dealers are ordering at the rate of 400 per month, and a car that anyone who has $3500 can buy.

All this came about because Ian Garrad, who heads Rootes' West Coast distribution organization, was impressed by the good things Ford's Fairlane-series V-8 was doing for sundry automobiles. It occurred to him that Sunbeam's Alpine sports car might respond well to a transfusion of V-8 muscle. To settle the question, Garrad commissioned Ken Miles, Shelby-American's

SUNBEAM TIGER

team manager, to change the idea into reality. Within two weeks Miles had produced the first prototype of the car that was to become the Sunbeam "Tiger": an Alpine stuffed full of Ford V-8 and three-speed automatic transmission.

This initial effort was a trifle ragged, having been pieced together rather hastily, but it did demonstrate that the fundamental idea was sound, which encouraged Garrad to have a second, more polished prototype built. The task was assigned to the Shelby organization itself, as they do have some experience in packing Ford's little V-8 into British sports cars. Pack they did. Not just the V-8, but this time one of Ford's four-speed, all-synchro transmissions as well, and with results that were even better than with the automatic (which should surprise no one).

At that point, the time for prototypes and conversation was over. The next job was to sell the parent company in England the idea—and that was to take some doing. The home office was decidedly cool to Mr. Garrad and his hot-rodder's scheme, and it was not until Ian tucked the second prototype under his arm and made the trek to the factory that anyone got interested. What happened was that Garrad arranged for Lord Rootes (Himself) to drive the embryo Tiger, which was something of a gamble as Sir William doesn't really care very much for driving and is normally whisked about in a vast, silent sedan by a liveried chauffeur.

However, the old boy did drive the Tiger, and was so impressed that he immediately set an army of secretaries to work trying to get Henry Ford (why deal with underlings, right?) on the telephone. Mr. Ford, when reached, replied that he would be delighted to supply Rootes with engines, and with that the Sunbeam Tiger became a reality for all us eager sports car buyers and enthusiasts.

Since that time, of course, Chrysler Corporation has bought up 30% of the Rootes parent company, and many people speculated that the deal would spell the end of the Rootes-Ford tie-in. Not so, says management, and Tigers will be Ford-powered while the supply lasts (i.e., until the end of its production run).

Now then, you will appreciate that big V-8 engines do not plop into little cars without causing a few waves, and a lot of changes had to be made in the basic Sunbeam automobile before production could begin. Among these was a complete redesign of the unitized body/chassis structure, particularly in the area of the cowl. The outer body panels were not changed, but much of the interior sheet metal was altered in form and gauge to create additional strength and space for the wider engine. The alterations must have been successful, for the Tiger feels remarkably solid, with none of the cowl shake that is one of the less attractive features of many convertibles.

Some changes in the chassis were required. The Alpine has Burman recirculating-ball, worm-and-nut type steering gear, while the Tiger is fitted with rack and pinion steering. We rather imagine that this change in specification was made because the Ford engine leans into some of the space occupied by the Burman steering box in the Alpine.

The new steering system is installed in front of the cross member which carries the suspension, and pockets have been cut in the steel pressing to clear the ends of the rack. The pinion is connected to the steering column via a short universal-jointed rod. The Alpine's steering winds over 3.3 turns, lock to lock, and the Tiger's goes 3.1 turns, which would make it seem that

66

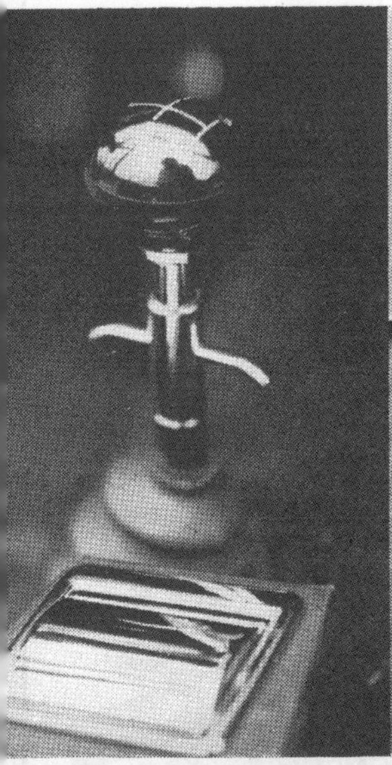

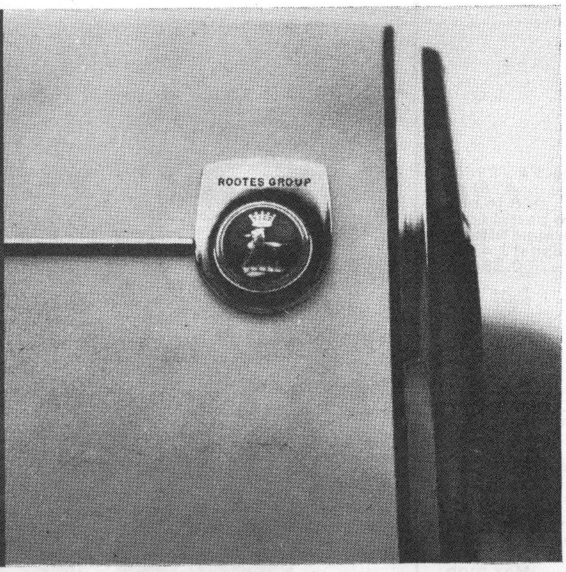
ROOTES GROUP

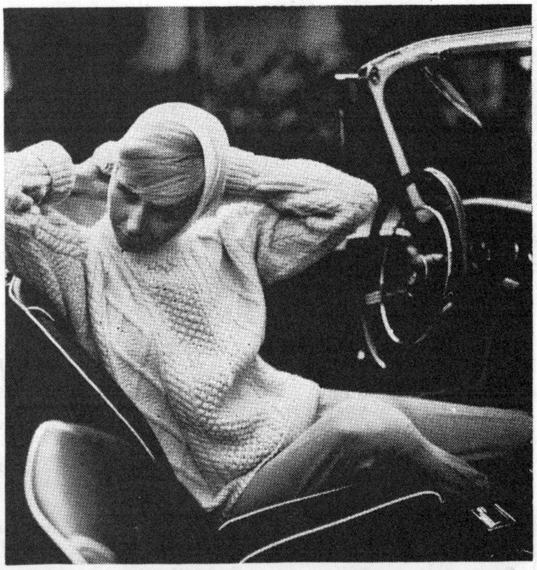

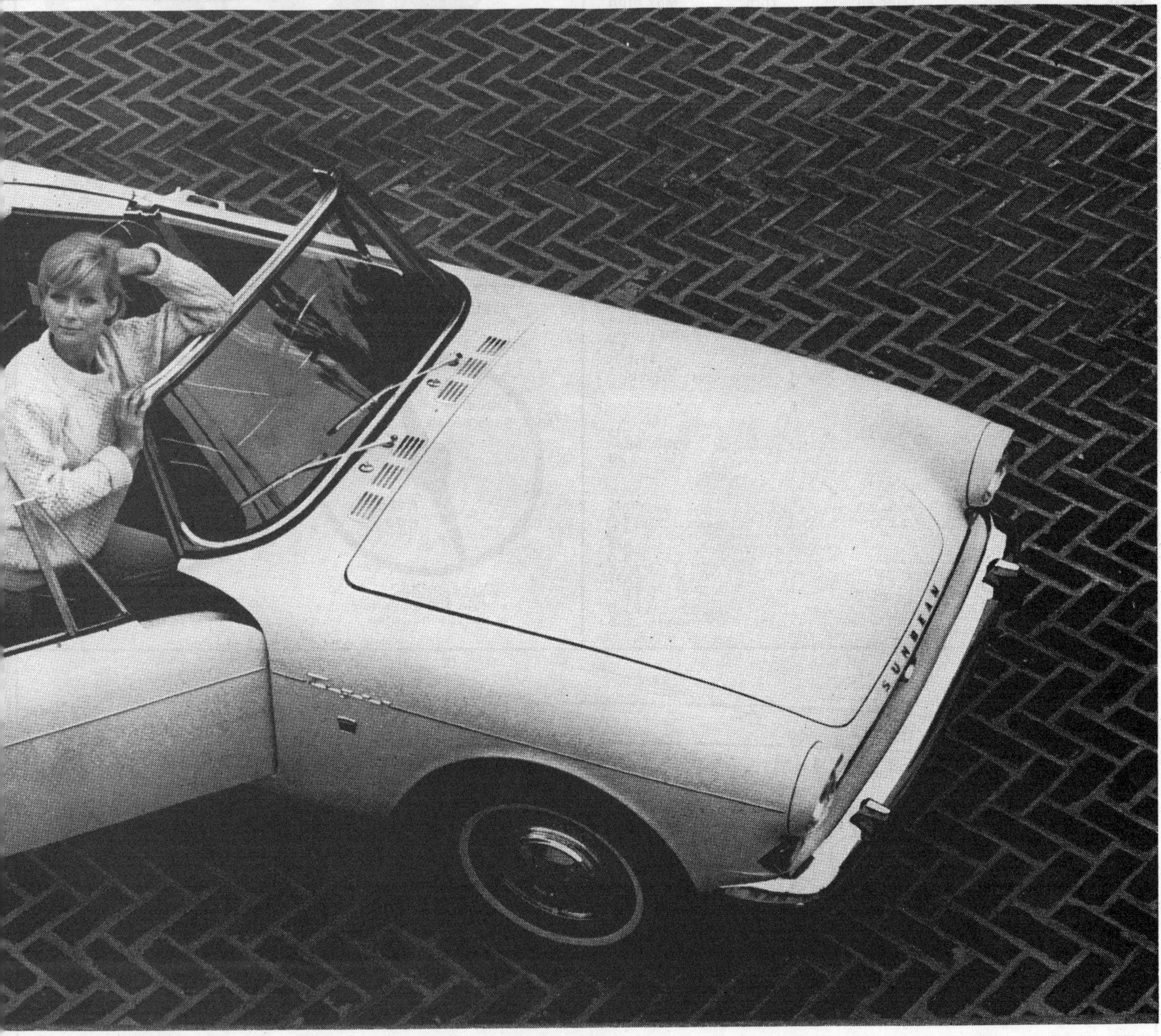
SUNBEAM

Road Research Report:

Importer: Rootes Motors, Inc.
505 Park Avenue
New York, N.Y. 10022

PRICES
Price as tested: $3499 POE West Coast

ENGINE
Water-cooled V-8, cast iron block, 5 main bearings
Bore x stroke.................................3.80 x 2.87 in, 96.5 x 73 mm
Displacement.....................................260 cu in, 4261 cc
Compression ratio.....................................8.8 to one
Carburetion.....................................Single two-barrel Ford
Valve gear........Pushrod-operated overhead valves (hydraulic lifters)
Valve diameter.....................................Intake 1.67 in, exhaust 1.45 in
Valve lift.....................................0.380 in
Valve timing:
  Intake opens.....................................21° BTC
  Intake closes.....................................51° ABC
  Exhaust opens.....................................57° BBC
  Exhaust closes.....................................15° ATC
Power (SAE).....................................164 bhp @ 4400 rpm
Torque.....................................258 lbs-ft @ 2200 rpm
Specific power output.........0.63 bhp per cu in, 38.5 bhp per liter
Usable range of engine speeds.....................................1000–5000 rpm
Electrical system.........12-Volt, 67 amp-hr battery, 42 amp generator
Fuel recommended.....................................Regular
Mileage.....................................18–22 mpg
Range on 13.5-gallon tank.....................................245–300 miles

DRIVE TRAIN
Clutch.....................................10-inch single dry plate
Transmission.....................................4-speed all-synchro

Gear	Ratio	Over-all	mph/1000 rpm	Max mph
Rev	2.32	6.68	—10.8	—54
1st	2.32	6.68	10.8	54
2nd	1.69	4.87	14.7	73.5
3rd	1.29	3.72	19.2	96
4th	1.00	2.88	24.8	124

Final drive ratio.....................................2.88 to one

CHASSIS
Unit construction, all-steel structure.
Wheelbase.....................................86 in
Track.....................................F 51.75, R 48.5 in
Length.....................................155.5 in
Width.....................................60.5 in
Height.....................................51.5 in
Ground clearance.....................................4.0 in
Dry weight.....................................2600 lbs
Curb weight.....................................2660 lbs
Test weight.....................................2930 lbs
Weight distribution front/rear.....................................51.7/48.3%
Pounds per bhp (test weight).....................................17.9
Suspension F: Ind., unequal-length wishbones and coil springs, stabilizer bar.
  R: Rigid axle, semi-elliptic leaf springs and panhard rod.
Brakes..Girling 9.85-in discs front, 9-in drums rear, 295 sq in swept area
Steering.....................................Rack and pinion
Turns, lock to lock.....................................3.1
Turning circle.....................................37.5 ft
Tires.....................................5.90 x 13
Revs per mile.....................................768

MAINTENANCE
Crankcase capacity.....................................4 qts
Oil change interval.....................................5000 miles
Grease fittings.....................................0

ACCELERATION
Zero to	Seconds
30 mph	3.5
40 mph	4.8
50 mph	6.5
60 mph	8.6
70 mph	10.8
80 mph	13.7
90 mph	16.7
100 mph	21.0
Standing ¼-mile	89 mph in 16.5

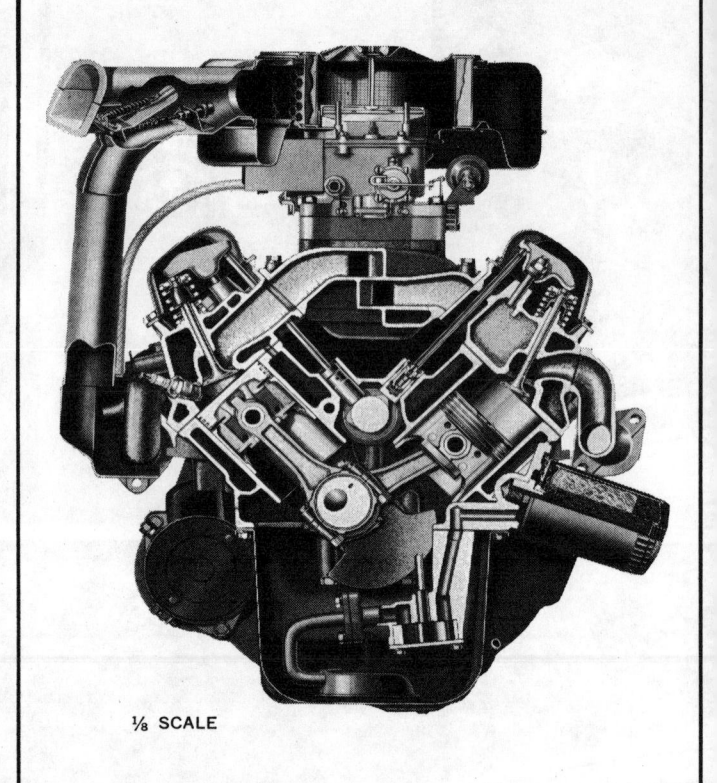

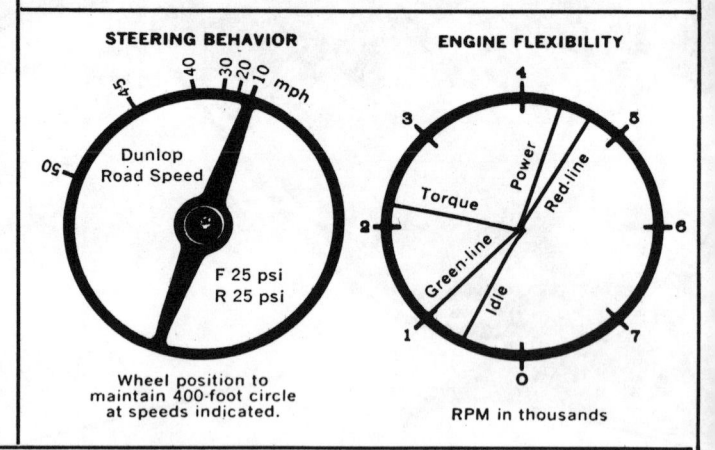

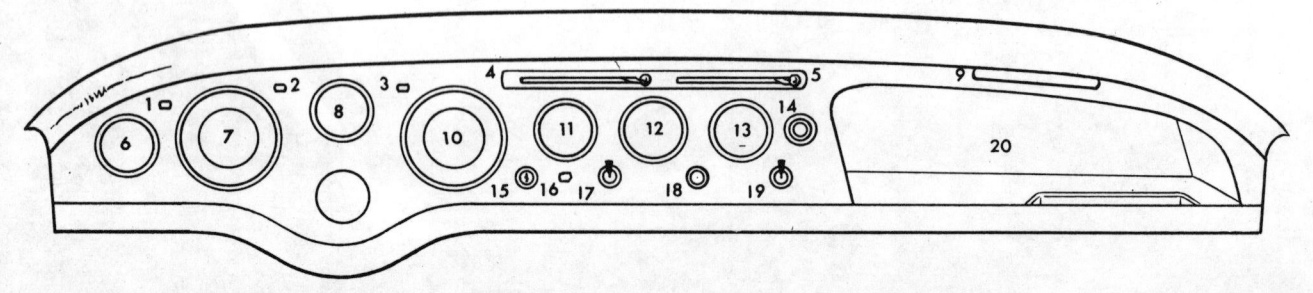

⅛ SCALE

STEERING BEHAVIOR

Dunlop Road Speed
F 25 psi
R 25 psi
Wheel position to maintain 400-foot circle at speeds indicated.

ENGINE FLEXIBILITY

RPM in thousands

(1) Oil pressure warning light, (2) Main beam tell-tale light, (3) Turn signal warning light, (4) Heater regulator, (5) Defroster regulator, (6) Ammeter, (7) Tachometer, (8) Oil pressure gauge, (9) Map light, (10) Speedometer and odometer, (11) Water temperature gauge, (12) Clock, (13) Fuel gauge, (14) Cigar lighter, (15) Ignition key, (16) Ignition light, (17) Headlights, (18) Windshield washer, (19) Wipers (two-speed), (20) Glove box.

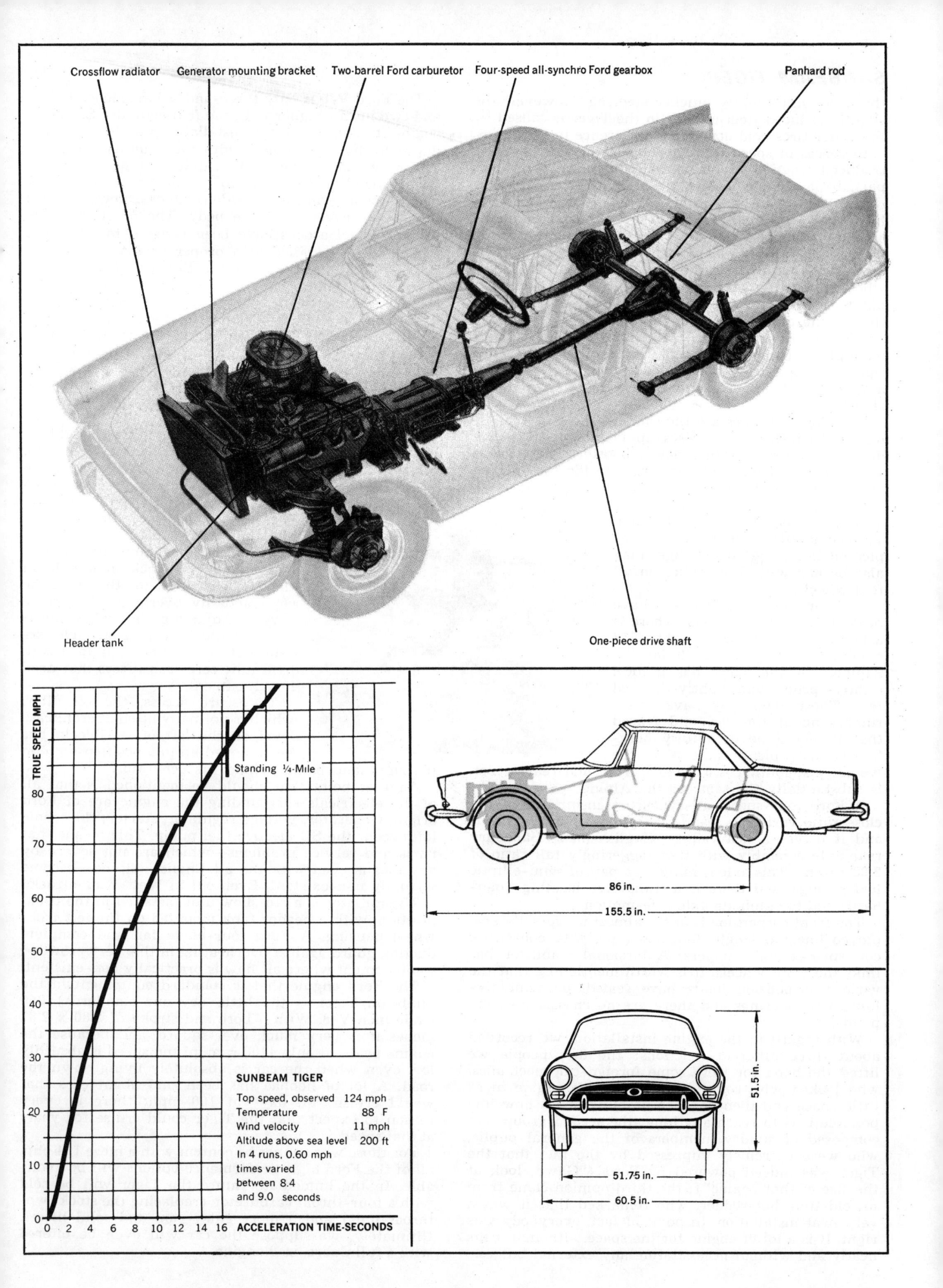

Crossflow radiator — Generator mounting bracket — Two-barrel Ford carburetor — Four-speed all-synchro Ford gearbox — Panhard rod

Header tank

One-piece drive shaft

SUNBEAM TIGER
Top speed, observed   124 mph
Temperature   88 F
Wind velocity   11 mph
Altitude above sea level   200 ft
In 4 runs, 0.60 mph
times varied
between 8.4
and 9.0 seconds

TRUE SPEED MPH

Standing ¼-Mile

ACCELERATION TIME-SECONDS

86 in.
155.5 in.

51.75 in.
60.5 in.
51.5 in.

69

SUNBEAM TIGER

the Tiger has slightly quicker steering. However, the slightly reduced steering lock in the Tiger is caused by the wider tires, and not by any difference in the ratios.

Increases in speed, weight and horsepower have introduced traction problems, and these are solved, in part, by a change to larger-section tires and wider-rimmed wheels. The wheels are, by the way, made of heavier gauge material. Wire wheels will be available, as will cast magnesium alloy wheels—at some increase in price over the standard steel wheels. You might be interested to know that the Tiger comes with different wheel cover discs (the sales literature calls them nave plates; we like to think of them as knave plates) and that is one of the few outward clues that distinguish the Tiger (ROAR!) from the Alpine (meow!). These nave plates (or knave plates; your choice) have a design that suggests—or perhaps we should say—*hints* at a wire wheel because wire wheels equal Sports Car, right?

The Tiger's brakes are the same as those of the Alpine; 9.85-inch Girling discs up front and nine-inch drums at the rear, with a power booster. There probably isn't room for anything larger inside the 13-inch wheels; but it doesn't matter—the brakes are entirely satisfactory for even very fast and furious touring. The competition oriented will be pleased to know that the Tiger may also be had with disc brakes on all four wheels.

Both springs and dampers have been stiffened in the Tiger. There is a fair increase in curb weight, 2653 pounds; compared to 2220 for the Alpine, yet the Tiger has a nice, tightly-sprung and tightly-damped feel. Those who may have heard rumors about the car, and feared that it would be dreadfully nose-heavy, will please note that the weight distribution is 51.7/48.3, front and rear, which is substantially the same as the Alpine.

A Ford four-speed, all-synchro transmission of the close-ratio variety is standard equipment in the Tiger, and it drives a heavy-duty, English-made Salisbury rear axle assembly with the staggeringly tall ratio of 2.88-to-one. This axle is hung on a pair of semi-elliptic leaf springs, and there is a transverse locating (panhard) rod to eliminate axle side-motion.

The front suspension is of the almost universally employed unequal-length A-frame type, with concentric coil springs and dampers. A torsional stabilizer bar links the front wheels. It is worth mentioning that the various suspension joints have sealed, permanently-lubricated bearings and there are no chassis greasing points.

With regard to the engine installation, we recorded about three different reactions: the first people we lifted the hood for were some foreign-car mechanics, who looked with some awe at so much engine in so little space and then began grumbling about how impossible it is to reach anything; the second group was composed of sundry members of the general public, who were extremely impressed by the fact that the Tiger was indeed powered by Ford ("Gawd, look at the size of that engine"); the third opinion came from an old-time hot-rodder, who remarked that it was a very neat installation. In point of fact, everybody was right. It is a lot of engine for the space, although it fits neatly and without necessitating any external bulges.

The Ford V-8 is only three-and-a-half inches longer and two inches higher than the four-cylinder Sunbeam engine it replaces, so the installation problem was reduced to finding enough width for it under the hood. The only main structural modification necessary involved bending the cowl to accommodate the larger clutch housing and to provide some clearance between the rocker covers and the body. The inner supports for the wheel arches have been lowered to allow the engine to be installed at a proper height.

The mounting points for the Burman steering gear used in the Alpine have been equipped with a set of cast iron brackets to carry the forward engine mountings. They are of the rubber-in-shear type as used on all production Fords, and carry the engine at machined surfaces on the under side of each bank of cylinders. The rear engine mounting is a waffle-type Ford rubber block which rests in a fabricated steel box welded to a cross member bolted to the base structure under the transmission casing.

You can't get at everything as easily as would be ideal: the rear spark plug on the left bank of cylinders, for instance, must be reached through a hole in the firewall—which is covered by a rubber bung. All of the plumbing has been routed in a very tidy fashion, and there is nothing "hacksaw and hammer" about the underhood area. The engine sits back in a hole in the cowl structure, and the top of the cowl actually overhangs the valve covers. Adjusting the valve clearances would be a real struggle except that the engine is equipped with hydraulic zero-lash lifters that need no adjustment.

To assure access, the oil filter, which is normally fitted at crankcase level on the left of the block, has been moved up to a position high on the righthand bank, behind the generator.

Another point that should be mentioned is that all of the electricals surrounding the engine are of Ford origin. Generator, voltage regulator, starter; the whole lot, except the SU electric fuel pump. This means that parts and service problems—which are not severe by any means even with the all-English Alpine—become virtually non-existent. Even out in West Wagontrack.

The radiator is a crossflow unit installed in the usual position, with a header tank mounted on the left front wheel housing. A Ford four-blade fan and complete ducting guard against overheating in this very crowded compartment where air flow is practically non-existent.

The Ford engine that is standard equipment in the Sunbeam Tiger is the little (by our standards) 260 cubic inch V-8. With a bore and stroke of 3.80 x 2.87 inches it is very much over-square, and because the engine peaks at only 4400 rpm, piston speed is absurdly low even when the car is absolutely flying down the road. A lot of hoohaa has been said about cars that would cruise "all day" at 100 mph; there is every reason to expect that the Tiger could cruise for years at that speed.

For those who cannot be content with a mere 164 bhp, all of the Ford high-performance options will be available. In the immediate future the Tiger will be sold with a four-throat carburetor (replacing the stock two-throat unit) and a more gutsy cam and solid lifters. Ultimately, we suppose the car will even be offered with a full Cobra-ized engine,

Webers and all. However, except for the really determined competition driver, the fullhouse version may not be precisely what the Tiger needs. In its present form, the added horsepower simply makes the car a lot more responsive; give it, say, 150 more horsepower and we suspect that they will have to change the name from Tiger to Godzilla.

Inside, the Tiger is just as posh and comfortable as the Alpine, which makes it pretty splendid. It has the new-type Alpine seats, which are adjustable up and down, fore and aft, and there is even an adjustment for recline. Indeed, in one regard it is even more comfortable than the Alpine; the Ford transmission is smaller, and as a consequence the transmission tunnel is lower and not as wide, so it intrudes less on passenger space.

A full complement of instruments is supplied. There is an electronic tachometer and matching (in appearance) speedometer; both are marvelously easy to read. The tachometer, by the way, gives dead steady readings, with no dance or wiggle at the needle. The speedometer has the usual odometer, which proved very accurate, and also has a trip-meter. There are also "real" water temperature and oil pressure gauges (no colored lights) and a fuel gauge marked off in gallons, which is a little something others would do well to copy. It tells you how much gasoline remains in the tank, rather than ¼, ½, ¾ or full, and as the Tiger travels almost exactly 20 miles on a gallon of fuel under most driving conditions, it is easy to know very quickly if there is enough fuel remaining.

Another neat trick is the way the warning lights for the turn indicators and high/low beam have been provided with dimmer lids. The colored lenses over these lights have thick and thin sections, and for night driving, the driver can flick the thick part of the lens down over the bulb. And too, there are two-speed windshield wipers; a windshield washer; passenger grab handle, and a hooded map-reading light. All very plush and civilized.

Not quite enough leg room has been provided for really tall drivers, but anyone 6'2" or shorter can get quite comfortable in the Tiger. The seat can be jacked into a variety of shapes and position, and the steering wheel hub can be unscrewed a bit to release a splined portion of the column so that the wheel can be positioned nearer or farther to suit the driver's tastes. The steering wheel supplied with the Tiger is the wood-rimmed item found in the Alpine GT, but praise be, we have been spared the walnut fascia. The instrument panel is covered with an excellent, non-reflective black vinyl synthetic cloth.

The Tiger's heating/defrosting equipment is all that one could ask, but when the controls are set for a nice blast of cool, fresh air, all one gets is a pitiful little sigh from the system. This is altogether inadequate for warm weather, for the engine transmits a lot of heat right through the firewall and cockpit temperatures soar at anything less than 50 mph. More air, gentlemen, please.

Neither did we care very much for the rear-view mirror, which is well placed but is of the de-magnifying type, which means that you can see a great deal of what's astern but can't determine what it *is*, nor how far away. It's a poor setup.

The Tiger's top is, well . . . an English sports car top. This is another of those man-hour devices (need we explain that term?) that has more joints than an Alaskan king-crab, but, when finally erect, does do the job of keeping the car's occupants warm and dry. The top on our test car had a tendency to flap, but that may have been only because the unseasonably warm weather made the material sag slightly. In any case, the top serves its primary function very well, and those who want to yield up a few extra dollars can have a hard-top as well.

The Sunbeam's trunk space has been rearranged again, the spare is back under the flooring. The Tiger has a monstrously large battery, and the floor has a square hump to clear the top of the battery. The filler caps on this battery have little nipples that plug into a rubber hose that is supposed to carry off fumes and any spilled acid, but it seems that this scheme is less than perfect. The hose in question could not be made to stay in place in our test car; by the time we returned the car, fumes and splashed electrolyte were corroding merrily away at the base panel in the trunk. The trunk lid is spring-balanced, and can be opened by merely punching the release button, which we liked.

Fuel storage is in a pair of tanks located inside the rear fenders, both filling from a single inlet on the right fender. The filler cap is of the hinged, quick-release type, and it is shaped so that it fairs into the top of the fender. The cap can't be mislaid and it certainly is a racy-looking device.

Frankly, we approached the Sunbeam Tiger with considerable skepticism. There have been numerous small cars that great, chuffing domestic engines did little to improve, and we feared that this might be the case. We could have saved our fears for something else; the Sunbeam has been utterly transformed by the change in engines, and it is a transformation that is all to the good.

In the first place, the Ford engine gives the car a smoothness and tractability that is not possible with the relatively highly tuned 1600cc Rootes-engined Alpine. The Ford engine will haul the car smartly away from 1000 rpm in top gear, and it is possible to drive the Tiger using fourth gear only—although this admittedly requires a lot of clutch slipping when starting from rest. More important, the Tiger will sprint around that slow truck in flying fashion without any rowing at the gear lever and with a minimum of time spent out in the "wrong" lane. There is just so much torque on tap that the transmission can be ignored —unless you happen to feel sporting and want to make full use of the mechanism.

Secondly, the level of the performance is pushed upward to a point that would be impossible with the original engine—no matter how highly tuned it might be. The Tiger does the standing-start ¼-mile in 16.5 seconds, and will pull past the 4700 rpm red-line in top gear. It is a genuine 120-mph automobile, and it does it with no fuss whatever. The acceleration times, incidentally, would all be probably three-quarters of a second lower if the car was

CONTINUED ON PAGE 159

SUNBEAM ALPINE IV
Further refinements for an old favorite

THE SUNBEAM ALPINE Series IV reflects Rootes Motors' traditional practice of bringing out a basic model and then developing and improving it over a period of several years. The "modern" Alpine, introduced in 1959, has established a good reputation in this country as a lively and competitive production category racing car as well as a comfortable, durable and well built sports/touring model. This latest version, the Series IV, promises to continue that tradition.

In outward appearance, the Series IV Alpine is distinguishable by two major changes. First, the rear fender line has been lowered and squared off to do away with the high-pointed, sweptback fenders of the earlier versions. And the air intake at the front of the car has been restyled, with a simple crossbar across the grille opening. There are also minor changes in appearance, such as the new snap-top fuel filler cap, but these are the subtle sort of dress-up improvements that only an Alpine buff would be aware of.

The other changes made in the Series IV are of the non-visible variety. Most important, the 90-bhp engine is now used in the hardtop "gran turismo" as well as in the roadster "sports tourer." The 90-bhp (instead of 83) engine can now be used in the hardtop because the new cast iron exhaust manifold (light gauge sheet metal earlier) accomplishes sufficient sound damping to make it suitable for the more genteel version. Other refinements include the adoption of the long-term-lubrication program popularized by the American manufacturers (rubber and/or nylon bushings at those points which formerly required periodic lubrication) and extended interval oil changes. In addition, the mechanical tachometer of previous models has been replaced by an electric model and the warning lamps now have openings that can be adjusted to suit the driver's preference.

Most interesting of the mechanical changes is that the Alpine IV is now available with a 3-speed automatic transmission. This is obviously a concession to the increasing number of drivers who have never mastered the intricacies of a manually operated transmission or would rather not work so hard in heavy traffic. It is also available with the traditional 4-speed manual transmission, with or without overdrive, for those drivers who prefer to select their own shift points.

The automatic used in the Alpine IV is the Borg-Warner Type 35, the same as that used in the Hillman Super Minx also made by Rootes. It is a 3-speed unit that will not puzzle any American driver who is familiar with automatic transmissions, except that the control stem is mounted on the driveshaft tunnel. The stalk of this control appears a bit anemic at first glance, little resembling the beefy shift levers usually found on driveshaft tunnels. On operating the control handle, however, the driver soon learns that a light touch is best for gear selection if an unwanted slot is not to be engaged.

Because the torque of the 1.6-liter Alpine engine is modest (93 lb-ft at 3500 rpm), the 3-speed automatic adds absolutely nothing to the performance of the car. With the accelerator pressed to the floor, the Alpine shifts at about 5000 rpm. At the shift, there is a noticeable change in engine note and a conclusive drop in revs. Then it climbs back up to 5000 and shifts again. The acceleration is adequate but hardly neck-snapping and an Alpine with a 4-speed manual transmission should be about a second faster through a quarter-mile drag. Going up, or down, through the gears, the changes are made smoothly and quickly and the only annoyance we found was a tendency to lurch back, then forward, when the lever was moved from "Park" down through "R," "N" and into "D." This was especially irksome when the engine was warming up on fast idle and may be one of the things you have to get used to with this type of transmission.

Except for the automatic transmission, the driving of the Alpine is much the same as we remembered from the Series III. There was one change made that we didn't like, however, and that resulted from a softening of the suspension. The earlier car had an excellent ride, we thought, and the new, softer springs simply emphasize the tendency of the car to "float" at fast touring speeds when slightly undulating or "wavy" road surfaces are encountered.

Other than these changes, the Series IV Alpine remains basically the same as the Series III. The driving position is still one of the best in the business, the servo-assisted disc/drum (front/rear) brakes are fully up to their job, the trunk is roomy and uncluttered and everything about the car reflects the builder's conscientious attempt to produce a sports/touring car that will be appreciated by the discriminating driver.

ROAD TEST RESULTS

PRICE
List price.................$2749
Price as tested...........$3148

GENERAL
Curb weight, lb.............2280
Weight distribution (with
　driver), front/rear, %....49/51
Wheelbase, in..............86.0
Track, front/rear......51.0/48.5
Overall length............155.0
　Width..................60.5
　Height.................51.5
Frontal area, sq. ft........17.3
Steering type....recirculating ball
　Turns, lock to lock........3.5
　Turning circle, ft..........34
Brake type............disc/drum
　Swept area, sq. in.........295
Tire size.............6.00 x 13

ACCOMMODATION
Normal capacity, persons......2
Seat width, in.........2 x 19.5
Head room, in...............39
Seat back adjustment, degrees..30
Entrance height, in...........48
Stepover height, in.........16.5
Door width, in.............40.5
Driver comfort rating:
　For driver 69 in. tall......90
　For driver 72 in. tall......90
　For driver 75 in. tall......85
(85-100, good; 70-85, fair; under 70, poor)

SPECIFICATIONS
Engine, no. cyl., type......4-ohv
Bore & stroke, in......3.21 x 3.00
Displacement, cc..........1592
　Equivalent cu in........97.1
Compression ratio..........9.1:1
Bhp @ rpm............90 @ 5000
　Equivalent mph...........88
Torque @ rpm, lb-ft..93 @ 3500
　Equivalent mph...........61
Transmission type......automatic
　No. forward speeds..........3
Final drive ratio..........3.89:1

FUEL
Type fuel required.......premium
Fuel tank size, gal.........13.5
Normal mi per gal.........18-22

PERFORMANCE
Top speed, high gear, mph....90
Acceleration, 0-30 mph, sec...6.2
　0-40 mph.................8.9
　0-50 mph................12.3
　0-60 mph................16.5
　0-80 mph................35.0
Passing test, 50-70 mph....11.2
Standing ¼-mi..............21.0
　Speed at end, mph..........67

SPEEDOMETER ERROR
30 mph indicated......actual 28.4
60 mph....................57.2

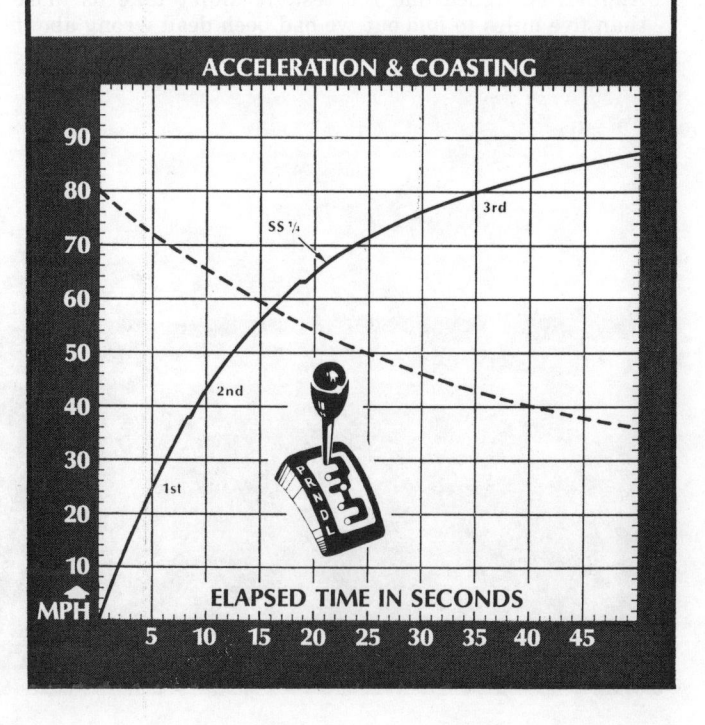

ACCELERATION & COASTING

ROAD TEST:
SUNBEAM TIGER

Very few will pull this Tiger's tail!

NEARLY TWO YEARS AGO A COBRA-INSPIRED IDEA SMOTE IAN GARRAD, West Coast manager of Rootes: What about putting one of the healthy little Fairlane V-8's in his Sunbeam Alpine? The car lacks only in suds to become a high-performance tourer á la Cobra, Sting Ray, or XKE. It already has the handling comfort, and stopping power. Besides, he strongly suspected he could market such a hybrid for a price *well* below the competition. To further investigate the possibility, two prototypes were constructed. One built by Carroll Shelby was to be as well-engineered as possible. One assigned to Ken Miles (since employed by Shelby) was to be converted as cheaply as possible. Ken dumped his engine in over the front crossmember, as more logical placement necessitated considerable modification to the firewall—the route that Shelby took. We never drove Ken's prototype, but we did have a secret hop in the Shelby car over a year ago. It went, alright—almost as well as a full-optioned Sting Ray. But anything but a straight line was Panicsville. The engine sat high and not very far back, promoting body-walk and horrible understeering. Undaunted by our opinion, Garrad sent the "good" prototype back to England for factory evaluation.

It took a long time (as these things often do) but the factory sorted out the problems, one by one, and the first boatload of production Sunbeam Tigers arrived in late August. Assigned one for test, it didn't take us more than five miles to find out we had been dead wrong about our evaluation of the results. Further, Ian was dead right about the price he could market the cars for—$3499. Rootes assigned the body/chassis modifications to Jensen (the Alpine is a unit-constructed vehicle) and somehow came up with the room to move the V-8 further back and lower. A track bar was installed to hold the rear axle in position, and spring and shock rates were adjusted to the ideal. Result: The fine points came shining through.

Currently, there are two versions available, one using the 260-inch V-8, the other using the 289 high-performance engine. We'll bring you a test report on the superhot next issue. The standard job, because of its low price, is much more exciting news. First, we knew the chassis was a solid, rugged unit, although the fact is not easily discernible with the standard 1600-cc engine. You just can't apply that much force. The Fairlane conversion, including the four-speed transmission and modified suspension, weighs roughly 200 pounds more, but it makes an amazing difference in the feel of the car. The extra weight in the chassis enabled a better unsprung weight ratio, especially since it is moved further rearward than originally. This, in turn, allows better wheel control with a relatively unsophisticated suspension (live rear axle) and the Rootes folks have parlayed the advantages into a downright luxurious ride for a car that gets around corners as well as the Tiger does. Unlike other conversions we've driven, a doubling of torque has only made the Sunbeam feel *more* solid than ever.

PHOTOS: DARREL NORBERGER

Tip-off to the potent "sleeper" is the insignia on the front fenders. Despite crowded engine compartment, below, the V-8 stayed cool under all conditions. Master cylinders are on left side of firewall, but brake booster is moved to the right side. Overflow filler tank in foreground.

SUNBEAM TIGER

Excepting sturdy gearshift lever, interior of the Tiger is much the same as the Series IV. Steering column is adjustable, as are seatbacks and pedals. The cockpit is comfortable, roomy. Tach is redlined at 4800.

Spare tire and battery are concealed beneath the trunk floor. Gas tanks are in the fenders with quick-release cap on right side. There's more than adequate space for luggage needs as compared to earlier series.

The V8 is really tucked under the firewall and makes things a bit sticky for maintenance. Cast rocker covers are not standard; part of an $80 dress-up kit. Two-barrel carburetor is stock on the 260-inch engine.

Since the V-8 is "inset" under the cowl, the first thing we were looking for was overheating—there isn't much room for the air to exit. A freeway traffic jam in an ambient of 110 degrees F. only produced a reading of 190 degrees F. on the water temperature gauge. The cockpit got warm, heated by the dual exhaust pipes and mufflers beneath the floor, but in a similar jam at 95 degrees the cockpit remained cool. Another point—modifying the firewall—has had no ill effects on the very spacious footroom in regular Alpines.

After driving the Tiger on the street for several hundred miles, we took it to Willow Springs for acceleration runs and track evaluation. The relatively high final-drive ratio didn't make it easy to get off the line, but the 0-60 mph time of nine seconds flat was impressive enough, especially since the same ratio enables high-speed cruising at 3800 rpm. What was mildly understeer on the streets turned into final oversteer on the tricky Willow Springs circuit. It was *mild* oversteer, nothing violent, indicating that it shouldn't be too much sweat to make a real competitive handler out of the Tiger with heavy-duty suspension options and racing tires. If you examine the SCCA options list for the car, you'll find that considerable thought has long since been devoted to just such an occurrence. One thing that *does* show signs of strain under such conditions is brakes. There were no problems in hot-lapping, but stopping and turning around from our series of acceleration runs produced brake smoke and some trace of fade after the fourth fast stop; something we never encountered racing the then-E-Production Alpine. For highway use this will definitely not be a problem. It'll complete at least one stop from its top speed of over 135 mph and, given reasonable cool-offs, will continue to stop. Should you anticipate harder usage than this, Rootes has competition pads and linings readily available.

From the standpoint of steering pressure, the Tiger is amazingly light on its feet. The adjustable steering column permits you to get just the right wheel adjustment for best grip and the understeer of *near*-maximum cornering is well under control. Get closer to the ultimate and the firmness will be welcome as the understeer turns to oversteer. Again, there is nothing violent or spooky about this change—it's very honest and apparent. At racetrack speeds and first-gear acceleration around a tight corner, it is easy to "pick up a wheel" and spin rubber. Frankly, we didn't find this annoying, but there's a limited-slip differential available should you want to eliminate the condition. In all other respects, the car is fine, equals the standard Alpine in handling traits (which is quite a compliment in itself) and even exceeds it when it comes to wet-road conditions.

If you're the sadistic type (as apparently we are) the Tiger is worth its price just to bug the street racers. For such sport we recommend you remove the Tiger emblem on the side of the car. They'll soon learn to suspect Alpines and be looking for it. Meanwhile, it's a ball to frustrate owners of both import and super-hot domestic iron. You can play with them cat-and-mouse style.

About the only drawback we found in the Tiger is that it'll be a bear to work on. The engine is literally buried under the cowl. It looks like you'd have to pull the engine to remove a cylinder head. However, the Fairlane is a strong engine and definitely understressed in this application. The *need* to pull a head should be extremely rare.

All in all, the Sunbeam Tiger is amazing value for its price. It's got everything you'd expect from a high-performance GT or sports car costing twice as much. Rootes dealers have a waiting list already, so you better get in line fast. — *Jerry Titus*

A fast Sweeper at Willow produces almost neutral steering from the Tiger. Body-roll is very moderate though car is equipped with standard suspension.

SUNBEAM TIGER ROAD TEST 18/64

PERFORMANCE:
0-30	3.1 sec.	0-70	11.9 sec.
0-40	4.9 sec.	0-80	15.0 sec.
0-50	7.2 sec.	0-90	18.1 sec.
0-60	9.0 sec.	0-100	22.8 sec.

Standing ¼ mile .... 16.3 sec. @ 85 mph
Top Speed (av. two-way run) .... 135 mph

Speed Error 30   40   50   60   70   80   90
Actual 29   39   49   60   70   80   89

Fuel Consumption   Recommended Shift Points
Test: .... 17 mpg   Max. 1st .... 42 mph
Average: .... 19 mpg   Max. 2nd .... 65 mph
                                    Max. 3rd .... 80 mph
RPM Red-line .... 4600 rpm

Speed Ranges in gears:
1st .... 0 to 42 mph   3rd .... 20 to 80 mph
2nd .... 10 to 65 mph   4th .... 30 to top mph

Brake Test: 71 Average % G, over 10 stops. Fade encountered on 4th stop.

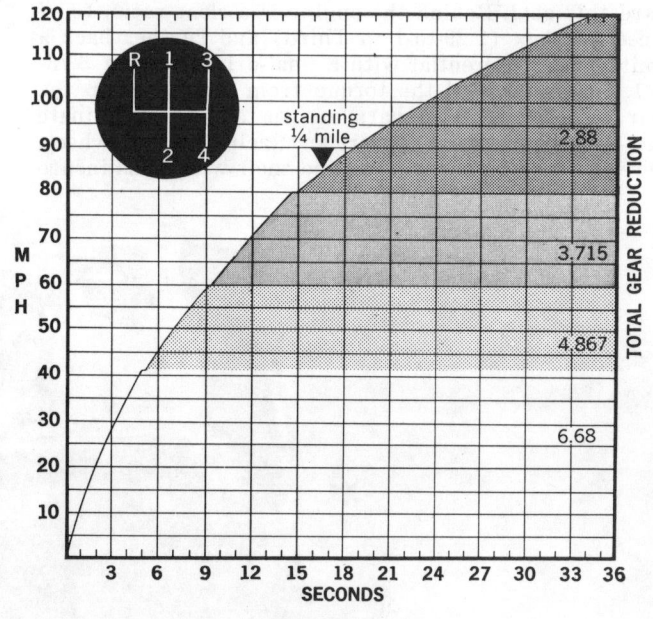

Vehicle .... Sunbeam
Model .... Tiger
Price (as tested) .... $3499 POE N.Y.
Options .... None

ENGINE:
Type .... Ford Fairlane V-8
Head .... Iron, removable
Valves .... OHVA, pushrod/rocker
Max. bhp .... 164 @ 4400 rpm
Max. Torque .... 258 lbs. ft. @ 2200 rpm
Bore .... 3.8 in. 96.5 mm.
Stroke .... 2.87 in. 73 mm.
Displacement .... 260 cu. in. 4259 cc.
Compression Ratio .... 8.8 to 1
Induction System .... Single, 2-barrel carburetor
Exhaust System .... Cast-iron headers to 2 pipes and mufflers
Electrical System .... 12 volt distributor ignition

CLUTCH:
Single disc, dry
Diameter .... 10 in.
Actuation .... Hydraulic

DIFFERENTIAL:
Hypoid
Ratio .... 2.88 to 1
Drive Axles (type) .... enclosed semi-floating

STEERING:
Rack and pinion, adjustable column
Turns Lock to Lock 3⅛
Turn Circle .... 38 ft.

BRAKES:
Girling disc front/drum rear
Drum Diameter .... 9 in.
Disc Diameter .... 9.85 in.
Swept Area .... 295 sq. in.

TRANSMISSION:
Four-speed, full-synchro
Ratios: 1st .... 2.32 to 1
        2nd .... 1.69 to 1
        3rd .... 1.29 to 1
        4th .... 1.00 to 1

CHASSIS:
Frame: .... Unit, with sub assemblies
Body: .... Steel, integral
Front Suspension: ... I.F.S. unequal arm, coil springs, tube shocks, sway bar
Rear Suspension: ..... Live, axle leaf springs, tube shocks, Panhard rod
Tire Size & Type: .... 5.90 x 13 Dunlop RS5

WEIGHTS AND MEASURES:
Wheelbase: .... 86 in.   Ground Clearance .... 4 in.
Front Track: .... 51.75 in.   Curb Weight .... 2525 lbs.
Rear Track: .... 48.5 in.   Test Weight .... 2780 lbs.
Overall Height .... 51.5 in.   Crankcase .... 4 qts.
Overall Width .... 60.5 in.   Cooling System .... N.A.
Overall Length .... 156 in.   Gas Tank .... 13½ gals.

[Acceleration chart: MPH vs Seconds, showing standing ¼ mile at ~16.3 sec @ 85 mph. Total Gear Reduction: 2.88, 3.715, 4.867, 6.68]

REFERENCE FACTORS:
Bhp per Cubic Inch 0.63
Lbs. per bhp 15.3
Piston Speed @ Peak rpm .... 2838 ft./min.
Sq. In. Swept Brake area per Lb. 0.116

77

ROAD TEST 20/64

Red Hot Sunbeam TIGER

IN LAST ISSUE'S ROAD TEST OF THE STANDARD SUNBEAM TIGER, we described it as a high-performance sports car. The optioned Tiger is that and much more. It has the real explosive acceleration qualities of a big Modified or a strictly-for-dragging hot rod; about as wild a machine as you'd ever want to drive on the streets. Its docility, however, is more than acceptable if you don't want to use the power. And here we'd like to point out we made a boo-boo in the last article by stating the 289-inch Fairlane will be available. It won't. Only the various 260 versions will. And that's plenty!

Secret to the engine's output is its Stage One kit. This consists of a four-barrel carburetor atop an aluminum manifold, Ford's high-performance solid-lifter camshaft, heavy-duty valve springs, and a dual-point distributor. The knowledgeable reader will quickly recognize this as a hop-up with no sacrifice in reliability. Engine noise is increased a bit due to the solid lifters, and gas mileage gets a kick in the teeth if you're heavy-footed, but the normal virtues of the Fairlane are otherwise unaltered ... except for a third more power, that is.

Power, in itself, isn't worth a whole lot if you can't properly apply it, so the remainder of the driveline and the suspension system have been logically tailored toward this goal. Behind the engine is a close-ratio, four-speed gearbox (1.29-to-1 in Third) and further back a limited-slip differential with a final-drive ratio of 3.73-to-1. To prevent all the torque from wrapping up the rear springs, traction bars are installed to eliminate axle-housing rotation. American Racing's alloy wheels were installed on our test car and their wide rims insure proper tire profile, get maximum power to the ground.

Heavy-duty shocks and swaybar assure that the roadability is up to the horsepower. To some degrees, the limited-slip increases understeer, but the extra power makes this easy to control. The hot version handles every bit as well as the stock one, which is not often the case when you increase the power in a given chassis.

Our standing-start acceleration runs were a distinct pleasure. The car gets off the line very nicely, with just the right amount of wheelspin and no fishtailing. We varied our shift-points; 5500 in 1st, 5800 in 2nd, and 6000 in 3rd. This combination seemed to keep the engine in the most useable torque/horsepower range.

The Tiger's future looks bright from every standpoint. Most important, there is a tremendous amount of interest in this particular model by the factory folks. Its attractive price makes it equally interesting to the car-buying public. From our standpoint, these make it interesting enough to consider it THE sports car of 1964, though we shy away from such a designation. There's little doubt you'll be seeing a lot of them, both on the road and in competition. Options abound that make it more than suitable for the latter endeavor. We particularly like the options combination in our test car. Totalled, they bring the list price up to some $800 over the basic model—still well below the outlay for comparable performance.—*Jerry Titus*.

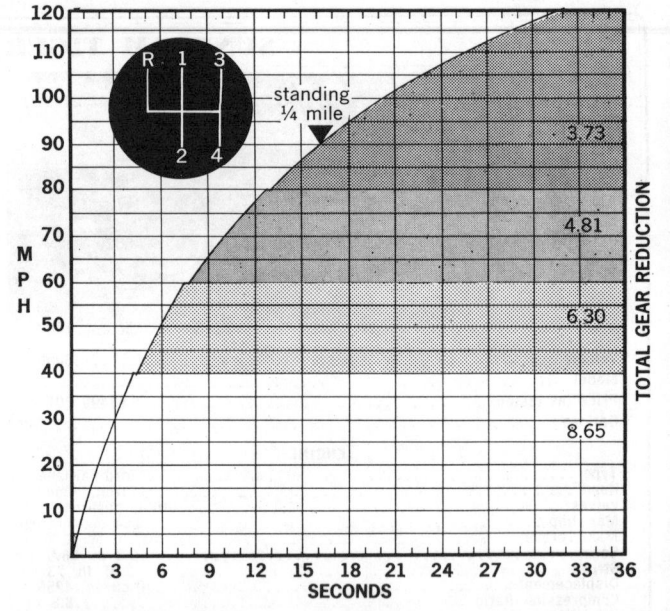

With high-performance options this Tiger is set to chew up Cobras and Sting Rays!

Power on, at right, the optioned Tiger takes a nasty turn in good shape. Above, stripes on the tail are metal tape. Wheels are American Mags. Below, the busy engine compartment has an overflow tank, oil filter, windshield washer, and power brake booster; the only power option on the car. Convertible top is much improved in both construction and its operation.

Photos: Darryl Norenberg

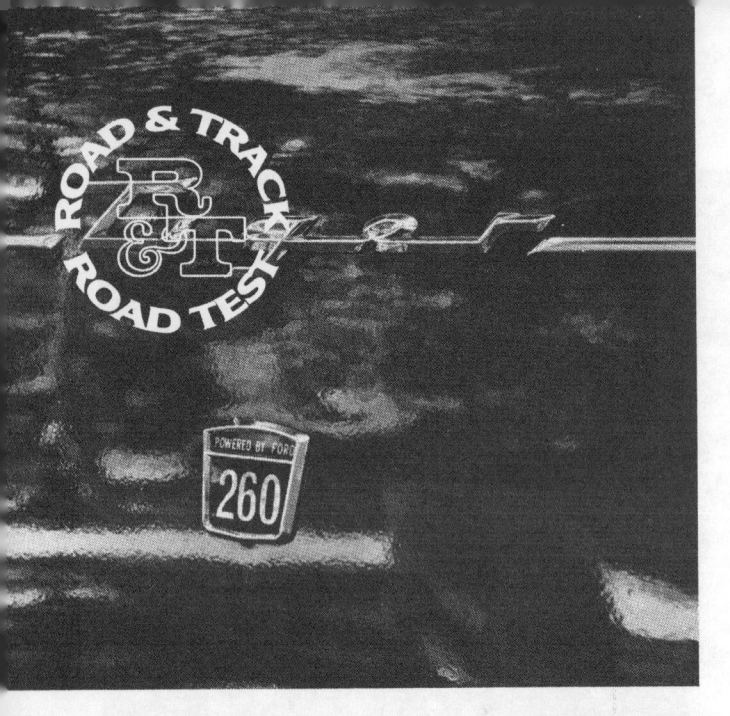

Sunbeam Tiger

Performance, comfort and reliability at low cost—what more can one ask?

ADMITTEDLY, THE IDEA of taking a well-bred European chassis and inserting into it a good-sized American V-8 is not a new one. Sydney Allard did it with considerable competition success for several seasons, the Facel Vega built in France uses a big Chrysler engine, Iso in Italy is putting a 327-cu. in. Chevrolet into a nice 2-plus-2, Jensen and Bristol in England put other engines in their already established chassis and, without doubt, the most successful combination is the Carroll Shelby redesigned AC chassis and body into which he inserted the "small" Ford V-8 engine. Now it has been done again, with a Ford engine introduced into the chassis of the Series IV Sunbeam Alpine. And it is a combination that seems almost certain of finding favor wherever the new car, called the Sunbeam Tiger, is sold.

The idea for the new car came from West Coast Rootes manager Ian Garrard, a tall, native-born Britisher who came to the U.S. 13 years ago and learned his lessons well about the American market. Garrard was largely responsible for building a good competition image for the Sunbeam Alpine on the West Coast, giving meaningful support to drivers who campaigned the marque, and doing much to change the impression of the previous Sunbeam Alpine, which had been regarded more as a sporty car than a sports car.

It has been over two years since Garrard commissioned the insertion of Ford V-8s into a pair of Alpine chassis. Ken Miles did one of these jobs while he was still running his own shop and the other was done in the then-not-too-busy Cobra works of Carroll Shelby. The Shelby job had a 4-speed manual transmission, the Miles car a simple 2-speed automatic. These cars were pretty much hacked together, no real development work being done on them after the bit of shoving and squeezing required to insert the engine and gearbox. Garrard then took the Shelby-built car to England, handed it to his confreres at Rootes Group and said, in effect, "This is a car we can sell in America." If there was any skepticism about the suitability of the mating, and you know there must have been, driving the car quickly dispelled it and production plans went forward.

In appearance, the Tiger is indistinguishable from the Series IV Alpine (which we have reviewed on page 33) except for very discreet trim flashes ("Tiger" appears only in the spelled-out chrome trim strip in front of the doors), the little shields saying "260 Ford," and the distinctive wheel covers that are peculiar to the Tiger and not used on the IV. The people package is also the same on the Tiger and it is still one of the most comfortable sports cars available today.

In body styles, the Tiger will be available as a pure roadster with foldaway top (stowed away with great neatness behind folding panels) and with the detachable hardtop. It will not be available with the permanent hardtop and the de luxe trim of the Sunbeam Alpine Grand Touring model. Other than these trim items, though, the Tiger comes with all those civilized appurtenances for which we have always praised the Alpine—roll-up windows, complete instrumentation, seats that are adjustable for leanback as well as fore and aft, adjustable steering wheel and so on.

In appearance, inside the passenger compartment, the only indication of there being something different about this Tiger is the stubby American-looking shift lever poking up out of the driveshaft hump. Otherwise everything looks very Alpiney.

A tug on the hood release and lifting the lid over the engine compartment never failed to bring appreciative ooohs and ahhhs wherever we practiced this. Yes, you could say that there is little waste around the engine. In fact, you could say further that it fits very snugly. And, no, we wouldn't like to try to change the plugs—especially while the engine was hot.

The standard engine for the Tiger is the 260-cu-in. Ford V-8 from the Fairlane. This engine, in standard form, has a bore and stroke of 3.80 x 2.87 and with a single 2-barrel carburetor puts out 164 hp at 4400 rpm. It has hydraulic lifters and is a nice, completely tractable, uncomplicated engine with a compression ratio of 8.8:1. For the Tiger installation there is no change made in the engine except that an additional header tank has been added for radiator water and a flat, low-restriction paper air cleaner is used. A change was required in the steering to provide additional clearance and the car is now equipped with rack and pinion, with 3.2 turns lock-to-lock and a turning circle of just over 36 ft. The gearbox is the standard American 4-speed all-synchro that is awfully hard to beat. It is crisp, sharp, positive, accurate, a delight to use. Some drivers might prefer to add an inch or two extension on this handle, though, as the knob is slightly lower than the top of the central map box lid and reaching over it without dragging the wrist takes a bit of practice.

The suspension of the Tiger is the same as the Series IV Alpine, independent with unequal A-arms in front, live axle with semi-elliptic springs in the rear. The spring settings are

Sunbeam Tiger

AT A GLANCE...

Price as tested	$3598
Engine	V-8, ohv, 4262 cc, 164 bhp
Curb weight, lb.	2565
Top speed, mph	118
Acceleration, 0–60 mph, sec	7.8
Passing test, 50–70 mph, sec	4.4
Average fuel consumption, mpg	20

Sunbeam Tiger

considerably stiffer than on the present Series IV Alpine, making the ride firm, well controlled and comfortable.

Due to similarity in the choice of engine and transmission, one tends to compare the Tiger with the Cobra. In our test of the Cobra (June 1964), we described it as "a squat, mean, and brutal piece of machinery," commented on its lack of creature comforts and minimal weather equipment, but noted that "one can forgive almost anything for the sheer exhilaration of its performance." In comparison, the Tiger is much more docile than its name suggests, it is hard to fault from the standpoint of comfort, and our impression was that the 164-bhp engine was entirely adequate for the car.

Of course, as with all Ford engines, there is an almost infinite variety of performance options, and we were able to sample a 245-bhp version of the car. The additional power was obtained mainly by a different cam, and a 4-barrel carburetor with appropriate manifolding. Applying this power to the road presented a problem and resulted in a bad case of axle tramp if we engaged the clutch suddenly. However, this was cured by fitting Traction Masters, which will probably become standard equipment on the modified cars.

The price of the 245-bhp version has not yet been definitely established, although it will be in the region of an additional $250. Up to about 60 mph, the additional power does not really earn its money, but after 60 mph the modified car comes into its own and, as a glance at the acceleration curve will show, 90 mph comes up in 15 sec, as opposed to 19 sec for the standard version.

Despite the advantage of the additional top-end performance, we felt that the 245-bhp engine was unnecessary and unsuited to the general concept of the Sunbeam Tiger as a comfortable and refined sports/touring car. In 164-bhp form, the performance and handling of the car are just about ideal for the purpose for which it is intended. High cruising speeds can be maintained effortlessly over long periods, the suspension provides a satisfactory combination of comfort and good roadholding, the brakes are entirely adequate for emergency stops, and the car as a whole fulfills its purpose remarkably well. However, if one starts to use the full potential of the 245-bhp engine, the 590-13 tires seem inadequate, the suspension needs additional strengthening, and one gets the impression of imposing upon the car to an unnecessary degree.

We have registered our enthusiasm on several occasions in the past for the Ford V-8 engine and the superb all-synchro 4-speed transmission which goes with it. When these units are installed in a car such as the Alpine, which combines good sporting characteristics with all the comforts of home, the result cannot fail to please—particularly at only $3500.

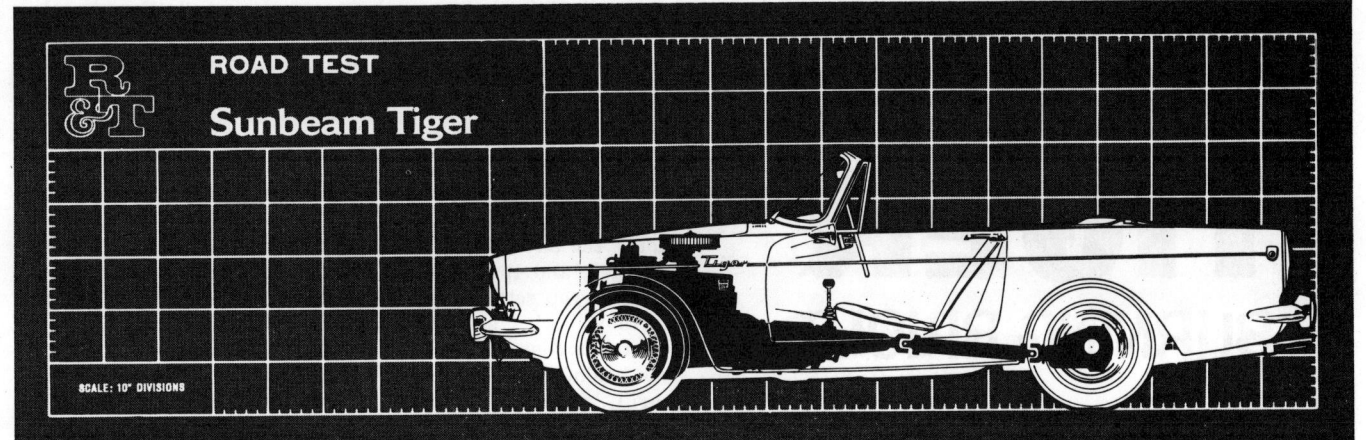

ROAD TEST
Sunbeam Tiger

SCALE: 10" DIVISIONS

PRICE
List price.................$3499
Price as tested............$3598

ENGINE
No. cylinders & type.....V-8, ohv
Bore x stroke, in......3.80 x 2.87
Displacement, cc............4262
Equivalent cu in............260
Compression ratio..........8.8:1
Bhp @ rpm............164 @ 4400
Equivalent mph.............107
Torque @ rpm, lb-ft...258 @ 2200
Equivalent mph..............53
Carburetors, no. & make....1 Ford
No. barrels & dia......2-1.438
Type fuel required.......regular

DRIVE TRAIN
Clutch type.......dry single plate
Diameter, in...............10.0
Gear ratios, 4th (1.00).....2.88:1
3rd (1.29)................3.72:1
2nd (1.69)................4.87:1
1st (2.32)................6.68:1
Sychromesh.............on all 4
Differential type.........hypoid
Ratio....................2.88:1
Optional ratios..............six

CHASSIS & SUSPENSION
Frame type........unit with body
Brake type, front/rear..disc/drum
Swept area, sq in..........295
Tire size................5.90-13
Steering type......rack & pinion
Turns, lock to lock..........3.2
Turning circle, ft..........35.6
Front suspension: independent with A-arms, coil springs, tube shocks, anti-roll bar.
Rear suspension: live axle, semi-elliptical springs, tube shocks.

ACCOMMODATION
Normal capacity, persons........2
Seat width, front, in........2 x 18
Head room....................39
Seat back adjustment, deg.....30
Entrance height, in...........48
Step-over height.............16.5
Door width, front/rear.......40.5
Driver comfort rating:
For driver 69-in. tall........90
For driver 72-in. tall........85
For driver 75-in. tall........85
(85–100, good; 70–85, fair; under 70, poor)

GENERAL
Curb weight, lb.............2565
Test weight.................2965
Weight distribution (with driver), front/rear, %...........51/49
Wheelbase, in................86
Track, front/rear........51/48.5
Overall length, in...........156
Width......................60.5
Height.....................51.5
Frontal area, sq ft.........17.3
Ground clearance, in.........4.5
Overhang, front/rear......28/42
Departure angle (no load), deg..15
Usable trunk space, cu ft.....6.0
Fuel tank capacity, gal.....13.5

INSTRUMENTATION
Instruments: 5000-rpm tachometer, 140-mph speedometer, oil pressure, water temperature, fuel.
Warning lights: ignition, high beam, turn indicator.

MISCELLANEOUS
Body styles available: roadster (as tested) and removable hardtop.

ACCESSORIES
Included in list price: reclining seats, windshield washers, seat-belt anchors, adjustable steering column.
Available at extra cost: tonneau cover, heater, clock, lighter, whitewalls, etc. Also numerous performance options.

CALCULATED DATA
Lb/hp (test weight).........18.1
Cu ft/ton mi...............125.2
Mph/1000 rpm (high gear)...24.3
Engine revs/mi.............2468
Piston travel, ft/mi.......1182
Rpm @ 2500 ft/min..........5217
Equivalent mph.............126
R&T wear index..............29.2

MAINTENANCE
Crankcase capacity, qt..........5
Change interval, mi........6000
Oil filter type.............paper
Change interval, mi........6000
Chassis lube interval, mi...6000
Tire pressure, psi.........31/31

ROAD TEST RESULTS

ACCELERATION
0-30 mph, sec................3.1
0-40 mph....................4.3
0-50 mph....................5.8
0-60 mph....................7.8
0-70 mph...................10.7
0-80 mph...................14.4
0-100 mph..................23.7
Passing test, 50-70 mph......4.4
Standing ¼ mi...............16.0
Speed at end, mph............84

TOP SPEEDS
High gear (4850), mph........118
3rd (5000)..................92
2nd (5000)..................72
1st (5000)..................53

GRADE CLIMBING
(Tapley data)
4th gear, max gradient, %....16
3rd.........................23
2nd.........................29
1st....................off scale
Total drag at 60 mph, lb.....89

SPEEDOMETER ERROR
30 mph indicated.....actual 28.1
40 mph....................37.5
60 mph....................56.2
80 mph....................75.0
100 mph...................93.8

FUEL CONSUMPTION
Normal driving, mpg........18-22
Cruising range, mi......240-295

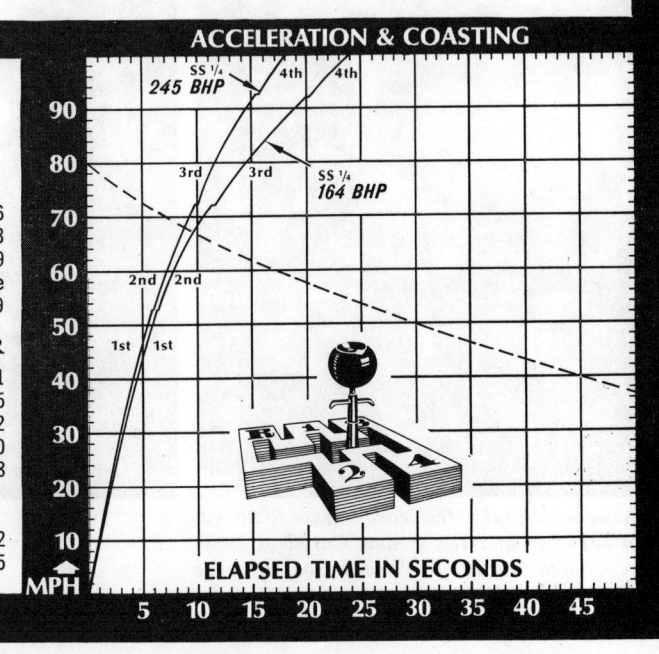

ACCELERATION & COASTING
SS ¼ 245 BHP
SS ¼ 164 BHP

ELAPSED TIME IN SECONDS

TIGER TIGER BURNING BRIGHT

When is not a hot rod a hot rod?
When it's a Sunbeam Tiger

by Dick Wells ■ Not too long ago the tiger was just another animal, regarded as a beast of the jungle, or at least an attraction at the local zoo. Recently, however, this beautiful creature has been associated, in one way or another, with everything from men's hair-dressing to something you "... put in your gas tank"; or use to complement performance, such as with a certain Wide-Track Tiger.

Today another breed of tiger has caught the public's eye. It's a new car model. And for those who may be inclined to doubt the advisability of naming something on four wheels a Tiger, and thus link the animal's related attributes, we suggest you settle back into the new Sunbeam Tiger's comfortable bucket seat, take command by grabbing the stem of its four-speed trans, and mash the throttle to activate the business end of this exciting package. You're in for a thrill, 'cause here's a number that packs the wallop of an American hot rod, yet incorporates those features commonly inherent in an imported sports car.

Basically, the Tiger is a Sunbeam Alpine sports import with a Ford 260 tucked neatly beneath the bonnet. Its history dates back to January of 1963 when Rootes Motors

"Showroom fresh" test car turned 17.20 e.t. (2 bbl carb) in quarter at new Carlsbad strip, should run easy 15's with non-slip rear end, drag tires, tuning, etc. Traction bars, installed on our Tiger, were considered a must.

Snug, but nice. Installation results in a true "sleeper" on the road. If the owner prefers to service his own car, he's in trouble with spark plugs, although openings in firewall afford access to the rear, hidden plugs.

84

officials in the United States began a serious examination of possible ways of producing an ultra high performance sports car without building one from the ground up. A complete engineering appraisal was made of all possible American V8's in terms of suitability, and the 260 cubic inch Ford Fairlane thin wall, cast iron V8 was selected for a variety of reasons. First, the engine is light. Weight was a premium consideration and the 260 featherweight was attractive for the light-car installation.

Second, the engine would fit the Alpine chassis with a minimum of chassis alterations. This was a definite advantage since the Alpine had at that time three years of competition experience behind it, proving its chassis and running gear durability: husky enough to take the added zap of a hot V8. And third, the Ford 260 was favorable because of the enormity of hop-up options readily available, an unlimited number of which are manufactured and marketed by Ford Motor Company.

By spring of 1963, Carroll Shelby, of Shelby-American Cobra fame, was commissioned to go the route once more and install the Ford V8 in the Alpine chassis. Rootes Motors of Los Angeles took possession of the first prototype (a late '62 Alpine) and, satisfied with the combination and its commendable performance, shipped the Anglo-American roadster back to its home in England for approval of the Rootes factory engineering staff and board of directors.

First to drive the car at the Sunbeam Talbot Limited factory, Coventry, England, was chief executive Lord Rootes himself who is reported to have disappeared in a cloud of burning rubber smoke on his first test ride, returning as excited as a high school student with his first car. Weeks later, an order was placed for 4,000 Ford 260 engines for the first production year (this figure was doubled shortly thereafter, due to the car's overwhelmingly favorable acceptance). And that's how a 4-wheeled tiger was born.

As indicated, the Tiger is a European sports car combined with an American V8 and it must therefore be judged accordingly. The Alpine enjoys the same heritage as all Rootes produced cars: a quality vehicle resulting from rigid manufacturing standards. On a comparative basis, its styling is far more dashing than many imports, although the Euro-
(Continued on following page)

In top photo, HRM's Eric Dahlquist (left) and Dick Wells check out 260 Ford. Tank at left of compartment is cooling system reservoir; coolant capacity is 16.2 quarts. In lower photo, the Tiger's neatly arranged passenger compartment.

Second test car carried hop-up goodies; 4-bbl, Cobra cam, mag wheels, etc., ran 15-second e.t.'s "box stock" at Pomona drags with Gary McKeand driving. This one should be real good on quarter when "uncaged" through strip tuning.

LEFT — Trunk compartment is surprisingly adequate; beneath floor, spare tire, tools and 12-volt battery. Convertible top is manually operated.

TIGER, TIGER

pean flavor is retained. Appointments are not lavish, but are trim and very complementary to the overall styling. Unit construction is featured, including chassis and body cross-bracing for strength and rigidity, with light weight and a low center of gravity the expected outcome. Not occupied, the car — with the Ford 260 installed — is advertised at 2,525 pounds (our test car tipped the scales at 2,550); dry, it is just 2,407. Overall length is 156 inches, with an 86-inch wheelbase.

Positioned in the flairs of the rear fenders are two fuel tanks which carry a combined total of 13.5 gallons; a very convenient quick-release hinged filler cap is used. An electric fuel pump, which issues an audible clicking inside the car at low speeds, mounts beneath the trunk compartment.

Front suspension is fully independent, employing coil springs and swinging links. Thick rubber pads between springs and abutments minimize the transfer of any possible road noise and vibration; the car is comparatively quiet, beyond its attention-getting exhaust gurgle when the windows are open. Direct-action shocks are housed in the center of each coil spring and a torsion bar sway eliminator is fitted between the lower links. Steering is rack and pinion type.

Rear suspension is by semi-elliptic leaf springs and direct action shocks which afford adequate control. The English-built Dana rear axle is semi-floating with hypoid final drive (2.88 ratio in our test car). A stabilizer has been incorporated to maintain transverse axle location.

Braking is good, the result of Girling 9.85-inch disc brakes at the front (standard equipment), with 9-inch di-

Telescopic steering column (standard), adjustable seats and back permit driver to tailor best position at wheel. The car is very maneuverable in traffic due to responsive 260 Ford engine, quick steering and 156" overall length.

ameter drum brakes rear. The system is obviously more than adequate for a car of this weight.

A peek under the front-hinged hood and one immediately assumes that the 260 was dropped in through a funnel; the compartment is completely filled up and some regular service procedures, such as changing spark plugs, won't be as easy as the owner might hope. On the other hand, the 260 lends itself well to the arrangment in some service areas with its typically American front-mount distributor, for example, so no major problem here.

The engine carries the same specs as that used in Ford's American offerings. The 260 displacement is the result of a 3.80 bore, 2.87-inch stroke, with a reported 164 horsepower at 4400 rpm sans power options, with two-barrel carb. The engine is economical (we averaged 19.57 mpg during the test on premium gas) and, as performance figures disclose, carries the little Alpine very efficiently.

In the driver's compartment we find features which are again in the European tradition. A pair of bucket seats, designed to comfortably cradle most "frames," flank the abbreviated-length, short-travel stick on the floor. The driver faces a well-planned instrument panel with gages that are quick and easy to read, not the least of which is a stock 6000-rpm tachometer. Unless

photos by Eric Rickman and Dick Wells

accustomed to the close sports car pedal arrangement, a driver newly introduced to the Tiger might encounter some difficulty, but this is quickly overcome and one soon adjusts to the setup. The seats are individually adjustable and the backs adjust to reclining positions. This feature, coupled with an adjustable length steering wheel, allows the driver to tailor his position for best driving.

Generally, the Alpine rates with the best of them in overall quality. From its genuine leather interior to the excellent fit of body panels the car is very appealing; the workmanship is exceptionally good. The convertible top (a hardtop is also available) is completely watertight even in a heavy downpour and, although air ventilation isn't the best (no side "wing" vents), the problem is quickly solved by folding away the top, or removing its hardtop, whatever the case may be.

But the true test comes in driving, when the 260 gets a chance to flex its muscles, and the "feel" of the car can be enjoyed. The engine starts easily whether hot or cold; the driver is positioned in a manner that affords good vision all around — all four fenders are visible without difficulty — and the stick is within easy reach. Once away, the driver is immediately aware of the car's potential power and ease of handling. Buzzing along in traffic, the Tiger proves its superiority over larger cars of comparable power, for it is very agile, responds quickly and is therefore ideal for city travel. Handling is excellent, although on wet surfaces it does tend to become a bit queasy in turns and some care must be taken by the driver. It recovers nicely, however, from controlled slides, and gives a true sports car feel.

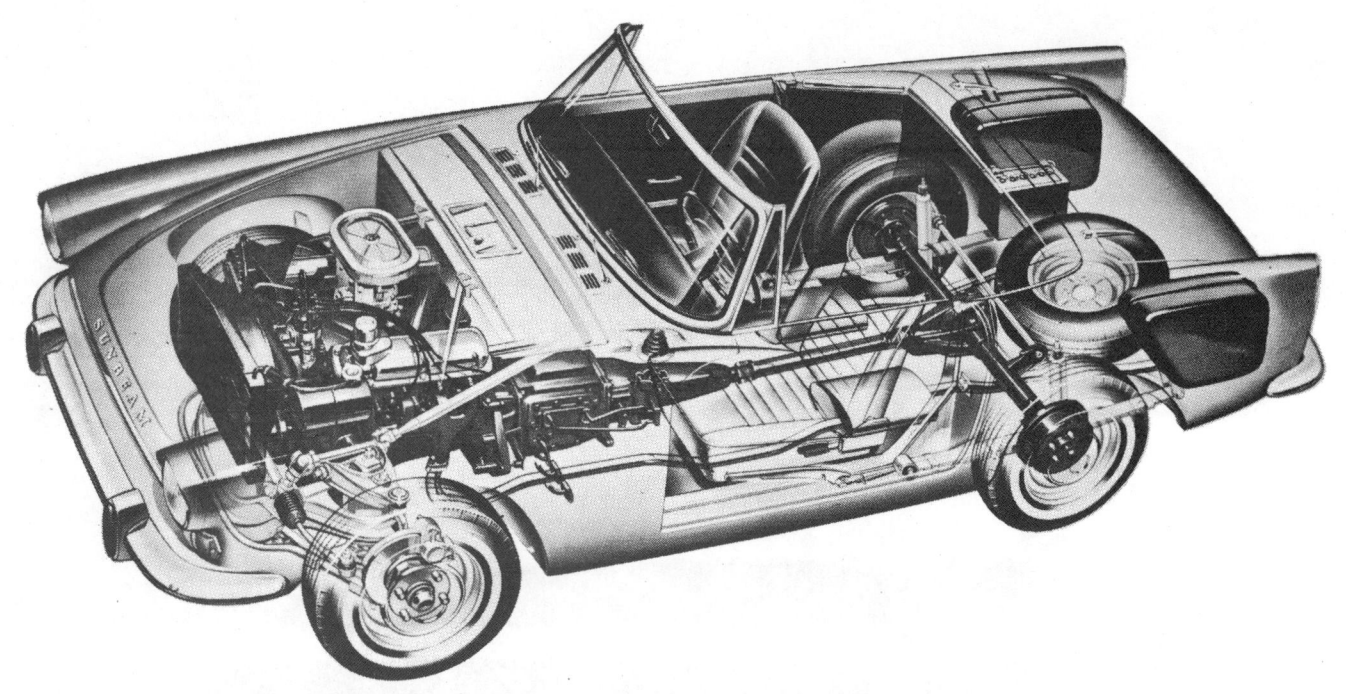

The Ford four-speed trans shifts smoothly, even in power shift situations, and is an all synchromesh unit with a safety mechanism to prevent accidental engagement of reverse. Ratios are: first, 2.32; second, 1.69; third, 1.29; and fourth, 1:1. Even with the 2.88 axle ratio in fourth, the car lugs down well, will recover acceleration without bucking. Of course, this isn't a recommended practice, but it does illustrate the 260's more-than-adequate delivery of torque. The clutch is boosted through use of a slave cylinder.

Those accustomed to the American car ride and steering will promptly detect a certain stiffness in the Tiger. The ride is by no means spongy; in fact, quite firm as one might expect. And the rack and pinion steering is truck-like; fine for straightaway driving, but it takes some arm-power to park, and to turn in tight corners at crawling speeds. Steering ratio is 3.1 turns of the wheel, lock-to-lock.

Our first test car was the two-barrel carb model, not equipped with any of the multitude of performance options available, except for traction bars which were considered a must . . . the way we drove it most of the time. HOT ROD's Tech Editor, Eric Dahlquist, exposed the Tiger to a drag strip test during a special press conference held prior to the grand opening of the new Carlsbad Dragway at Carlsbad, California. With air cleaner in place and no speed tuning whatsoever, Eric managed a 17.20 elapsed time with a top speed of 79.22 mph for the quarter-mile.

Reactions of press representatives at Carlsbad were very much like those experienced when driving the car on the street; few expect to see a Sunbeam turn on like that. The car will, how-

Sunbeam Tiger design features include unitized construction, resulting in solid "feel" and rattle-free body. Ford 260 mates to Ford 4-speed trans via 10-in. hydraulically boosted clutch. Most of options offered are performance items.

ever, do much better. Bill Coffey, of San Bernardino Sports Cars Limited, reported to us that his own Tiger, the "stock" two barrel car, turned a 16.54 e.t. at 89.00 mph with no special work done to it. It was, in fact, without traction bars and equipped with street tires.

All members of HOT ROD's staff eventually drove the "standard" Tiger during its test and enthusiasm was at a high tempo. We all agree that it's a good handling, exhilarating performing little bomb that acts like a miser in the economy department. So excited were we with the car that the Los Angeles Rootes cars distributor was contacted to borrow a Tiger with the power package installed. Included in the options are high-performance Cobra cam, solid lifters, 4-barrel (Holley) carb, heavy-duty valve springs, distributor modification kit and a replacement tach (up to 8000 rpm). A little more than $300 can be spent for hop-up and dress-up items, but the fob price of the Tiger without options is down to $3499, another very appealing characteristic of the car.

We were lucky enough to be loaned a performance model and, upon getting it, learned that many early "running change" improvements are being made. The upholstery in the second car was slightly different and we were told that those Tigers now being produced include a simulated wood dash which would richen the car's interior. Also, the brake and clutch pedals have been "spread out" to afford more convenient driver operation, and some Tigers now being delivered have the Borg-Warner T-10 four-speed.

Next move was to cut a trail to the Pomona Drag Strip for a try at the quarter during the strip's 1964-'65 season opening event. Again, a "showroom fresh" car that wasn't set up for the drags; street tires were used (6.50 x 13 rear, 5.90 x 13 front), jetting and timing, etc., were left as is. This one had a 3.76 rear end ratio, as opposed to the 2.88:1 we had in our first car, and a much taller trans low gear ratio which didn't help at the drags. Mag wheels were installed (not included in the $300 options package mentioned earlier) as well as a couple of racing stripes across the rear deck which literally "let the cat out of the bag."

The Tiger fell into G/Stock, under National Hot Rod Association '64 rules, and did quite well on its first outing. L.A. rodder Gary McKeand drove for us and managed a best elapsed time of 15.66 seconds with a top speed of 88.84 mph, giving a pretty fair indication of the car's drag potential.

Although there are now a couple of American made cars in a similar price/performance category, we concluded that the Sunbeam Tiger should be considered, particularly among those watch-the-budget shoppers who are looking for a good performing car with sports car handling. It's fun to drive and most of those who try to take the car from a stop sign turn out to be just "tiger food." We certainly don't endorse street racing, but it's hard to resist once in a while, 'specially if you've got a "Tiger by the tail!" ■■

FORD MAKES A TIGER OF THE SUNBEAM

STUFF IN A FORD V-8 AND YOU'VE GOT A TIGER BY THE TAIL

by Bob McVay, *Assistant Technical Editor*

THE IDEA CAME from Ian Garrad, Western U.S. Manager for Rootes of England. He drove the first Sunbeam Tiger prototype, hastily built by Ken Miles, and loved it. Then he enlisted the technical know-how of the Shelby-American organization to incorporate needed changes for a production model. Lord Rootes himself drove the second prototype in England and—you guessed it—he too fell under the Tiger's spell.

The rest is all history. Grueling tests in Africa, Europe, and America, negotiations with Ford for the first 4000 engines, and two years of work sorting things out finally let the first boatload of Tigers reach our shores. They were eagerly snapped up by anxious buyers. Rootes has since doubled their target production to meet the demand.

The beauty of Garrad's idea is that it makes good sense. The Sunbeam Alpine has proven a sturdy, comfortable sports car by gathering more than its share of trophies under the able guidance of such notables as Don Sesslar in the Midwest and Ken Miles and Jerry Titus on the West Coast, to mention only a few.

Ford's lightweight, cast-iron, 260-cubic-inch V-8 is also a proven factor. You can't beat cubic inches. With the standard two-barrel carb, it's rated at 164 hp and puts out 250 pounds-feet of torque. The engine fits without increasing the car's weight by much (horsepower and torque have been doubled, with only a 300-pound weight increase).

Until the Tiger was born, this kind of sports car performance just wasn't available for $3499. In standard touring trim, the Tiger has a 2.88 rear axle coupled to either a Warner T-10 or a Ford-built four-speed gearbox. It can also be ordered with Ford's three-speed automatic.

To give some hint of the Tiger's versatility and how customers can match it to their driving needs, three different transmission ratios and eight rear axle ratios are available. A 4.55 ratio tops the axle option list for the guy who simply *must* have the quickest Tiger out of the jungle.

With the standard 2.88 axle, our test Tiger managed over 20 mpg at legal cruising speeds. This dropped down to 13 during hard test driving. Fifteen mpg was the average for city traffic, which proves performance and economy *can* be compatible. Twin rear fender tanks hold 13½ gallons.

The Sunbeam Tiger isn't just a sports car with a big V-8 shoe-horned under the hood. Everything that needed strengthening was beefed up to handle the doubled power and torque.

Engine compartment is stuffed full of Ford V-8 power. Standard two-barrel carb, 164-hp V-8 provides sparkling performance with 20-mpg economy. Getting at the left rear spark plug requires removing a firewall panel and some physical gymnastics.

Dual exhausts, beefed-up suspension, and optional traction bars make Sunbeam Tiger feel and sound like a thoroughbred.

Heavier anti-roll bar, beefed-up front suspension, and disc brakes (front only) help Tiger handle its doubled horsepower.

PHOTOS BY DARRYL NORENBERG, PAT BROLLIER

TENACIOUS TIGER GOT A GOOD GRIP ON THE ROAD, SHOWED LITTLE LEAN. GREAT POWER RESERVE ADDED TO CONTROL IN FAST CORNERING.

SUNBEAM TIGER

Heavier springs and shocks, stronger spindles, A-arms, and wheels were some of the modifications. A large-capacity radiator kept our Tiger's engine temperature below 210° even during performance testing on a very hot day at Willow Springs Raceway.

Engine, clutch, and transmission are Ford (except for the Warner gearset already mentioned). The rear end is a Salisbury unit. Ford's 260-inch V-8 gives the touring Tiger more than adequate power and acceleration. Our spec chart bears this out, but that's only half the story.

Most sports car drivers pride themselves on their ability with the gearbox. These drivers will especially enjoy going up or down through the Tiger's well selected, all-synchromesh ratios, but they don't have to shift unless they want to. For all normal driving, even with two people and luggage aboard, only first and fourth are really necessary. First gear was good for 54 mph if held to the red line. In fourth, the car could be lugged down to a low 500 rpm, around 10 mph, yet it would still accelerate smoothly and strongly. Using all four gears was especially pleasing to our ears, thanks to the Tiger's dual exhaust system. Passing acceleration in any gear, at any speed under 110 mph, was as fierce as we could want.

In other words, the Sunbeam Tiger is a charger in standard trim, but Rootes makes provisions for even more performance if you want more. A Stage I kit, consisting of a wilder cam, solid lifters, an aluminum four-barrel carb mounted on an aluminum manifold, and heavy-duty valve springs, adds 81 hp more. Two four-barrel carbs can also be fitted, as they can to most Ford V-8 engines. And, going off the deep end, racing enthusiasts can gain maximum performance by fitting Weber carbs just like Shelby's racing Cobras.

Girling 9.85-inch-diameter discs up front, with nine-inch drums at the rear, provided adequate braking for our test Tiger. Since the V-8 has been moved slightly farther back toward the firewall than the four-banger, the Tiger has the edge on braking, with slightly better weight distribution. Again, the racing enthusiast hasn't been forgotten. Discs on all four wheels are optional.

The Tiger corners flat and fast under all conditions, without undue rear-end squat or nose dive under acceleration or braking forces. Steering has been changed to accommodate the V-8 installation. The Tiger uses rack-and-pinion steering, with only 3.2 turns between locks. A bit heavier than the Series IV Alpine's Burman recirculating ball mechanism, our Tiger's steering provided excellent road feel and a minimum of wheelspin during fast driving at Willow Springs. Handling was as near neutral as we've tried, but there's a certain amount of understeer when cornering near the limit of adhesion.

Dunlop Road Speed tires are standard equipment for the touring Tiger. A belted-tread tire would give even better traction on the road or track. As we drove it, and as most buyers will, the Dunlop tires are adequate for normal driving.

Our test car was fitted with Traction-Masters, which helped noticeably during hard acceleration, braking, and cornering. Without them, the Tiger shows spring wrap-up and rear-wheel hop during maximum acceleration.

It looks to us like Rootes has a winner in their Sunbeam Tiger. With a comfortable, roomy interior, fully instrumented dash, and outstanding performance, the Tiger's a lot of sports car for $3499. That's about as much fun as anyone can buy for the price. It's only a few hundred dollars above popular four-cylinder two-seaters and a lot less than some. Naturally, the Tiger's performance will be compared with Cobra's and Corvette's, but it's priced a good $1000 or more below either. /MT

Like all Sunbeam roadsters, Tiger has complete instrumentation, roomy, comfortable reclining seats, adjustable steering wheel.

SUNBEAM TIGER
2-door, 2-passenger roadster

OPTIONS ON CAR TESTED: Heater/defroster, windshield washers, tonneau cover, whitewalls
BASE PRICE: $3499
PRICE AS TESTED: $3649 (plus tax and license)
ODOMETER READING AT START OF TEST: 3500 miles
RECOMMENDED ENGINE RED LINE: 5500 rpm

PERFORMANCE

ACCELERATION (2 aboard)
0-30 mph.................................3.4 secs.
0-45 mph.................................5.6
0-60 mph.................................8.9

PASSING TIMES AND DISTANCES
40-60 mph.........................5.5 secs., 402 ft.
50-70 mph.........................6.6 secs., 580 ft.

Standing start ¼-mile 16.7 secs. and 85 mph
Speeds in gears @ 5500 rpm
1st ....54 mph   3rd ....90 mph
2nd ....71 mph   4th ....115 mph
                                (observed) @ 5100 rpm

Speedometer Error on Test Car
Car's speedometer reading 30 45 50 61 71 83
Weston electric speedometer .. 30 45 50 60 70 80
Observed miles per hour per 1000 rpm in top gear ....22.5 mph
Stopping Distances — from 30 mph, 34.5 ft.; from 60 mph, 151 ft.

SPECIFICATIONS FROM MANUFACTURER

Engine
Ohv V-8
Bore: 3.80 ins.
Stroke: 2.87 ins.
Displacement: 260 cu. ins.
Compression ratio: 8.8:1
Horsepower: 164 @ 4400 rpm
Horsepower per cubic inch: 0.63
Torque: 250 lbs.-ft. @ 2200 rpm
Carburetion: 1 2-bbl.
Ignition: 12-volt coil

Gearbox
4-speed manual, all-synchro (Warner T-10); floorshift

Driveshaft
1-piece, open tube

Suspension
Front: Independent, with upper and lower A-arms, coil springs, double-acting tubular shocks, and anti-roll bar
Rear: Solid axle, with semi-elliptic leaf springs and double-acting, tubular shocks, panhard rod. (Optional Traction-Masters on test car.)

Differential
Hypoid, semi-floating
Standard ratio: 2.88:1

Steering
Rack and pinion, with adjustable, telescoping wheel
Turning diameter: 35.0 ft.
Turns lock to lock: 3.2

Wheels and Tires
4-lug, steel disc wheels
5.90 x 13 Dunlop Road Speed tubed whitewall tires

Brakes
Girling servo-assisted discs front; drums rear
Front: 9.85-in. dia. discs
Rear: 9-in. dia. x 1.74-in.-wide cast-iron drums
Swept area: 295 sq. ins.

Body and Frame
Unit construction
Wheelbase: 86.0 ins.
Track: front, 51.0 ins.; rear, 48.5 ins.
Overall length: 156.0 ins.
Overall width: 60.5 ins.
Overall height: 51.5 ins.
Curb weight: 2550 lbs.

Sunbeam Tiger: Right-hand drive

Interior of the Tiger is neat and well equipped. Note the gear-lever for the all-synchromesh Borg-Warner gearbox, reclining seats and adjustable steering column

AFTER almost a full year's production confined entirely to l.h.d. versions for the United States market, the Sunbeam Tiger has at last been released for sale in r.h.d. form in this country. So scarce indeed has the supply of right-hand drive cars been that the Rootes Competition department has been forced to use l.h.d. cars so far for this successful competition car.

The Tiger joins the ever-growing band of models which fits one or other of the ubiquitous range of Ford V8 engines (even though Chrysler have become large shareholders in the Rootes organization since the car was developed), in this case being offered with a 4,261 c.c. unit producing a very modest 164 b.h.p. (gross), but with formidable torque of 258 lb. ft (gross) at 2,200 r.p.m.

A four-speed all-synchromesh Borg-Warner gearbox is specified, and the Salisbury hypoid back axle is very high geared at 2·88 to 1. A limited-slip differential is optional.

In many ways the Sunbeam Tiger is closely related to the Alpine Series IV, and indeed is scarcely distinguishable from the exterior except by close study of the badges and by looking for the "Tiger" and "260" motifs—the latter representing the size of this Ford engine in cubic inches—and the thin chrome strip down each side, plus (of course) two exhaust pipes.

Suspension is substantially re-worked, and a new front cross member has been added, together with larger disc brakes and calipers. Rack-and-pinion steering is also specified. New rear springs and dampers have been designed to cope with the torque and loads in the much more robust rear-axle unit.

Twin fuel tanks of 11·25 gal. total are fitted to this large-engined car, and the tyres are only 5·90-13 in.

It will be remembered that the Sunbeam Tiger has already made quite a name for itself in international motor sport, having taken the first three places in its class in the Geneva Rally last autumn, and was well driven into fourth place overall in the Monte Carlo Rally in January by Peter Harper and Ian Hall.

Price in England is £1,446 (£1,195 without tax) and there are several extras (including a smart hardtop) available.

The Tiger is very similar to the Alpine Series IV in this view. Recognition points include twin exhaust pipes and the "Tiger" motif on the front wings

Sunbeam Tiger 260 4,261 c.c.

Autocar Road Test
NUMBER 2025

AT A GLANCE: Well-equipped, easy-going sports car with plenty of power and vee-8 smoothness; high gearing gives relaxed cruising at 100 m.p.h.; predictable handling, but some steering feed-back and poor turning circles; powerful servo brakes; moderate fuel consumption.

The optional hardtop is particularly neat in design and fitting. Rear quarterlights open, but the ones on the doors are fixed. Below: Controls and instruments are well placed and everything is well within reach

MANUFACTURER:
Sunbeam - Talbot Ltd., Ryton - on - Dunsmore, Coventry.

PRICES:
Basic	...	£1,195 0s. 0d
Purchase Tax	...	£250 10s. 5d
Total (in G.B.)	...	£1,445 10s. 5d

Extras (inc. P.T.)
Hardtop	...	£60 8s. 4d
Fog and spot lamps (each)		£3 12s. 6d
Radiomobile	...	£29 3s. 8d
Seat belts (each)	...	£4 15s. 0d

PERFORMANCE SUMMARY
Mean maximum speed	... 117 m.p.h.
Standing start ¼-mile	... 17·0 sec
0-60 m.p.h.	... 9·5 sec
30-70 m.p.h. in 3rd gear	... 9·8 sec
Overall fuel consumption	16·9 m.p.g.
Miles per tankful	... 190

IF ever there was a car to prove that big, lazy engines are better than small, busy ones, then the Sunbeam Tiger is it. Here is a model, little different from the latest Alpine IV except in the all-important matter of its power unit and transmission, which has been effectively transformed from a two-seater tourer to a thrust-in-the-back sports car with a great striding gait and an unburstable mechanical quality.

The idea of "mill switching," as the Americans call it, is not new, but for a large British manufacturer to install a foreign engine from a rival firm in one of their own cars is unprecedented. That the changed car should feel so balanced brings as much credit to the basic Alpine design as to the characteristics of the new engine and the development of its installation.

93

Autocar Road Test 2025

MAKE: **Sunbeam Tiger 260**
TYPE: **4,261 c.c.**

Speed range, gear ratios and time in seconds

m.p.h.	Top (2·88)	Third (3·72)	Second (4·86)	First (6·68)
10—30	6·6	5·1	3·8	3·0
20—40	5·8	4·8	3·4	2·7
30—50	5·8	4·5	3·7	3·2
40—60	6·0	4·6	4·4	—
50—70	6·8	5·3	5·5	—
60—80	7·7	6·1	—	—
70—90	9·0	9·8	—	—
80—100	11·9	—	—	—
90—110	19·2	—	—	—

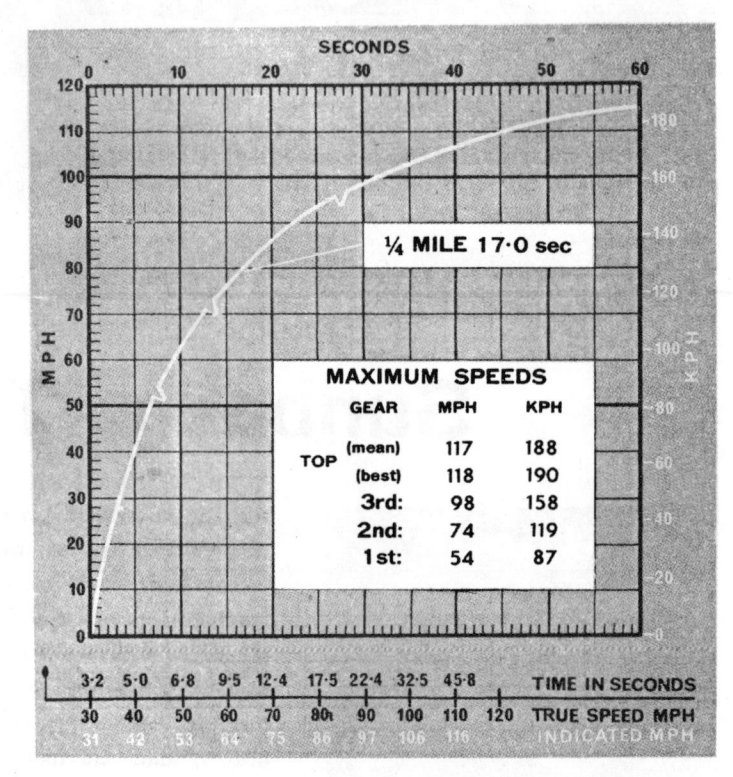

TEST CONDITIONS
Weather ... Dry with 8-15 m.p.h. wind
Temperature ... 6 deg. C (43 deg. F)
Barometer, 29·40in. Hg. Dry concrete and tarmac surfaces

WEIGHT
Kerb weight (with oil, water and half-full fuel tank): 23·6cwt (2,644lb-1,202kg)
Front-rear distribution, per cent ... F, 51; R. 49
Laden as tested ... 26·6cwt (2,980lb-1,354kg)

TURNING CIRCLES
Between kerbs ... L, 37ft 2in.; R, 37ft 9in.
Between walls ... L. 38ft. 8in.; R. 39ft. 3in.
Steering wheel turns lock to lock ... 3·3

PERFORMANCE DATA
Top gear m.p.h. per 1,000 r.p.m. ... 23·9
Mean piston speed at max. power ... 2,110 ft/min
Engine revs. at mean max. speed ... 4,900 r.p.m.
B.h.p. (gross) per ton laden ... 123

FUEL CONSUMPTION
At constant speeds
30 m.p.h. ... 33·9 m.p.g.
40 „ ... 31·8 „
50 „ ... 29·1 „
60 „ ... 26·7 „
70 „ ... 24·2 „
80 „ ... 21·1 „
90 „ ... 19·0 „
100 „ ... 15·5 „

Overall m.p.g. ... 16·9 (16·7 litres/100km)
Normal range m.p.g. ... 15-22 (18·8-12·8 litres/100km)
Test distance ... 1,568 miles
Estimated (DIN) m.p.g. ... 22·1 (12·8 litres/100km)
Grade ... Premium (96-98RM)

OIL CONSUMPTION
SAE 10W/30 ... 12,000 m.p.g.

¼ MILE 17·0 sec

MAXIMUM SPEEDS

GEAR	MPH	KPH
TOP (mean)	117	188
(best)	118	190
3rd:	98	158
2nd:	74	119
1st:	54	87

TIME IN SECONDS	3·2	5·0	6·8	9·5	12·4	17·5	22·4	32·5	45·8
TRUE SPEED MPH	30	40	50	60	70	80	90	100	110	120
INDICATED MPH	31	42	53	64	75	86	97	106	116

BRAKES (from 30 m.p.h. in neutral)

Pedal load	Retardation	Equiv. distance
25lb	0·25g	120ft
50lb	0·52g	58ft
75lb	0·80g	38ft
100lb	0·90g	33ft
125lb	0·98g	30·7ft
Handbrake	0·42g	72ft

Clutch Pedal load and travel ... 60lb and 5in.

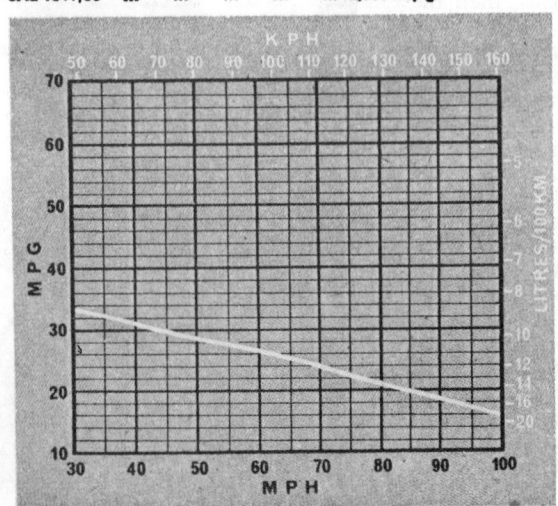

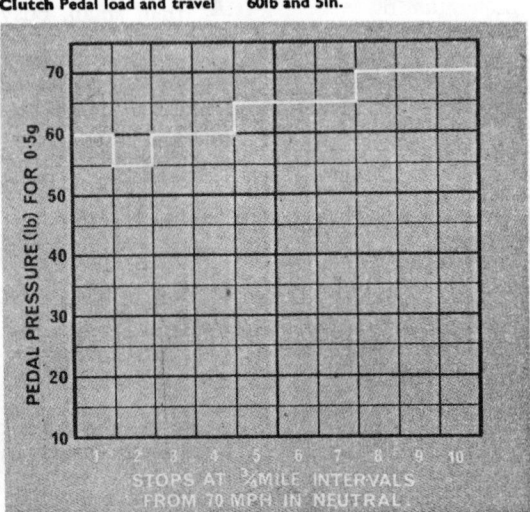

94

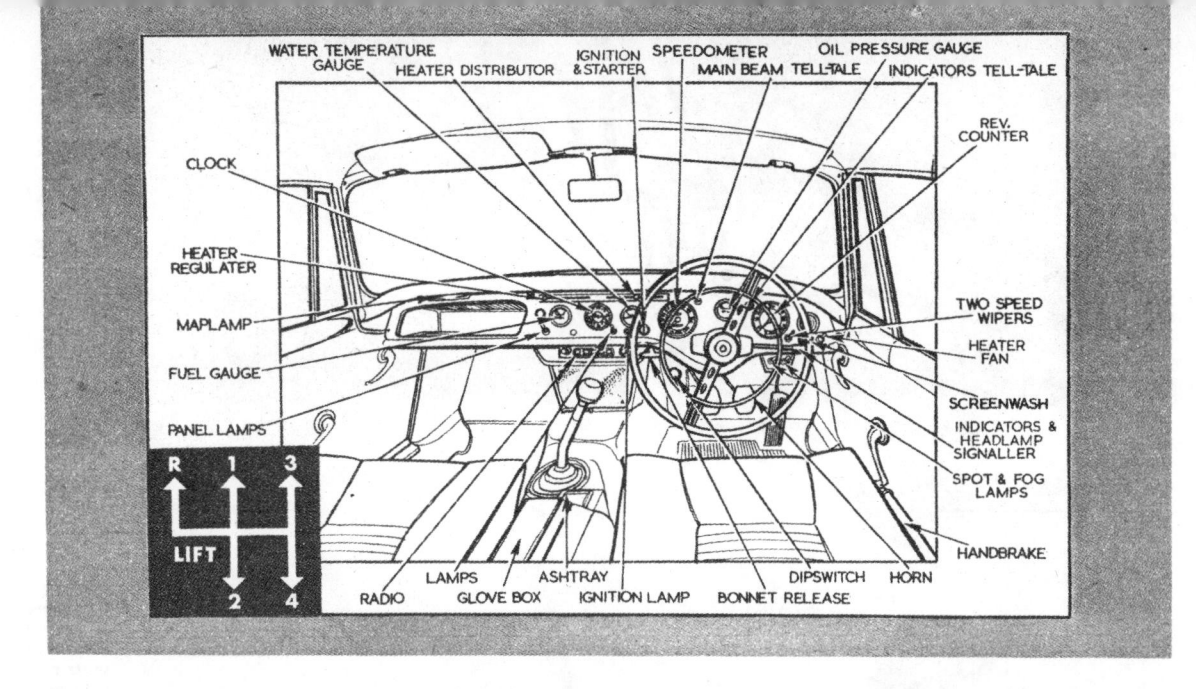

Briefly, a 4.2-litre Ford V8 Fairlane engine with Borg-Warner 4-speed manual gearbox has been squeezed into the Sunbeam Alpine. The final-drive gearing has been raised from 3.89 to 2.88 to 1, giving 23.9 m.p.h. per 1,000 r.p.m. in top gear instead of 17.8—an increase of 34 per cent. Other engineering changes have been a cross-flow radiator with larger matrix area and remote header tank, and rack-and-pinion steering (instead of recirculating-ball type) to give more clearance for the engine; the battery has been moved into the boot alongside the spare wheel.

Power and Performance

In terms of power the Ford engine develops 164 b.h.p. gross, just under double that of the Alpine (88 gross), at 600 r.p.m. fewer. Much more significant, however, is the peak torque figure of 258 lb. ft. which is well on the way to being three times that of the Alpine (94 net). The penalty for this is an increase in weight of some 4cwt, distributed evenly between front and rear. The effect is electrifying, with acceleration times from rest to 80 m.p.h. almost halved and a maximum speed raised 20 m.p.h. to 117. Yet the Tiger is as sweet and docile as the best in family cars, and can manage a standing-start quarter-mile using top gear only in 21.5sec, just 1sec *less* than a flat-out run in the automatic Alpine we tested last May.

The non-sporting characteristics (and origins) of the engine are felt when accelerating, for although the rev counter has its red sector from 4,700 upwards the pull falls off progressively from about 1,000 r.p.m. fewer and normally one never needs even to approach the limit. This impression is confirmed by the times for 20 m.p.h. increments in third, which suddenly tail off above 70 m.p.h. (3,800 r.p.m.). As soon as one gets used to this, learning to change up early when accelerating and not to bother with a down-shift unless the speed has really dropped, the Tiger is a rapid and exceedingly enjoyable car to drive.

Narrow though the rev band might be, the speed ranges in the gears are unusually wide. First has a maximum of 54 m.p.h. when required and top will pull quite smoothly from 10 m.p.h. so it is no strain to miss out a ratio, or maybe two on occasions. The spacing of the ratios could not be more even, with almost exactly 20 m.p.h. between the limits for each.

Although first is very high, no skill is needed to get the car away from rest. The engine idles at around 700 r.p.m. and with a diaphragm spring and centrifugal assistance the big, 10in. dia. clutch can be eased in without touching the accelerator, when the car will "creep" happily with no throttle at 7 m.p.h. We found the best technique for sprint take-offs was to use about 4,000 r.p.m. to get the wheels spinning on dry tarmac, leaving only very short black lines behind.

Cornering

In the wet, rather more delicate control is needed to avoid violent axle tramp which, if allowed to persist, might damage the rear suspension. Once the wheels are turning and the clutch is fully home, the throttle can be opened wide even in first or second without any snaking or rear-end twitchiness, provided the car is pointing straight. Cornering on slippery surfaces calls for caution, as expected, although within a very short time one learns just how far the tail will kick out and to anticipate it early with steering correction.

This technique of power drifting, even in the dry, is particularly easy to control with the Tiger. One runs into corners on the overrun to a point just short of the apex, then unwinds the lock and stamps on the throttle at the same time. The tail slides out just so far and then stops on its own as the weight transfers back under power and adds to the rear wheel grip. On the M.I.R.A. road circuit we tried this type of cornering without applying any correction and found that the radius of the turn tightened up appreciably, but otherwise the car maintained a safe, predictable course.

Steering

Normally when driving round bends at a steady speed the handling has just a trace of understeer with strong self-centring action. This gives good stability at speed, although in a gusty cross-wind we found steering responses a little delayed above 90 m.p.h. There is a good deal of feed-back to the wheel rim from road irregularities, and one senses that the engineers have had to compromise in designing this new steering. At full lock there seems to be an unusual degree of tyre scrub and the front repeatedly swings wider than one expects when turning slowly into narrow gateways. The mean turning circle of 37ft. 6in. between kerbs is over 5ft. more than for an ordinary Alpine; this makes the ratio on the Tiger (3.3 turns lock-to-lock) about the same as that of the Alpine (3.6).

For ride comfort also the Tiger feels much like the Alpine. There is a good balance between firm control of the wheels for tidy handling and soft movements to absorb shocks. Certain types of rough surface can catch the back-end by surprise, especially on a corner when the tail will patter sideways a foot or so. The Panhard rod added to the Tiger no doubt reduces this tendency, but better location of the axle by radius arms is needed.

Starting the engine from cold is always simple and immediate. Once

95

Sunbeam Tiger 260

On the passenger side there is a false toeboard under the carpet, and both seats can be adjusted for rake and reclined by releasing the lever on the outside of the cushion

the throttle has been pressed to cock the automatic choke, the vee-8 bursts into life with a purposeful throb and then idles smoothly. No warming up period is necessary before the engine will pull strongly and without hesitation. Once or twice after prolonged idling in hot weather restarting was delayed, and care then had to be taken not to pump the accelerator and flood the cylinders. According to the handbook, water temperature should be between 85 and 100 deg. C. and most of the time our car ran at 95. This high reading on the gauge, which crept up to 100 (not boiling because of the pressurization) during maximum speed runs, may cause some concern unless one has read about the hot thermostat.

Fuel Consumption

During our three-week test everyone used the performance when they could so the overall consumption for 1,568 miles was 16.9 m.p.g. The corresponding estimated (DIN) figure (based on steady-speed measurements) is 22.1 and we had no difficulty in getting 20 m.p.g. on the road with a little restraint. The range between refills therefore can vary from only about 180 to as much as 240 miles; however, the usual Rootes "dead reckoning" fuel gauge is fitted with a scale marked in gallons (and litres) so there is never any doubt about the level in the twin 5½ gal. tanks.

Above about 80 m.p.h. there is considerable wind roar with the (optional) hardtop in place. With the standard hood erected there is much more noise generally, but no flapping; in open trim buffeting is not unpleasant and there is an exciting jet-like whistle above 60 m.p.h. Motoring with the car in these three different forms emphasizes the near-absence of mechanical noise from the engine and the unusually subdued exhaust beat. One never has to soft-pedal through towns at night, the only noise coming from the car being that muffled waffle which characterizes the vee-8.

The hardtop (which matches the car paint only if ordered with a new car—otherwise it is black) is easily taken off provided one can enlist a helper. It has opening rear quarterlights which help considerably in getting a comfortable degree of ventilation, since the front ones on the doors are fixed. The twin sunvizors must be removed before undoing the overcentre clips on the screen rail, and it is all too easy to break their pivot lugs when putting the roof back on.

Behind a hinged tonneau panel the folding p.v.c. hood is hidden out of sight, and once the knack is mastered, it is quick and simple to erect. It gives unusually snug and weathertight protection, although the blind rear quarters sometimes make it difficult when trickling into a main road at an oblique angle.

Tiger brakes are identical with those of the Alpine, and cope extremely well with the extra performance. Front discs are 9.85 in. dia.

Spare wheel and heavy-duty battery are normally hidden under the boot floor which lifts up or out as required

For quick identification only the thin chrome line down each side and the two exhaust pipes give away the Tiger.

and there is a vacuum servo to lighten the load. Almost 1·0g retardation was recorded quite easily, and the results of our fade test from 70 m.p.h. showed little increase in pedal pressures. A slightly distorted disc caused some juddering when the brakes got really hot, but no efficiency was lost, the trouble being an isolated fault rather than a design or material weakness. Most of the time the brakes felt smooth and powerful, although one or two of our staff commented that the higher gearing and increased engine inertia made them feel less sensitive than those on the Alpine.

The handbrake managed a creditable 0·42g stop on its own, and made light work of holding the car facing either way on a 1-in-3 hill. There was plenty of torque, despite the high first gear, to get the car going again very easily on this gradient.

To accommodate the large Ford engine a few inches of toe room have been lost, but this is barely noticeable to a driver of average leg length. All the adjustments of the Alpine are retained except the one for the pedal cluster, both seats being adjustable for reach, cushion angle and backrest rake. In addition the steering column has a telescopic range of about 3in. On the left there is a false toeboard for the passenger to brace his feet against.

Driving Position

The seats have excellent contours and grip the hips well during fast cornering. One can adapt the driving position to any shape or style and the only adverse comment concerned slightly cramped clearance between the bottom of the wheel rim and some drivers' thighs when lifting off the throttle for braking. Pedal arcs are well planned and the 60lb clutch load did not feel heavy.

With the seat right back the gear lever is at armstretch in first and third, and it would be better with a few degrees more backward crank. The Borg-Warner synchromesh is powerful and faultless, although gear changes feel notchy unless the clutch is right on the floor.

In front of the driver and across the dashboard are all the instruments including a clock, and on the right there is a blanked hole for the optional ammeter. The heater has a two-speed booster fan which encourages a comforting, warm draught round the lower regions when the roof is off in fresh weather. There are no independent cold air ventilators and even with everything switched off a good deal of engine and transmission heat is transmitted through to the footwells. Theoretically the heater ducts should pass cold air with the water tap closed, but on our car there was always a dribble of warmth.

At night the headlamps give illu-

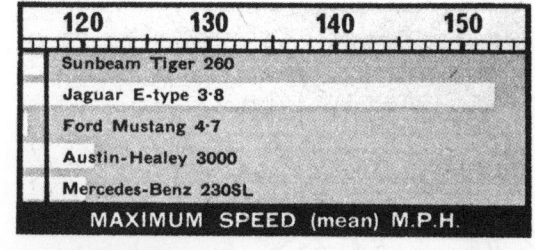

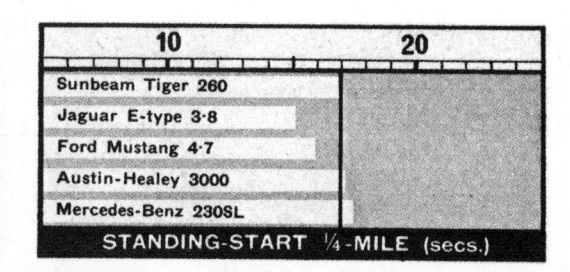

HOW THE SUNBEAM TIGER 260 COMPARES:

MAXIMUM SPEED (mean) M.P.H.
- Sunbeam Tiger 260
- Jaguar E-type 3·8
- Ford Mustang 4·7
- Austin-Healey 3000
- Mercedes-Benz 230SL

STANDING-START ¼-MILE (secs.)
- Sunbeam Tiger 260
- Jaguar E-type 3·8
- Ford Mustang 4·7
- Austin-Healey 3000
- Mercedes-Benz 230SL

0–60 M.P.H. SECONDS
- Sunbeam Tiger 260
- Jaguar E-type 3·8
- Ford Mustang 4·7
- Austin-Healey 3000
- Mercedes-Benz 230SL

M.P.G. Overall and Estimated (DIN)
- Sunbeam Tiger
- Jaguar E-type
- Ford Mustang
- Austin-Healey
- Mercedes-Benz

mination well up to the performance of the car, with long range on main beam and a good spread when dipped. A headlamp flasher—so necessary on motorways these days—is a standard fitting. The windscreen wipers have two speeds and use a double-bladed U-section rubber which does not lift off the glass right up to the maximum speed.

There is no doubt that the Tiger is somewhat misnamed, for it has nothing of the wild and dangerous man-eater about it and is really only as fierce as a pussy-cat. A woman would find it easy to control. Yet for the man who loves power it has a fascination, because it does all that it can do without fuss, noise or effort. It has a certain surprise quality too, most onlookers dismissing the car as just another Alpine until, suddenly, with only an impressive "whoosh" it's gone, up the road and away before they have time for that second look. It's a car one parks with reluctance, such is the fun in driving it.

SPECIFICATION : SUNBEAM TIGER 260 — FRONT ENGINE REAR-WHEEL DRIVE

ENGINE
- Cylinders ... 8 in 90 deg vee
- Cooling system ... Water; pump, fan and thermostat
- Bore ... 96·5mm (3·80in.)
- Stroke ... 73·0mm (2·87in.)
- Displacement ... 4,261 c.c. (260 cu. in.)
- Valve gear ... Overhead, pushrods and rockers.
- Compression ratio 8·8-to-1
- Carburettor ... Ford twin-choke
- Fuel pump ... S.U. electric
- Oil filter ... Ford full-flow
- Max. power ... 164 b.h.p. (gross) at 4,400 r.p.m.
- Max torque ... 258 lb. ft (gross) at 2,200 r.p.m.

TRANSMISSION
- Clutch ... Ford, single dry plate, 10in. dia.
- Gearbox ... 4 speed, all synchromesh
- Gear ratios ... Top 1·0; Third 1·29; Second 1·69; First 2·32; Reverse 2·32.
- Final drive ... Hypoid 2·88 to 1

CHASSIS AND BODY
- Construction ... Integral chassis with steel body

SUSPENSION
- Front ... Independent, coil springs and wishbones, anti-roll bar, telescopic dampers
- Rear ... Live axle, half-elliptic leaf springs Panhard rod, telescopic dampers
- Steering ... Engineering Productions, rack and pinion. Wheel dia. 15·5in.

BRAKES
- Make and type ... Girling, disc front, drum rear
- Servo ... Girling vacuum type
- Dimensions ... F, 9·85in. dia; R, 9·0in. dia; 1·75in. wide shoes.
- Swept area ... F, 196 sq. in. R, 99 sq. in. Total 295 sq. in. (222 sq. in. per ton laden).

WHEELS
- Type ... Pressed steel disc 4·5in. wide rim
- Tyres ... Dunlop RS5 tubeless. 5·90—13in.

EQUIPMENT
- Battery ... 12-volt 67-amp. hr.
- Generator ... Ford 360W
- Headlamps ... Lucas sealed beam 60/45 watt.
- Reversing lamp ... Extra
- Electric fuses ... 2
- Screen wipers ... 2-speed, self-parking
- Screen washer ... Standard, manual plunger
- Interior heater ... Standard, fresh-air
- Safety belts ... Extra, built-in anchorages
- Interior trim ... P.v.c.
- Floor covering ... Carpet
- Starting-handle ... No provision
- Jack ... Screw pillar
- Jacking points ... 4 corner sockets
- Other bodies ... None

MAINTENANCE
- Fuel tank ... 11·25 Imp. gallons (no reserve)
- Cooling system ... 27 pints (including heater)
- Engine sump ... 8·5 pints (3·9 litres) SAE 10W/30 Change oil every 6,000 miles; Change filter element every 6,000 miles
- Gearbox ... 3·25 pints SAE80EP. No oil change.
- Final drive ... 2·5 pints SAE90EP. Change oil every 6,000 miles
- Grease ... No points
- Tyre pressures ... F and R, 26 p.s.i. (normal driving) F and R, 32 p.s.i. (fast driving.)

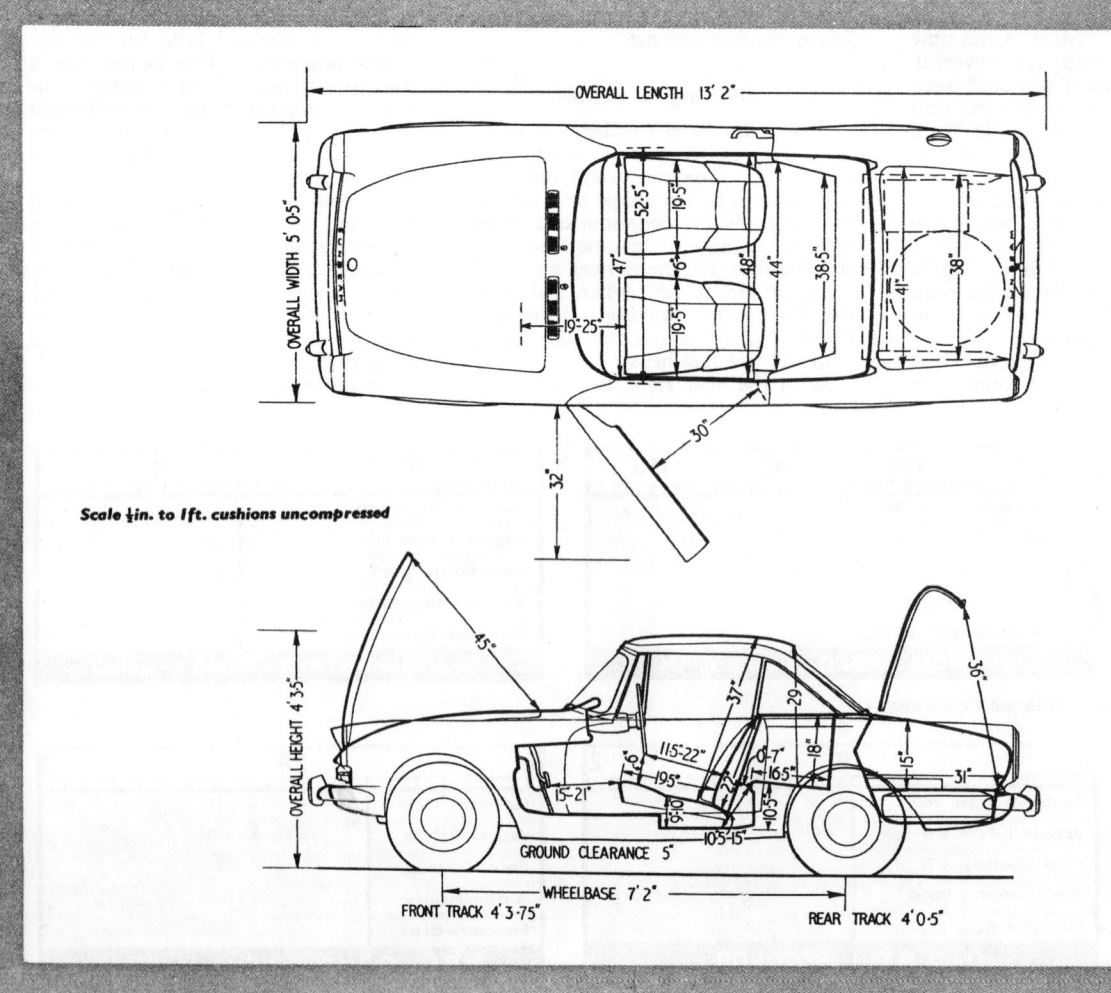

Scale ¼in. to 1ft. cushions uncompressed

THE SUNBEAM TIGER

Brief Impressions

WHEN I first heard about the Sunbeam Tiger project, the idea of putting a Ford V8 engine into a Sunbeam Alpine made me shudder a bit, for though the Alpine is a sound enough car it can hardly be considered a classic high speed vehicle and I visualised this rather genteel 2-seater roadster suddenly finding itself possessed of 300 b.h.p. like a Shelby-Cobra. The next acquaintance with the idea was the sight of the rather rorty-looking Le Mans cars, with alloy wheels, cared hub caps, stark trim, rowdy exhaust systems and holes and bulges all over the bodywork. Consequently, when the Editor said I could borrow a Sunbeam Tiger for a day I automatically visualised a car that was going to be a bit of a riot, with a thundering great V8 engine and so much power that it would be an embarrassment on the open road. Imagine my surprise when I went to collect it and found a very normal-looking Sunbeam Alpine hard-top, normal-looking except for larger section tyres and the name Tiger on the side. At first I was disappointed because I thought I was going to get a Rootes version of a Shelby-Cobra, but I soon re-adjusted my ideas and realised that whereas the Shelby-Cobras are great fun, they are not exactly practical, but this Tiger was not only practical and usable but surprisingly pleasant. The 4.2-litre Ford V8 engine is absolutely standard and is fitted into the Alpine bonnet space so neatly that you would think it was specially made for it and there are no air scoops, power bulges or what-have-you, so that the result is the best sort of Q-car. Even the V8 exhaust noise is very subdued and you can glide about the place looking like an innocuous Alpine at first glance, and when an M.G.-B or TR4 appears in the mirror you just waft away in top gear, leaving them looking very surprised. With 258 lb. ft. torque at 2,200 r.p.m. the wafting away is very impressive and there is no noise or fuss.

The mention of o.h.v. Ford V8 immediately conjures up four double-choke Webers, massive exhaust pipes, 7,000 r.p.m. and 300-350 b.h.p., but Ford also make a very cooking o.h.v. V8 that gives 164 b.h.p. at 4,400 r.p.m. without the slightest sound, and this is the unit in the Tiger. A Borg-Warner 4-speed manual gearbox is coupled to the V8 engine and a short rigid central lever controls it in a lumpy sort of fashion, as gearboxes go, but the torque of the engine makes the use of the gearbox almost unnecessary. For maximum acceleration it paid to forget 3rd gear and after winding it up in 2nd a quick " round the corner " change into top brought you onto the peak of the torque curve and the car then really got along pretty well. The stability was much better than I imagined and although the ride was choppy and the suspension uninspired it was quite usable as a fast roadster and gave confidence to hold it flat-out. Rootes blurb-sheets claim 125 m.p.h. but the one I borrowed would not even show that on its speedo. However, it did hold 4,400 r.p.m. along the Stevenage by-pass, which is peak power engine speed, and a calculated 105 m.p.h. on the 2.88 to 1 rear axle, but it felt as if it would have gone on all day at that speed. Bearing in mind that it weighed 23½ cwt. (2,632 lb.) in running trim, with radio, heater, hard-top and all mod. con. it is unlikely that 164 b.h.p. would push it along any better. The torque output is another matter altogether, and 258 lb. ft. make it a very quick car about the place, the typical Rootes handling and steering being alright for road use, in and out of the traffic on the open road.

To find out if it did accelerate I took it along to the B.D.R.A. practice day on a beam-timed ¼-mile standing-start and it did a best of 16.34 sec. in the dry and consistently beat 17 sec., which was not bad for a fully-equipped roadster. On a damp track it was impossible to do a fierce take-off as the cart-sprung rear axle stamped up and down like a jack-rabbit. Figures are not the best thing for the Tiger, its behaviour and manner of going being far more impressive, the engine being unbelievably quiet and smooth and the torque making the car extremely flexible and restful to drive. There is rather a lot of wind noise around the windscreen pillars, which is accentuated in the hard-top version, and this, coupled with the jolting and pounding from the suspension, makes you feel you are really charging along, and when you think you must be doing 80 or 90 m.p.h. in the dark you put the panel light on to find you are doing 65-70 m.p.h.! This must make it an essentially safe car in inexperienced hands and with an all-in price of £1,445 10s. 5d., of which £250 10s. 5d. goes to the Government, it will certainly be found in many inexperienced hands. At such a low price it must surely sell like " hot cakes," or should it be " hot rods "! Now that it is available on the British market it seems unlikely that Rootes will sell any more Alpines, for this Anglo-American-bastard 2-seater is such good value for money, giving an effortless 100 m.p.h. anywhere and a maximum speed that is also its cruising speed, while the engine should last for ever. — D. S. J.

FRAZER NASH CAR CLUB

Owners of post-war Frazer Nash sports cars met at the home of Barbara Marshall and Betty Haig on March 14th to discuss the formation of a Club which would enable race meetings for these cars to be held (the V.S.C.C. caters for post-war historic racing cars, but not for post-war classic sports cars). It was agreed to form a club of the above name, with Michael Burn as Chairman, Betty Haig as Hon. Secretary and Hugh Cundey as Treasurer. Miss Haig, who had been running the post-war Frazer Nash Register, from which this new Club has stemmed, said that 24 cars had been registered to date. The subscription to the F.N.C.C. is 10s. and the Secretary's address is: Shellingford House, Shellingford, Nr. Farningham, Berks. An early race meeting at Castle Combe will probably be co-promoted with the Porsche Owners' Club.

THE REAL SUNBEAM TIGER, 1925.—4-litre supercharged V12, 305 b.h.p., weight 18 cwt.

ROOTES' SUNBEAM TIGER, 1965.—4.2-litre non-supercharged V8, 164 b.h.p., weight 23½ cwt.

A Tiger for Rallying

As prepared for international rallying, Rootes' Ford-powered Tiger has even sharper claws

BY HENRY N. MANNEY

THE SUNBEAM ALPINE has long been referred to among its friends as the "Sports Husky," its chassis being derived from the utility van of that name, and thus there was some alarm when Rootes announced its intention of jamming a whacking great Ford V-8 therein. Boulevard sports, tired of rowing themselves along with the gear lever, applauded this decision but those with competition in mind had dark thoughts of the Dreaded Understeer. When the car actually appeared, it proved to be quite a pleasant automobile indeed, but even so the inclusion of three Tigers in the Monte Carlo Rally entry lists provoked much laughter. Collapse of stout party, as two of the three were among the select number of finishers, one made ftd on a special stage, and they wound up first and second in their GT class besides Peter Harper being fourth overall.

As to our mind this was the success story of the year, we made haste to contact the celebrated Marcus Chambers, COMCOMPROOTES, and try one of these diabolical devices. It turned out that Harper's would be available after he finished some Swedish ice racing and so it came to pass that in company with Gethin Bradley we tore ourselves away from a good cuppa tea and set sail for Stevenage and Mr. Harper's agency for guess which make of automobile. The Tiger was in what the used-car boys call "performance tested" condition with glass out of the headlights, a graunch on the rear wing (courtesy Pat Moss-Carlsson) a generous coating of Swedish dirt, rally plates, and a full set of Weathermaster snow tires with studs. This particular sort, explained Peter while he idly picked a few rusty ones out of the spare, wasn't too much use (they were all leaning at an angle of 45°), and he preferred the Scason type.

I then had the job of driving this studded monster to the works at Coventry while Gethers followed in the spacious and comfortable Humber wagon with which we had arrived, lunch then being scheduled with Marcus whilst proper tires were slammed on and a quick wash job was administered. As its conduct with studs on a dry road is not really relevant, I will content myself with saying that it showed a strong disinclination to deviate from a straight line and that it is easy to see why Peter and Andrew Cowan had to use the handbrake on all downhill hairpins to get the back end around. Combined with this tetchiness was an extremely short rear end ratio, which meant that if power were to be turned on in short corners in third in the amounts one would use, say, in my Lancia, one progressed in a series of zigs and zags. It says a lot for the soundness of the car, though, that it fired first kick, the only untoward mechanical noise was a slight tappet click, and the Ford 4-speed gearbox shifted as sweetly as ever.

Naturally enough, the rally Tiger differs in certain aspects from a street one, the chief external clue being an impression of bulk caused by the oversize 13 x 5 mag wheels and fat tires. The engine has been Cobra-ized, the clutch is also a Cobra unit and the box a Ford with special higher ratio internals as the Warner parts are not available in Britain. There is, of course, a Salisbury Powr-Lok limited slip diff which wore a 3.77:1 ratio for the Monte, and suspension consists of Husky export springs with Rapier rally dampers plus a 0.75-in. stabilizer bar. The brakes carry Ferodo DS-11 on the front and VG-95 at the rear, those back cylinders also being bored out to 0.875-in., a larger water radiator plus an oil radiator is fitted, a 26-gallon tank roosts in the boot to the exclusion of all else save a spare tire (a second spare parks on the lid), the exhaust system is higher up, and the electrical system boasts alternators to take care of all the iodine lights. There doesn't seem to have been much lightening of the bodywork which tends to be not over-heavy on the Alpine anyway, but even so the rally car must scale more than a normal one by virtue of the extra equipment.

Most of this is in the office, so important on international rallies, and it is extremely interesting to see just what is considered necessary. First off, since nobody can drive if he can't see the road, there are a multitude of switches controlling extra iodine driving lights and/or foglamps, sectional instrument lighting, the navigator's map light, the wire-heated screen front and rear, and de-icing squirts for the screen and driving lights too, no less. This last is because frozen snow cast up by cars in front forms on the lenses, causing an appreciable drop in illumination. Also fitted is a very handy plastic molded sheet nine inches high running closely around the inside of the screen to channel the defroster air. For the navigator's benefit, a pair of Heuers, one stop watch and one master clock, rest on a padded mount on the dash above the Halda twinmaster and, as an extra refinement, an additional rear-view mirror in case someone is following closely. The driver's side is more simple with a floor-mounted dip switch, a stalk flasher to the left of the wheel, a handy knee rest covering the window and door handles, and a tach in front of his eyes with "6000"' marked in red.

After lunch and inspection of the 998-cc rally Imps (one with a V-8 Ford poised nearby), Gethin and I stepped aboard and settled ourselves in the comfortable seats, finding out simultaneously that there was really more legroom than we needed and that we actually needed a cushion. Or else my overcoat, which I had had before. Clutching stop watch and Leica in hand, we then rumbled out through the works gate in second (such was the modest idle and low gears) and blatted off in the gap between two cloth-capped gents on bicycles en route to the pub. To say the least, the Tiger is a stimulating machine to drive in traffic as notwithstanding Shelby's trick cam there is a flattish power curve up to max revs (by which time you are too fast for traffic); just as well, too, for a peaky one would have been embarrassing on ice. Naturally enough the Tiger was a trifle noisier than the normal one due to the increased breathing and several squeaks, groans, and rattles brought on by the special stages, but I wouldn't say that an intercom was really necessary for those of normal hearing. Otherwise, its competition history did not reveal itself except for a rather heavy centrifugal clutch which needed to be pushed right down, a hardish ride, the brakes being a bit tired, and the front wheels bouncing a bit from weak shocks. None of these were terribly obtrusive and in fact the Tiger was dead simple to drive.

First off we went along some tricky bits so that we could get the odd picture; the handling seemed to be okay as far as we went (Marcus doesn't appreciate bent motor cars) but the slightly vague steering and dead handling characteristics made me wish that I had it for a week to gain more acquaintance. On fast swerves it went around all right if with a strong sensation of being propelled forcefully by the rear wheels, but there was no apparent understeer, oversteer, or anything—it just went. I suppose that one has to go a lot faster to find out its eventual behavior and on a damp road at 4 P.M. neither of us was prepared to do that. Suffice to say that the Tiger is not an understeering pig but lots of poke in a small package. Later on, in search of a suitable place to do acceleration figures, we negotiated several roundabouts and there the car did require some forethought to get the front end pointed away from the grass and into the corner. Reflections on the limited-slip diff and cures thereof produced the answer, though, and sundry squirts of throttle in third were found to do the trick. Like the heavier sort of front-driver, it very much liked the power on when any sharpish curve was contemplated.

Acceleration runs were lots of fun, as we would wait until some pursuing vehicle was within a hundred yards and then disappear into the distance. A moderate amount of throttle produced the best results on getaway as too little (below 2500) bogged it down and too much caused a bout of wheelspin with consequent sidewise attitude until the diff took hold. The back axle, much to our surprise, didn't begin to tramp and the most difficult bit was keeping one eye on the tach and the other out the windshield, as 6000 rpm came up far too quickly for comfort, by which time we were up the chuff of some unwary Mini. Top speed runs, limited by the redline as it was still accelerating vigorously at 6000 in top, showed that the Tiger was very steady at those speeds and was even steerable, the only indication of speed being a sizable amount of row from under the bonnet. The water temp rose to just under 100° C early on and stayed there, oil pressure was generally about 2.2 kg cm sq, and nothing smelled hot. Altogether quite a car and just what England needs with its crowded traffic conditions— good acceleration to reduce that awful time out passing Ford Zephyrs and heavy trucks while the oncoming column bears down. I've said it before and I'll say it again—there ain't any substitute for cubic inches. Please can we have it again, Mr. Chambers?

ROAD TEST No. 17/65

Sunbeam Tiger

Successful marriage of big V-8 with comfortable sports tourer. Good flexibility, performance and handling more than compensate for bumpy ride on poor surfaces.

THE first point to establish is that the Tiger is not just an Alpine with a V-8 engine shoehorned in (although it is a fairly tight fit) but a separate car in its own right. The changes are many, all enabling the extra power to be used safely and reliably, and the newcomer need not encroach upon the market for the more stately touring Alpine. The Tiger is a sports car of the most masculine kind, not in the strength needed to drive it, but in its character—141 effortless horsepower from a lazy V-8 will produce really quick acceleration when wanted or it can be throttled down to potter quietly in top gear at less than 1,000 r.p.m.

It is this dual character that makes the Tiger so attractive to a wide variety of people, or the same person in a variety of moods. Sporting enthusiasts can use all the gears and all the performance, including 0–60 m.p.h. in 9.4 sec. and a maximum over 115 m.p.h., with safe sure-footed handling and only an overall consumption of 17.8 m.p.g. to deter them. Less power-conscious people will like the easy tractability which includes the ability to go from rest to ninety in third gear. The cost of this chameleon is £1,446.

Considering the inherent limitations of the suspension design—a leaf sprung rear axle with no additional location—the roadholding is outstanding. On good roads the throttle can really be used to advantage in a completely controllable fashion, be the surface wet or dry, either to provoke the tail for amusement or to generate the ultimate cornering power. On bad roads the ride gets choppy, the steering kicks and the body shakes but it still holds the road and goes where you point it.

A grand touring interior is rather belied by high speed wind roar with the hardtop in position, but one expects a certain amount of noise from a sports car and with the hood down folded under a neat panel behind the occasional single transverse rear seat, the Tiger is great fun.

Performance and Economy

Despite Chrysler's financial interest in Rootes, the Ford engine is still used and will continue to be fitted to the Tiger. Only 141 b.h.p. from 4.2 litres is a very low specific output, but this is the least tuned version of a V-8 which in its most powerful production form can produce over 100 b.h.p. more. American knowledge of thin-wall casting techniques keeps the weight down to a reasonable level—the Tiger with all its extra strength is 3¼ cwt. heavier, but the weight distribution is slightly nearer 50/50 than the Alpine.

Moving the engine a bit farther back does not help accessibility, but Rootes dealers equipped with a few special tools will have no difficulties in reaching essential service items such as plugs and the oil filter.

The advantages of the low output, with maximum power at only 4,400 r.p.m., are good torque throughout the range from under 1,000 r.p.m. to around 5,000 r.p.m.—the useful limit in acceleration tests—a remarkable degree of mechanical silence helped also by hydraulic valve lifters, and the ability to retain tune with a minimum of attention over a maximum period.

PRICE:—£1,195 plus £250 10s. 5d. equals £1,445 10s. 5d.
(Hardtop extra £50 plus £10 8s. 4d. equals £60 8s. 4d.)

Closed GT car with airy hardtop easily converts to sports car. You can tell it is a Tiger by the chrome stripe on the side.

Performance figures are impressive: only just outside the select band who reach 100 m.p.h. in under 30 seconds. Acceleration tails off a little after this towards the maximum at 116.4 m.p.h. but it is quite happy, apart from some wind roar, to cruise in motorway style around 110 m.p.h. or so, a mere 4,700 r.p.m.

At the effortless end of the scale, top gear performance starts easily below 20 m.p.h. and just surges onwards to the maximum. Pottering in town, the Tiger is almost silent but the distant whuffle of the V-8 is a constant reminder of power in hand for all emergencies, even in top gear.

Cold starting is easy on the automatic choke whatever the weather. It takes some time to reach running temperature and well over two miles of gentle driving before the choke releases the fast idle setting, but there is no hesitancy during this period. For warm starting it is vital not to give a preliminary squirt on the throttle which, with the fierce accelerator pumps on the Carter carburetter, is enough to quench it. Several seconds of churning are then needed to clear the cylinders. The same problem can cause the engine to stutter if the accelerator is floored at under 500 r.p.m.

Standing starts can easily produce a great deal of useless wheelspin with too many revs, while too few would allow the Dunlop RS5s to grip too quickly and the car would falter. A nice balance used about 2,500 r.p.m. before letting in the clutch and we then used 5,000 r.p.m. in the gears when power began to drop off noticeably, although the engine sounded perfectly at ease.

Although the petrol consumption can be fairly heavy, probably between our overall figure at 17.8 and our touring figure of 21.7 m.p.g., much of this is offset by a readiness to run on mixture grade petrol, an equivalent saving of nearly 2 m.p.g. over super premium.

Transmission

One doesn't really need close ratio gears with such a flat power curve for most normal motoring, but for the man in a hurry their choice is first class. With a first gear capable of about 50 m.p.h. a lazy change from first to top is the town normal. Thereafter it is unnecessary to change down except for the tightest corners, when a surfeit of power can easily save a lot of steering. With a bit of gentle clutch slip one can even start in third.

The gear lever sits solidly and conveniently on the wide transmission tunnel. Synchromesh on all four ratios is absolutely unbeatable and obstructs the change until it is synchronized, giving an erroneous impression of heaviness when in fact it can be almost a two finger affair if a bit of patience is used, together with some throttle to prevent the revs dropping too far. At high speeds the centrifugally assisted clutch becomes noticeably heavier, but this is a very good compromise of lightness for traffic use with good gripping for hard work.

The lower ratios, particularly first, produce some noise and there is some back axle whine noticeable only at steady speeds up to 60 m.p.h. or so, but it is unnoticeable as soon as any load in transmitted. An easy start was made on the 1 in 3 hill.

Handling and Brakes

The first impression gained in car park manoeuvring is the surprising lightness of the steering. For the Tiger a rack-and-pinion system has replaced the Alpine's rather complicated steering layout, partly as a space saver and partly for the known advantages of sensitivity and no lost mechanical effort. In fact, it is almost too sensitive with considerable kick-back and chatter on bumpy roads; there seems to be a case for a hydraulic steering damper which would not detract from the present virtues of easy accurate placing and the ability to sense the need for correction almost before it is required.

Initial understeer (accentuated by almost parallel steering arms) changes progressively and controllably to final oversteer, the degree of which depends on throttle position. Much of the credit for such good manners—equally good in the wet—must go to the Dunlop RS5s. There is no tyre squeal except for the curious noise on ridged concrete roads. If tail sliding does occur through too sudden use of throttle the car comes straight as soon as the throttle is eased and the steering straightened, or if a corner is entered too quickly on a trailing throttle astute acceleration will restore control. In fact you can put the car at almost incredible angles to the direction of travel and still regain control, which we noticed particularly in snow.

If the tyres are left at their high speed pressures of 32 lbs./sq.in., the car feels considerably less sure-footed on rough roads and tends to get wheel patter at either or both ends in a very tiresome manner; with the pressures reduced to the normal 26 lbs./sq.in. the result is much more tolerable—bumps are still noticeable but not noise-provoking. Fast take-offs in the wet can also provoke tremendous axle tramp but in the dry the RS5s grip so well that this does not happen—so well, in fact, that we wrongly suspected a limited slip differential.

A further contribution to the well balanced feel of the

Continued on the next page

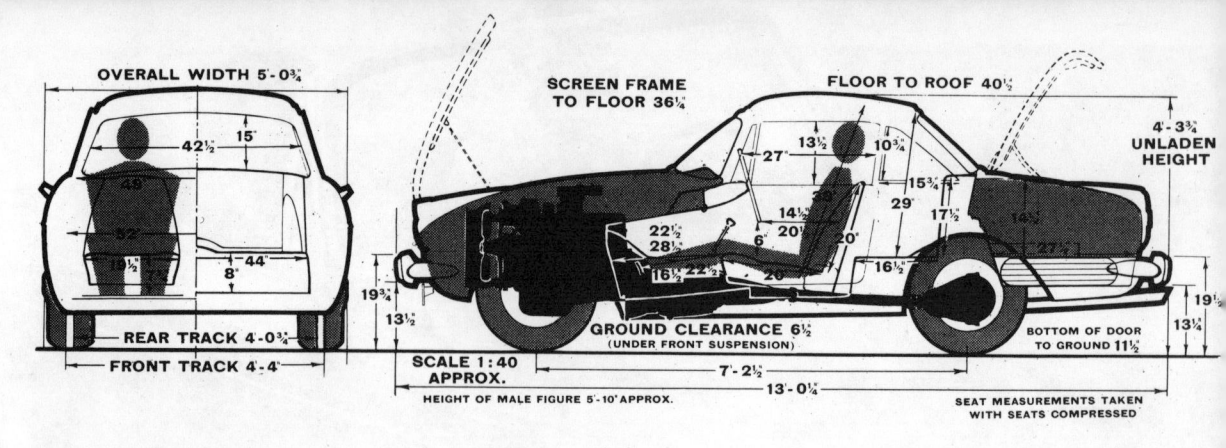

handling must come from the strong front anti-roll bar which confers considerable roll stiffness without too much understeer.

Although the servo-assisted brakes are heavy by modern standards at 130 lbs. for a maximum 1g stop, they do not feel out of place in a masculine sports car. Our 20 stops from 73 m.p.h. fade test produced some smell and squeal towards the end with a 15 lb. pressure rise, but there was no loss of confidence. Two trips through the water splash made no apparent difference.

Comfort and Control

On good roads the tremendously confident handling complements the pleasantly firm ride. Bad roads do upset the ride, but they have to be very bad before this unbalances one's impression of the car.

The seats are excellent with very good side support and most sizes could find the right fore and aft position; the steering column adjustment is a useful addition although its tendency to foul people's knees could be eliminated with a raised column or a smaller wheel, and the driving position made that much better. Large closely spaced pedals are well placed for heel and toe operations. The handbrake on the right is easy to use but obstructs the window winder when it is on.

There is some draught with the hood off and noise stays at a reasonable level up to 90 m.p.h. An extra whistle appears when the wireless aerial is fully raised at this speed. So long as one does not feel inclined to listen to the radio or to converse it is easy to maintain the Tiger's 100 plus m.p.h. with either the hardtop or the flap-free soft top.

With a water mixture temperature control, the heater is not instantly adjustable and one tends to spend too much time between hot and cold before finding a satisfactory compromise for the weather, but the output is good and it demists well. With the hard top, visibility is almost as good as in an open car, with no blind spots, and the rear view mirror keeps one well informed of progress aft. With the soft top, blind spots on the rear quarters are initially worrying after the hard top's superb airiness. The lights are adequate even for this car's performance.

Fittings and Furniture

A traditional range of fully visible instruments is typical of Rootes's products; the horn ring and the headlamp flasher are particularly easy to use. The rear occasional seat is really quite unusable as such, and is more useful as carry-cot space or extra GT luggage room. Any person of above average size rubs his head against the hard or soft tops.

As sold, the Tiger soft top is remarkably well finished and reasonably simple to erect—folding it away behind the panel

1, washer reservoir. 2, petrol filter. 3, dipstick. 4, alternator. 5. coil. 6, brake fluid reservoir. 7, clutch fluid reservoir. 8, air cleaner. 9, distributor. 10. oil filter. 11, sealed cooling system expansion tank. 12, oil filler. 13, brake servo.

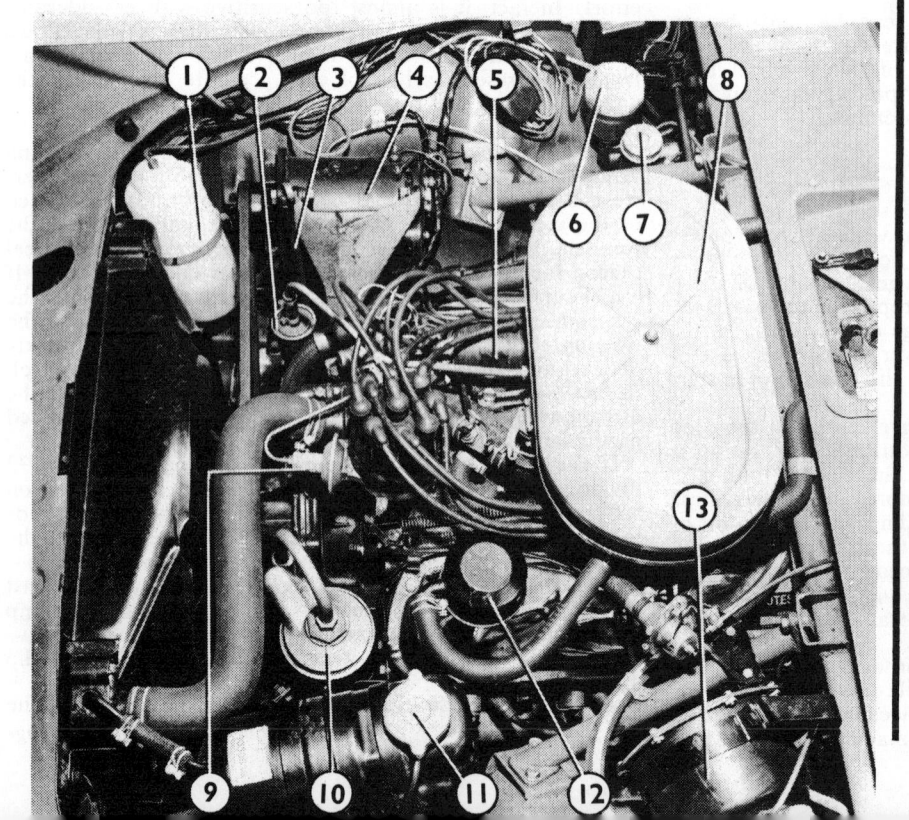

Performance

Test Data: World copyright reserved; no unauthorized reproduction in whole or in part

Conditions

Weather: Dry with variable winds, 0–30 m.p.h.
Temperature: 50°–52°F, Barometer 29.30 in Hg
Surface: Dry tarmacadam
Fuel: 97 octane

Maximum speeds

	m.p.h.
Mean of opposite runs	116.4
Best one way ¼-mile	117.5
3rd gear	91
2nd gear at 5,000 r.p.m.	70
1st gear	50
"Maximile" Speed: (Timed quarter mile after 1 mile accelerating from rest)	
Mean	111.1
Best	111.1

Acceleration times

m.p.h.	sec.
0–30	3.7
0–40	5.1
0–50	6.8
0–60	9.4
0–70	12.5
0–80	17.1
0–90	22.6
0–100	30.6
Standing quarter mile	17.4

The left pile (4.3 cu.ft) fits in the boot and the right (3.4 cu.ft) goes easily behind the seats without obstructing the view rearwards. Tools, spare wheel and battery are under the flat floor which is retained by two Dzus fasteners (undone with a halfpenny).

Semi-bucket seats have a good range of adjustment. The space behind is better used for luggage than people.

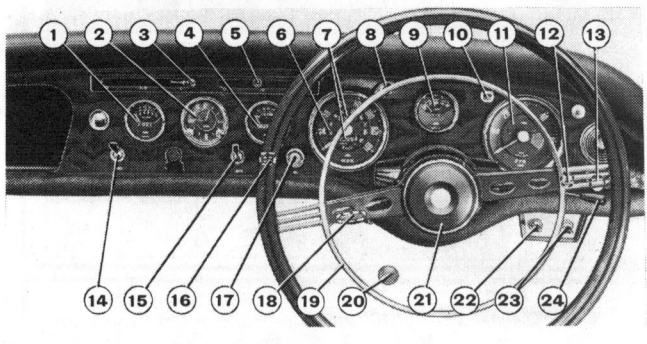

1, fuel gauge. 2, clock. 3, heater temperature control. 4, water temperature gauge. 5, heater direction control. 6, speedometer. 7, trip and total mileage recorders. 8, indicator warning light. 9, oil pressure gauge. 10, main beam tell-tale. 11, rev. counter. 12, wipers. 13, windscreen washer. 14, panel light. 15, lights. 16, ignition warning light. 17, ignition/starter switch. 18, bonnet release. 19, horn ring. 20, dip switch. 21, steering column adjustment. 22, fog light. 23, spot light. 24, indicator arm/flasher.

in the rear compartment takes considerably more practice. The hardtop is held with four over centre clips and requires two people to remove it since it is too large, though not too heavy, for one man's arm span. Although no lid is provided for the facia glove locker, the central arm rest holds a useful lockable box.

In the boot there is reasonable space—not so much as the Alpine because of its larger spare wheel and battery; both are concealed under the flat floor, with the neatly clipped jack, wheel brace and nominal tool roll.

Safety belts (listed extras) were provided in the test car. Otherwise safety considerations were confined to liberal padding—along the facia top and bottom; the mirror edge is framed and the sun visors are soft. Perhaps the greatest safety factor is the ability to accelerate quickly out of any trouble whatever gear you happen to be in.

Continued on the next page

m.p.h.	Top sec.	3rd sec.
10-30	—	5.0
20-40	6.1	4.6
30-50	5.5	4.4
40-60	6.1	4.9
50-70	7.0	5.4
60-80	8.0	6.8
70-90	9.1	10.0
80-100	13.2	—

Brakes
Pedal pressure, deceleration and equivalent stopping distance from 30 m.p.h.

lb.	g	ft.
25	.26	115
50	.52	58
75	.74	40½
100	.94	32
130	1.00	30
Handbrake	.42	71

Fade
TEST 1. 20 stops at ½g deceleration at 1 min. intervals from a speed midway between 30 m.p.h. and max. speed (= 73 m.p.h.)

	lb.
Pedal force at beginning	45
Pedal force at 10th stop	55
Pedal force at 20th	60

Clutch
Free pedal movement . . . . . = ½ in.
Additional movement to disengage clutch completely . . . . . = 3½ in.
Maximum pedal load . . . . . = 45 lb.

Hill climbing
At steady speed   lb./ton
Top   1 in 5.8   (Tapley 380)
3rd   1 in 4.4   (Tapley 500)
2nd   1 in 3.3   (Tapley 645)

Fuel consumption
m.p.g.
Touring (consumption midway between 30 m.p.h. and maximum, less 5% for acceleration) 21.7
Overall 17.8
= 15.9 litres/100 k.m.
Total test distance . . . . . 3,455 miles
Fuel tank capacity (maker's figure) . 11¼ gal.

Steering
Turning circle between kerbs: ft.
Left 34½
Right 36½
Turns of steering wheel from lock to lock . 3.2
Steering wheel deflection for 50 ft. diameter circle = 1.0 turns

Speedometer
Indicated	10	20	30	40	50	60
True	10	20	30	40	49½	59
Indicated	70	80	90	100	110	
True	68	78	87	96	105	

Distance recorder . . . . . ½% slow

Weight
Kerb weight (unladen with fuel for approximately 50 miles) . . . . 23.1 cwt.
Front/rear distribution 52½/47½
Weight laden as tested . . . . . 26.8 cwt.

Parkability
Gap needed to clear a 6 ft. obstruction parked in front

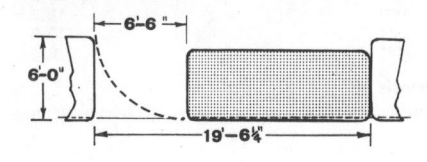

How they run...

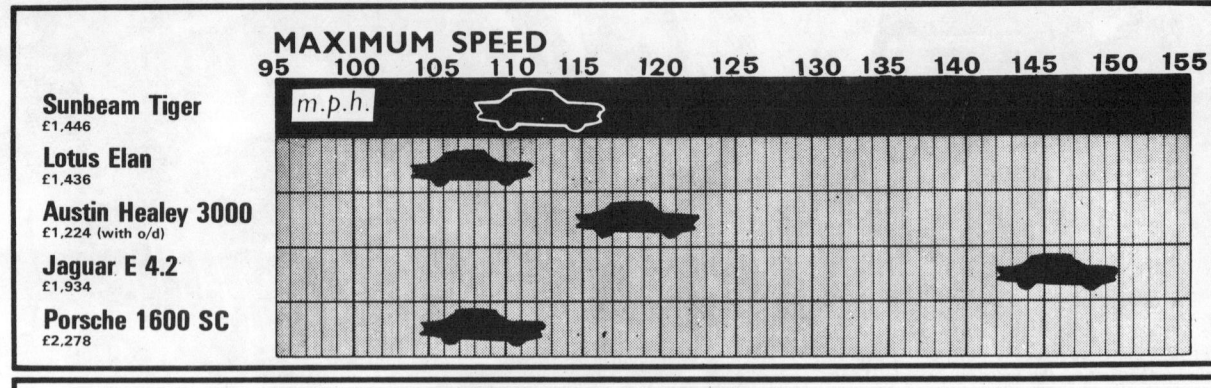

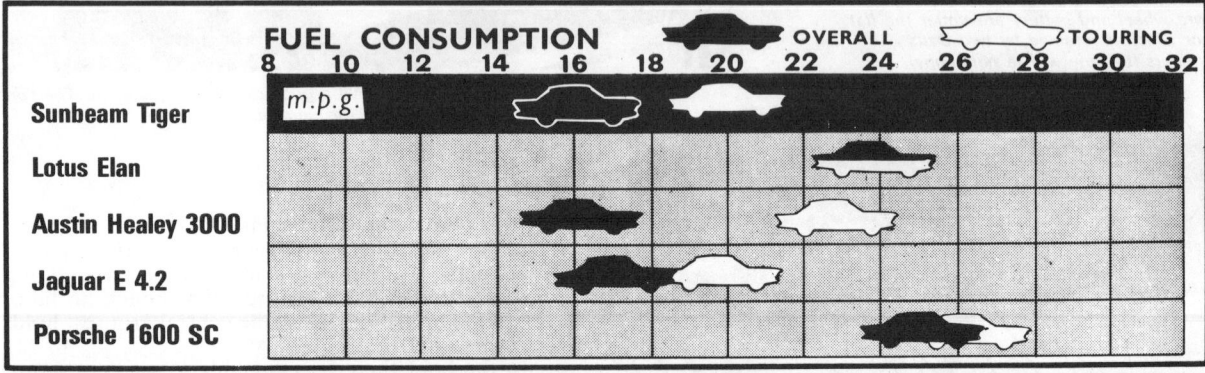

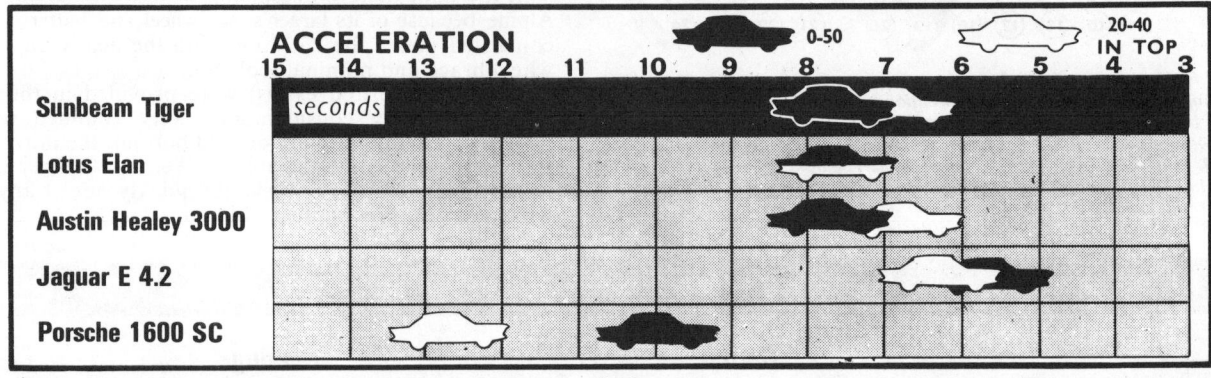

MAXIMUM SPEED (m.p.h.)

Car	Price	Max Speed
Sunbeam Tiger	£1,446	~112
Lotus Elan	£1,436	~105
Austin Healey 3000	£1,224 (with o/d)	~120
Jaguar E 4.2	£1,934	~145
Porsche 1600 SC	£2,278	~107

FUEL CONSUMPTION (m.p.g.) — ■ Overall / ☐ Touring

Car	Overall	Touring
Sunbeam Tiger	~17	~21
Lotus Elan	—	~25
Austin Healey 3000	~16	~23
Jaguar E 4.2	~18	~22
Porsche 1600 SC	~26	~28

ACCELERATION (seconds) — ■ 0–50 / ☐ 20–40 in top

Car	0–50	20–40 in top
Sunbeam Tiger	~7	~6
Lotus Elan	~7	—
Austin Healey 3000	~7	~7
Jaguar E 4.2	~6	~5
Porsche 1600 SC	~9	~13

MAKE Sunbeam: TYPE Tiger: MAKER Sunbeam Talbot Ltd., Ryton-on-Dunsmore, Coventry

Engine
- Cylinders . . . V-8
- Bore and stroke . . . 96.5 mm x 73 mm
- Cubic capacity . . . 4,261 c.c.
- Valves . . . pushrod o.h.v.
- Compression ratio . . . 8.8 : 1
- Carburetter . . . Ford 2 choke
- Fuel pump . . . SU electric
- Oil filter . . . Ford full-flow
- Max. power (net) . . . 141 b.h.p. at 4,400 r.p.m.
- Max. torque (net) . . . 258 lb. ft. at 2,200 r.p.m.

Transmission
- Clutch . . . 10 in. dia. s.d.p. centrifugally assisted
- Top gear (s/m) . . . 1.00
- 3rd gear (s/m) . . . 1.29
- 2nd gear (s/m) . . . 1.69
- 1st gear (s/m) . . . 2.36
- Reverse . . . 2.36
- Final drive . . . Hypoid bevel 2.88 : 1
- M.p.h. at 1,000 r.p.m. in:—
  - Top gear . . . 23.5
  - 3rd gear . . . 18.2
  - 2nd gear . . . 13.9
  - 1st gear . . . 9.9

Chassis
- Construction . . . Steel platform

Brakes
- Type . . . Girling hydraulic disc/drum with vacuum servo
- Dimensions . . . 9.85 in. dia. discs. 9 in. dia. drums
- Total swept area . . . 295 sq. in.

Suspension and steering
- Front . . . Independent with wishbones and coil springs. Anti-roll bar
- Rear . . . Live axle with semi-elliptic leaf springs
- Shock absorbers:
  - Front } . . . Armstrong telescopic
  - Rear }
- Steering gear . . . E.P. rack and pinion
- Tyres . . . Dunlop RS5 5.90—13

Coachwork and equipment
- Starting handle . . . None
- Jack . . . Mechanical pillar
- Jacking points . . . 4 corner sockets
- Battery . . . Below boot floor. 12v. 67 amp.-hr. Negative earth
- Number of electrical fuses . . . 2
- Indicators . . . Self-cancelling flashers
- Screen wipers . . . Self parking, two speed
- Screen washers . . . Manual plunger
- Sun visors . . . Two
- Locks:
  - With ignition key . . . Either door
  - With other keys . . . Boot lid and glove locker
- Interior heater . . . Fresh air
- Extras . . . Hardtop, whitewall tyres, tonneau cover, and range of Rootes accessories
- Upholstery . . . P.V.C.
- Floor covering . . . Carpet
- Alternative body types . . . None

Maintenance
- Sump . . . 8½ pints S.A.E. 10W/30
- Gearbox . . . 3¼ pints S.A.E. 80EP
- Rear axle . . . 2½ pints S.A.E. 90EP
- Steering gear . . . 90EP
- Cooling system . . . 27 pints (3 drain taps)
- Chassis lubrication . . . No greasing points
- Ignition timing . . . 6° b.t.d.c.
- Contact breaker gap . . . .015 in.
- Sparking plug type . . . Autolite BF42
- Sparking plug gap 032/.036
- Tappet clearances . . . hydraulic
- Front wheel toe-in . . . 125 in.
- Castor angle . . . 4° 40′
- Tyre pressures . . . 26 lbs. sq. in. front and rear up to 110 m.p.h. 32 lbs. sq. in. front and rear over 110 m.p.h.

SUNBEAM UNLEASH THE TIGER

V8
4·2 litre engine
0-60 m.p.h. in 9·2 secs
top speed over 120 m.p.h.

At last! Powerful performance and placid personality in one car – the Sunbeam Tiger, now available to discerning drivers who appreciate ease of driving with fantastic acceleration, road holding and handling. 164 bhp project the Tiger from 0-60 mph in 9·2 seconds with a top speed above 120 mph. Spur this performance through 4 well-chosen gears; or pad along knowing there's power enough for top gear acceleration from 20 mph. Add firm suspension, extremely good fuel economy, rack-and-pinion steering, servo-assisted brakes with front discs, plus fully-adjustable seats, walnut facia and full instrumentation and you've got the supreme sports car for race track, rally circuit, motorway or town traffic. £1,445.10.5 inc £250.10.5 pt.

BY APPOINTMENT TO
HER MAJESTY THE QUEEN
MOTOR VEHICLE
MANUFACTURERS
ROOTES MOTORS LIMITED

ROOTES MOTORS LIMITED

LONDON SHOWROOMS AND EXPORT
DIVISION ROOTES LIMITED DEVONSHIRE
HOUSE PICCADILLY LONDON W1

SUNBEAM TIGER'S RECORD TO DATE...

1965 Monte Carlo Rally
1st and 2nd Over 2,500 cc GT Class   4th Overall

1964 Geneva Rally   1st 2nd 3rd   Over 2,500 cc GT Class.

1964 Pacific Divisional Championships
1st in Class 'B' production event.

1964 US 200-Mile National Sports Car Race
1st in Class   2nd overall

Also Dutch National 24-hour Speed Record   February 9th, 1965.

SUNBEAM TIGER

SUNBEAM TIGER

We put Karen Snow, who normally campaigns cars of the AH Sprite Class behind the wheel of our test Tiger for a time trial in New Jersey. As luck would have it there were no other cars competing in the Tiger's class and she found herself running against Jag XKE's and Corvettes. An XKE took first in class but Karen beat out several Corvettes for a clean fifth place.

PHOTOS BY JIM GRAY AND THE EDITOR

This Ford V-8 engine puts out 164 HP stock, can go to over 200 with special tuning kits.

▶ Mmmmmmmmm, Boy! There is just no substitute for cubes! This was the reaction of one of the fellows here in the office to the Sunbeam Tiger. We had given it perhaps just a bit too much accelerator going away from a stop light and pinned him back against the passenger seat. While, unlike the dragster coterie, we don't adhere to this particular axiom there is no denying that 260 cubic inches powering a 2500 pound car makes for snappy performance all the way down the pike. We can only think of the Sunbeam Tiger as a sanforized Cobra.

Now, we are aware that driving to the supermarket in an automobile like this just does not give you any idea of its potential. We looked around for someone who does a little more than just drive to the nursery school and chose Karen Snow to make sure we were not overly enthusiastic about the car for reasons of our own. Karen races a Sprite and does it well. We allowed her to run it in a time trial, hovering close to her all day to pick up her impressions.

Alpines she had seen and even driven so the exterior was not particularly new to her. She was more than pleased with the interior especially the seating. She had no trouble reaching the pedals, found driving easy with "no steering wheel in the chest" and "thoroughly enjoyed hopping easily in to the car without the usual necessary contortions I'm accustomed to."

Several things contribute to this: the door opens wide, and the bucket seats seem almost to wrap around you once you sit down. Support for the thigh is excellent and the gear shift lever is positioned so that a minimum of effort is required and absolute no reaching entailed. As Karen put it, "No lunge into 3rd gear."

We keep drifting back to that power pack, though, because it was the most impressive facet of this Rootes offering. Although a trip through the gears is as smooth as

The same Tiger on display at the Bridgehampton races. Most deceptive in exterior in appearance, that front hood houses a 260 cu. in. Ford V-8 engine and we found the acceleration, in any gear, just short of incredible.

Karen tapes on racing numerals prior to her runs through the traps.

ABOVE: "I must admit," Karen says, "to this being one of the rare occasions when my 5'3" person really fit comfortably in a car. No straining to depress the clutch pedal, no steering wheel in the chest, no lunge into 3rd gear. Great!" LEFT: Two shots of the trunk. Karen sits in space where spare is stored flat under cover shown at left.

109

SUNBEAM TIGER

Tiger has independent suspension with coil springs up front, semi-elliptic leaves in back and telescopic shocks all around. Steering is rack and pinion.

RIGHT: Karen moves up to start for first run. Course was loose dirt and gravel, but dry. (See photos immediately right of this one.)

silk, the car goes forward as if it were being kicked in the rear. This forward thrust is accompanied with a barely audible engine "thrummm" delightful to hear and most deceptive to anyone waiting beside you at a red light, secure in the misguided knowledge that they can "dust you off" when the green comes up. With the Tiger, you go away from them permanently! None of this business about catching you in the long haul!

Karen felt that the power was a bit excessive for the car's handling ability, at least in the street job. We don't quite agree, considering the restrictions placed on you by the legal limits to which you normally adhere on our roads and streets. In spite of what we regard as a BIG engine up front, the car steers quite well, with independent front wheel suspension well beefed up for the extra weight and rack and pinion steering. Take a good look at the phantom view accompanying this story. Although the springing is with coils up front, the rear is semi-elliptic but you can actually see in this photo just how well it was all arranged. The ride is excellent overall with a stability we honestly enjoyed.

The dashboard is nicely designed with a full compliment of instruments, padded for safety with this padding encompassing the passenger grab rail. There is an air of luxury permeating the Tiger backed up by solid performance (Rootes claims it will cruise at 115 miles per hour). With a price around $3500 the Tiger should appeal to "the young in heart" who like performance in the Jag XKE and Corvette category but must buy with a budget in mind.

This, of course, is not a car that you would expect to read about in P.I.C. primarily because one doesn't think about it in terms of economy. We feel, though, that when the Sunbeam Imp and Sports sedans have relatives lige the Tiger, one cannot ignore it. There are several imports these days that sell for three to six hundred dollars more than the Tiger and we think that prospective buyers will take this into consideration when they go shopping for "powered" sports cars.

LEFT: Here she comes flying down last straight. BELOW: Tiger shows little lean as Karen goes into series of full lock turns at speed. Panhard stabilizer bar is used to improve handling.

Still cornering hard, she follows flagman's directions to complete full, tight circle. Here, she felt steering was a bit slow, but not sloppy.

Around the pylons once more before a drive to the finish with mandatory full braking after passing timer. Karen reported brakes excellent, transmission quick, positive.

SUNBEAM TIGER

A most appealing high-performance machine from Rootes

By GREGOR GRANT

When it was learned that Carroll Shelby, inspired by Ian Garrad of the U.S.A. section of the Rootes Group, had installed a V8 Ford engine in an Alpine chassis, people naturally thought that Rootes were on the verge of producing a hairy sports car in the Cobra tradition. This impression was carried a stage forward when the Sunbeam Tigers appeared at Le Mans, with raucous exhausts and decidedly prototype G.T. characteristics.

However, when fully equipped road versions were entered in the 1964 Geneva Rally, they had begun to look far more civilized vehicles than the Le Mans cars. In the 1965 Monte, they were very efficient looking and the Peter Harper/Ian Hall car finished fourth overall.

Now the Sunbeam Tiger 260 has gone into production, and an extremely pleasant motor car it turns out to be. It is no rip-snorting sports car, but a most appealing high-performance machine, with admirable flexibility and commendable silence. Top gear performance is exceptionally good and it will apparently cruise at over 100 m.p.h. on the motorways for ever. Having owned Alpines, the difference between a four-cylinder and an eight-cylinder engine struck me as being similar to a prop-engined and a jet-propelled aeroplane, in smoothness and "hit-in-the-back" take-off!

The Tiger is a very stable machine, completely unaffected by side winds at all speeds. It is only when roads are bumpy that a certain amount of skittishness takes place—especially on fast bends, which on average smooth surfaces can otherwise be taken very rapidly indeed.

On sharpish corners the Tiger is not quite so happy and one must think in terms of *doucement* when applying power in the lower ratios. In John Bolster's view: "Sudden axle tramp may cause total rear-end breakaway and there is evidence of roll-steering of the rear axle, in an understeering sense, which may cause the car to veer to the left when going suddenly on to the over-run."

It was discovered early on that "racing" starts produced pronounced axle tramp and that the ideal method of driving the car was to trickle off, and then to take full advantage of the immense torque of the V8 engine. In other words, the rigid axle employed is eminently satisfactory for sensible driving, but will react somewhat viciously if harsh methods are employed.

Otherwise there are no obvious criticisms of a car which is so much better than the four-cylinder Alpines that it is doubtful whether or not the latter will continue to be sold in any

the use of minimum 93 octane fuel.

Undoubtedly Rootes really have got something in the Tiger, and one must suppose that the next step will be to examine the possibilities of i.r.s.—at least before the rumoured 4.7 is offered as an alternative.

In the U.S.A. road conditions should be ideal for the Sunbeam Tiger. The appearance will appeal to prospective purchasers, particularly as other road-users will believe that they are coming up against a standard Alpine. How surprised Grannie and her Cadillac will be when the Tiger rushes off into the distance!

Anyway, I was so impressed with the Tiger that I have just acquired a hard top version!

SPECIFICATION AND PERFORMANCE DATA

Engine: V8, 96.5 x 73 mm. (4,261 c.c.); o.h.v. (push-rod); 164 b.h.p. at 4,400 r.p.m.; 8.8 to 1 c.r.; double-choke Carter carburetter; pump-assisted, centrifugal cooling.

Transmission: Single dry-plate 10 ins. clutch; hypoid rear axle; four-speed all-synchromesh gearbox; ratios 2.88, 3.715, 4.867 and 6.88 to 1. Reverse, 6.68.

Suspension: Independent front, with helical springs and wishbones, enclosed telescopic dampers; semi-elliptic rear direct acting dampers; Panhard stabilizer rod.

General: Rack-and-pinion (greaseless) steering; telescopic wood-rim steering wheel; Girling 9.85 ins. disc brakes (front), 9 ins. drums (rear), Servo assistance; 5.50 x 13 ins. (tubed) Dunlop RS5 tyres; pressed steel wheels; 11½-gallon rear petrol tank, with quick-release filler cap, SU petrol pump; 12-volt electrical and ignition equipment; heater-cum-ventilator; two-speed wipers; speedometer with trip recorder; r.p.m. counter; oil pressure, water temperature and petrol gauges; anchorages for safety harnesses.

Dimensions, etc.: Length, 13 ft. 0 ins.; height, 4 ft. 3½ ins.; width, 5 ft. 0½ ins.; wheelbase, 7 ft. 2 ins; turning circle, 36½ ft. (right), 34½ ft. (left); weight, as tested, 26 cwt. 4 lb.

Performance: Maximum speed (mean), 116.8 m.p.h. Speeds in gears: first, 50 m.p.h.; second, 69 m.p.h.; third, 90 m.p.h. Acceleration: 0-30 m.p.h., 3 secs.; 0-50 m.p.h., 5.6 secs.; 0-60 m.p.h., 7.6 secs.; 0-80 m.p.h., 13.8 secs.; 0-100 m.p.h., 25.2 secs. Petrol consumption (overall), 21.2 m.p.g. Speedometer errors (correct figures in parentheses): 30 m.p.h. (30); 50 m.p.h. (50); 60 m.p.h. (58); 80 m.p.h. (76); 90 m.p.h. (83); 100 m.p.h. (90).

Extra equipment available: Hard-top; tonneau cover; radio, clock, cigar lighter, safety belts.

Makers: Sunbeam-Talbot, Ltd., Ryton-on-Dunsmore, Coventry.

Price: £1,445 10s. 5d. (incl. £250 10s. 5d. P.T.).

---

considerable quantity. Value for value, the Tiger offers comfort, good appearance, adequate general handling, excellent brakes, smoothness and silence, a most efficient four-speed all-synchromesh gearbox and comprehensive equipment.

The highest praise must be given to the all-weather equipment on the model tested. With hood erected, there were no rattles, no draughts, and it was completely water-tight in the heaviest of rain. A hard-top is also available and is similar to that offered on the Alpine. By installing the spare wheel under the luggage platform, a fairly roomy boot has been obtained.

All-in-all, it is a very handsome car, well-planned and what is more important nowadays, immaculately finished, both inside and outside.

As regards technical specification, the data panel includes all necessary information. When taking figures on the car originally, it was believed that a 4.7-litre engine had been installed, in place of the standard 4.2. Some remarkable figures were obtained, but this was found to be due to inaccurate stop-watches, due to go back for checking.

Anyway John Bolster took over using more accurate equipment, and the figures were more consistent with those anticipated with the given power-output, weight and axle ratio. The speedometer was accurate up to 50 m.p.h., 2 m.p.h. fast at 60, 4 at 80, 7 at 90 and 10 at 100. All performance figures were taken with the tachometer needle just entering the "red"—around 4,800 r.p.m.

Mean maximum speed was 116.8 m.p.h., and the standing quarter took just 16.6 secs. From standstill to 100 m.p.h. occupied 25.2 secs., with the Tiger still accelerating. For a 4.2 litre car, the engine is anything but thirsty, and overall consumption (mainly B.P. Super Plus) worked out at 21.2 m.p.g. The makers themselves recommend

ACCELERATION GRAPH

SUNBEAM TIGER — MAX. SPEED 116.8 M.P.H.

113

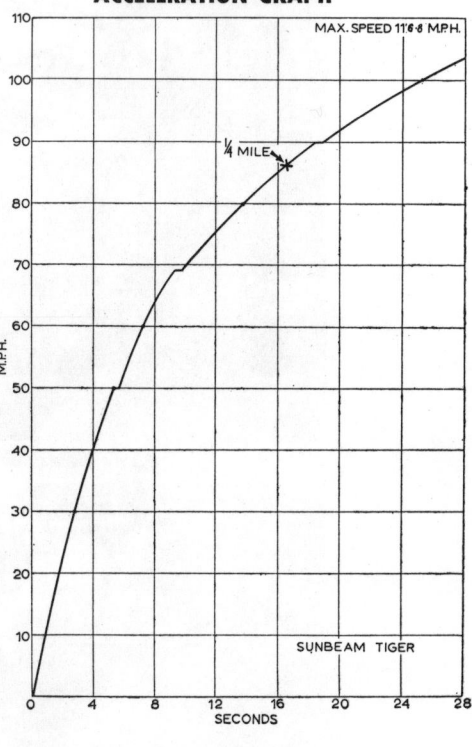

TIGERS CAN BE TAMED

BELOW: Oil check for the works rally Tiger Doug drove to Geneva. Seven headlamps turned night into day, but dipping wasn't easy. BOTTOM PHOTO: Journey's end. Note de-icing panel in back window, extra spare mounted on the boot.

Sunbeam Tiger V8s will so

EVER since its introduction at the 1964 New York motor show, the Sunbeam Tiger V8 had been working solely for the Yankee dollar. In March this year, however, Rootes decided to remove the "U.S.A. only" tag and make their top glamor sports car available elsewhere.

"Elsewhere," they told me, would include Australia — and the Tigers would be released there in a matter of weeks. So I asked how soon I could have a car to trip-test for **Modern Motor**.

The request couldn't have come at a better time. The Geneva Salon was coming up, and Rootes wanted to exhibit the Tiger which Peter Harper drove into fourth place in this year's Monte Carlo Rally. Would I like to drive it over for them?

That's how I came to be standing at Lydd Airport one bitterly cold

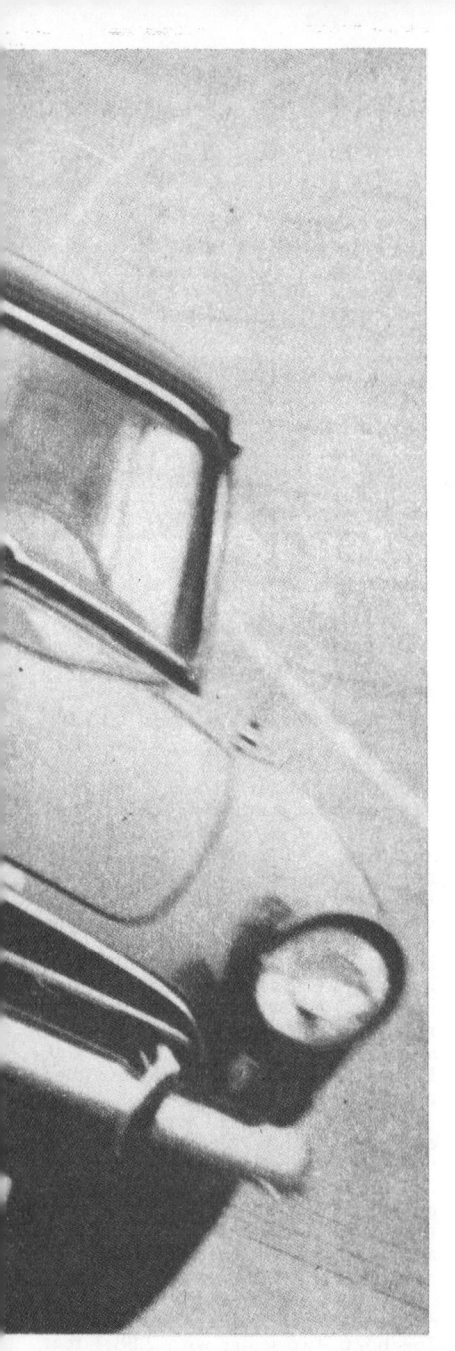

LEFT: Sunbeam Tiger under test. Maximum with stock-standard engine and gearing is 141 m.p.h., but rally cars are geared down to gain acceleration.

RIGHT: More instruments and controls than a Lancaster — all meant to be used. Floor shift works a Ford 4-speed box.

BELOW: 4.2-litre V8 with four-choke carby fits tightly into engine bay. It develops 164 b.h.p. in standard form.

e sold in Australia. Doug Armstrong has trip-tested one, tells you all about them

morning in March, waiting while the crew of the Bristol Airfreighter warmed up its engines.

My companion for the trip was Rootes P.R. man Gethin Bradley. As we waited, he filled me in on the details of the car I was about to drive.

The Sunbeam Tiger was developed from a most unlikely beginning—the underbody of the plodding, unglamorous Hillman Husky, which Rootes used as the basis for the 88 b.h.p., 100 m.p.h. Sunbeam Alpine sports car, introduced in 1959.

Then American high-performance machinery expert Carroll Shelby was called in to take the development a stage further. He replaced the Alpine's four-cylinder engine with a 4.2-litre Ford (Fairlane) V8 coupled to a three-speed automatic transmission, beefed up the rest of the car to suit, and the result was the Sunbeam Tiger.

The late Lord Rootes liked Shelby's prototype and approved it for production, except that he had the automatic drive replaced by a four-speed manual gearbox. This was before Rootes allied themselves with Chrysler — but the Ford V8 suits the car so well that it's expected to be retained.

The standard Tiger puts out 164 b.h.p. at 4400 r.p.m., and a staggering 258 ft./lb. of torque at a mere 2200. Final-drive ratio is 2.88:1, producing 23.5 m.p.h. per 1000 revs in top gear — a theoretical maximum of 141 m.p.h., since the car's rev-counter is red-lined at 6000.

Acceleration isn't lacking, as you can imagine; but Rootes' Competitions Department wanted even more get-up-and-go for the rally, so the two cars prepared for it were modified accordingly.

The 4.2-litre lightweight Ford V8s were fitted with "Cobra kit" camshafts, heads and valves from Ford's 4.7-litre unit, plus enlarged and polished ports, heavy-duty valve springs and screwed-in rocker posts. Using a four-choke Holley carburettor in place of the standard two-choke, the rally engine gave around 200 b.h.p., and with 3.77:1 final-drive and Salisbury Powr-Lok diff it was quite a bomb—but a controllable one.

The new torque figure was never worked out — but although the diff ratio on Harper's Tiger was changed to 3.54:1 for our Geneva trip, there was still enough hurry-up left to snap your head back when accelerating, even at 90 m.p.h.

The Channel crossing took only 18 minutes — but the hour's difference

115

SUNBEAM TIGER

between Continental and British "winter time" meant it was 11.30 a.m. when we finally set out from Le Touquet, with 400 miles to cover to our night stop at Arbois, in France's Jura Mountains.

Peter Harper, who took this particular car to a class victory in the Monte, is an ex-R.A.F. pilot. After driving the Tiger for a couple of miles, I didn't think he could be anything else. The cockpit had more instruments than a Lancaster, and there was full safety harness for "pilot" and crew. Bradley and I were ringed with plastic tanks and electric motors to wash and defrost our windscreens —plus another to de-ice the headlamp glasses. The boot was so full of fuel tank (25 gallons) and spare wheel there was precious little space for anything else, and there were enough iodine-vapor lights fitted to land at 140 m.p.h. To complete the illusion, this Tiger would accelerate like a VC10—providing you could reach the clutch pedal.

I wouldn't have classed Harper as a very tall man but he must be all legs. His "long-arm" driving position, with the steering wheel down to the bottom of its column adjustment, suited me fine, but the pedals were only just in reach—and that clutch pedal was good and heavy.

The 3.54 diff ratio produced 19.25 m.p.h. per 1000 revs in top, representing a permissible maximum of 115.5 m.p.h.—and I found that red line on the tacho very useful, for the needle was only too willing to hit the 6000 mark. It got there so eagerly that I thought it wiser to sit around 5500 r.p.m. on long straights, considering 106 m.p.h. quite fast enough.

What really surprised me was the flexibilty of the rally engine. Top gear would take us through town traffic without snatch or fuss and the Tiger would accelerate like mad from as low as 10 m.p.h. — still in top gear, yet with never a ping.

The weather in France was filthy, and when we emerged from a half-hour lunch stop at Peronne, it was snowing heavily — a pleasant prospect, with another 300 miles to go!

On we went through Soissons, Chateau-Thierry, Troyes, and into the Seine Valley around Chatillon. The snow stopped and the Tiger pressed on. The hard-to-reach clutch pedal was a nuisance, but it brought out the V8's fantastic low and medium-speed pulling capabilities, for I found myself changing-down only when the car had almost reached the last chonk. Under all other circumstances it would pull like a train in top.

The other side of Dijon the terrain began to gain height. The roads were in a very bad state from the winter's frosts and snows, and the surface was a mass of potholes. For a car with only 7ft. 2in. wheelbase and competition suspension, the Tiger rode the bumps well — and there were times when we hit the holes pretty fast. The simple live axle was greatly assisted by the restraining Panhard rod—standard on the Tiger.

The potholes and puddles threw plenty of dirty water over the windscreen (which had not only a Triplex heating element built-in, but two "stick-on" heaters as well), but we had all the equipment to deal with it. A touch of one switch sent a stream of water over the glass, and another switch set off a squirt of glycol for de-icing. First time I switched on the washer, I was convinced I was driving an aeroplane, for the whirr of the electric motor (18in. away beneath the rear window) sounded for all the world as though the wheels were being retracted. I'm sure there was a bank-and-turn indicator among all those instruments somewhere!

Darkness began to fall soon after Dijon, and as we had neither amber headlights (requested, but not enforced, by the French) nor right-hand dipping arrangement, we worked out a special drill.

Iodine-vapor headlights are non-dippable, so the Tiger was wired with two separate pass-lights. We twisted the pass-lights to provide dip, and this arrangement w o r k e d well, for although the lamps were white, the French drivers didn't retaliate—and, believe me, I have been nearly driven off the road by "camionistes" (French for truckies) who hadn't liked the dip of my lights!

Racing the Clock

Time was marching on, and we had a date with a wonderful dinner at the Rotisserie de la Balance in Arbois. We decided to use all the incredible array of seven headlamps, including the central iodine-vapor "tar-melter" and the smaller spots on the bumpers. The central horror and the spots were controlled by switches on the Tiger's centre armrest/console, and the head dip by conventional foot switch. We would blind along with all lights blazing, then, at a shout from me, Gethin would douse the spots and the tar-melter, and I would dip the foot switch.

After the first two operations I learned the thing to do was dip and brake at the same time, for after seven lights with three iodine-vapor units, driving on two conventional pass-lamps was almost like being left in the dark.

We made Arbois by 7.45 p.m., despite a stop for coffee and cognac, and another for fuel. The Tiger returned just over 17 m.p.g. for an on-the-road average of 55 m.p.h. and objected not at all to the French "Super" (I use the inverted commas in their most literal sense). The Balance restaurant provided food and wine that were out of this world, and we fell into bed feeling all was well with the trip.

The Tiger slept out in the freezing temperatures but was away at the first touch of the button next morning, and a check on the rapier-like dipstick showed that oil consumption was nil.

It was really freezing as we thundered away in bright sunshine and began the ascent toward Pontarlier over the Cossonay Pass. As we got higher, the ice ruts became incredibly deep; at one point, I'm quite sure the Tiger was steering itself on its twin silencers. The roads were so narrow and iced that it was impossible to stop and take photographs.

Mindful that the car had to be exhibited on the Rootes stand in Geneva, I took it very gently. It would have been a shame to bend the model after having got so far. No, it was a case of hold that Tiger — and so intent was I on taking it easy that I motored over the pass, ice, snow and all, in top gear. What a fantastic machine!

A stop at the top for one last cafe-cognac, and we began the descent, to reach the French/Swiss frontier at Vallorbe at about 10 a.m. Down into Morges (next door to Lausanne), and we took the new Lausanne-Geneva autoroute. We averaged just on 100 m.p.h. down this 38-mile motorway, the Tiger shaking off a few Alfa drivers as they sped towards the city.

At 11 a.m. we checked in at our hotels, and the surprising amount of luggage we had managed to cram into the Tiger was unloaded. By afternoon, the Tiger was sitting on its show stand for all the world to see, and Rootes' publicity manager breathed a sigh of relief.

The car had given us a safe but exciting run to Geneva and had virtually done the journey in top gear. No oil was used, fuel consumption averaged out at 17.5 m.p.g., even though we'd done a lot of climbing and had seen 6000 come up on the rev-counter several times.

A real fire-breather, yet always docile and easy to drive. The standard 164 b.h.p. two-seater with 2.88:1 rear end should be a joy.

What does the normal Tiger cost? Basic U.K. price (without tax) is £1195 stg. for the roadster, so the Australian tag should be around £2400 tax-paid — or a bit over £2500 with the hardtop.

FOOTNOTE: I can foresee two further developments for the Tiger. 1.—Its 4.2-litre V8 differs from the 4.7-litre unit only in bore size — and Shelby has been getting a reliable 365 b.h.p. from the latter. What's the betting we'll see some 4.7-litre Tigers, perhaps in this year's Le Mans 24-hour race? 2.—Rootes may well go back to Shelby's original idea and offer the option of automatic drive on the Tiger; this would be in line with their general policy, since automatic Alpines are already available.

CARS & CAR CONVERSIONS

FEATURE ROAD TEST

SUNBEAM TIGER

A TIGER THAT LEAVES ITS STRIPES ON THE ROAD

WHEN all's said and done, the Sunbeam Tiger works out at one helluva lotta car for fourteen hundred quid. There's no doubt, too, that the idea behind the car is a darned good one: you take a compact, reasonably small two-seater and stuff a dirty big Ford V8 engine in the sharp end. Which means that you've got plenty of power for performance, workable dimensions for negotiating jams in the traffic and a pretty low overall weight which means that the engine is hardly ever doing any real work—it ought to last for ever and ever, mechanically. If this sounds too near perfect, then your thinking is on the right lines. The two biggest snags are in the suspension and in the body itself: lets take the last one first. The Alpine body is set up for a maximum speed of something in the low or middle nineties, which takes a fair length of time to reach. Under these conditions its all hunky and pretty dory too. But if you change all that to a Tiger 90 miles an hour becomes a speed which you can virtually knock off in third gear, and after that, top gear gives you another thirty miles an hour. And things ain't so good —the wind noise above this speed is shattering. Motorway cruising at around the ton practically makes conversation impossible, and it is extremely wearing on driver and passenger. Then there's the suspension. Only minor changes are made in the standard Alpine layout, and you've still got the live axle and cart springs, with a Panhard rod. With the power that the Tiger's got this simply won't do, and you start wishing the makers had heard of independence—or at the very least a limited slip diff—every time a shower of rain falls. But this isn't the only trouble: on wet roads the whole car's behaviour is unusually exciting—the weight of 4.2 litres of Ford V8 engine in the front helps to promote rather strenuous understeer with

117

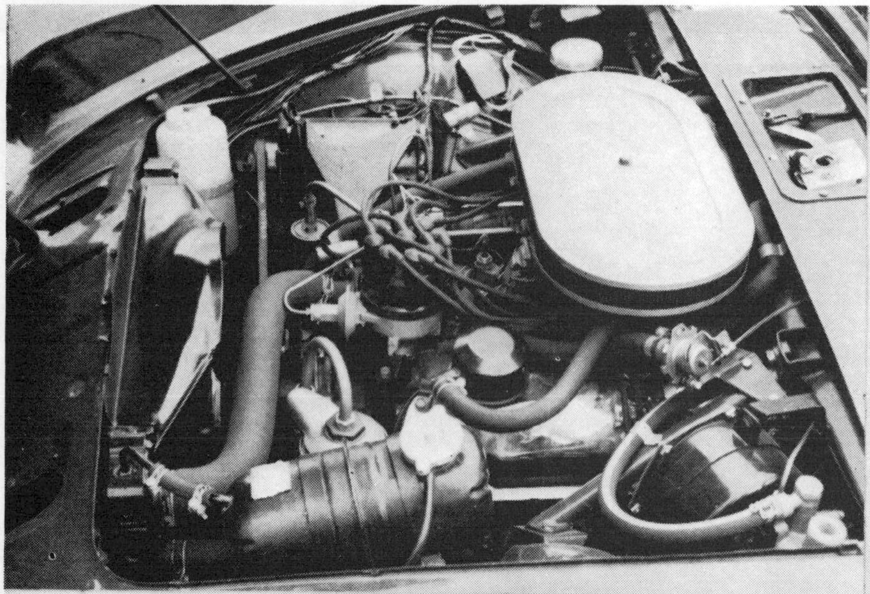

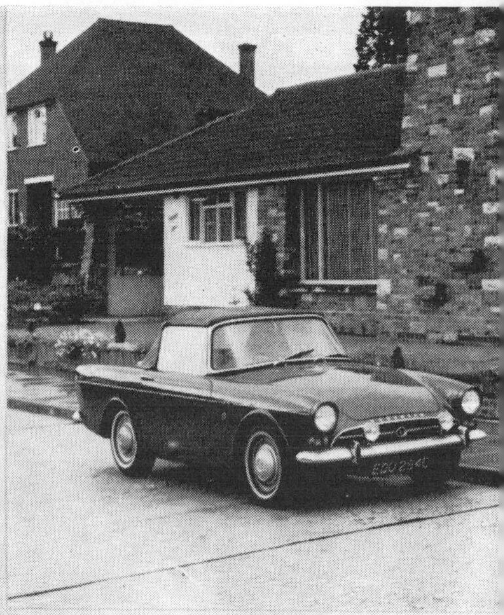

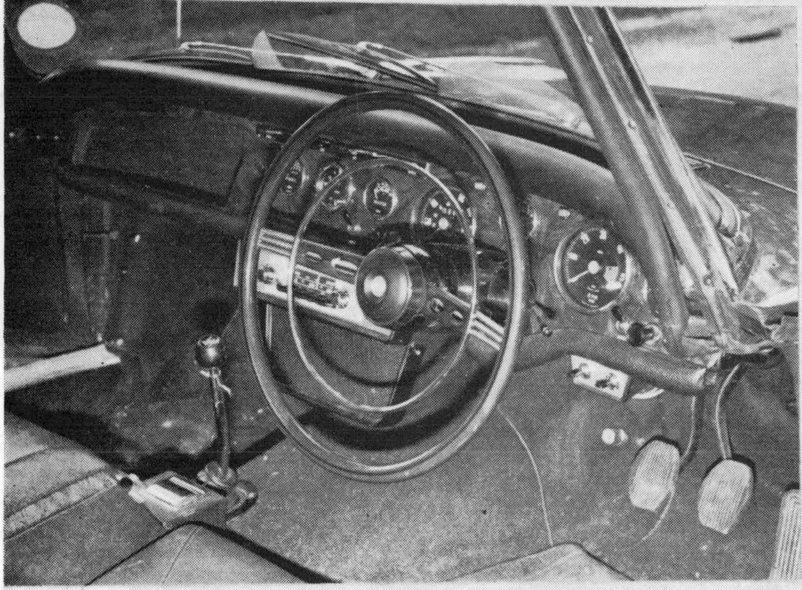

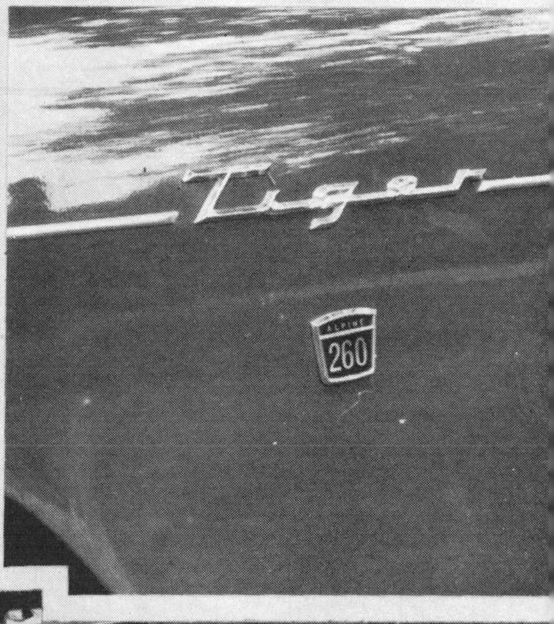
Tiger
ALPINE
260

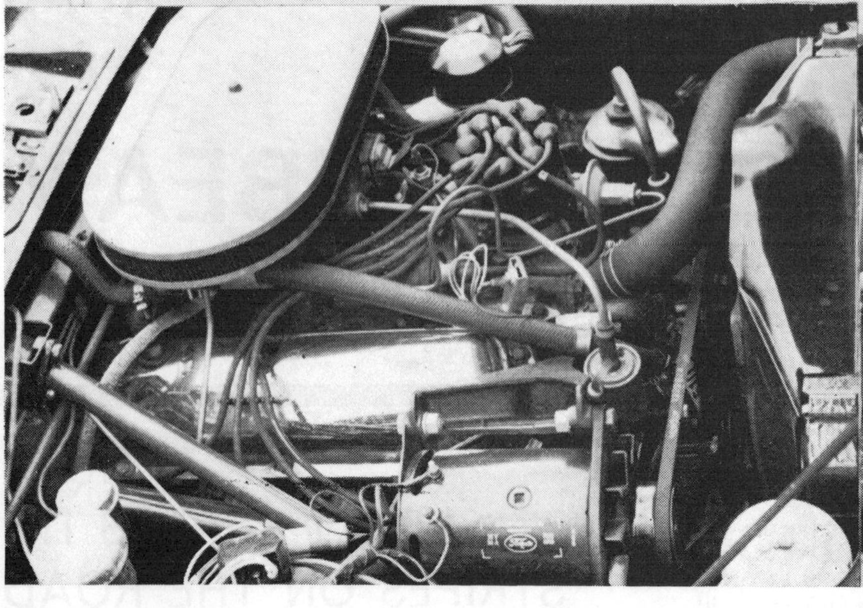

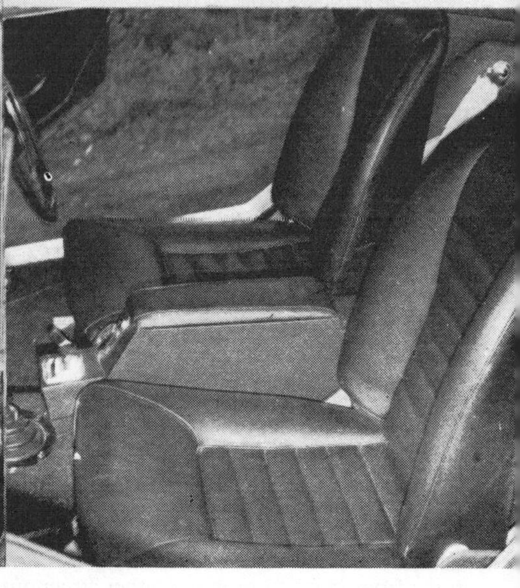

SUNBEAM TIGER

the power off, and you need to be pretty cautious the first few times you balance this with the application of the right foot. Clumsy use of the power can have the tail round to meet the front fairly easily even in the dry, and in the wet it really wants watching.

So much for the snags. On the credit side the marriage is not completely unsuccessful. The Tiger hasn't really got as much power as all that—although it sometimes feels as if it has too much—and in fact the quoted gross output is only 164 b.h.p., at the relatively low crankshaft speed of 4,400 r.p.m. But what it has got is very high torque at very low speed—the quoted figure of 258 lb. ft. (at only 2,200 r.p.m.) compares with 260 lb. ft. 4,000 r.p.m. for the much more powerful "E"-type Jaguar engine. Thus, like most American V8's, its overall feeling is one of complete effortlessness and great smoothness, with impressive urge from idling speed upwards. Mechanically it is fairly quiet, with twin exhaust pipes giving off a nice throaty burble in the best "woofly" V-manner, and of course never has to scream its head off at high revs. In an almost vintage manner the rev-counter is red-lined at 4,800 r.p.m.!

There is an automatic choke for the dual-throat carburettor, and starting is first-time always. Idling is smooth and silent, and the very short-stroke power unit is almost uncannily flexible—if the car is moving at all then top gear will do very nicely, thank-you, in the same sort of way as the Ford Mustang, although free use of the Ford gearbox will make it go and then some.

The gearbox is a four-speed unit with synchromesh on all forward gears, and the ratios, which give maximum speeds in the gears of around 50, 70 and 90 m.p.h. are almost ideally spaced. The 121 m.p.h. we got out of it for maximum speed indicates that the car isn't exactly low-geared, and the box is quiet. The change, though, is maybe a bit on the heavy side, but the lever has a short movement and hits the right cogs every time. For pedestrian motoring most of them can be dispensed with, going straight into top from second or even first in traffic. It will accelerate smoothly and strongly from ten miles an hour in top gear, which may not equate to your idea of a sports car power unit but which certainly makes life pleasanter in rush-hour traffic.

The suspension is something we've already gone on about a bit. In general layout it is the same as that of the standard Alpine, though naturally a bit beefed-up, especially at the front. The brakes, for which relief many thanks, are perfectly up to the job. The same disc front, drum rear combinations as on the Alpine is used, with a servo which results in a nice firm pedal, not too hard and not too soft for our taste. Really hard braking from maximum speed gets the pedal travel increasing a bit, and occasionally during the test we found the left front brake coming on a bit early. By and large, however, the anchors are up to the job, and the car remains perfectly steady under heavy braking from high speed.

Like all Rootes Group cars, the interior of the Tiger is very nicely fitted up. The driving position can be adjusted to suit you by means of seats with reclining back-rest, plenty of fore and aft movement, and there is an adjustable column for moving the wheel about. There is full instrumentation, with matching speedometer and rev-counter, oil pressure, fuel and water temperature gauges, an ammeter and a clock—the speedometer reads up to 140 m.p.h., by the way, which gives you plenty of scope! We rather liked the steering wheel but didn't much care for the steering, which is light but, at 3½ turns from lock to lock, a bit on the low-geared side, we felt, for so fast a car. Visibility is good except through the completely blind rear quarters on the convertible version we tested, and we thought little of the interior ventilation: on a long journey in warm weather, with the hood up, the inside of the car gets pretty warm, and there seems to be no way of getting enough cool air in from outside. The terrible wind noise at speed we mentioned earlier gets even worse if you open a window, so the only thing to do is to sit and stifle. Those quarter-lights you can see in the pictures are a rather pointless exercise in obscuring vision, by the way—they don't even open, and for that matter aren't, meant to.

Once you get used to it, the Tiger is a pretty nice car to drive for all that. The wind noise absolutely ruined its high-speed cruising potential so far as we were concerned, but at lesser speeds on twisty roads it is pretty good fun. This is definitely not the car for an inexperienced driver—you might be lucky, but we reckon harm could come to a young lad who didn't know what he was doing in the Tiger. But if you approach it with some degree of responsibility and experience it is possible to get from A to B pretty quickly without undue effort. There is vigorous acceleration from 100 m.p.h. simply as a result of pressing the loud pedal, while from a standing start the getaway, provided you can overcome the wheelspin, is pretty impressive. From a standstill, 60 m.p.h. comes up in ten seconds, and ninety in 22 seconds; while the top gear performance is outstanding among cars in the Tiger's price bracket—40-60 wants six seconds, 60 to 80 only 7½ and 70-90 less than ten, which by rapid arithmetic will tell you that if you emerge from a 40 m.p.h. speed limit zone in top gear at exactly 40 m.p.h. and simply push a bit harder on the pedal, exactly 13½ seconds will tick away before you are doing a respectable 80 m.p.h. So far as petrol goes, we got 20 to the gallon all told, which isn't bad, while very hard driving, including the taking of figures, brought this down to a worst figure of 17 m.p.g.—not really so bad for 120 plus performance.

Looking at our battered finger-nails reminds us of one further grouse—the hood. When we had the car the weather was fine, so down came the hood—and our finger-nails still bear the scars. Once you've got the thing down it stows away neatly behind and under all sorts of complicated panels, but getting it there is hell. Getting it up isn't much better, and while this sort of thing may be permissible in California, where so far as one can discover it never rains unexpectedly—if it rains at all, in lil ole England it matters—if it came on to rain while the hood was stowed the car would be full of water before you got the damn thing up again.

But still, as we said to begin with—when all's said and done, the Sunbeam Tiger is a helluva lotta car for the money.

This should be your most familiar view of the Tiger. If it's not he isn't trying, or you are.

Cars on Test

SUNBEAM TIGER

Engine: V8-cylinder, 96·5 mm. × 73 mm.; 4,261 c.c.; pushrod-operated o.h.v.; compression ratio 8·8 to 1; twin-choke carburettor; 164 b.h.p. at 4,400 r.p.m.
Transmission: Four-speed and reverse gearbox, synchromesh on all forward gears with floor-mounted central gearlever.
Suspension: Front, independent, with coil springs and wishbones; anti-roll bar and telescopic shock absorbers. Rear, semi-elliptic leaf springs and telescopic shock absorbers. Tyres: 5·90 × 13.
Brakes: Front, Girling 9·8 in. discs; rear, 9 in. drums, with vacuum-servo assistance.
Dimensions: Overall length, 13 ft. 0 in.; overall width, 5 ft. 0½ in.; overall height, 4 ft. 3½ in.; ground clearance, 4½ in.; kerb weight 22½ cwt.

PERFORMANCE

	m.p.h.			secs.
MAXIMUM SPEED	— 122	ACCELERATION	0–30 —	4·0
Mean of two ways	— 121		0–40 —	5·5
SPEEDS IN GEARS First	— 50		0–50 —	7·4
Second	— 70		0–60 —	10·0
Third	— 90		0–70 —	13·0
			0–80 —	16·0
			0–90 —	22·1
Fuel consumption: 20 m.p.g.		Standing quarter-mile	—	17·5

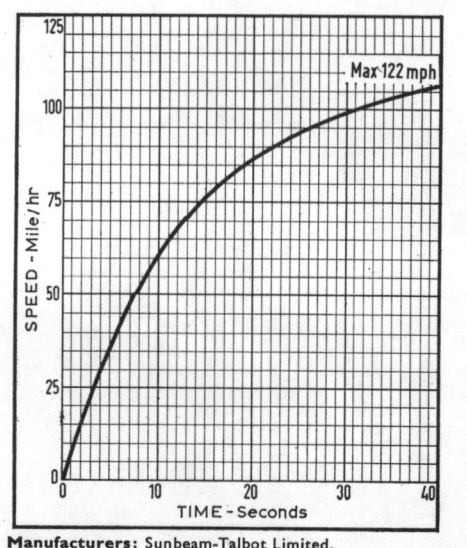

Manufacturers: Sunbeam-Talbot Limited, Ryton-on-Dunsmore, Coventry.
Price: (Including tax) £1,445 10s. 5d.

SUNBEAM TIGER

Take one well-developed British-made chassis, add one smooth-running American-made V-8 engine and transmission combination and you come up with one of the sweetest sport car packages yet! This particular Anglo-American combo is called a Sunbeam Tiger. This Tiger will purr or roar, but more on this later.

The Sunbeam Tiger owes its existence to the foresight of Ian Garrad, West Coast manager for the Rootes Group, builder of the well-known Sunbeam and Hillman cars, and Carroll Shelby, famous for his Shelby-Cobra Championship sports car. Garrard had long felt that there was an excellent market in this country for an ultra high performance sports car in the Sunbeam line to supplement their very fine Alpine model.

One day just two short years ago Garrard saw Shelby's Cobra-Fords trounce all opposition in a California sports car race. Right there Garrard saw the answer to his dream—if the Alpine chassis could be fitted with the Ford 260 cubic inch V-8 Fairlane engine he would have a winner. He rightly felt that the 260's lightweight, compactness, availability of parts, and easy-to-get speed options would satisfy the most demanding sports car enthusiast.

He also figured it would be capable of 125 mph (which it will do), have the Alpine excellent handling characteristics, offer vivid acceleration, keep Alpine's exceptional creature comforts and sell for less than any other competitor from Europe or Detroit.

Garrard took the idea to Shelby and by the end of May, 1963, the first prototype was buzzing around the Riverside Raceway. Ken Miles was consulted on the chassis and suspension of the portotype. Only minor mods were needed to bring the car around to the desired result. By July 1963, and after much in-town and out-on-the-Desert testing, the Tiger was deemed ready for appraisals by Rootes' Board of Directors. You would have to live under the British system for a while to imagine what a test for the Tiger this must have been. Just think, an engine from one of the "colonies"! After a trial spin by Lord Rootes himself, over hill and dale and virtually England's only super highway, the Tiger passed inspection.

There are many changes in the Tiger over the Alpine, many changes which were made in order to tuck the little V-8 in where a straight-four had been. The 260 V-8 is only 3½ inches longer and two inches higher than the four, so the main problem was to find extra side space. The extra space was made by bending the cowl structure to accommodate the larger clutch housing and the rocker covers. Wheel arch supports were lowered to allow lowering of the V-8 engine to its proper height.

The first reaction on looking into the engine compartment is nothing short of wonderment! However, after a more careful look one can see that it is a very neat job and it isn't impossible to work on after all. What amazed me most of all was that the engine could be tucked under the cowl and still afford the passenger and driver as much foot room as before. Also, this is one case where hydraulic lifters are appreciated because they won't need adjustment, which avoids consequent hassle in getting at the shrouded valve covers.

The new rack and pinion steering system replaces the Burman recirculating-ball, worm-and-nut system and is fitted in front of the front cross member. The pinion is connected to the steering shaft by a universal-jointed rod, which incidentally lends a safety factor in front end crashes by allowing the column to fold at this point rather than spear the driver! Steering is very accurate and precise.

Suspension is made up of the usual coil front and leaf rear type springs, the rear having a panhard rod for additional side location. This panhard rod no doubt accounted for the good stability in a 45 mph cross wind encountered during our test. A sway bar steadies up the front end in the usual fashion. Suspension joints are sealed, permanently-lubricated bearings and there are no greasing points on the chassis.

The power train begins with the 164 bhp, 260 cubic inch, Ford V-8. It has a bore of 3.80 inches and a stroke of 2.87 inches. The engine peaks out at a tame 4400 rpm and is exceptionally smooth throughout its power range. A hotter version with a 4-barrel carb will be offered later, but we believe the standard version to be the ideal set up for a car that will spend most of its time on earth at a speed somewhere this side of 125 mph for the greater part of its life!

The gearbox is also Ford-made and is a dandy. It is fitted with close ratios and needs to be used only when the driver is so inclined simply because the engine is so smooth and flexible. The power unit is lashed up ahead of a 2.88 to 1 rear axle ratio, which at first glance would seem to be outrageously low. Most sports cars in this country compete with gear ratios more like 4.56 to 1 or 4.11 to 1. Those ratios are great for stump-pulling and elapsed time at the drag strip or for spurting down short straights on closed sports car circuits. However, for the guy who wants to cruise in comfort at high speed and without the engine thrashing away hour after hour, this 2.88 to 1 ratio makes terrific sense! The four speed gearbox can be put to some use on mountain roads with this 2.88 to 1 gear set. As an example, slow mountain corners are left behind very quickly in second gear. If a hill should be next up, the driver snags third gear and hauls ashes up like it didn't exist! Then if the hill is exceptionally long and straight, the driver pops into fourth gear and vaults ahead at an ever-increasing crescendo. Wowie! That's what a sports car is for in my book!

Performance is plenty adequate with the aforementioned standard rear end ratio. No doubt acceleration would be even better with stump-pulling ratios, but then you would get some rear axle tramp. Traction master rear spring stabil-

SUNBEAM ST TIGER
POWERED BY FORD

HERE'S THE AMERICAN BUILT V-8 THAT MAKES THIS TIGER PURR

izer bars will cure this problem and are supposed to be an option.

The Sunbeam Tiger is about the most comfortable sports car around and has features that very few of its competitors offer. The seating is about the most adjustable of any available. The steering wheel hub can be unscrewed slightly to release a splined end on the column so the wheel can be placed to suit the driver. We shoved it all the way in to get that "arms-out" position that affords the driver more elbow room for quick maneuvering.

Handling is great! The short wheelbase, 86 inches, makes the Tiger a winner in the tight stuff, especially with the torque from Ford's little V-8 to help poke you around. The fast corners require more attention, but still are very stable. Attention to tire pressures could introduce a bit more understeer in the front for faster bends if the driver wanted it. The standard set-up is just fine for our taste. Competition drivers would want the optional mag wheels and bigger donuts for maximum effort on the corners. It is amazing how Rootes managed to keep the fore to aft weight ratio to 51% to 49% on a short wheelbase of 86 inches and still have all that room inside the car!

The staggering thing about the Tiger is its price. It reaches our shores for a dollar under $3500, and reaches inland destinations with many goodies for just over $3700. Some of those goodies not already mentioned are: 2-speed electric wipers, vacuum servo power brakes (disc front, drum rear), heater and defroster, and one of the most complete instrument panels we've seen.

The Tiger operates on regular gas and pushes itself along with gas mileage varying between 15 and 23 miles per gallon depending on whether you want your Tiger to purr or roar. We think Mr. Garrard came up with a winner! It is already a success and those British are going to have to tool up to handle more Ford V-8s in those little Alpines. I wonder what that will do to our balance of payment problems?

SUNBEAM TIGER SPECIFICATIONS
List price, P.O.E.	$3499
Curb weight, lbs.	2660
Test weight	2850
Tire size	5.90 x 13
Brakes, front/rear	disc/drum
Engine type	water-cooled V-8
Displacement, cc.	4261
Cubic inches	260
Compression ratio	8.8 to 1
Bore and stroke, inches	3.80 x 2.87
Horsepower, SAE	164 @ 4400 rpm
Max. Torque	258 lbs.-ft. @ 2200 rpm

EXTERIOR DIMENSIONS
Wheelbase	86 in.
Tread, front/rear	51.75/48.5 in.
Length, overall	155.5 in.
Width	60.5 in.
Height	51.5 in.

INTERIOR DIMENSIONS
Headroom	39 in.
Seat width	2 x 18 in.

GEAR RATIOS
4th (1.00)	2.88
3rd (1.29)	3.72
2nd (1.69)	4.87
1st (2.32)	6.68

ACCELERATION (6,000 FT. ALTITUDE)
0-30 mph, seconds	3.4
0-40	4.6
0-50	6.4
0-60	8.4
0-70	11.1
0-80	14.8
0-100	23.9
Standing start ¼ mile	16.6 secs.
Speed at end ¼ mile	87 mph

THE 4.2-LITRE V8 SUNBEAM TIGER

A Handsome Compact Anglo-American Sports Car with the Emphasis on Effortless Acceleration

ACCELERATION CONTRAST.—The Sunbeam Tiger, to which acceleration is second nature, with a much more staid companion, in the form of The Mechanical Tar Spraying & Gritting Co. Ltd.'s Fowler steam-roller, No. 15969, in use last month in Berkshire.

THE use of American vee-eight power units in British high-performance cars is an interesting development likely to increase—Bristol, Jensen, A.C. Cobra, and a number of big sports/racing cars of even more limited output use such engines. But whereas the emphasis has been either on luxury travel or competition performance of a hairy kind, the Sunbeam Tiger 260 conceived by the Chrysler-Rootes Group is a practical, road-going sports car. No combination of American vee-eight in a British chassis could be happier, for the snug installation of the " cooking " 141 (net) b.h.p., 4,261-c.c. push-rod-o.h.v. Ford V8 engine, coupled to a Borg-Warner gearbox, in the long-established and otherwise mainly unaltered Sunbeam Alpine transformed this somewhat harsh but fast and compact sports car into a very accelerative, extremely effortless motor car without in anyway changing its sporting characteristics.

Jensen Motors of West Bromwich did the structural modifications necessary to install the Ford engine into the confined under-bonnet space and MOTOR SPORT commented on the new Sunbeam Tiger last April, when the Continental Correspondent drove a perfectly normal example over an electrically-timed s.s. ¼-mile in 16.34 sec.

This gave a clear indication of the performance of the new hybrid, and D. S. J. was, in general, favourably impressed, as I was, especially when, going to Goodwood in the car, I found it possible to wuffle up South Harting hill in the 2.8-to-1 top gear and later enjoyed the smooth surge of acceleration on one of the quickest journeys I have made between the Sussex circuit and home.

We now present a full road-test report on this interesting and desirable Rootes Group sports car, discussing it in detail. It is virtually the former 4-cylinder Sunbeam Alpine re-engined, and is a pure 2-seater sports car with a seat behind the two front seats for the occasional doubled-up passenger, dog, or luggage, although there is a spacious boot for the last-named. Outwardly the car is recognisable as a Tiger only by the " Tiger 260 " badges on sides and tail (the 260 represents the engine's swept volume in cubic inches) and the " Tiger " scroll incorporated in the plated strip along the waistline, over which the " Sunbeam " lettering front and back takes precedence—it is *not* necessary to run the car exclusively on Esso. From the recognition aspect the discerning will also note the twin exhaust pipes. There are " Rootes Group Sunbeam " badges on the sides of the tail, and the old Talbot badge on the radiator grille, so this is a well be-badged car, but the badges are small and discreet. The key-ring carries the old Sunbeam-Talbot badge.

As one expects of Rootes' products, the interior of the Tiger is tastefully appointed. The driver's and passenger's seats are tight-fitting, separate, bucket-type seats, the backs adjustable in rather wide stages after side handles have been lifted and then pressed down to lock the seat-back in the desired position. The backs fold forward onto the cushions to give rather restricted access to the back compartment. In view of the short wheelbase the back axle intrudes into the cushion of this back shelf and the car is best regarded as purely a 2-seater. The steering column is adjustable after unlocking a large knob on top of the steering wheel and this, in conjunction with the adjustable seat, enables a comfortable driving position to be selected, with choice of " Caracciola " or " Farina " stance. It is also possible to adjust the small, polished-wood-rimmed spring-spoke wheel so that it is low enough not to obstruct the forward view. The wheel carries a full horn-ring, sounding a powerful horn.

Visibility is good, over a plain bonnet, although the screen pillars are somewhat thick. The gearbox tunnel is as wide as formerly, so that the pedals are very slightly biased to the o/s, but there is room for the clutch foot, resting on the lamps' dipping button, beside the clutch pedal. Clutch and brake pedals are of pendant-type, the accelerator a treadle.

Between the front seats is a very useful, lockable stowage-box with padded lid, which endeared itself to me because it accepted a Rolleiflex camera and lightmeter. Just ahead of this there is a lidded ash-tray, on the transmission tunnel, and immediately in front of this rises the well-placed gear-lever, with gaitered base. The floor is thickly carpeted, with a rubbing-mat for the driver's feet; it was hanging loose above the accelerator pedal.

The instruments are spaced out along a facia of polished walnut veneer, well crash-padded above and below. Before the driver are the 140-m.p.h. speedometer with total and trip odometers and the tachometer reading to 6,000 r.p.m., with the red-section from 4,700 r.p.m. Between these is the oil-gauge. These are British Jaeger instruments, very clearly calibrated, the speedometer reading in k.p.h. as well as in m.p.h. and the needles moving in complementary arcs. To the left of the tachometer there is a Lucas ammeter and on the centre of the panel are located the Jaeger fuel and water temperature gauges, also fully calibrated, the former in litres as well as gallons, the latter in deg. C. and deg. F., with a not-completely-dependable Smiths clock (which is an extra) between them. Above these three small dials the twin heating and ventilating horizontal controls quadrants are neatly located. Warning lamps and the flick-switches for lamps, panel lighting and the two Lumax fog-lamps fitted to the test car, are scattered, but the wipers and adjacent washers-button are conveniently positioned for the fingers of the right hand, as is the flick-switch for the heater blower. The fog-lamp switches are on a little panel of their own, below the facia, and rather obstructive in a crash. On the left-hand side of the facia there is a large open cubby-hole, with a map-lamp which has its own switch, above it. There is a choke label but, as the Ford engine has an automatic choke, the hole is blanked off.

Not every sports car has anti-dazzle vizors, but these, of soft padded type, are provided on the Sunbeam Tiger, although there is no vanity mirror, and, although detachable, the vizors do not swivel. Below the facia on the test car the excellent push-button Radiomobile radio and speaker were fitted.

On the left of the steering column a slender stalk looks after the turn-indicators and daylight lamps-flashing. The hand-brake lever lies well out of the way, horizontally, on the right of the driver's seat, where it is immediately to hand, but savages the knuckles if it happens to be in the " on " position while the

124

TIGER DETAILS.—Left view shows the well-appointed interior, comfortable seats, central gear-lever and acceptable facia of the car, that on the right the size of the luggage boot, with spare wheel and battery stowed under the floor.

driver's large window winder is being operated. These winders need five turns to lower fully the window glasses. The very wide doors, with good "keeps," provide for easy entry and exit and have push-button external handles, simple metal "pulls" and lever-type inside handles which lift up to open the doors. The luggage-boot lid has external plated hinges and the efficient quick-action fuel filler is recessed in the o/s of the body. The bumper over-riders are rubber capped in the modern style, and the appearance is embellished by wheel trims, through which the tyre valves protrude, and whitewall Dunlops.

The bonnet panel has to be propped open. The boot has a slam-type lock, but does not require the use of the key to open it unless purposely locked. The boot is shallow but long, and should take all the luggage the occupants of a car of this type normally take with them. The spare wheel lives horizontally under the floor, with the 12 volt 67 amp./hour battery beside it, the lid of the latter intruding only slightly into the luggage compartment. The test car was equipped with Irvin-Rootes safety-belts.

Naturally, modifications were necessary to the front-end of the Alpine to enable the Ford V8 engine to be installed, this engine being a fine example of modern thinwall iron-casting techniques, so that, while developing a gross b.h.p. of 164, and 258 lb. ft. torque at only 2,200 r.p.m., it is of notably low weight. This engine retains its Carter 2-barrel carburetter, and, having a c.r. of 8.8 to 1, will consume premium fuels. A new cross-flow radiator is used, fuel is fed electrically, and there are two entirely separate exhaust systems, each with its own silencer and plated tail-pipe. Petrol is contained in two tanks, one in each back wing, but they feed as one, giving a capacity of 11¼ gallons.

The transmission is entirely new, a hydraulically-operated clutch conveying the drive to a 4-speed all-syncromesh Borg-Warner gearbox, while a heavy-duty propeller shaft drives a high-performance Salisbury hypoid back axle with the satisfyingly high ratio of 2.88 to 1. To cope with the extra weight of the engine the Alpine i.f.s. has higher-rate coil-springs and the damper settings have been changed. The front disc/rear drum servo-assisted braking system is unchanged but a modified front cross-member carries a new rack-and-pinion steering unit.

On the road this Sunbeam Tiger handles and responds like a typical sports car, and possesses that fine flow of smooth power that is associated with a big-capacity multi-cylinder vee power unit, acceleration producing scarcely any sound other than the characteristic note from the exhausts. The Tiger's most impressive feature is its excellent, effortless acceleration, even from very low speeds in top gear. The accompanying table quotes the figures for standing-start pick-up, but only driving experience of the Sunbeam-Powered-By-Ford can convey how enjoyable this smooth flow of power makes the car on the road, and how rapidly the Tiger disposes of traffic tangles. The rear-view mirror, incidentally, is of the dangerous "diminishing" type, quite unnecessary with acceleration of this kind!

Some idea of the potency of this Sunbeam-Ford's pick-up in top gear can be conveyed by quoting further acceleration times—30-50 m.p.h. occupies 5½ sec., 60-80 m.p.h. only 8 sec. It will pull from 12 m.p.h. (500 r.p.m.) in top gear. The s.s. ¼-mile time was not quite so good as that obtained by D. S. J. in another Tiger but he was alone in the car, whereas we timed the car two-up, with a fairly full tank of petrol—many runs of 17 sec. were made without exceeding 4,700 r.p.m. At this speed the genuine maxima in the gears are, respectively, 42, 66 and 87 m.p.h. Taking the engine 300 r.p.m. "into the red" gives an impressive 90+ in 3rd gear.

On good roads the handling is excellent, although care has to be taken to get the car straight before opening the throttle in the lower gears on a slippery surface! Normally it is usual to roll away in 2nd gear and go straight into top, the acceleration still being entirely adequate for most situations. The gear-lever has a large knob labelled with the gear positions and a neat lift-up catch to prevent reverse being selected inadvertently. It is a "mechanical," notchy change, heavily spring-loaded towards the high-gear positions, but with good syncromesh on all four forward speeds. Third gear is commendably quiet, but there is slight 1st and 2nd gear howl and back-axle whine. The clutch has a rather long travel, is not too heavy for a sports car, and is moderately smooth. Both front wings are in full view of an average-height driver.

The steering is light, once on the move, accurate, perhaps a bit "dead," with gentle castor-return action. It is usefully "quick" steering, geared 3⅛ turns, lock-to-lock, with no lost motion. A great deal of fierce kick-back is transmitted through the wheel, which is shiny and slippery but has token finger grips. As the suspension, being stiff enough to kill all noticeable roll except where direction is changed very suddenly as the car is being furiously accelerated, gives a rough, rattly ride on bad roads, the Sunbeam Tiger is a sports car somewhat in the vintage image. Even on good roads the ride is lively and, in spite of stiff springs,

The Alpine-like appearance of the accelerative Ford-powered Sunbeam Tiger is apparent in this view. Note the Lumax fog and spot lamps and wind-up glass side windows.

125

Tight fit! This Tiger has a Ford under its bonnet. The polished valve covers are normally an extra on this power unit.

the nose dips under heavy braking, deflecting the headlamp beams. The front-end becomes squidgy under these conditions. There is not overpronounced understeer, the normal cornering trend being pleasantly neutral. I am told that the suspension is impossible on European back routes, but it is quite acceptable in Britain, especially as the snug-fitting driving seat, if unyielding, is quite comfortable on long runs, while passengers praised the comfort of their seat. Elbow room for the driver's right arm is restricted. The steering lock is restricted also, particularly to the right, resulting in a turning circle of 36½ ft.

The back axle, on half-elliptic leaf-springs without any other location, can be made to tramp furiously if too-fierce bottom-gear take-off is indulged in, and the Dunlop RS5 nylon tyres can be made to spin relatively easily. The brakes are light to apply and adequate, but for prolonged mountain driving it is possible that something larger than the 9.85 in. discs and 9-in. drums might be an improvement. It is possible that a larger tyre size than 5.90 × 13 might also be desirable for really hard motoring, but only the most spirited cornering provokes protest from these RS5s. The speedometer was virtually accurate when checked at 50 and 60 m.p.h.

Taken all round, this mating of American vee-eight engine and popular British sports car has very definitely succeeded. The Sunbeam Tiger is fascinating to drive and offers really good and *usable* performance for a total outlay of £1,445 10s. 5d., particularly as no skimping has been indulged in to gain a few more m.p.h. or greater acceleration, the Tiger weighing, with its very adequate equipment and finish, over 22 cwt. The weather protection is excellent, and the hood, although tedious to stow in its metal rear locker, does not drum and looks durable. Its rear quarters do constitute a blind-spot in certain situations, however. The glass door-windows do not create much draught when open; the quarter-lights are fixed. A hard-top is available for an extra £60 8s. 4d., inclusive of tax.

The headlamp beam is rather cut off when dipped and the full-beam warning light is dazzling. There is bright and dim panel lighting but neither this, nor the map-light, illuminates the heater controls.

The Sunbeam Tiger will poodle along at 15 m.p.h. in its high top gear or accelerate splendidly to a maximum of 116 m.p.h., and it cruises effortlessly at any speed up to maximum. At 90 m.p.h. on the Motorways the engine is turning over at less than 4,000 r.p.m. and oil-pressure is normally 50 lb./sq. in. Water temperature is rather high, at 85° C., but I never made the radiator boil. As to petrol consumption, pottering around, enjoying the easy top-gear performance, I got 19.2 m.p.g., and on a fast main road drive, speed restricted only by the appalling traffic hold-ups on the notorious A31 Winchester-Bournemouth road, the figure improved to 22.0 m.p.g., so it should normally be possible to obtain better than 20 m.p.g.

A full tank of petrol lasted 203 miles, but consumption would have been increased by the recording of acceleration figures, and something like 225 miles should normally be possible. The electric pump primes an empty tank efficiently. After 700 miles no oil had been used. To inspect the impressive machinery the bonnet top has to be lifted and propped up. The long dip-stick is accessible, in a tunnel behind the alternator.

THE SUNBEAM TIGER 260

Engine : Eight cylinders in 90° vee formation, 96.5 × 73 mm. (4,261 c.c.). Push-rod-operated overhead valves. 8.8-to-1 compression-ratio. 141 (net) b.h.p. at 4,400 r.p.m.
Gear ratios : First, 6.8 to 1; 2nd, 4.86 to 1; 3rd, 3.71 to 1; top, 2.88 to 1.
Tyres : 5.90 × 13 Dunlop RS5 on bolt-on steel disc wheels.
Weight : 1 ton 1 cwt. 1 qtr. 27 lb. (dry weight).
Steering ratio : 3⅛ turns, lock-to-lock.
Fuel capacity : 11¼ gallons. (Range approx. 225 miles.)
Wheelbase : 7 ft. 2 in.
Track : Front, 4 ft. 4 in.; rear, 4 ft. 0¾ in.
Dimensions : 13 ft. 0 in. × 5 ft. 0½ in. × 4 ft. 3½ in. (high-hood up).
Price : £1,195 (£1,445 10s. 5d. inclusive of purchase tax).
Makers : Sunbeam-Talbot Ltd., Ryton-on-Dunsmore, Coventry, England.

Performance Data

Acceleration :

0-40 m.p.h.	..	4.7 sec.	0-70 m.p.h.	..	12.5 sec.
0-50 ,,	..	6.8 ,,	0-80 ,,	..	15.5 ,,
0-60 ,,	..	9.0 ,,	0-90 ,,	..	20.6 ,,
s.s. ¼-mile	..	17.0 sec.			

Speed in gears : First, 42 m.p.h.; 2nd, 66 m.p.h.; 3rd, 87 m.p.h.; top, 116 m.p.h.

To sum up, the Sunbeam Tiger V8 is a most entertaining sports car, and one possessing performance which makes it a very fast car indeed in terms of average speeds and, in the right hands, a very safe one. Its engine should be extremely durable, being so lightly-stressed, and it provides the fluid power output and "there-and-gone" acceleration I encountered first in the side-valve 3.6-litre Ford V8 some years before the war. At its selling price of less than £1,500 this well-finished, sensibly-equipped Rootes Group product, in something of the vintage tradition remembering the steering kick-back and hard suspension and respectably high power/weight ratio, is indeed an excellent addition to the ranks of British sports cars. Most of the minor shortcomings referred to above have been inherited from the Alpine and may well be designed out as the Tiger is developed further, but had the Alpine not been used as a basis the price would presumably have been far higher. While an engineer might raise an eyebrow at some of the installation details and the Sunbeam Tiger, like the Daimler SP250, has a better engine than chassis, taken all round it is an excellent investment, admirably suited to modern traffic conditions.—W. B.

Seen at the Vintage Prescott Meeting—Arnold-Forster rear-ends!

NOW UP TO 1725cc

● The Editor tries the latest in Sunbeam Alpines ●

THE ONLY CHANGE worth talking about on the Sunbeam Alpine for the coming twelve months—or maybe longer—is the fitting of the bigger and, naturally, pokier power unit. Apart from that the mixture is "similar", as our friend the barman said, but the difference is enough to make it into a much quicker car in terms of acceleration. Maximum speed hasn't gone up by much, if any: Rootes have mentioned a figure in excess of the ton as top whack, but we couldn't do better than something in the high nineties. But the acceleration is a different story altogether, and when we are saddled with Foolish Frazer's overall speed limit it will be acceleration that counts. Since this report appears after Christmas we had better say, for the benefit of any spies that may be reading it, that the performance figures and the rest of the test were achieved back in the days of freedom, in dear old 1965.

So what's it all about then? It's a four-cylinder unit still, developed, naturally, from the dear old banger which Rootes engineers have been causing to possess more and more cubic centimetres and more and more horses for as long as most of them can remember. It has a five-bearing crankshaft and an alloy cylinder head, which gives it a compression ratio of 9·2 to 1, just fractionally higher than the old 1600 engine. The bore is the same as the former engine at 81·5 mm., and the extra capacity comes from a longer stroke of 82·55 mm., compared with the 76·2 mm. of the 1592 c.c. motor. The gasworks takes the form of twin Stromberg CD 150s; an oil cooler is a standard fitting. Maximum power is increased from 82 b.h.p. at 5,000 r.p.m. to 100 at five-five, and the torque goes up from 94 lb. ft. at 3,500 r.p.m. to an impressive 110 lb. ft. at three-seven. All of which makes it go a bit, and although it's true to say that a MiniCooper S would stay with it on acceleration and beat it in maximum speed, it must be admitted that these things are a damned sight more comfortable in the Alpine. And if you're going to sign away your birthright to an insurance company you might as well have something which at least *looks* like a sports car.

There are one or two snags to the bigger engine, one of which had us puzzled. Rootes tell us that it's got them puzzled too, and it seems to be common to all the alloy-head 1725s. What the problem is concerns starting from cold—starting from hot is wizard, but if the engine is cold, you yank out the choke and bingo, it fires pretty well first time. But it then needs the choke until, literally, full normal running temperature is shown on the gauge—a matter of 85 degrees C. And if you happen to be batting along on a chilly morn and the temperature drops a trifle, as well it might, you'll run into the most colossal "flat spot". Obviously the first place to look is the mixture, but we can't believe that Rootes haven't tried this, so it must be something else. A pity, because it can be a bit of a pest to have an engine that won't pull properly (unless the choke is far enough out to double the idling speed) for about seven miles.

In other respects the engine delivers the goods. Idling is pretty fast normally, at about a thousand revs., and the extra torque does wonders for the flexibility. It is fully possible to prance about at around 25 m.p.h. in overdrive top, and while we frankly fail to see the point of this exercise as a practical means of getting from A to B, it must mean something. You notice the biggest benefits in acceleration. Maximum speed has gone up only by a couple of miles an hour—after all, the axle ratio isn't altered—but you get there a hell of a lot quicker, and using a few more revs. isn't really "on" unless you have a very long straight road in front. In spite of that, the extra urge will push it along at a one-way best of 97 m.p.h. compared with under 95 for the 1600 model.

Outwardly the car hasn't changed at all, the only difference to be seen is the engine capacity on the shields, one on each wing and a third on the boot lid.

The engine is fitted with an alternator which is capable of 'holding' all the electrics on the car.

At first glance the engine compartment is a mass of pipes and tubes, in fact, the accessibility is good.

When it comes to leaving the start, however, the bigger engine is really in business. Conditions weren't exactly ideal for acceleration testing, but even so we found a pretty dramatic improvement. Like knocking nine seconds off the 0–80 time, for instance. The improvement gets bigger and better and more and more the faster you try to go, and while the Alpine still isn't what we'd call a really fast car, at least with the 1725 engine you don't have to suffer humiliations from Cortina G.T.s and things. From rest to sixty wants just over eleven seconds, nearly three seconds better than the 1600; from rest to seventy knocks off more than four seconds to bring the time down to 15.4, and from rest to 80 you know about already.

The fuel consumption isn't a lot worse. From the 1600 we found our consumption ranged between 22 and 25 miles to the gallon, whereas the 1725 did a regular and consistent 20 m.p.g. no matter what we did with it.

The other item of note about the car is the fitting of a 35 amp. alternator instead of the dynamo, and apart from largely theoretical advantages in terms of weight and space-saving, we reckon that this is The Thing. Not only does it provide a charge from the bottom up, so to speak, but it would balance pretty well everything electrical on the test car:

we tried sidelights, headlights, screen-wipers, radio and heater fan, and threw in a couple of fog-lights as well, with the result that so long as the engine was doing 1500 revs. or more the discharge of this sizeable collection of amps-drainers was perfectly balanced by the alternator's input. Very nice in nasty weather.

In other respects it is a Sunbeam Alpine. The handling isn't altered, there is still the terrible wind-noise (with the soft-top) at anything over about seventy (Mr. Frazer will presumably save them the trouble of having to sort this one out) and, apart from anything else, the Alpine is still one of the most comfortable and best-equipped fast touring cars in captivity. Think of it: Full-reclining, widely adjustable seats; an adjustable steering column; well-placed pedals; a full kit of instruments, mounted where you can see 'em; headlight flashers; two-speed screen wipers; a two-speed heater fan (even if it is one of the noisest going); plenty of space for bits and pieces; overdrive on third and top; and most of these are standard fittings, with a few others thrown in. If you have the overdrive you get a lower back axle ratio of 4.22 to 1, instead of the normal 3.89. Price? There has to be a snag—it'll cost you the best part of nine hundred quid to put it on the road.

Cars on Test

SUNBEAM ALPINE 1725

Engine: Four-cylinder, 81.5 mm. × 82.55 mm.; 1,725 c.c.; compression ratio 9.2 to 1; pushrod-operated overhead valves; light alloy cylinder head; twin Stromberg CD150 carburettors; 100 b.h.p. at 5,500 r.p.m.

Transmission: Four-speed and reverse gearbox (overdrive on third and top on test car) with synchromesh on all forward gears. Floor-mounted centre change.

Suspension: Front, independent, with swinging links and coil springs, anti-roll bar and telescopic shock absorbers; Rear, semi-elliptic leaf springs.

Brakes: Front, Girling 9.85 in. discs; 9 in. drums rear, with vacuum servo.

Dimensions: Overall length, 13 ft.; overall width, 5 ft. 0½ in.; overall height, 4 ft. 3½ ins.; ground clearance, 4½ ins.; weight, 19¼ cwt.

PERFORMANCE

	m.p.h.		secs.
MAXIMUM SPEED	97	ACCELERATION	0–30— 3.2
Mean of two ways	96.5		0–40— 5.4
			0–50— 7.8
SPEEDS IN GEARS	First—30		0–60—11.3
	Second—48		0–70—15.4
	Third—78		0–80—21.2

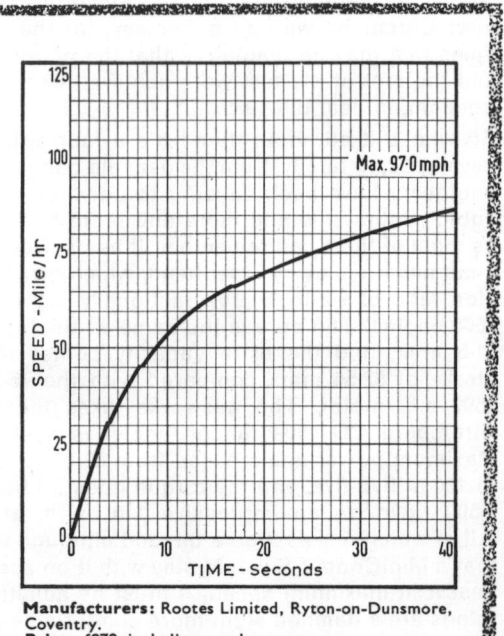

Manufacturers: Rootes Limited, Ryton-on-Dunsmore, Coventry.
Price: £878, including purchase tax.

THE SUNBEAM ALPINE IS, AND HAS BEEN FOR A NUMBER OF YEARS, A *VERY* NICE CAR. When asked to describe the attributes of a good sports car, it's one of the first to pop into our minds as an ideal example. We suspect the marques' qualities go largely unappreciated by many sports car fans, as it is not an exciting car like its muscular brother, the Tiger, nor a unique design like several others. Yet it is undeniably outstanding when its individual points, including the price tag, are totalled.

Rootes' latest in the Alpine line, the Series V, offers only detail improvements, but they are important details...an additional 125 cc's, a five-main bearing crankshaft, a new oil pickup, different gear ratios, and a new convertible top. All these improvements are made without an increase in its low price. While the base is $2399, accessories such as the radio, heater, tonneau cover, seat belts, and so on raised the list price of our test car to $2650, including delivery and handling. Considering the many deluxe features included as standard—an oil cooler, excellent upholstery, fully-adjustable seats, whitewall tires, and a very high standard of finish, this figure makes it a very sound competitor in its field.

The new five-main block looks much like the older one externally, with its narrow configuration, cast-iron material, and separate full-flow filter. A development stemming directly from racing experience, the oil-pump pickup has been moved to the front of the sump, eliminating the possibility of partial bearing starvation under hard braking conditions. The carburetors, formerly downdraft Zeniths that had several problems, are now 1½-inch Stromberg diaphragm-type sidedrafts. They offer far more direct fuel/air routing, don't have external accelerator-pump linkage that wears, and—thus far

SUNBEAM ALPINE SERIES V

*When someone asks you, "Just what IS a sports car?"
the Sunbeam Alpine is the perfect answer!*

By JERRY TITUS

SUNBEAM ALPINE SERIES V

—seem to hold their screws better. Somewhere in the process of all these changes it looks like the new model averages about the same gasoline mileage, despite the increase in cubics, and it is logical to assume they have something to do with this as well. The redline has been moved up to 6000 rpm, but the peak is well below that.

New gear ratios, combined with a 3.89 final drive, are not unlike the older ones in effect. Those familiar with the Sunbeam box will attest to its being a nice transmission, with fairly firm but positive and consistent shifts. There was a big gap between second and third. Other than that, it was fine. This one has a lesser gap there—it's still fairly wide—but the *first* cog seems a bit high for smooth starts, especially when the engine's cold. There's one thing you'll surely appreciate if you're a fast up-&-down-shifter—they've relocated reverse over and down to the *right* instead of to the left, thereby eliminating the possibility of getting into the reverse slot on a fast 3-2 backshift. It used to require a 'lockout' on the race cars.

Rootes improves their convertible top with each new series, and this one is no exception. The big change concerns elimination of the metal panel into which the top was concealed it its down position. The area behind the seats would hold a pair of three-year-olds comfortably, or quite a few packages. It was necessary to dismount either so you could move the panels and let the top down. The panels scraped each other and, invariably, you picked up deep scratches. 'Tis no longer true. The top-well is permanent, as is a very expensive-looking boot. The top folds in completely, the padded boot snaps in place, and everything looks great. Up, the top looks good, fits tight, but is not greatly improved from a wind-noise standpoint. Let's face it, *any* rag top has wind noise, but this one looked so good we expected less.

The ride, as we commented when testing the Series IV, is about as good as you could expect from a live-rear-axle car. This one is just as good. So's the handling. We've always liked the Alpine's dependable stability, even at rather ridculous speeds. For some reason, while they appear unchanged, the Dunlop tires had less wet-weather bite than we remembered—kind of greasy. But the dry-surface bite is fine.

Alpine's don't really start running until they get over 2000 miles on the clock and our test car had only 300. Because of this, we didn't notice the larger engine size making much difference where we expected it—in torque. But the times were improved, even so. There were also noticeable improvements in lower engine noise, less vibration, and smoother idling.

I don't know much more we can say about the new Alpine. Even if you aren't in the market, make it a point to drive one so's you have an idea what we're talking about when we describe it as an example of what a good production sports car should be. Notice the finish, the ruggedness, the excellent stopping power and stability. It's bound to impress you, no matter what you drive. Maybe they're overdue for a restyle or a new design. It's hard to make a change when you have a good product.

1725-cc SUNBEAM ALPINE

The Alpine Gets a New Engine with 5 Main Bearings and 99 bhp

THE MOST INTERESTING feature of the latest Sunbeam Alpine is the new engine. It is still a 4-cyl in-line overhead valve design but it is slightly larger in displacement, with 1725 vs. 1592 cc, and about 10% more power. The external dimensions of the engine are the same as before (obtained by keeping the cylinder bores at 81.5 mm), but there are now five main bearings instead of three and the increased displacement was obtained by lengthening the stroke from 76.2 to 82.6 mm.

The new 1725-cc engine is being used by Rootes in four of its models, the Hillman Minx, Super Minx, Sunbeam Rapier and Alpine V. There are three stages of tune, ranging from 69.5 bhp in the Hillmans (Hillmen?) to 99 for the Alpine V. An aluminum sports-type head with more efficient porting is used on the Rapier and Alpine versions and the Alpine has a pair of Stromberg CD carburetors in place of the more conservative air-fuel mixture instruments on the other models. The new engine is also faster-turning, developing its maximum power at 5500 rpm, 500 more than the 1592-cc engine in the Series IV. An oil cooler of the finned pipe variety is fitted as standard and the electrical system has been switched to use negative ground.

The torque of the new engine is now 103 lb-ft at 3700 rpm compared with 93 at 3500 in the previous version. This makes a worthwhile improvement in the high gear performance of the new Alpine. Our test car was fitted with the 4.22:1 final drive ratio so the around-town snap was appreciably greater than on the last Alpine we drove. This short-

1725-cc SUNBEAM ALPINE

legged ratio is ordinarily used with overdrive ($156 extra) and we think it would be excellent if you could snick into overdrive for cruising. Which we couldn't. Otherwise, the 4.22:1 ratio results in a buzziness we don't care for. The standard 3.89:1 final drive would be better with the standard 4-speed in this respect as it would give 17.4 mph per 1000 rpm in high gear compared with the 16.1 mph/1000 of the 4.22:1.

There are a number of less significant changes in the Alpine V. There's now a much appreciated air vent on each side of the cockpit, the rear brakes (drum) are self-adjusting and the space behind the seats has been carpeted, so it seems like storage space, rather than being upholstered to resemble a vestigial seat. The folded-down top is also now covered with a snap-down fabric apron rather than the neat folding panels of the Series IV.

The only exterior changes in the new version are badges that read "1725" instead of "IV." It is still a pleasant car to look at, and is not seriously dated, even though the basic body style was introduced in 1959. It handles well enough to make exuberant driving a pleasure, the all-synchro gearbox works smoothly and the combination of disc brakes in the front and drums at the rear will stop you in good fashion. It is also an unusually comfortable sports car for the taller driver.

For a sports car of this price range, there are several nice luxury touches, like the handsome flip-top gas cap, instruments that are easy to read and pleasant to look at, a map light over the glove bin on the dash, padded map compartment between the seats, and so on. The only complaint we had about comfort and convenience was that the roadster doesn't come with sun visors. A curious oversight.

Things we like about the Alpine V include the luggage space. The trunk is huge compared with that of most sports cars and is of a shape that accepts 24 and 26-in. suitcases standing up. Remarkable. There is also enough additional storage space behind the seats to make a long weekend or a vacation trip a practical possibility. We also liked the fuel consumption of our test car. We got an honest 30 mpg on an 800-mi trip at moderate cruising speeds and the worst tankful we used didn't go under 25 mpg. This is excellent indeed and makes us wonder what might be possible in overdrive.

To sum it up, we can think of nothing more appropriate to say than that the Alpine V has retained the virtues of the previous versions and added a few new ones which assure that it continues to be one of the most civilized of the contemporary sports cars. We like it.

1725-cc SUNBEAM ALPINE AT A GLANCE...

Price as tested	$2594
Engine	4 cyl, ohv, 1724 cc, 99 bhp
Curb weight, lb	2220
Top speed, mph	96
Acceleration, 0-60 mph, sec	14.0
50-70 mph (3rd gear)	8.8
Average fuel consumption, mpg	28

132

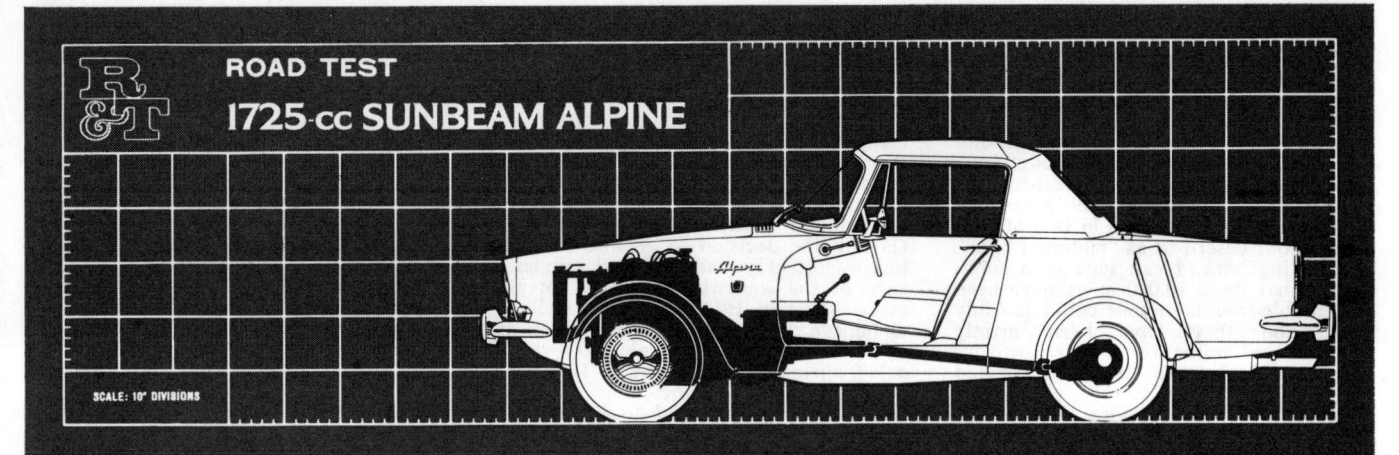

R&T ROAD TEST
1725-cc SUNBEAM ALPINE

SCALE: 10" DIVISIONS

PRICE
Basic list.................$2399
As tested................$2594

ENGINE
No. cyl. & type........4-cyl, ohv
Bore x stroke, mm....81.5 x 82.6
   In......................3.21 x 3.25
Displacement, cc/cu in.1724/105.2
Compression ratio..........9.1:1
Bhp @ rpm..............99 @ 5500
   Equivalent mph..............88
Torque @ rpm, lb-ft...103 @ 3700
   Equivalent mph..............59
Carburetors.......2 Stromberg CD
Barrel diameter.............1.50
Type fuel required........premium

DRIVE TRAIN
Clutch type......single-plate, dry
   Diameter, in................7.5
Gear ratios: 4th (1.00).....4.22:1
   3rd (1.29)................5.46:1
   2nd (1.99)................8.42:1
   1st (3.12)................13.2:1
Synchromesh..............on all 4
Differential type..........hypoid
   Ratio......................4.22:1
   Optional ratios............3.89:1

CHASSIS & SUSPENSION
Frame type........unit with body
Brake type............disc/drum
   Swept area, sq in..........295
Tire size...............6.00-13
   Make..............Dunlop C-41
Steering type....recirculating ball
   Turns, lock-to-lock..........3.5
   Turning circle, ft............34
Front suspension: independent with A-arms, coil springs, tube shocks, anti-roll bar.
Rear suspension: live axle, semi-elliptic leaf springs, tube shocks.

ACCOMMODATION
Normal capacity, persons........2
   Occasional capacity...........3
Seat width, front, in........2 x 18
Head room....................39.0
Seat back adjustment, deg.....30
Entrance height, in..........47.7
Step-over height.............16.5
Door width...................40.5
Driver comfort rating:
   Driver 69 in. tall............90
   Driver 72 in. tall............90
   Driver 75 in. tall............85
   (85-100, good; 70-85, fair; under 70, poor)

GENERAL
Curb weight, lb............2220
Test weight................2590
Weight distribution (with driver), front/rear, %....49/51
Wheelbase, in..............86.0
Track, front/rear......51.0/48.5
Overall length.............155.3
Width......................60.5
Height.....................51.5
Frontal area, sq ft.........17.3
Ground clearance, in........4.3
Overhang, front/rear......28/42
Departure angle, deg........15
Usable trunk space, cu ft....6.0
Fuel tank capacity, gal....13.2

INSTRUMENTATION
Instruments: 7000-rpm tachometer, 120-mph speedometer, trip odometer, oil pressure, water temperature, fuel level.
Warning lights: ignition, high beam, directionals.

MISCELLANEOUS
Body styles available: roadster (as tested), hardtop.

CALCULATED DATA
Lb/hp (test wt)..............26.1
Mph/1000 rpm (4th gear).....16.1
Engine revs/mi (60 mph)....3725
Piston travel, ft/mi.........2020
Rpm @ 2500 ft/min..........4610
   Equivalent mph..............74
Cu ft/ton mi................85.0
R&T wear index..............75

EXTRA COST OPTIONS
Heater, tonneau cover, seat belts, radio, overdrive, wire wheels, Dunlop SP-41 tires.

MAINTENANCE
Crankcase capacity, qt.......4.8
   Change interval, mi......6000
Oil filter type...........full flow
   Change interval, mi......6000
Chassis lube interval, mi..6000

ROAD TEST RESULTS

ACCELERATION
Time to speed, sec:
   0-30 mph..................4.2
   0-40 mph..................6.8
   0-50 mph..................9.8
   0-60 mph.................14.0
   0-70 mph.................19.0
   0-80 mph.................25.0
   50-70 mph (3rd gear)......8.8
Time to distance, sec:
   0-100 ft..................3.6
   0-500 ft.................10.3
   ¼-mile...................19.3
Speed at end, mph..........70.5
Passing exposure time, sec:
   To pass car going 50 mph...8.0

FUEL CONSUMPTION
Normal driving, mpg......25-30
Cruising range, mi......300-360

SPEEDS IN GEARS
High gear (5900), mph........96
   3rd (6000)..................75
   2nd (6000)..................49
   1st (6000)..................31

BRAKES
Panic stop from 80 mph:
   Deceleration, % G..........85
   Control...................fair
Parking: hold 30% grade.....yes
Overall brake rating........good

SPEEDOMETER ERROR
30 mph indicated......actual 27.8
40 mph.....................36.5
60 mph.....................56.1
80 mph.....................74.0
Odometer correction factor..0.970

ACCELERATION & COASTING

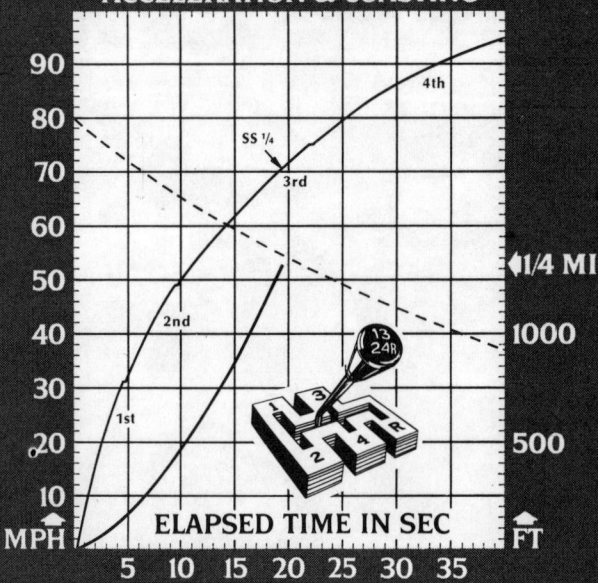

Having reached 10,000 miles on the clock since August, 1965, I can now assess the true potentiality of the 4.2-litre V8 Sunbeam Tiger. In purchasing one of these cars through my good friend Norman Garrad of the Rootes Group, I must admit that it was entirely due to experiences with a road-test car that I placed the order. This was for a hard top version, finished in that attracttive colour described as "midnight blue".

Looking back, I can state with confidence that these 10,000 miles have been as trouble-free as anyone could possibly wish—and they have been mainly pretty rapid miles, for a large percentage of the distance has been covered on the Continent of Europe, where they have a more realistic idea of where to apply speed limits.

My sole mishap was when somehow or other water contaminated the petrol tank, and the engine died away at the motorway end of the North Circular. Rootes of Ladbroke Hall speedily sent a rescue vehicle, and not only did they transport the crippled vehicle to the service depot for a thorough clean-out of the fuel system, but also supplied me with a car to take care of an important business appointment. The only other bothers have been a noisy windscreen wiper motor, and a faulty rear boot lock.

The V8 Tiger was the inspiration of John Panks, then on the West Coast of U.S.A. Fitting a 4.2-litre Ford V8 engine seemed to many people to be a crazy plan altogether, but after Carroll Shelby got busy with a prototype, and many thousands of miles were covered, the possibilities of such a hybrid became evident. So much so that Brian Rootes was enchanted with the project and, in consultation with Panks and with Ian Garrad, the decision to go into production was quickly made. With the appearance of the somewhat noisy prototypes at Le Mans in 1964, folk were inclined to believe that the car was too much of a "racer", and something akin to a solid-axle version of a Cobra. However, when the production machines were released, they were found to be entirely different. People who tried them discovered that they were quiet, extremely comfortable, entirely effortless in performance, and had none of the drawbacks associated with increasing power-output by a vast amount, on what looked to be a perfectly normal Sunbeam Alpine chassis.

Although the design was basically Alpine, there were many changes not obvious to the naked eye. The chassis was strengthened considerably, suspension altered, more powerful braking (with servo assistance) provided, and rack-and-pinion steering adopted. Transmission was also entirely new, via a heavy-duty centrifugally assisted clutch, four-speed all-synchromesh Ford gearbox, and an immensely strong final drive with a ratio of 2.88 to 1.

General handling was remarkably good, although heavy-footedness did tend to promote axle tramp, and also wheelspin. Driven sensibly the Tiger displayed no obvious vices whatsoever, and speedily impressed one with its ability to maintain incredibly high cruising speeds, with no conscious effort on the part of the silky power-unit.

Rootes were wise to insist on a standard Ford unit. It would have been so easy to go for high-compression heads, solid valve-lifters, four-barrel carburetters, high-lift camshaft and all the rest of the speed equipment paraphernalia—and what would have been the end-product? A near sports-racer, with orthodox two-seater coachwork, which would have little or no appeal to owners who demand sports-car performance, but without all the noise and fuss of a modified machine!

The V8 engine scarcely needs to work hard at all. At 4,000 r.p.m. in top, the machine is cruising just on 95 m.p.h. After I had passed 5,000 miles, the engine appeared to rev more freely than before, and on the splendid Antwerp-Hasselt autoroute I found myself cruising at just over 5,000 r.p.m. or something over 118 m.p.h., but this produced a penalty of increased petrol consumption. With a 4.2-litre engine prospective owners might well be deterred on the score of fairly heavy consumption. In point of fact, the car has proved to be far more economical than was anticipated and, since new, has averaged precisely 22½ m.p.g. I suppose this is due to the habit I have adopted in normal running of changing up from bottom into top. At 100 m.p.h. cruising on M1 before that stupid limit was introduced, fuel was consumed at the rate of 16 m.p.g. Nevertheless one does not require to run on super-

'10,000 miles in a Tiger'

Effortless and trouble-free motoring in a V8 version of the Sunbeam Alpine

By GREGOR GRANT

TIGER IN THE PADDOCK. *The Managing Editor with the Tiger in the paddock at the Le Mans test weekend.*

premium fuel (although I invariably do so), so the saving all round can be quite considerable.

As for oil consumption, between changes (Castrol XL), I have added only one half-pint, which is yet another advantage of having a lightly stressed power-plant. During the running-in period (about 1,500 miles), the cooling system required regular topping up, and the engine was inclined to run hot in traffic. All this has now disappeared, and I cannot remember when the system required any additional water. Again, when fairly new, the automatic choke seemed to take an inordinately long time to cut out, and the engine was inclined to stall in traffic. Following the first 500 miles service, this was rectified, and carburation is now beyond criticism.

Tyre wear has been remarkably light, and although I have newly changed the Dunlop RS5s for another product of the same company, there were several thousands of miles left on the covers. The Autolite sparking plugs were satisfactory, and owners may not care to change over to another preferred type as removal is not exactly without its problems. Nevertheless, should replacements be required, I would recommend Champion F9Y grade.

Accessibility is not one of the strong points of the Tiger's engine compartment, and it is indeed fortunate that the V8 unit is so reliable. However, normal maintenance is comparatively straightforward, and the only part of the engine that might require checking is the fan belt tension. The car also has rather a special type of SU petrol pump, and should owners familiar with the normal SU feel tempted to take one apart, my advice is "don't". It is quite a tricky job to reassemble, as an owner I met recently found out to his cost.

Brake lining wear has been surprisingly light and, so far, I have not found it necessary to replace pads or linings, or even to adjust the handbrake. The rear dampers may shortly be due for replacement, but even so, I have yet to bump the axle against the stops. I had one fright, when a horrible grinding noise suggested rear axle failure. This turned out to be the simple matter of a retaining bolt for the handbrake cable coming adrift and allowing the cable to foul the inside of the wheel.

The finish has been, on the whole, admirable, with no sign of deterioration on the bright parts, such as I have seen in other makes of car purchased around the same period as the Tiger. After being completely waterproof for months, water began to seep into the interior and thence to my trouser-legs. This was traced to some of the packing "goo" which seals the rubber conduits above the door having disintegrated. Five minutes' work soon put this right.

Generally I have the hard top *in situ*, but on several occasions have had the hood erected. This is somewhat tricky to do at first, but one quickly learns the procedure, and the result is as snug and close-fitting a structure as I have ever found on an open car.

Paintwork is first-rate, and requires very infrequent application of one of the many high-grade polishes that are available nowadays. Incidentally, I have found Turtlewax to be extremely effective, and is much freer from rain-spotting than many competitive brands.

Many owners have their own theories regarding tyre pressures. With the RS5s, I kept them at 28 p.s.i., rising to 32 p.s.i. for motorways (pre-70 m.p.h. era). Keeping the latter pressure makes the car more bumpy than one would like, particularly when driving one-up and with nothing in the luggage boot.

The lighting equipment is better than average, and the only addition I have made is one of the later Lucas foglamps, mounted on the nearside of the badge-bar (extra). I have also acquired a tonneau cover, which necessitates the fitting of extra studs. The heating system has been exemplary, and once the engine has attained its normal working temperature, demisting is 100 per cent. efficient.

The gearbox has remained a sheer delight to use, and the transmission on the whole is commendably quiet. However, a slight "buzz-buzz" has developed in second gear, which oddly enough I found on the original test car. The upholstery (p.v.c.) reacts well to modern cleaners, and can soon be restored to showroom condition (I found the Moly product extremely good).

The engine keeps extremely clean, as befits a completely oil-tight unit. Changing the intake filter is an extremely simple operation, and the battery's location in the luggage boot encourages regular inspection and topping up.

Well, there it is, and I am now looking forward to the next 10,000 miles. With such a tremendously heavy programme of events, this mileage will doubtless be covered in a comparatively short time and, if the Tiger provides the same sort of trouble-free motoring that it has given me, I shall consider it to be an excellent investment.

For readers who may be interested, the all-up weight, ready for the road (full 11½ gallons tank, tools, etc.) is 26½ cwt. This is with the hard top, and with the hood stowed. Best timed maximum speed has been 119 m.p.h., and the swiftest standing quarter-mile, 16.9 secs. The Tiger costs £1,195 plus £250 10s. 5d. p.t., and the hard top sets one back £60 8s. 4d. with p.t. Not a great deal to pay for such a splendid motor-car, which, when the word gets round, must sell in ever-increasing numbers.

Since having its 10,000 miles go-over, the Tiger has been modified with a Panhard rod at the rear, interior-controlled Armstrong wing mirrors and Dunlop Yellow Spot tyres. On a very fast run to Le Mans and back, the suspension and general handling are immensely improved over the standard production lay-out.

135

ROAD TEST
NUMBER 2079

Sunbeam Alpine Series V 1,725 c.c.

AT A GLANCE: Established Rootes two-seater now fitted with latest five-main-bearing engine. Performance and economy improved, with less fuss. Close-ratio gearbox with optional overdrive gives a good choice of ratios. Comfortable ride and fully adjustable driving position. Safe, predictable handling and powerful, but heavy, brakes. Full range of equipment, not all of it included in basic price. Good value for money.

MANUFACTURER
Sunbeam-Talbot Ltd., Ryton-on-Dunsmore, Coventry.

PRICES
Basic	£725 0s 0d
Purchase Tax	£152 12s 1d
Total (in G.B.)	£877 12s 1d

EXTRAS (INC. P.T.)
Overdrive	£51 7s 1d
Heater	£18 2s 6d
Whitewall Dunlop Road Speed tyres	£12 16s 9d
Seat belts (each)	£3 19s 6d
Ammeter	£3 6s 0d
Clock	£7 15s 4d
Fog lamps (each)	£5 7s 9d

PERFORMANCE SUMMARY
Mean maximum speed	98 m.p.h.
Standing start quarter mile	19.1 sec
0-60 m.p.h.	13.6 sec
30-70 m.p.h. (through gears)	13.9 sec
Overall fuel consumption	25.5 m.p.g.
Miles per tankful	280

SPORTS car fashions, equipment and fittings have changed a lot in the past decade. One of the first models to break with the old he-man tradition, by offering wind-up windows, comfortable seating and plenty of space, was the Sunbeam Alpine. Introduced in 1959 with a structure based largely on a Hillman Husky floor, 1,494 c.c. 78 b.h.p. Sunbeam Rapier engine and gearbox, the Alpine has been revised several times in the intervening seven years. The engine became 1,592 c.c. for Series II, reclining seats and a smart GT hardtop model appeared in Series III, while a new hood mechanism, together with the trimming down of tail fins identified Series IV. The latest revision—to Series V—places more emphasis on mechanical improvements than before. In common with other Rootes models for 1966, the engine has been given a longer-stroke, five-main-bearing crankshaft which increases capacity to 1,725 c.c.; however, only the Alpine is fitted with twin constant-vacuum Stromberg 150CD carburettors. Though the gearbox has included synchromesh on bottom for nearly two years, the latest car has its own special close-ratio set matched to the new engine tune.

Thus equipped, along with the optional overdrive, adjustable steering column and a wide range of instruments, the Series V Alpine is a thoroughly practical sporting car offering nearly saloon car comforts at a very reasonable price. Indeed, since 1959, despite all the mechanical and styling changes, the basic price of this open sports car has increased by only £40, to £725, which is no mean achievement.

In spite of the progressive power increases and a careful control on all-up weight, Alpines are not really much quicker now than ever they were. Unfortunately we cannot make comparisons with our Series IV test car, as this was the heavier GT model with optional automatic transmission (no longer available on Series V). The last open car we tried was a Series II back in 1960, and the last manual car a series III in September 1963. Acceleration through the gears, and performance in any one gear has been marginally improved, although the real gain of the new close ratio box has been to make the latest car less fussy to drive. Even when using overdrive, and under favourable wind conditions, 100 m.p.h. was barely possible; 90 m.p.h. was none the less a comfortable cruising speed on motorways and could be maintained with little strain.

The Alpine is normally sold without overdrive, and a 3.89 axle ratio, while our test car had the overdrive and 4.22 axle ratio that goes with it. The

136

Autocar Road Test 2079

MAKE: SUNBEAM

TYPE: Alpine Series V

WEIGHT
Kerb weight (with oil, water, and half-full fuel tank): 20·0 cwt (2,246lb–1,020kg)
Front-rear distribution, per cent: F, 51·6; R, 48·4
Laden as tested .. 23·0 cwt (2,582lb–1,172kg)

TURNING CIRCLES
Between kerbs .. L, 31ft 8in; R, 33ft 2in.
Between walls .. L, 33ft 6in.; R, 34ft 11in.
Steering wheel turns lock-to-lock .. .. 3·6

PERFORMANCE DATA
Top gear m.p.h. per 1,000 r.p.m. .. 16·3
Overdrive top gear m.p.h. per 1,000 r.p.m. 20·3
Mean piston speed at max power 2,980 ft/min.
Engine revs at mean maximum speed (overdrive) 4,825 r.p.m.
B.h.p. per ton laden .. .. 80·0

OIL CONSUMPTION
Miles per pint (SAE 20W) 220

FUEL CONSUMPTION
At constant speeds: top and overdrive

m.p.h.	Top m.p.g.	O.D. Top m.p.g.	m.p.h.	Top m.p.g.	O.D. Top m.p.g.
30	44·5	48·2	70	28·0	31·7
40	39·6	44·5	80	23·4	27·6
50	35·7	39·6	90	19·4	23·4
60	31·2	34·8			

Overall m.p.g. 25·5 m.p.g. (11·1 litres/100 km)
Normal range m.p.g. .. 23-30 (12·3-9·4 litres/100km)
Test distance (corrected) .. 1,317 miles
Estimated (DIN) m.p.g. 28·8 (9·8 litres/100km)
Grade .. .. Premium (96·2-98·6 RM)

TEST CONDITIONS
Weather Dry and overcast, with 5-10 m.p.h. wind
Barometer .. .. .. 29·5in. Hg.
Temperature .. .. 7 deg. C. (45 deg. F.)
Surfaces .. .. Dry concrete and asphalt

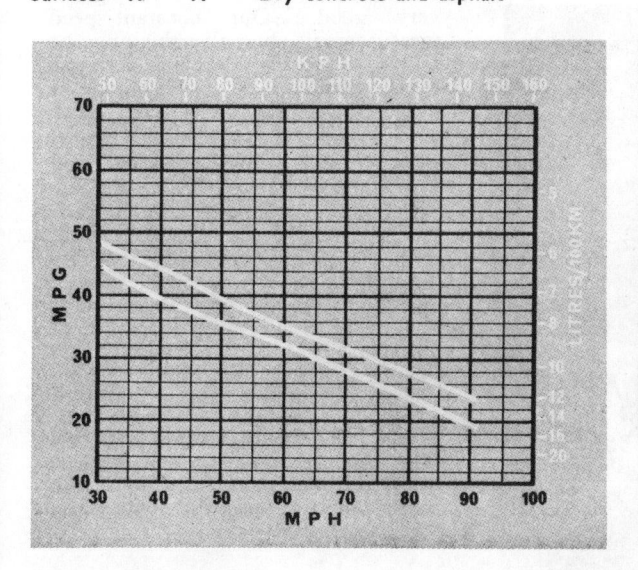

Speed range, gear ratios and time in seconds

m.p.h.	O.D. Top (3·38)	Top (4·22)	O.D. Third (4·39)	Third (5·47)	Second (8·40)	First (13·17)
10—30	—	—	—	9·0	5·0	3·2
20—40	16·2	11·0	10·7	7·7	4·4	—
30—50	16·6	10·0	9·8	7·0	—	—
40—60	16·6	10·1	9·5	7·4	—	—
50—70	17·1	10·5	11·4	10·3	—	—
60—80	20·7	13·1	16·1	—	—	—
70—90	—	24·3	25·7	—	—	—

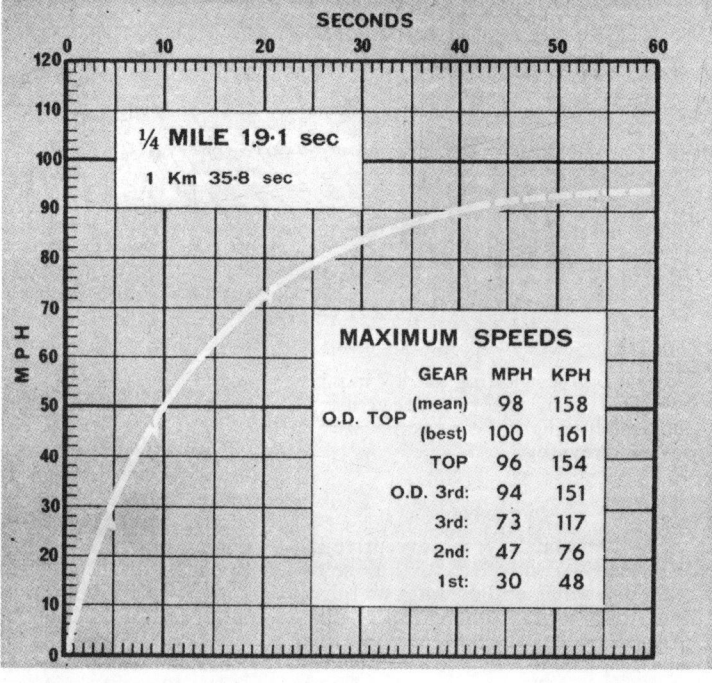

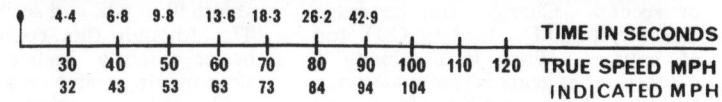

¼ MILE 19·1 sec
1 Km 35·8 sec

MAXIMUM SPEEDS

GEAR	MPH	KPH
O.D. TOP (mean)	98	158
(best)	100	161
TOP	96	154
O.D. 3rd:	94	151
3rd:	73	117
2nd:	47	76
1st:	30	48

TIME IN SECONDS: 4·4 / 6·8 / 9·8 / 13·6 / 18·3 / 26·2 / 42·9
TRUE SPEED MPH: 30 / 40 / 50 / 60 / 70 / 80 / 90 / 100 / 110 / 120
INDICATED MPH: 32 / 43 / 53 / 63 / 73 / 84 / 94 / 104

BRAKES

(from 30 m.p.h. in neutral)

Pedal load	Retardation	Equiv. distance
25lb	0·23g	131ft
50lb	0·45g	67ft
75lb	0·72g	42ft
100lb	0·88g	34ft
125lb	0·90g	33ft
150lb	1·00g	30·1ft
Handbrake	0·35g	86ft

CLUTCH Pedal load and travel: 32lb and 5in.

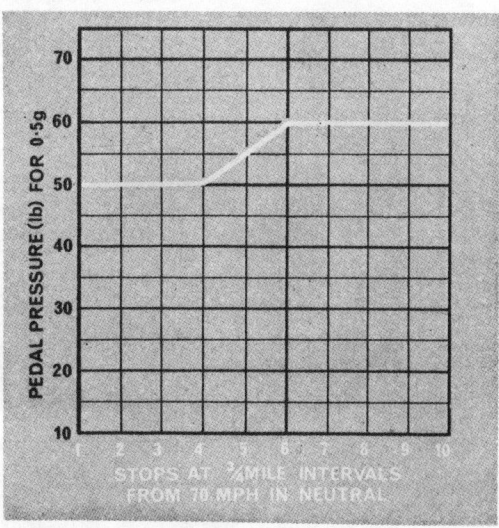

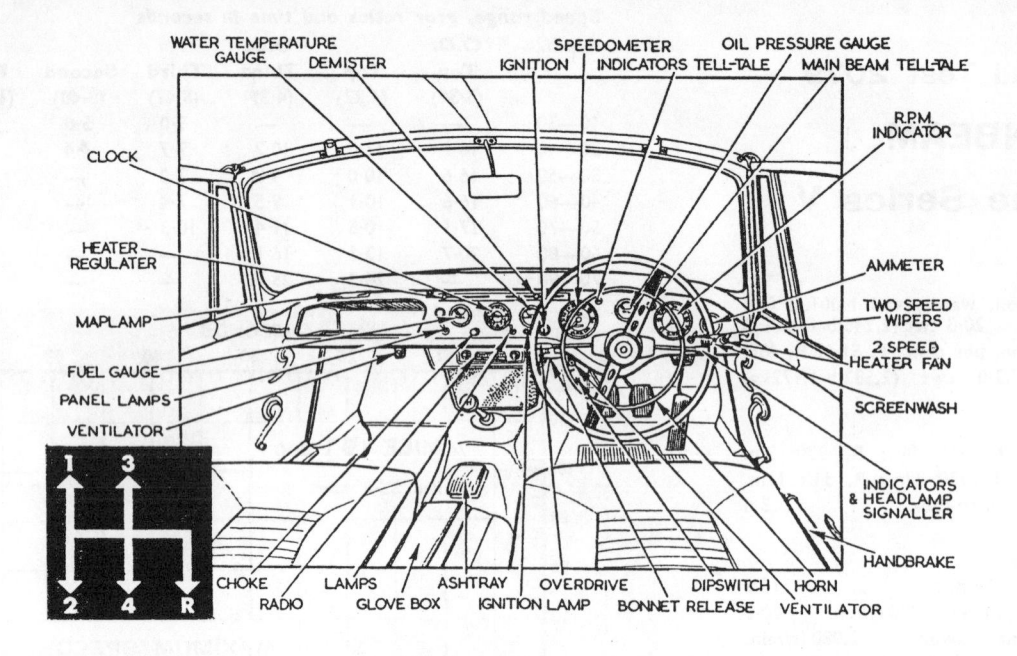

3·89 ratio gives gearing at 18·7 m.p.h. per 1,000 r.p.m. in top, and a genuine 100 m.p.h. might be possible without over-revving.

Overdrive

The optional Laycock overdrive is electrically controlled by a self-centring switch, and operates on third and top; it is automatically disengaged when changing out of the top-3rd plane of the gate into bottom or second. Changes can be made direct from O.D. third to O.D. top of course. What is nominally a 6-speed set of gears is spoilt—as often happens—by overdrive third and direct top having almost the same ratio. Acceleration figures in O.D. third were a little better than in direct top up to 70 m.p.h.; above this speed the extra friction in the overdrive made direct top more efficient. O.D. third was good for 94 m.p.h., and top 96 m.p.h.

Compared with the Series III, acceleration through the gears is a little better, more particularly at higher speeds where wind resistance begins to take effect. From 0-60 m.p.h. takes 13·6sec (Series III took 14·9), while a standing-start quarter-mile needs 19·1sec (19·8sec). The special close-ratio gearbox has well-planned steps; bottom is good for about 30 m.p.h. and second goes on to 47, although this could have been better slightly higher for passing slow-moving traffic on winding roads.

The Alpine engine is only mildly tuned—with 53 b.h.p./litre—and is a very docile unit for slow, town work. Carburation is good and the engine runs evenly at all speeds; however towards the end of the test period the plugs gave trouble and had to be replaced. It pulls strongly without snatch from as low as 1,000 r.p.m., and is still breathing well when the rev counter needle enters the danger zone starting at 6,000 r.p.m. (We limited speeds in all the gears to this figure.) There was quite a lot of induction noise and our road test car produced a painful grating resonance through the throttle linkage, which eventually fell apart.

The Alpine is easy to start from cold, but needs a lot of choke during the first few minutes running. Difficult hot-starting was one of the troubles with the earlier Sunbeam Alpines; we were particularly pleased to find that the Stromberg carburettors seem to have cured this at last.

Fuel Consumption

Most of our staff like driving comfortable sporting cars, and one or two found excuses to rush off on journeys in the Sunbeam. Nearly everyone drove it quickly where traffic conditions allowed, so that the overall fuel consumption figure—25·5 m.p.g.—is very good. Our constant-speed measurements show that this must be a very carefully developed engine tune; consumption at 30 m.p.h. in overdrive top gear is 48·4 m.p.g. Even at 70 m.p.h. we recorded 31·7 m.p.g. and overdrive always gives an extra 10 m.p.h. cruising speed at no extra fuel cost. Super-premium petrol is not needed, the aluminium cylinder head, with its 9·2 compression ratio, dealing with premium grade without protest. The average Alpine owner, who may not use all the performance all the time, should chalk up to 28 m.p.g. without effort and should manage 300 miles on a tankful of petrol.

The flush-fitting, snap-action, fuel filler cap in the offside rear wing is neat, and accepted full flow from pump nozzles until the twin tanks were nearly full.

The Alpine Series V is the only Rootes model to have twin Stromberg 150CD carburettors. Piping from the cylinder head to inlet manifold looks after closed-circuit crankcase breathing

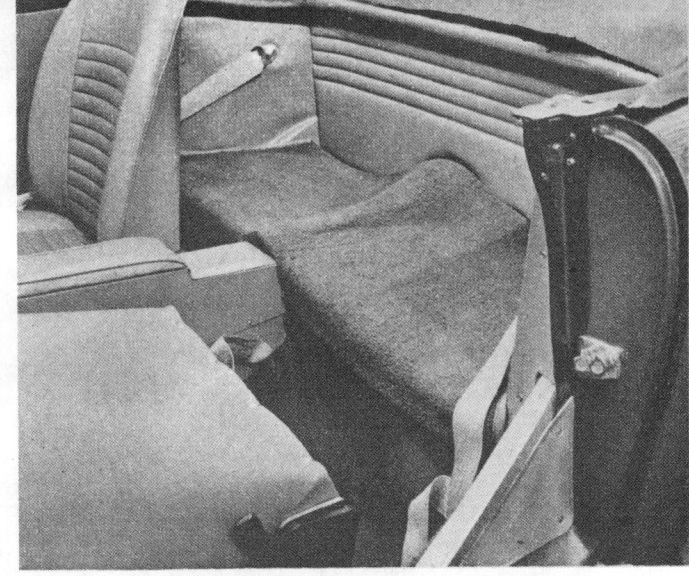

Above:
By stowing the spare wheel vertically, there is a reasonable amount of luggage space. Twin fuel tanks are fitted, one in each rear wing. The bumper over-riders are rubber padded

Above right:
This carpeted shelf behind the front seats is not meant to carry people, as there is no legroom. Its base lifts to reveal the battery. The hood is concealed under the tonneau when folded

Right:
Facia of the open Sunbeam Alpine is trimmed with leathercloth. The heater, clock, radio and ammeter are all extras. The glove box between the front seats is lockable

Suspension is supple, and reminds one of several continental sports cars rather than its obvious British competitors. The optional Road Speed tyres help the basically very sound suspension balance to produce really safe, predictable road holding. The steering is low geared, and strongly self-centring; this gives the impression of considerable understeer when entering sharp bends. Twisting roads are best tackled with some verve because the combination of a fairly heavy car and a front-end which tends to plough safely towards the outside of bends makes a normal approach hard work. In fact, the car is well-balanced enough to allow it to be set up in advance and help the tail to come round. On a long bend, the understeer gradually and predictably changes to a more neutral attitude, which is almost automatically corrected by slight wheel movements.

Suspension

That this is after all a fairly firmly sprung sports car becomes apparent when driving over rough ground. On the M.I.R.A. washboard surface the body felt especially rigid at normal speeds, although anything below 20 m.p.h. caused the scuttle and screen to shake around quite appreciably. At 60 m.p.h. there was virtually no vibration at all. Ride on the *pavé* was good, but the simple rear suspension (by half-elliptic springs and a live axle) has limitations of movement and control; there was appreciable axle-hop, and these movements tended to tweak the rear of the car sideways quite abruptly. Long-wave pitches proved rather unpleasant, as the car bucked up at the rear first, above 50 m.p.h.

All that needs to be said about the brakes is that they are a servo-assisted Girling, mixed disc-drum system. Firm and progressive, with excellent "feel" and apparently very resistant to fade, they are as safe and predictable as we would expect. Surprisingly high pedal pressures are required from the servo-assisted system for it takes a manly push of 150lb to record 1·0g braking.

Leverage on the pull-up handbrake, mounted snugly between the driver's door and the seat, is almost ideal, but a strong tug is needed to prevent the car from rolling back on a 1-in-3 test hill. Restart was easy and immediate. Use of the handbrake in emergencies would only produce about 0·25g. The window winding handle has at last been moved so that it is now well clear of the handbrake lever.

Driving Position

Drivers of all shapes and sizes quickly make themselves comfortable in the Alpine, for the driving position is adjustable in several ways. Not only can the seats be moved back and forward as usual (through 6in.), and their deep backrests adjusted for rake through a wide range, but the steering column is adjustable for reach and the pedal cluster can be moved with the aid of a spanner. Steering column adjustment is particularly simple. The boss in the centre of the wheel is turned to release the clamp, and the wheel can then be moved back and forth through 2·5in. and locked in any intermediate position. Padded rolls on the seat cushion and backrest locate driver and passenger very securely; no effort is needed to hold oneself in place when cornering hard

AUTOCAR, 13 May 1966

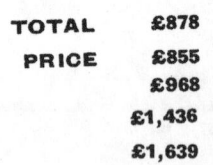

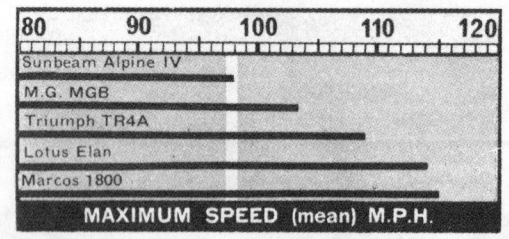

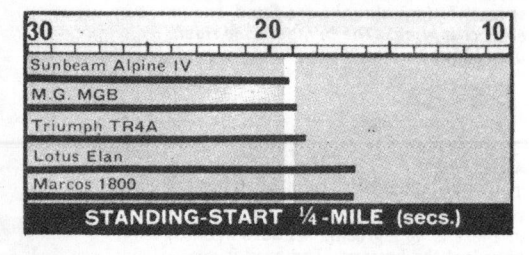

HOW THE SUNBEAM ALPINE SERIES V COMPARES:

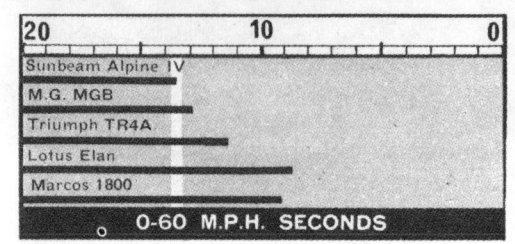

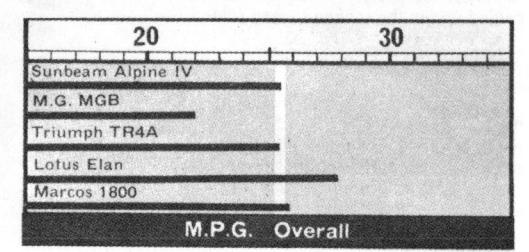

TOTAL PRICE	MAXIMUM SPEED (mean) M.P.H.	STANDING-START ¼-MILE (secs.)	0-60 M.P.H. SECONDS	M.P.G. Overall
£878 Sunbeam Alpine IV				
£855 M.G. MGB				
£968 Triumph TR4A				
£1,436 Lotus Elan				
£1,639 Marcos 1800				

Sunbeam Alpine V...

With front seats in their normal position, there is really no room for people to sit on the carpeted shelf behind. One adult might just squeeze in—sideways and uncomfortably—for short distances, but children would manage better, as with the hood up headroom is limited. The base of the shelf lifts to reveal the battery, well away from engine and transmission heat.

Stowage Space

This shelf is really intended as extra stowage space for coats and maybe a picnic hamper. There is a small open compartment in front of the passenger (with a map reading lamp above it, and a grab handle in its padded lip), while an oblong, locking box is mounted between the seats as an armrest. Neither is big enough, however, for a camera or lady's handbag.

Road test Alpines usually arrive with a full range of instruments and of these the ammeter and accurate clock are still extras. Blanking plates are easily removed to fit them into the leathercloth covered panel. (On the alternative GT model the facia is polished walnut). Rootes instruments are always crisply styled and plainly calibrated with white figures on a black ground, and Dayglo red pointers. The fuel gauge is marked in gallons and litres, and the speedometer has a secondary kilometer scale. The all-important oil pressure gauge is immediately in front of the driver, between the speedometer and rev counter, whereas the other minor instruments, controls and switches are scattered around the panel. Sensibly, the wiper switch and washer button are next to each other.

Headlamp mainbeam and indicator warning lights have roll-down lenses special to Rootes which can be adjusted like tiny translucent eyelids to reduce the glare at night. The overdrive tell-tale is no longer fitted.

Pedal layout is excellent. The organ-pedal throttle control enables easy heel-and-toe changes; when the left foot is not working the clutch it can be rested on the rubber cap of the dipswitch, tight up against the tunnel.

With such a well-planned interior, and luxuries such as the oil cooler and folding hood, we were surprised to find that a heater costs over £18 extra. (It is, however, standard on the GT.) Plenty of really warm air is supplied, but there are no face level vents, and it is impossible to send cool air on to the screen while heating the footwells. New on the Series V, however, are independent cold air vents which channel ram-air into the footwells at knee height, a refreshing feature for heat waves and hot climates.

Hood

The Alpine has always offered a neat, easily stowed hood, but there have been further refinements in the last couple of years. Stability and good sealing around the door glasses are assured by using rigid members from the screen to the hood pivots behind the seats (these bars fold down for stowage). A rigid bar with four positive fastenings fits snugly against the screen rail, and above the door glasses twin lengths of nylon burr zips bind the fabric to the fold-

140

ing rails and ensure an air-tight fit. When performed in the correct sequence, hood stowage is quick and easy. The hinged steel panels of earlier models have gone, and the hood now disappears into a short, full-width box with built-in tonneau cover which neatly covers the folded fabric, or the hole when the hood is erect.

Door glasses, with fixed quarter lights, and the deep screen, fend off most of the wind when the hood is down, but above about 70 m.p.h. there is quite a lot of turbulence and back draught.

Maintenance is down to a practical minimum. There are no greasing points at all, and oil changes are at 6,000-mile intervals. The dipstick is short and inaccessible, hiding between the distributor and the oil filter, and masked by the coil and a scuttle stiffening tube.

No one seriously expects sports cars to be draughty, noisy and uncomfortable these days. Complete weather protection, comfortable seats and adequate luggage room, with docile road manners and close to 100 m.p.h. are now demanded by the enthusiast. The Alpine Series V provides all these and, although approaching its seventh birthday in July, continual improvements in equipment and power output have maintained its competitive position. ■

SPECIFICATION : SUNBEAM ALPINE, SERIES V, FRONT ENGINE, REAR-WHEEL DRIVE

ENGINE
- Cylinders .. 4 in-line
- Cooling system .. Water; pump, fan and thermostat
- Bore .. 81·5mm (3·21in.)
- Stroke .. 82·55mm (3·25in.)
- Displacement .. 1,725 c.c. (105·2 cu. in.)
- Valve gear .. Overhead, pushrods and rockers
- Compression ratio 9·2-to-1
- Carburettors .. 2 Stromberg 150 CD
- Fuel pump .. AC mechanical
- Oil filter .. Fram full flow
- Max. power .. 92·5 b.h.p. (net) at 5,500 r.p.m.
- Max. torque .. 110 lb. ft. (net) at 3,700 r.p.m.

TRANSMISSION
- Clutch .. Borg and Beck diaphragm spring, 7·5in. dia.
- Gearbox .. 4-speed, all synchromesh
- Gear ratios .. OD Top 0·80; top 1·00; OD third 1·04; third 1·30; second 2·00; first 3·12; reverse 3·35
- Final drive .. Hypoid bevel, 4·22-to-1 (with overdrive)

CHASSIS AND BODY
- Construction .. Integral with pressed steel body

SUSPENSION
- Front .. Independent, coil springs and wishbones, anti-roll bar, telescopic dampers
- Rear .. Live-axle, half-elliptic leaf springs telescopic dampers

STEERING
- Type .. Burman, recirculating-ball. Wheel dia. 15·5in.

BRAKES
- Make and type .. Girling disc front, drum rear. Servo: Girling vacuum type
- Dimensions .. F, 9·85in. dia.; R, 9·0in. dia.; 1·75in. wide shoes
- Swept area .. F, 196 sq. in.; R, 99 sq. in. Total 295 sq. in. (256 sq. in.) per ton laden

WHEELS
- Type .. Pressed steel disc, five studs 4·5in. wide rim
- Tyres .. Dunlop C.41 tubeless—size 6·00 13in. (optional Dunlop RS5 5·90-13in. fitted to test car)

EQUIPMENT
- Battery .. 12-volt 43-amp. hr.
- Alternator .. Lucas 10AC, 35 amp.
- Headlamps .. Lucas sealed beam 60-45 watt
- Reversing lamp .. Extra
- Electric fuses .. 2
- Screen wipers .. 2-speed, self parking
- Screen washer .. Standard, manual plunger
- Interior heater .. Extra, fresh air type
- Safety belts .. Extra, anchorages built in
- Interior trim .. Pvc seats, Everflex hood
- Floor covering .. Rubber mats
- Starting handle .. No provision
- Jack .. Screw pillar
- Jacking points .. 4, at each corner
- Other bodies .. Hardtop G.T.

MAINTENANCE
- Fuel tank .. 11·25 Imp. gallons (no reserve) (50 litres)
- Cooling system .. 12·5 pints (including heater) (7·1 litres)
- Engine sump .. 8·25 pints (4·5 litres) SAE 20W or 10W/30 (including oil cooler) Change oil every 6,000 miles; change filter element every 6,000 miles
- Gearbox and overdrive .. 4·5 pints SAE 10/50. Change oil every 6,000 miles
- Final drive .. 1·75 pints SAE 90EP. Change oil every 6,000 miles
- Grease .. No points
- Tyre pressures .. F, 24; R, 24 p.s.i. (normal driving) F, 24; R, 26 p.s.i. (fast driving)

Scale ⅛in to 1ft cushions uncompressed

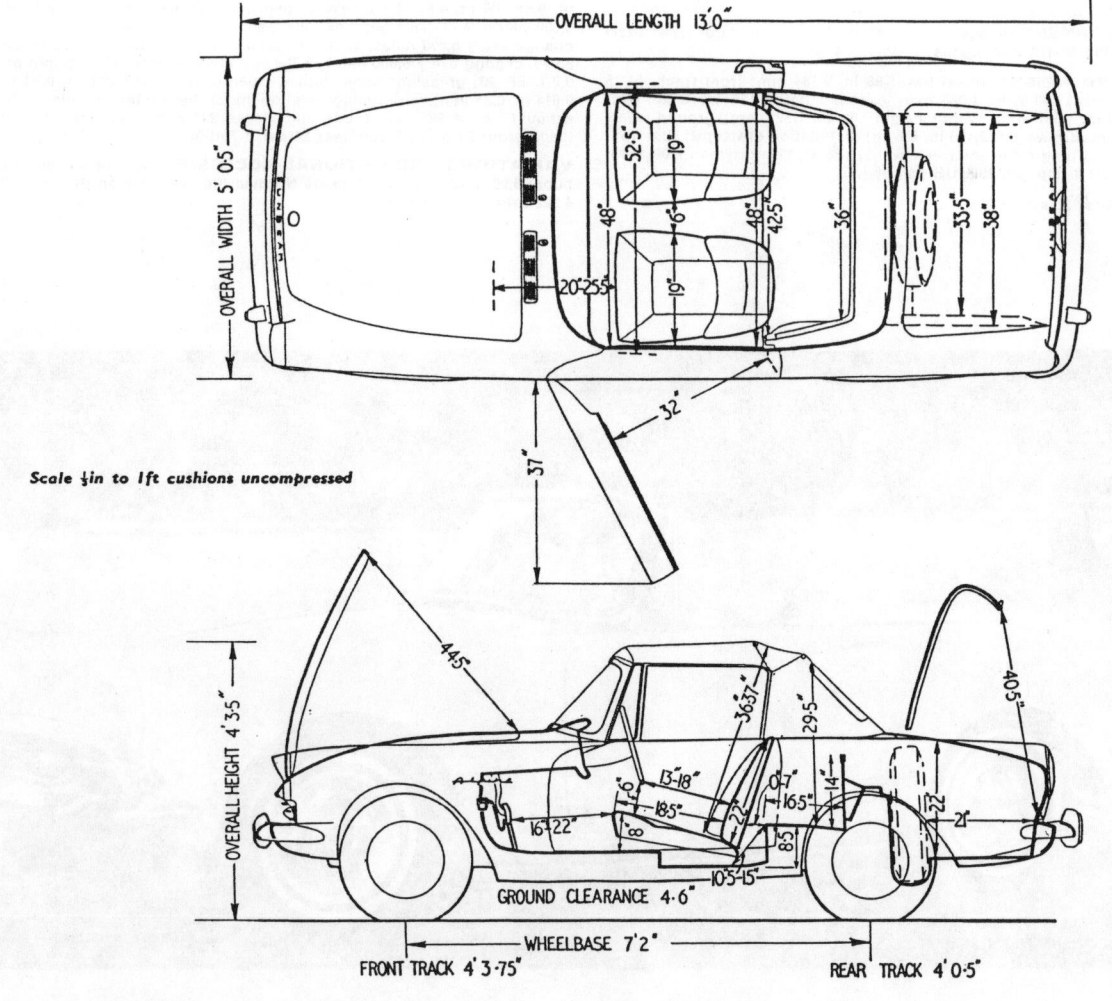

Sunbeam Alpine Series V
Sports Tourer

ENGINE CAPACITY 105.26 cu in, 1,725 cu cm
FUEL CONSUMPTION 28 m/imp gal, 23.3 m/US gal, 10.1 l × 100 km
SEATS 2 **MAX SPEED** 102 mph, 164.2 km/h
PRICE IN GB basic £ 725, total £ 877
PRICE IN USA $ 2,399

ENGINE front, 4 stroke; cylinders: 4, vertical, in line; bore and stroke: 3.21 × 3.25 in, 81.5 × 82.5 mm; engine capacity: 105.26 cu in, 1,725 cu cm; compression ratio: 9.2; max power (SAE): 100 hp at 5,500 rpm; max torque (SAE): 110 lb ft, 15.2 kg m at 3,700 rpm; max number of engine rpm: 6,200; specific power: 58 hp/l; cylinder block: cast iron; cylinder head: light alloy; crankshaft bearings: 5; valves: 2 per cylinder, overhead, in line, push-rods and rockers; camshafts: 1, side; lubrication: rotary pump, full flow filter; lubricating system capacity: 9 imp pt, 10.78 US pt, 5.1 l; carburation: 2 Zenith-Stromberg 150 CD semi-downdraught carburettors; fuel feed: mechanical pump; cooling system: water; cooling system capacity: 12.50 imp pt, 15.01 US pt, 7.1 l.

TRANSMISSION driving wheels: rear; clutch: single dry plate, hydraulically controlled; gearbox: mechanical; gears: 4 + reverse; synchromesh gears: I, II, III, IV; gearbox ratios: I 3.122, II 1.993, III 1.296, IV 1, rev 3.323; gear lever: central; final drive: hypoid bevel; axle ratio: 3.889.

CHASSIS integral; front suspension: independent, wishbones, coil springs, anti-roll bar, telescopic dampers; rear suspension: rigid axle, semi-elliptic leafsprings, telescopic dampers.

STEERING recirculating ball; turns of steering wheel lock to lock: 3.

BRAKES front disc (diameter 9.84 in, 250 mm), rear drum, servo; area rubbed by linings: front 196 sq in, 1,264.20 sq cm, rear 99 sq in, 638.55 sq cm, total 295 sq in, 1,902.75 sq cm.

ELECTRICAL EQUIPMENT voltage: 12 V; battery: 43 Ah; generator type: alternator, 35 Ah; ignition distributor: Lucas; headlamps: 2.

DIMENSIONS AND WEIGHT wheel base: 86 in, 2,184 mm; front track: 51.75 in, 1,314 mm; rear track: 48.65 in, 1,236 mm; overall length: 156 in, 3,962 mm; overall width: 60.50 in, 1,537 mm; overall height: 52 in, 1,321 mm; ground clearance: 4.25 in, 108 mm; dry weight: 2,108 lb, 956 kg; distribution of weight: 52% front axle, 48% rear axle; turning circle (between walls): 36 ft, 11 m; tyres: 6.00 × 13; fuel tank capacity: 11.2 imp gal, 13.5 US gal, 51 l.

BODY sports; doors: 2; seats: 2.

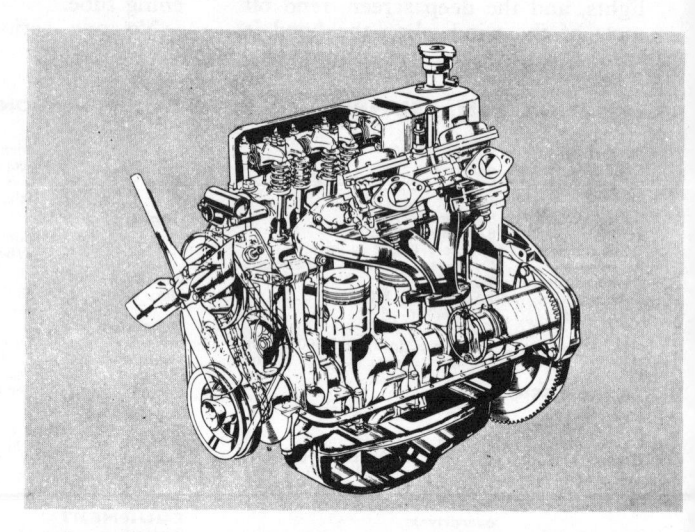

PERFORMANCE max speeds: 37 mph, 59.6 km/h in 1st gear; 57 mph, 91.8 km/h in 2nd gear; 88 mph, 141.7 km/h in 3rd gear; 102 mph, 164.2 km/h in 4th gear; power-weight ratio: 21.2 lb/hp, 9.6 kg/hp; carrying capacity: 375 lb, 170 kg; acceleration: 0—50 mph (0—80 km/h) 8.9 sec; speed in direct drive at 1,000 rpm: 17.8 mph, 28.7 km/h.

PRACTICAL INSTRUCTIONS fuel: 91-94 oct petrol; engine sump oil: 8 imp pt, 9.51 US pt, 4.5 l, SAE 10W-20 (winter) 20W-30 or 40 (summer), change every 6,000 miles, 9,700 km; gearbox oil: 3.50 imp pt, 4.23 US pt, 2 l, SAE 30W-20W, change every 6,000 miles, 9,700 km; final drive oil: 1.80 imp pt, 2.11 US pt, 1 l, EP 80-90, change every 6,000 miles, 9,700 km; steering box oil: 0.35 imp pt, 0.42 US pt, 0.2 l, EP 90; greasing: none; tappet clearances: inlet 0.012 in, 0.30 mm, exhaust 0.014 in, 0.36 mm; valve timing: inlet opens 29° before tdc and closes 63° after bdc, exhaust opens 69° before bdc and closes 23° after tdc; tyre pressure (medium load): front 24 psi, 1.7 atm, rear 24 psi, 1.7 atm.

VARIATIONS AND OPTIONAL ACCESSORIES wire wheels and knock-on hubs; 5.90 × 13 tyres; Laycock-de Normanville overdrive on III and IV (0.803 ratio), 4.222 axle ratio; hardtop.

MOTOR ROAD TEST No. 27/66 ● Sunbeam Alpine GT

This view of the Alpine has not changed very much over the years: earlier cars had a slatted grille and metal overriders on the bumper. The fog and spot lights are extras.

Civilized sports car

". . . its performance, handling, steering and transmission have all been upgraded to satisfy the more fastidious demands of the keen driver."

RIGHTLY or wrongly, the Sunbeam Alpine became known in its early days as a "gentleman's tourer"—which was a polite way of saying that it handled and went like a saloon (albeit a good saloon) while looking like a sports car. Since then, the trend in sports cars has been towards greater refinement while many saloons, backed by rally reputations, are leaning towards the enthusiastic market: the two have converged to such an extent that anything with two seats is now automatically sporting. Happily, we think the Alpine now justifies this label because its performance, handling, steering and transmission have all been upgraded after a programme of continous development, to satisfy the more fastidious demands of the keen driver. Rootes themselves prefer the GT label for the hard top model we tested and Sports Tourer for the cheaper soft top: with the first you get better trim, more room for children (or luggage) behind, but no alternative weather protection when the hard top is off. With the second (for which a hard top is also available at extra cost) the hood steals some of the already small back seats so the family man who likes fresh air has a difficult decision to make. Either way, you get a comfortable, civilized car with excellent front seats, a generally smooth and willing new 1,725 c.c. engine, an outstanding gearbox, and roadholding that, on smooth roads at least, would be educational to many people—especially early Alpine owners. It is not as fast as some competitive two seaters in the £1,000 bracket (the maximum speed is still below 100 m.p.h.) but there is compensation in greater economy, especially if overdrive is fitted. It is a likeable car that, without being sensationally good in any way, seems to make friends with all who drive or ride in it, whether they have sporting leanings or not.

Performance and economy

With 92.5 b.h.p., the Alpine has the most powerful of the four 1,725 c.c. engines (58.5 b.h.p. Minx/Gazelle, 65 b.h.p. Super Minx, 85 b.h.p. Sceptre/Vogue) and also by far the smoothest that we have yet experienced. On full choke it usually starts promptly when cold but even in mid-summer took a long time to warm up. For several miles, the choke on our test car had to be manipulated in and out according to speed and throttle opening to prevent either over-revving or cutting out altogether. Sometimes the starter had to be whirred several times before a warm engine would fire.

PRICE: £775 plus £163 5s. 5d. purchase tax equals £938 5s. 5d. Overdrive as fitted £54 7s. 6d. extra.

Sunbeam Alpine GT
continued

There is a fairly strong pull from 1,000 r.p.m. upwards (even though peak torque is not reached until 3,700 r.p.m.) so you don't have to linger for the power to "come in". Up to 5,000 r.p.m., it feels crisp and smooth but begins to get hysterically noisy and buzzy at higher speeds--so much so that most drivers settled for 5,000 r.p.m. as a normal ceiling. In any case, acceleration seems to tail off at very high engine speeds so the 6,000 r.p.m. red line on the rev counter is perhaps more for show than for practical use. Despite a claimed increase in power of 10 b.h.p. (about 10%) over the last manual Alpine we tested—one of the finned series III cars—the top speed has increased by only 1 m.p.h. and is disappointingly still just short of 100 m.p.h., although it needs only slightly favourable conditions to exceed this speed. There is a more marked improvement in acceleration especially in top gear acceleration which starts with a fairly strong 20-40 m.p.h. time of under 11 seconds and doesn't begin to tail away until after 70 m.p.h. The car is also quicker through the gears than before and up to 70 m.p.h. is level pegging all the way with its obvious and closest rival, the MGB GT.

These useful if not dramatic gains in performance have been matched by similar improvements to economy—a rare achievement. At 30 m.p.h. in overdrive top the car is doing well over 50 m.p.g.: even at 70 m.p.h. it is still as high as 35 m.p.g., a figure that conveniently corresponds to our touring consumption. So law-abiding people who use only modest acceleration in the lower gears will have light fuel bills; even hard drivers will probably not drop below our 25.6 m.p.g. overall. We used premium (98 octane) petrol without any pinking.

Transmission

Some people consider the latest gearbox to be a more worthwhile improvement than the new engine. Without being quite the best gearbox in existence, it is nonetheless hard to fault and pleased all who used it besides suiting a variety of cars with equal distinction—the Gazelle, Super Minx and Alpine for instance. Rootes have achieved such finesse with a light, smooth and easy gearchange (synchromesh on all four gears) and matched it to an equally light, smooth and short-travel clutch. The pair seem unusually well co-ordinated and pleasant to use.

With the optional overdrive fitted to our car, there are ostensibly six different ratios but since overdrive third and direct top are so close together it is perhaps more practical to regard it as a five-speed box with alternative means of selecting fourth. Some drivers were disappointed that the overdrive switch, a stalk on the left of the steering column, could not be worked simultaneously with the gear lever: others would have found it more natural to move the spring-loaded centre-return lever upwards (rather than down) to change up. On a light throttle or at modest speeds (up to 60 m.p.h.) upward changes are reasonably smooth; high-speed or down changes are best done while dipping the clutch to avoid an unpleasant jerk.

It needs two people to lift the hard top which is locked in place by four over-centre catches which need strong fingers to work.

Five-seater: there is comfortable room for three small children on the rear bench seat.

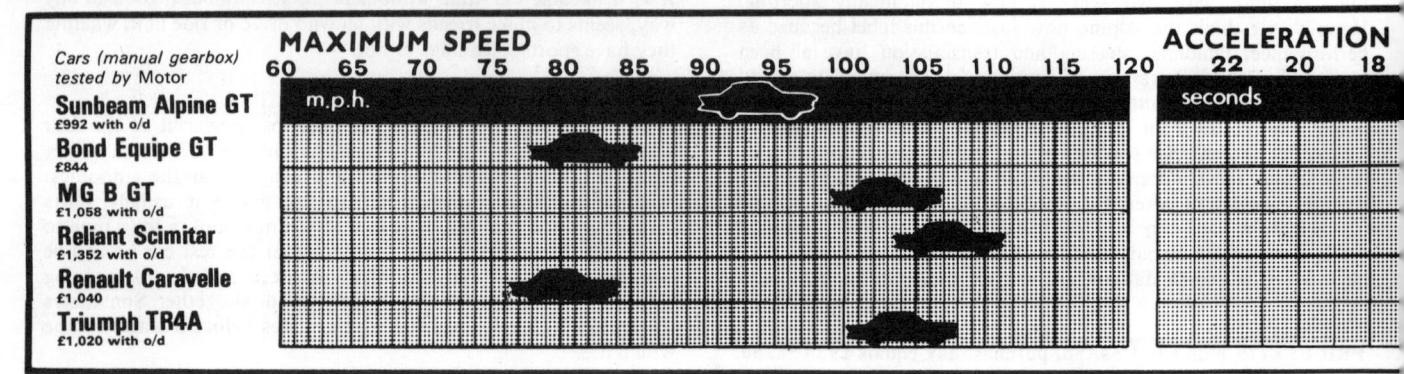

We thought the overdrive was a valuable extra; it is impossible to overtax the engine in overdrive top (20.4 m.p.h. per 1,000 r.p.m.) for even at a downhill 100 m.p.h., the engine is doing only 4,900 r.p.m.—1,100 r.p.m. below the limit. At 70 m.p.h., it is under 3,500 r.p.m. so the life expectancy of the engine ought to be high. First gear—a dragster ratio rather than a panic gear—would not start the car from rest on a 1 in 3 hill. There is no gear whine at all, either from the gearbox or the final drive.

Handling and brakes

The Alpine's handling, though not in the best sports car class, would impress saloon car drivers unaccustomed to flat cornering, squeal-free tyres (Dunlop RS5s), and fairly high-geared medium-weight steering that responds positively (but a little springly) to quite small wheel movements. As one driver said, the steering would be unrecognizable to any Rootes driver of five years ago. There is not nearly so much built-in understeer as on the closely related saloons so long-arm purists can hustle through a tight S bend without lifting a hand from the wheel. On a good surface, the car has reassuring "on rails" roadholding with little decelerative tyre scrub or premature tendency for the back to break away. Breakaway in the wet is progressive and very controllable on cross-ply tyres.

The roadholding deteriorates appreciably on poor surfaces and a bumpy corner will patter the wheels off course, make the body pitch and roll, and can induce severe axle tramp if you try any violent standing-start acceleration. These observations contradict what we said about the last Alpine (an automatic) we tested: the difference is probably due to the smoother and smaller delivery of power in the earlier car and what we suspect were light damper settings (or weak dampers) on the latest versions.

The brakes passed all our tests quite well though some people thought they were a little too heavy (despite servo assistance) and spongy. The handbrake was very strong.

Continued on the next page

Performance

Test Data: World copyright reserved; no unauthorized reproduction in whole or in part.

Conditions

Weather: Warm and mild, light breeze 0-5 m.p.h.
Temperature: 66°–70°F, Barometer 29.50 in. Hg.
Surface: Dry tarmacadam and concrete.
Fuel: Premium 98 octane (R.M.).

Maximum speeds

	m.p.h.
Mean lap speed banked circuit } direct top	98.0
Best one-way ¼-mile } direct top	100.00
O/d top gear	96.3
O/d 3rd gear	94.2
3rd gear (at 6,000 r.p.m.)	75.5
2nd gear	50.0
1st gear	31.0

"Maximile" speed (timed quarter mile after 1 mile accelerating from rest):
Mean 95.2
Best 95.8

Acceleration times

m.p.h.	sec.
0-30	3.9
0-40	6.5
0-50	8.9
0-60	13.0
0-70	17.9
0-80	25.5
Standing quarter mile	19.0

m.p.h.	O/d Top sec.	Top sec.	3rd sec.
10-30	—	—	8.4
20-40	14.7	10.7	7.5
30-50	15.0	10.1	6.8
40-60	15.6	10.2	7.5
50-70	17.3	11.6	9.0
60-80	21.8	13.5	12.2

Speedometer

Indicated	10	20	30	40	50	60	70	80	90
True	10	20	30	40½	50½	60½	70½	81	92

Distance recorder 1% fast

Hill climbing

At steady speed
		lb./ton
O/d top	1 in 15.1	(Tapley 145)
Top	1 in 9.7	(Tapley 230)
O/d 3rd	1 in 9.3	(Tapley 240)
3rd	1 in 6.8	(Tapley 325)
2nd	1 in 4.2	(Tapley 520)

Fuel consumption

Touring (consumption midway between 30 m.p.h. and maximum less 5% allowance for acceleration) .... 35.2 m.p.g.
Overall .... 25.6 m.p.g.
(= 11.0 litres/100 km.)
Total test distance .... 1,600 miles
Tank capacity (maker's figure) ..... 11 gals.

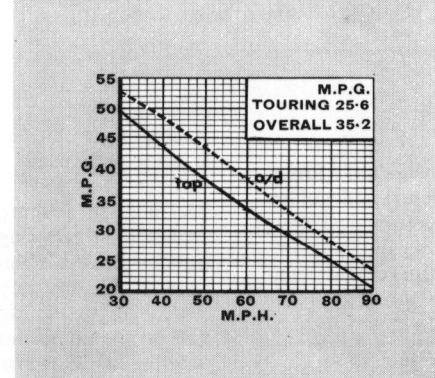

Steering

Turning circle between kerbs: ft.
Left 30.5
Right 32.0
Turns of steering wheel from lock to lock . 3¼
Steering wheel deflection for 50 ft. diameter circle = 0.95 turns

Brakes

Pedal pressure, deceleration and equivalent stopping distance from 30 m.p.h.

lb.	g	ft.
25	0.27	111
50	0.54	56
75	0.67	45
100	0.92	32½
120	0.98	30½
Handbrake	0.38	79

Fade test

20 stops at ½g deceleration at 1 min. intervals from a speed midway between 30 m.p.h. and maximum speed (= 64 m.p.h.).

	lb.
Pedal force at beginning	47
Pedal force at 10th stop	50
Pedal force at 20th stop	50

Clutch

Free pedal movement .... = 1 in.
Additional movement to disengage clutch completely .... = 3¼ in.
Maximum pedal load .... = 30 lb.

Weight

Kerb weight (unladen with fuel for approximately 50 miles) ..... 19.8 cwt.
Front/rear distribution 51/49
Weight laden as tested .... 23.6 cwt.

Parkability

Gap needed to clear a 6 ft. wide obstruction parked in front

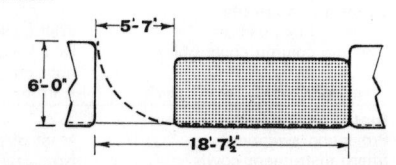

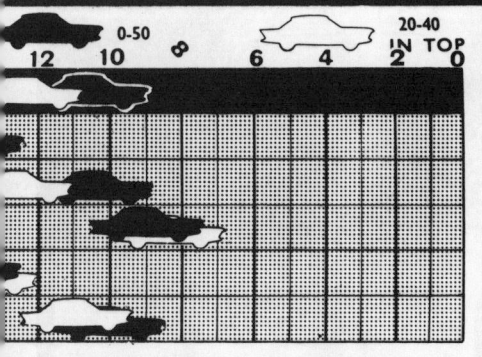

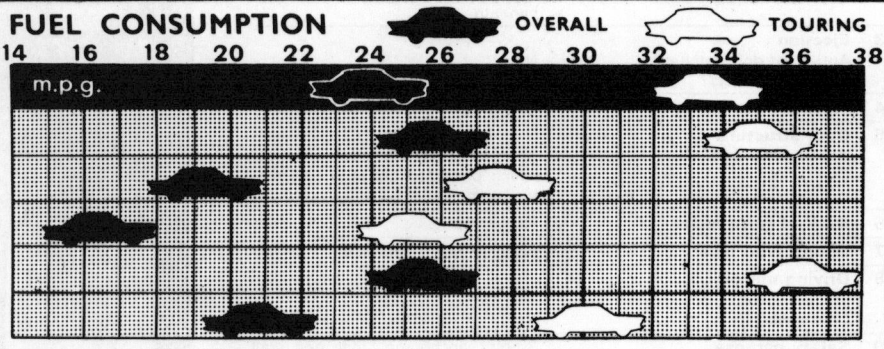

5'-7" / 6'-0" / 18'-7½"

145

Sunbeam Alpine GT
continued

The two comfortable bucket seats have a very wide range of adjustment: the steering column telescopes, too. One adult can sit sideways on the rear bench—preferably without the hardtop which restricts headroom behind.

Comfort and controls

Except on bad roads, the Alpine rides with the comfort of a firmly sprung saloon: on wavy or bumpy surfaces it can hop and wobble a bit but this is rare. Theoretically, there are seven practical ways of adjusting the driving position: the Alpine has four of them compared with the one or two of many other cars. Excellent semi-bucket seats can be moved bodily to and fro and, by reversing a block underneath, up and down, and the squabs have six angle settings—too widely spaced to be perfect—from upright to semi-reclining. In addition, the steering column can be telescoped 2½ inches after releasing the central knurled boss. Not surprisingly, all our drivers found they could tailor a generally relaxed and comfortable driving position, if not a perfect one. Since the pedals are offset to the right (to leave room for the floor dip-switch) tall people complained that their left leg fouled the bottom of the steering wheel when pressing the clutch. Another criticism was that the seat is too close to the door, restricting shoulder and elbow room (but, in compensation, increasing already good lateral support).

Gone is the rasping exhaust of the original Alpine yet this is still not a particularly quiet car. Engine noise—a deep crisp note

Safety check list

1	**Steering assembly**	
	Steering box position	Well back behind axle line
	Steering column collapsible?	By 2½ inches only if wheel adjusted right out
	Steering wheel boss padded?	A little
2	**Instrument panel**	
	Projecting switches?	Most of them
	Sharp instrument cowls?	No
	Effective padding?	On top, yes; vent controls protrude beneath
3	**Ejection**	
	Anti-burst door latches?	No
	Child-proof doors?	No, but only two doors
4	**Windscreen**	Zone toughened
5	**Door structure**	
	Handles, winders	Both project; the door handles, which point straight at one's knee, look very dangerous
6	**Back of front seats**	Firm padding
7	**Windscreen pillar**	Angular, minimal padding
8	**Driving mirror**	
	Framed?	Yes
	Collapsible?	No
9	**Safety harness**	3-point anchorage, rear one well behind and below shoulder

The boxes on the left will fit in the boot; those on the right stack on the rear bench inside. Total—an excellent 9.7 cu ft.

—is modest except at high revs, and there is virtually no audible tyre rumble, even on a coarse-textured road. But above 65 m.p.h. wind noise becomes loud and it is a bit overbearing at really high speeds.

As our pictures show, the GT, although far from being a four seater, can be used successfully as a family car provided that half the family are under three feet tall. Two-year-olds can sit comfortably on the back bench with both front seats right back. For older children, the front seats must be pushed forward at least one notch—little handicap for an adult passenger but tall drivers will be reluctant to make the sacrifice which will almost certainly bring their knees harder against the steering wheel. For easier access to the back, the front squabs flop forward under spring pressure by releasing a side lever; even so, most of our under-five assessors managed to get their feet firmly wedged between front and back seats when clambering in. One adult sitting sideways *could* tolerate a short journey in the back but the lack of legroom and headroom would make it very tiring.

Four over-centre catches and two locating lugs hold the neat hard-top in place: it could have been removed and replaced very quickly if one of the catches had not been impossibly stiff—probably due to misalignment of the screwed-on catch. Two people are needed to lift the top clear. There is no alternative soft-top shelter so it is a calculated risk to drive far from base in the open. Another disadvantage of fresh-air motoring is that there is noticeably more scuttle shake and body flexing on rough roads without the hard-top: it is surprising what four strong catches and a snug fit round the screen top do to the car's rigidity.

Interior heating is good, ventilation (with the top in place) adequate. There are no quarter lights but under-scuttle vents,

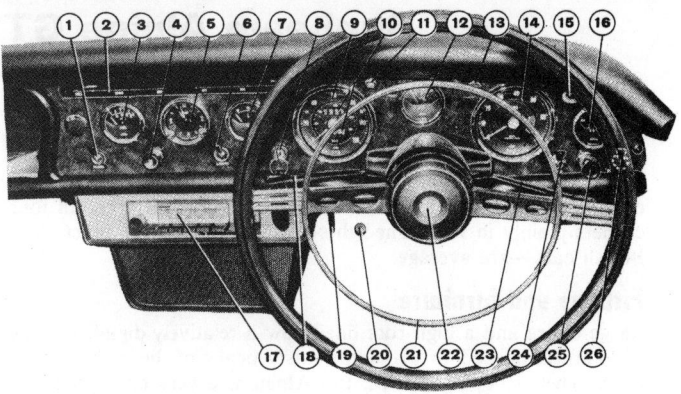

1, panel light. 2, heater controls. 3, petrol gauge. 4, choke. 5, clock (extra). 6, lights. 7, temperature gauge. 8, ignition/starter. 9, speedometer. 10, trip and total mileage recorder. 11, flasher tell tale. 12, oil pressure. 13, main beam warning light. 14, rev counter. 15, overdrive tell tale. 16, ammeter (extra). 17, radio (extra). 18, overdrive (extra). 19, bonnet release. 20, vent. 21, horn ring. 22, lock for steering wheel adjustment. 23, indicators and flasher. 24, wipers. 25, washers. 26, heater fan.

(either fully open or fully shut), let a strong ram-forced stream into the car which wafts across your lap, over your face and out through front-hinged extractor windows behind. It's a crude system compared with some fully adjustable fresh-air vents but apart from being a bit draughty, it seems to work quite effectively —or did until the driver's vent control broke.

Continued on the next page

Specification

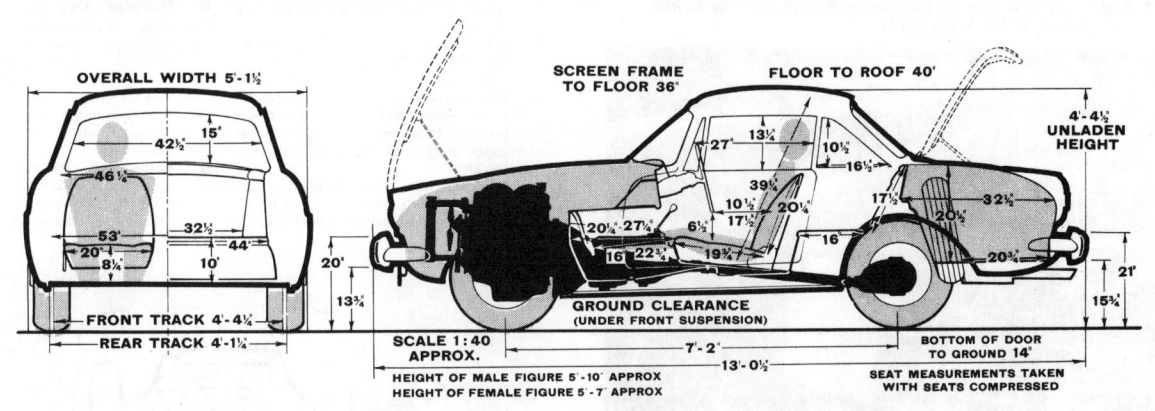

Engine
Cylinders	4
Bore and stroke	81.5 mm. x 82.5 mm.
Cubic capacity	1,725 c.c.
Valves	o.h.v. pushrod
Compression ratio	9.2:1
Carburetters	Two Stromberg 150 CD's
Fuel pump	AC mechanical
Oil filter	Fram full flow
Max. power (net)	92.5 b.h.p. at 5,500 r.p.m.
Max. Torque (net)	103 lb. ft. at 3,700 r.p.m.

Transmission
Clutch	Borg and Beck 7½ in. dia., diaphragm spring
Top gear (s/m)	1:1 (overdrive, 0.803:1)
3rd gear (s/m)	1.29:1 (overdrive, 1.04:1)
2nd gear (s/m)	1.97:1
1st gear (s/m)	3.12:1
Reverse	3.32:1
Overdrive	Laycock de Normanville
Final drive	Hypoid bevel 4.22:1 (3.89 without overdrive)

M.p.h. at 1,000 r.p.m. in:—
O/d top gear	20.4
Top gear	16.3
O/d 3rd gear	15.7
3rd gear	12.6
2nd gear	8.3
1st gear	5.2

Chassis
Construction . . . . Unitary body/chassis

Brakes
Type	Girling disc/drum with servo assistance
Dimensions	9.85 in. front discs, 9 in. rear drums

Friction areas:—
Front	20.8 sq. in. of lining operating on 196 sq. in. of discs
Rear	60.4 sq. in. of lining operating on 99 sq. in. of drums

Suspension and steering
Front	Independent by coil springs and wishbones with anti-roll bar
Rear	Semi-elliptic leaf springs and a live axle

Shock absorbers:—
Front } Armstrong telescopic
Rear }

Steering gear	Burman recirculating ball
Tyres	5.90—13 Dunlop Road Speed
Rim size	4½J

Coachwork and equipment
Starting handle	No
Jack	Mechanical pillar
Jacking points	4 corner sockets
Battery	12 volt negative earth 38 amp. hrs. capacity
Number of electrical fuses	2
Indicators	Self cancelling flashers
Screen wipers	2-speed self-parking electric
Screen washers	Manual plunger
Sun visors	2

Locks:—
With ignition key	Both doors
With other keys	Boot and facia cubby
Interior heater	Fresh air style fitted as standard
Major extras available	Overdrive, wire wheels, RS or SP tyres
Upholstery	Pvc
Floor covering	Carpet
Alternative body styles	Sports tourer (soft top)

Maintenance
Sump	8¼ pints SAE 20W
Gearbox	4½ pints with o/d SAE 20W
Rear axle	1¾ pints SAE 90EP
Steering gear	SAE 90EP
Cooling system	12½ pints
Chassis lubrication	None
Minimum service interval	3,000 miles
Ignition timing	6°–8° b.t.d.c.
Contact breaker gap	0.015 in.
Sparking plug gap	0.025 in.
Sparking plug type	Champion N9Y
Tappet clearances (hot)	Inlet 0.012 in.; Exhaust 0.014 in.
Valve timing	Inlet opens 29° b.t.d.c. Inlet closes 63° a.b.d.c. Exhaust opens 69° b.b.d.c. Exhaust closes 23° a.t.d.c.
Front wheel toe-in	⅛ in.
Camber angle	½°
Castor angle	4° 40'
Kingpin inclination	5½°
Tyre pressures	24 p.s.i. all round

Sunbeam Alpine GT
continued

There are no thick body panels above the waistline so all-round visibility is good. Reversing is particularly easy since the driver sits well behind the centre line of the car with all four corners plainly in view. The lights—similar to those on most other British cars—are average.

Fittings and furniture
Large doors and a high roof line allow a relatively dignified entry but care is needed to avoid the nasty peaks of the fixed quarter lights when stooping. Inside, the Alpine is a very cosy little car; like a well furnished parlour with comfortable seats, thick carpets and attractively sober decor. As in most Rootes cars, there is not a shoddy-looking fitting in sight. The scattered but logical mass of instruments and dials (some of them extras) on the polished walnut facia is the familiar Rootes design: so are the hooded tell-tale lights and unrecessed toggle switches, the furthest of which can just be reached without leaning forward. Only the overdrive stalk, indicator/flasher and horn ring are genuine finger-tip controls, while from the point of view of grip, the wooden steering wheel is purely decorative since the rim has been sprayed plastic-smooth. There are two useful interior lights—a general purpose one above the mirror (not a good place from a safety angle), the other serving as cubby light and map reader for the passenger. There is room for small oddments in the facia cubby and a central locker, the lid of which doubles as an arm rest. For a sports car, the boot is quite big and of course, there is more luggage space on the flat rear bench inside.

Thick, soft sun visors (which must be removed from spring-loaded sockets before taking the hard-top off) would protect against the hard-top catches, which are anyway flat-faced. The protruding visor brackets are probably more dangerous. Another safety criticism is that the seats are anchored only at the front and therefore free to tip in an accident. Lap and diagonal seat belts fitted to our car provide good wrap-over at shoulder height but with the seat right back it was difficult to pull the belt tight enough because the buckle had disappeared down the side of the seat.

Servicing and accessibility
Details of the 6,000-mile service cycle are summarized below but seasonal "extras" (at spring and autumn) are recommended for further checks (brake pads, anti-freeze, etc.) and maintenance (engine tune, headlamp alignment). The handbook says that comprehensive workshop manuals are available from any authorized Rootes dealer.

Without the grubby chore of greasing dozens of nipples, most of the routine maintenance can be done quite easily by a competent owner and accessibility under the front-hinged bonnet is quite good. The simple jack, which lifts from either the front or back of the car, is very easy to use.

1, crankcase breather filter. 2, starter solenoid. 3, twin air cleaners. 4, twin Stromberg carburetters. 5, windscreen washer bottle. 6, radiator filler cap. 7, brake fluid reservoir. 8, distributor. 9, coil. 10, dip switch. 11, petrol pump and filter. 12, brake servo.

Maintenance chart
1. **Engine.** Drain oil and refill when hot; renew oil filter; clean petrol pump filter; check tension of fan belt; check tightness of manifold and carburetter flanges; clean crankcase regulator (all at 6,000 miles). Renew air cleaners; check engine mounting bolts (12,000 miles).
2. **Clutch.** Lubricate clutch pedal pivot; lubricate slave cylinder clevis pin (6,000).
3. **Gearbox.** Lubricate gearchange linkage; drain gearbox and overdrive and refill; examine for leaks (6,000 miles).
4. **Rear axle and propeller shaft.** Drain when hot and refill; clean breather hole and examine for leaks; check prop shaft bolts for tightness (6,000).
5. **Brakes.** Lubricate pedal pivot; check hydraulic fluid level; lubricate handbrake linkage; adjust pedal stop if necessary; inspect pipes (6,000).
6. **Steering and suspension.** Check bolts for tightness—particularly bottom link fulcrum pin securing bolts; check seals and steering joints; check level in steering box (6,000).
7. **Wheels and tyres.** Repack front bearings with grease and check end float (12,000).
8. **Electrical.** Clean and adjust sparking plugs; check battery electrolyte; oil distributor automatic timing, grease cam, oil contact breaker pivot, shaft and cam bearing; check breaker gap (6,000). Check starter motor bolts; renew sparking plugs; clean battery terminals and smear with silicone compound.
9. **Body.** Oil door hinges, strikers, locks, bonnet and boot hinges; clean drain holes in lower edge of doors; check tightness of door dovetails.

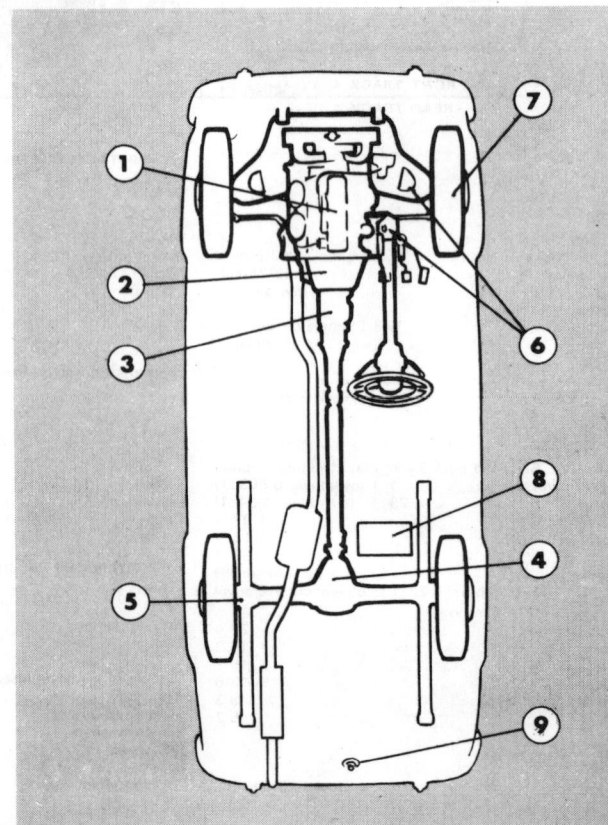

MAKE Sunbeam: **MODEL** Alpine GT: **MAKERS** Rootes Motors Ltd., Ryton-on-Dunsmore, near Coventry, Warwicks.

CHOICE OFF THE TRACK

CHRIS AMON'S
SUNBEAM TIGER

SINCE Grand Prix motor racing is looked upon as being the ultimate when we talk about driving, presumably racing drivers and the cars they use on the road must be worth looking into. After all, a man who demands the tops in technical finesse in the car he races is hardly likely to risk his neck in a questionable road car.

Chris Amon is a young man in a hurry to get to the top of the motor racing tree, and although he's only 23 he is getting up among the higher branches. This season he shared the winning Ford GT at Le Mans with his fellow New Zealander Bruce McLaren, and he has since been distinguishing himself with polished performances in a McLaren Elva in the CanAm "big banger" sports-racing car series in North America.

He uses a Sunbeam Tiger for commuting between his rented mansion in Surbiton and the McLaren factory in Colnbrook, and for long trips between racing circuits he finds the Tiger as near to his ideal as makes no difference—for the price.

"I bought a Tiger because it seemed to me to combine a simple engine with a lot of reliable horsepower, good performance and a general lack of fussiness in a car that was pleasant looking and comfortable.

"I think the car handles reasonably well. A lot of people tell me that it doesn't, but I must say that it goes round a corner as fast as I want to go without any problems. The braking is good. It stops in a straight line and stops from high speed well without any fade.

"I think that harder dampers would probably improve the handling, but they would also upset the ride, which would be a pity. Right now the Tiger combines reasonable handling with a good ride.

"I've done about 3,000 miles in the car and generally I've been very pleased with it. I like to travel fast when conditions permit it—away from speed limits—and the Tiger cruises pleasantly between 90 and 100 m.p.h. It gets up there quickly and is completely effortless. I was told before I bought it that it would be very noisy at speed, but with the hardtop on there is hardly any wind noise at all when you are driving fast."

Being a New Zealander Chris doesn't have a very high opinion of the English so-called summer weather and therefore he rarely uses the softtop. In fact he didn't even know he had a soft top with the car, folded behind its panels, until it was pointed out to him several days after he had bought it!

"The Ford engine is nice and simple. It starts easily and will pull virtually from a standstill in top gear without any jerking. Petrol consumption varies from around 15 to the gallon when I'm driving it hard, to around 21-22 m.p.g. when I'm just cruising around or on a trip. I think

IF Chris Amon is typical, racing drivers do not want to dice on public roads, but often they do have to travel fast and far. For his own personal transport he looks for reliability and comfort, good handling and effortlessness and gets annoyed with minor faults, as we all do. He thinks highly of automatic transmission

this is very economical when you consider the performance of the car. It uses hardly any oil, and it doesn't overheat in traffic. The gearbox was a bit stiff when it was new, but now it has freed up and is very pleasant. It isn't an exceptionally quick box, but for an ordinary road car it is certainly adequate.

"But there are one or two features of the Tiger that annoy me. They're just little things, but with a £1,500 motorcar you shouldn't have any worries! For instance, it comes with-

149

CHRIS AMON'S SUNBEAM TIGER...

out a cigarette lighter and mine has no sun vizors—these sort of things should be standard fittings on a car like this. The things that probably annoy me most are the troubles I have had with the window winders, the door locks, and the bonnet catch.

"The bonnet catch has been adjusted several times but I still have to wrestle with it to free the catch completely so that the bonnet will open. A little thing like this is infuriating, especially if you're in a hurry.

"The windows seem somehow to keep slipping off the winding mechanism, and make it hardly worth the trouble of attempting to raise or lower them. The door lock on the driver's door isn't any better. Sometimes you just have to put the key in, turn it, and the door opens with no drama at all, but at other times—like when it's pouring with rain and you don't have a coat—you have to resort to delicate juggling with the position of the door handle before you can even get the key into the lock!

"If Rootes can't trim a car like the Tiger in a better fashion than this, they will only have themselves to blame if sales drop off. And there aren't that many people about these days with £1,500 to spend. I think the Tiger is an extremely practical and quick road car, but when stupid little annoying troubles keep happening I sometimes feel like selling it tomorrow!"

Amon has a liking for fast cars and is in the pleasant position of being able to afford them even if he is hit hard by insurance on account of his tender age. He hasn't had a claim since he can remember, but the mere mention of the word "racing driver" will turn an insurance man pale and the premium will sky-rocket—even if you have just won Le Mans.

His last car was a 4.2 litre E-type convertible which he kept for only three weeks. Main reason for the quick change was the almost complete lack of luggage space. The E-type didn't meet the Amon requirements in the wet, and he says now that the Tiger is a much better all-round proposition. He has also owned a 1275 Mini-Cooper S, and while he says it is the best town transport you could buy, being both fast and economical, the noise and the boxy ride on a long trip became a little wearing.

Not being a young man who lets grass even think about growing under his feet, Amon was looking hard at some of the higher-class machinery at Earls Court and tantalizing some of the salesmen with what could have been one of those very rare "genuine enquiries."

"The Iso Grifo was one of the nicest cars I saw at the show. It was a well finished car, it looked great, and it combined some of the finer features of Italian automobile engineering with an exceptionally smooth, reliable and powerful American engine. A good point about the Iso is that it is available with automatic transmission. In this day and age it's becoming more and more important for driver comfort and ease as the roads become more congested and you spend more time on and off the clutch. Automatic transmission used to be something that the sports car men sniffed at, but the competition successes of the Chaparral and the tremendous potential of the new Ford J car that Bruce and I tested at Le Mans show that you don't have to have four on the floor to be with it any longer."

Eoin Young

BOOKS RECEIVED

The Vintage Car 1919-1930, by T. R. Nicholson. Published by B. T. Batsford Ltd., 4, Fitzhardinge Street, London, W.1. Price £2 5s.

Transport, by R. A. S. Hennessey. Published by B. T. Batsford Ltd., 4 Fitzhardinge Street, London, W.1. Price 15s.

Rover Memories, by Richard Hough and Michael Frostick. Published by George Allen and Unwin Ltd., 40 Museum Street, London, W.C.1. Price £1 10s.

Your Book About the Way a Car Works, by Harry Heywood and Patrick Macnaghten. Published by Faber and Faber Ltd., 24 Russell Square, London, W.C.1. Price 12s 6d.

"I Was There," 20 stories by the top sports writers of the *Daily and Sunday Telegraph*. Price 5s.

The Three Pointed Star, revised by Peter Hull. Published by Cassell and Co. Ltd., 35 Red Lion Square, London, W.C.1. Price £2 10s.

B.M.C. 1100, by P. Olyslager. Published by Thomas Nelson and Sons Ltd., 36 Park Street, London, W.1. Price 10s 6d.

FEATURE ROAD TEST

WORKS
SUNBEAM TIGER
A TIGER WITH TEETH

EVER dreamed of sitting behind the wheel of something really savage—something capable of spinning the wheels in top on a dry road, capable of leaving long black lines on the tarmac—something, in fact, which is the original hairy monster? So have we—and it doesn't matter how quickly the Mini can be made to go, it just ain't the same.

In fact, you can't really do it with a littl'un at all. What you want is lots of cylinders, lots of real poke and lots of lovely noise. For instance, you can do it beautifully in a Sunbeam Tiger of the right type—in this particular case, a works Tiger—Peter Harper's Tulip rally car, to be precise. A real brute of a car—not in fact as fast as all that but nevertheless juicing out a healthy increase in power over the standard 164 b.h.p., weighing, despite a lot of extra bits and pieces, probably a little less than the standard 22½ cwt., and one, way and another a car built for one purpose and one purpose only—competition. Not, in fact, the sort of car in which to take Auntie out for a Sunday afternoon's bluebell-picking.

From the outside it was pretty obvious that this was no ordinary Tiger. For a start, it was literally plastered with lights at both ends. Left-hand-drive, of course, which is usually favourite for continental events because it's easier for the bold intrepid pilot to overtake if he sits on the appropriate side—and in this car you do a fair amount of overtaking. The bodywork was standard, with the usual Tiger hard-top, apart from the holes to take all the lights, but the thing sat on Minilite wheels which were a dead give-away.

Hidden from the public eye, as you might say, were sundry other differences. For a start, the power unit—you know, the Ford V8 4,261 c.c. job which, under normal conditions, delivers 164 b.h.p. at four-four and the staggeringly high figure of 258 lb ft. of torque at only two-two (compare this with 260 lb. ft. for the 265 b.h.p. Jaguar engine if you like)—was equipped with a high-lift camshaft, solid tappets, single extra strong valve springs, polished ports and so on and had, of course, been fully balanced. Standard carbs and manifolding was retained, a competition distributor was fitted and the exhaust pipe was taken through the frame to stop it from being knocked off on the rough bits. Oh yes, and the car had an oil cooler on it. Not a lot, you might think, but enough to provide a healthy increase in power and still stay within the regulations. Balancing, port polishing and the camshaft meant that she would rev to six thousand, where the red mark was: the standard Tiger has a red mark on the tachometer at four-eight, so obviously something works differently!

The major snag with Tigers, in our experience, is the way they are stuck to the road—or not, as the case may be. Marcus Chambers and his men had sorted this little problem by fitting stiffer, high-rate front springs and stouter rear springs—in fact, those catalogued as export spring for the Hillman Husky. Laugh that off. Armstrong adjustable dampers all round appeared, from the ride, to be adjusted to the hard setting, too. Just in case all this took a bit of stopping, the brakes were fitted with DS11 front pads and VG95 rear linings, and a dual servo circuit had been arranged so that the standard under-the-bonnet servo unit operated on behalf of the front brakes, while a second servo, stuck behind the seats inside the car, looked after the back ones,

A dirty great rev counter the driver can see amongst other things.

This is the only car we have tested with a duplicate brake servo fitted on the back seat.

which it did to the accompaniment of a great deal of puffing and blowing.

Finally, the Rootes Competitions men had fitted the beast with the ultra-low (by Tiger standards) final drive ratio of 3·7 to 1, and a Powr-Lok limited-slip diff. A fuel tank holding (though not for very long) 18½ gallons, plus a dirty big and very robust roll-over bar, laced around under the hard-top, completed the spec, and we were, as they say, off.

Off isn't just the right word here. To say that she was running a bit rich is putting it somewhat mildly. No choke, of course, so a cautious pump on the pedal. The electrical fuel pumps went mad, the starter whirred, as they say, and absolutely nothing else happened. Flooded, of course. Usual drill—throttle wide open and try again—still no sign of life. So we left her for a bit and then, very gingerly, tried again. This time the jackpot—eight cylinders all working, and great scads of noise hurtling out of the twin tail-pipes. We learnt after that no matter whether she was hot or cold, you just didn't touch the loud pedal until she had fired, which in nearly every other case she did at once.

With the engine running, and firmly settled in the driver's share of two very comfortable seats, there seemed to be no excuse for not going somewhere. Too bad about the audience—if you will park a thing like this in a public car park, etc. etc. . . . . Pole her into first, and see what happens when you let the clutch out. You've guessed it—we took off down that (empty, fortunately) car park like we were starting at Le Mans at about five-past-four. Something else we'd learnt—you could, and preferably did, start off from the mark at little more than tick-over revs unless you were in a hurry.

The fairly small degree of modding permitted by class regs for the Tulip had done nothing to impair the extraordinary flexibility you get from a big American V8, and it was *possible* to drive the thing very gently indeed. Of course, this was bit hard on the plugs, and it didn't want a lot of traffic driving to get her firing on not more than six or seven. A quick blast of the throttle—lots of black smoke out of the back, lots of lovely noise everywhere—was sufficient to keep 'em going, though, and once clear of what Mr. Wilson likes, for some obscure reason, to call a "conurbation" it didn't take long to see what works Tigering was all about. The controls of the Tiger take a bit of working out at first when the Comps Dept. has finished with 'em. For a start, the standard rev-counter is disconnected—at least, it wasn't working—and a monstrous great thing of a replacement is struck up on the top of the facia where you can't fail to see it. Lighting and wiper are located on the arm-rest between the front seats instead of on the dash, there are various extra switches and knobs labelled, in many cases, "iodines" in big bold letters; the speedo, not surprisingly on a left-handed motorcar, was in k.p.h. and the fuel gauge and the rev-counter were together equipped with the fastest-moving needles this side of an aircraft. The usual "rally gear"—pockets for maps documents, tools, and an Avanti navigator's light—were all built-in.

So you get all this sorted out, stoke up the fire and start the engine—carefully, this time, so as not to do that flooding bit all over again. Not exactly an ideal traffic car, this, for all its flexibility: the plugs and things aren't all that happy at under about two thousand revs, which means that for a good deal of the time urban motoring means third gear. Third itself is good for a ton at maximum revs, and the gearing is such, with a 3·7 to 1 top, that a LOT of Power is available at pretty well any point in the engine speed range. In other words, burbling along is fine so long as you don't press too hard on the pedal on the exits from roundabouts—especially if it's wet.

It is pretty noisy in there and becomes very noisy in there once you get a few revs on board. Full acceleration through the gears becomes a bit of an endurance test for the ears as the full chatter of gearbox whine, exhaust noise and the clack of tappets gets in amongst you. But by God you're going—the limited slip diff limits the slip all right, and instead of one wheel spinning both of them will, with no trouble at all. In the wet, the car moves sideways as easily as it does forwards and the quick take-off makes for a busy driver. It's all part of the excitement—especially when you relate it to an acceleration of the order of eleven seconds from a standstill to the legal limit—8·8 from nothing to sixty, and 26 seconds from rest to the ton. You can do fifty in bottom gear, the legal seventy in second, while third gives you ninety and top—well, we never had a chance to try it on full chat in top gear. The standard car does 121 m.p.h., mean of opposite runs, and this one is probably about the same although, with the low axle ratio, it would get there faster.

The ride is hard and businesslike, to say the least. Every bump in the road communicates itself to the driver's bottom—you would probably be able to tell if you drove over a match, but we didn't actually try it: we hardly ever went slow enough to see a match right down there on the ground. This makes for a remarkable degree of controllability—the car handles so much better than a standard Tiger, despite the increased power, that it is difficult to believe

152

that they are the same car, only just a little bit different, if you follow.

The handling is entirely predictable: fast corners are taken in an attitude of understeer, and if you go too quickly round slower ones then you get oversteer and the behind comes round to meet the front. A quick flick of the command wheel and the situation is very largely under control again. In the wet, the car will adopt virtually any attitude you happen to want at a dab on the loud pedal—even in top, if you happen to be going quickly enough.

The brakes are pretty well twitched about, of course, and seem to be up to the job in hand. They don't, mark you, inspire confidence until they are warm—this is often the case with the "hard" friction materials but once you start using them they stop the car all right, and you never run out or even look like running out of anchors.

After dark—well, when the rest of the world is in darkness—you carry your own private daylight ration about with you. Standard headlights, plus a couple of small spots carried low down under the bumper, plus a pair of iodines for good measure tend to lighten the old darkness more than you might think possible. With the lot on it's a bit hard on anyone who happens to be looking towards you, and if you met an oncoming car under these circumstances you'd probably hear their screen melting. Still, the object of the exercise is to light the way, and it does this alright—you could land an aircraft down the "flarepath". In the same way, a whiff of iodines, to coin a phrase, is all that is necessary to move over the slower chap in front in daylight—if the worst comes to the worst, you simply give him a blast on the air-horns. If that doesn't move him, it would be no good trying dynamite—not loud enough.

Accepting, for a moment, that this tyre-squealing, rubber-burning snorting ball of 4·2-litre fire is all a young man desires to impress the birds (and, incidentally, himself) is there a snag? We don't count the racket, the harsh ride, the brutal acceleration—they are all part of the joy in this case. But there is, nevertheless, a snag. It's in that 18½ gallon tank, which needs filling up more often than the Editor's pint mug. The works Tiger is, to say the least, thirsty. This isn't much of a problem for Master Harper, of course, because one of the perks of being a works driver is that you don't have to buy the petrol. But it is a snag presumably for the likes of you and me, who do. Admittedly the car was running rich when we had it—probably a lot richer than it ought to have done. But even so, we boozed our way through the go-juice at the rate of a gallon of the stuff every fifteen British miles when driving normally, and about once in a dozen miles if you turned the tap on and went fast. Mr. Rootes Group says that this is too much, and that in proper trim it ought to do more than that.

All the same, though, given a pocket full of sufficient folding stuff to keep the beast's appetite satisfied, we can't think of a more exhilarating way to spend a journey than by doing it in this Tiger. Man alive, that beast's got real teeth!

Once again, your view.

Cars on Test

WORKS SUNBEAM TIGER

Engine: V8-cylinder, 96·5 mm. x 73 mm; 4, 261 c.c.; push-rod operated overhead valves; compression ratio 8·8 to 1; high-lift camshaft; solid tappets; stronger valve springs; polished ports, etc; twin choke-carburettor; competition distributor; fully balanced.

Transmission: Four-speed gearbox, synchromesh on all forward gears; 3·7 to 1 final drive; limited-slip differential.

Suspension: As standard Tiger, but with up-rated front springs; Hillman Husky special export rear springs; Armstrong adjustable dampers all round.

Brakes: As standard Tiger, but with separate circuits, dual servos and DS11 front pads, VG95 rear linings.

Dimensions: As standard Tiger.

PERFORMANCE

MAXIMUM SPEED:
Speeds in gears (at 6,000 r.p.m.)
First— 50 m.p.h.
Second— 70 m.p.h.
Third—100 m.p.h.

Fuel consumption: 12-15 m.p.g.

ACCELERATION
0– 30— 4·0 secs.
0– 40— 5·0
0– 50— 6·4
0– 60— 8·8
0– 70—11·0
0– 80—14·4
0– 90—19·5
0–100—26·0

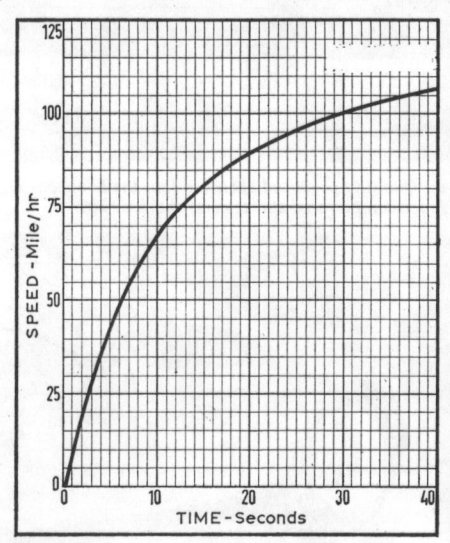

Car Prepared by: Rootes Competition Department, Coventry.

SHOEHORN JOBS 2

BY ERIC DYMOCK

Above: Quantity-produced shoehorn job, the Sunbeam Tiger. Below: Latest version of one of the first American-powered sports cars, the A.C. 289

THE SUNBEAM Tiger looks just like the Alpine. So much so, in fact, that the American market for which it was designed rather wishes it didn't. Americans want fire-eaters to *look* fire-eaters, not pretty but rather slow roadsters like the Alpine. Examination of the Tiger will show the problems of squeezing a large engine into a relatively small frame as applied to a car destined for large-quantity production.

Carroll Shelby seems to have a flair for this sort of thing, and it was he who first persuaded the Ford V8 into a Sunbeam Alpine. He sent his prototype along to the Rootes management who admit now that they were sceptical, but couldn't deny the thing worked, and worked well. Clearly, it was a possibility for production on a limited scale. There seemed to be a market for an Alpine that went a bit faster or, more important (especially in America) out-accelerated the opposition.

The production car was very similar to the prototype. Briefly, what was necessary first was to carve a large hole in the bulkhead. Even though, by virtue of Ford's thin wall casting techniques, the 4,261 c.c. V8 was relatively light at 639lb complete with clutch and gearbox, it replaced the Alpine unit which was only 397lb, so it *had* to go as far rearwards in the frame as possible. In any case, the Alpine has a sharply falling bonnet line and if unsightly bumps were to be avoided the engine had to be pushed farther back.

The bulkhead hole is filled with a low-volume-produced pressing, welded into place at the same time as the new transmission tunnel. This too is a low-volume pressing which changes the shape of the tunnel for the heavier gearbox which will transmit the extra power The Alpine has a remote control mechanism to bring the gear lever closer to the driver; the Tiger's lever grows straight out of the gearbox in much the same position in the car. It is slightly offset to the left, being a transmission of American origin but the inconvenience is hardly significant for British drivers. The original gearbox was made by Borg Warner; now it is Ford manufactured. An additional advantage in both units was a reduction in prop shaft length.

So the most important changes to the hull between the Alpine and Tiger are in the bulkhead and transmission tunnel. The two Ware struts which carry the suspension loads from the wheel arches up into the bulkhead, and stiffen the frame are retained. In any case they are detachable on the Alpine to allow engine removal and remain so on the Tiger. Engine mountings are strengthened and the front cross member is curved, but more significant, rack and pinion steering is installed because there is no room on the right wheel arch for the usual Alpine recirculating-ball steering box. Rootes insist that this was the only reason for the rack and pinion's adoption. It was not to make the car with the extra power more controllable and handle better, but merely because there was insufficient space for the ordinary steering box.

These are all the structural changes necessary to put a V8 in place of a four, but in this case the fit was an easy one. Much easier than, for example, it would be to get a Chrysler vee-8 into the same hull. In fact this operation is little short of impossible despite the obviousness of the idea. First, the Chrysler is too wide to fit between the wheel arches; second, the Ford's distributor is at the front, out of the way, while the Chrysler's is at the rear and would use up the space at present occupied by the heater. Which is why we are unlikely ever to see a Chrysler-engined Tiger.

The biggest problem once the engine was installed, was to get it to work without overheating. The Alpine radiator is low down at the front behind a shallow air intake, and with the larger vee-8 producing more heat and, therefore, needing more water and a larger cooling surface, the radiator had to be made larger in every direction. It only just fits. The expansion tank for the sealed cooling system has to be some distance away on the left side of the engine compartment. Even so, the efficiency of the cooling system, although adequate for normal conditions becomes marginal under heavy load in tropical countries, and the hot-climate export specification includes an electric fan ahead of the matrix to assist the air flow through it. The problem is at its worst at idling speeds after a fast run; there is a huge build-up of heat and the very bulk of the engine impedes the escape of air after it has passed through the radiator so the electric fan helps push more through.

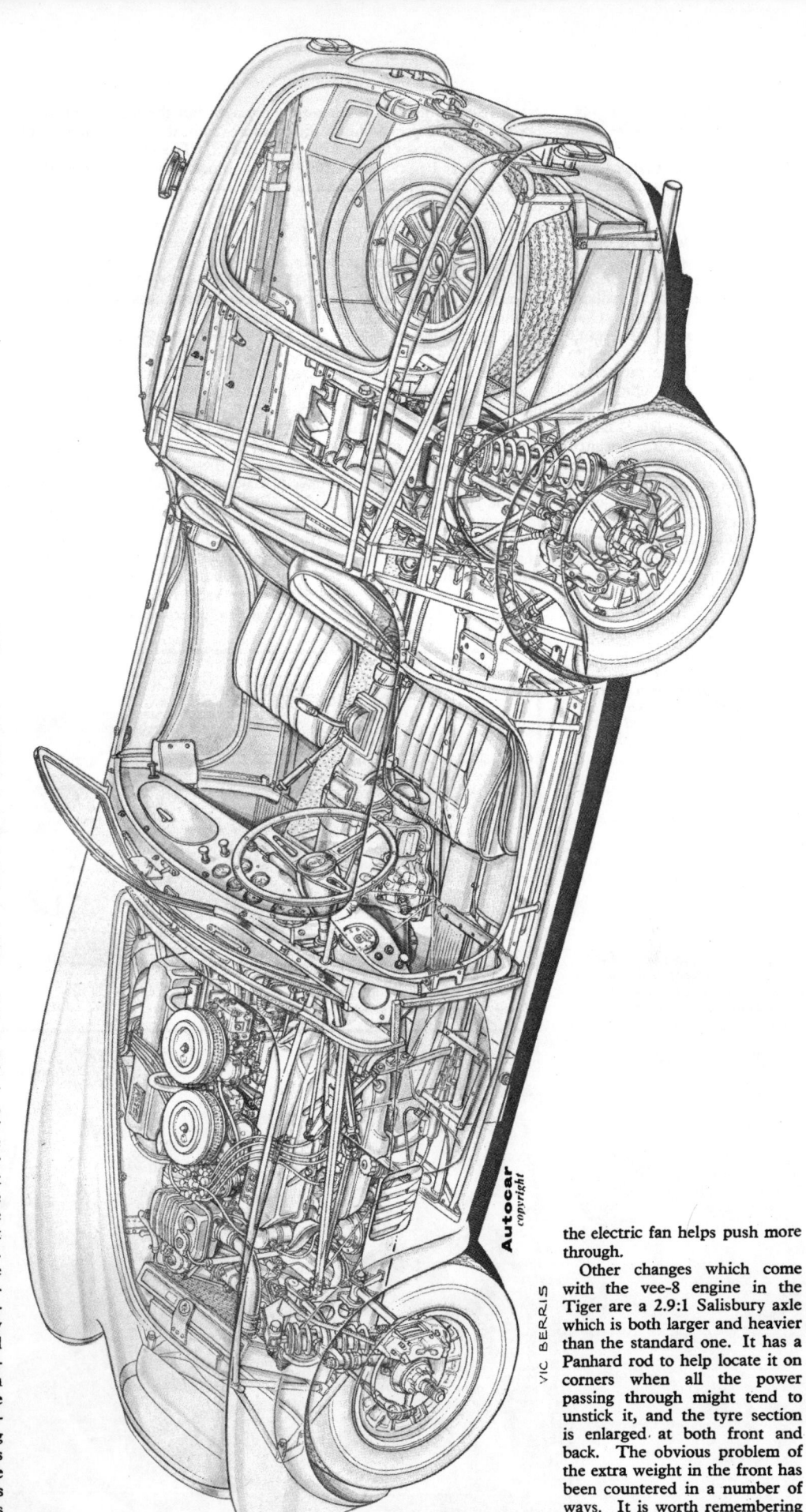

Other changes which come with the vee-8 engine in the Tiger are a 2.9:1 Salisbury axle which is both larger and heavier than the standard one. It has a Panhard rod to help locate it on corners when all the power passing through might tend to unstick it, and the tyre section is enlarged at both front and back. The obvious problem of the extra weight in the front has been countered in a number of ways. It is worth remembering that it is not the weight so much

SHOEHORN JOBS

as its distribution that counts. The engine is farther back in the frame. The back axle is heavier, and the battery is moved rearwards from under the space behind the seats to the boot. The spare wheel is laid on its side which reduces the boot capacity but moves the weight to the back. The result is that the Tiger's weight distribution is 51.5/48.5, while the Alpine's is 50/50. The actual weights are Tiger, 1,320/1,245lb; Alpine 1,098/1,086lb. The Tiger's brakes, designed principally for the American market, were held to be adequate with the addition of a heavier servo.

Peter Ware, until recently Rootes chief engineer, readily admits that had the Tiger been a volume produced car it might have justified a more sophisticated rear suspension, like perhaps a de Dion to eliminate the axle tramp you get accelerating hard. Apart from some trifling problems with the Panhard rod mountings which afflicted some early production cars, there have been very few problems in service. Of the idea that the Tiger experiment might be readily repeatable with perhaps a whole range of vee-8 options, Ware says that as time passes, this likelihood diminishes. When the Alpine was designed, cars tended to be "over-engineered," heavier than perhaps they needed to be, so that later on, you could put in a much more powerful engine without much difficulty. "If we were designing the Alpine today we should make it a whole lot lighter." And putting a very powerful engine in it might be a very different matter.

The other Carroll Shelby creation, the Cobra, also needed changes but the alterations were more radical for a number of reasons. The ladder-type frame was much easier to stiffen than the Alpine's hull. The frame tubes of the old AC Ace chassis were merely enlarged and the transverse leaf independent suspension gave way to coil springs and wishbones at each end. The main difference between Rootes and AC's problems being, of course, that in the former's case, the production of the "parent" model still went on; this was the reason for all the cutting and welding. But at the AC factory, manufacture of the old Ace stopped short, and they could have started making the beefier Cobra chassis almost the following day. This was easy with a simpler chassis made of tubes which need only the most elementary welding jig to make. The Alpine's tooling costs would have precluded a similar operation at Rootes.

The Cobra appeared with the 4·2-litre Ford engine in 260 b.h.p. form, and the whole chassis generally strengthened. The body shape was changed quite a lot, as you can do with individually built bodies without much trouble, although the style remained very much as before. So with a different transmission, a new, stronger chassis, drastic alterations to the suspension and even the bodywork, the Cobra only qualifies for inclusion among these other cars which have "grown" big engines by virtue of the fact that the change was accomplished over a relatively long time. Carroll Shelby had his first Cobra built on the Ace chassis and racing in 1961, but it was 1964 before one appeared at a London Motor Show and even though many had been built at Thames Ditton by then, the design had been evolved from the original stage by stage. ■

Cutaway of the Tiger showing how the engine has been mounted as far back as possible, with a large radiator matrix. As much weight as possible has been moved to the boot to balance the extra engine mass

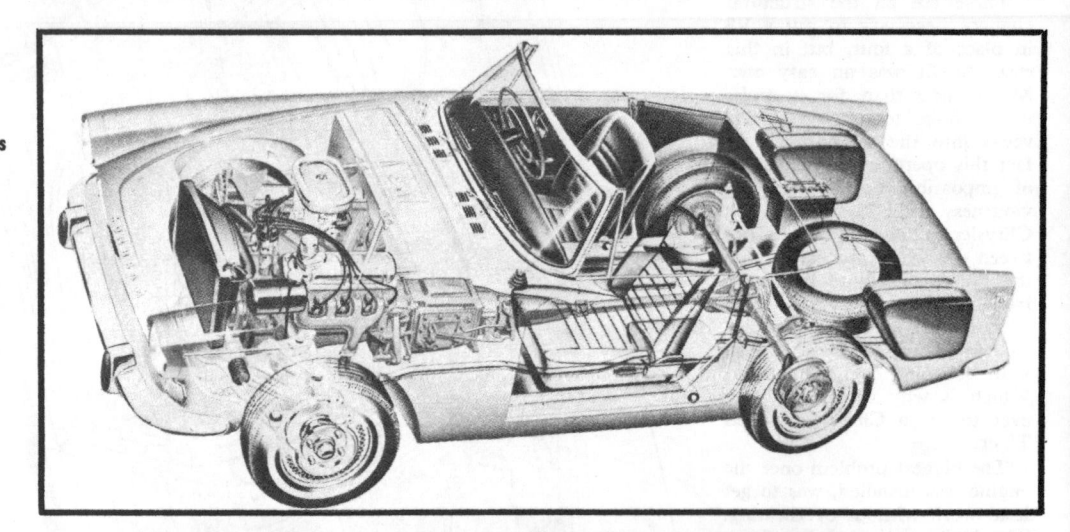

Eight-pints in a quart pot. Even the proverbial shoehorn would not be much help at removing the Ford engine from its tight fit in the Sunbeam Tiger

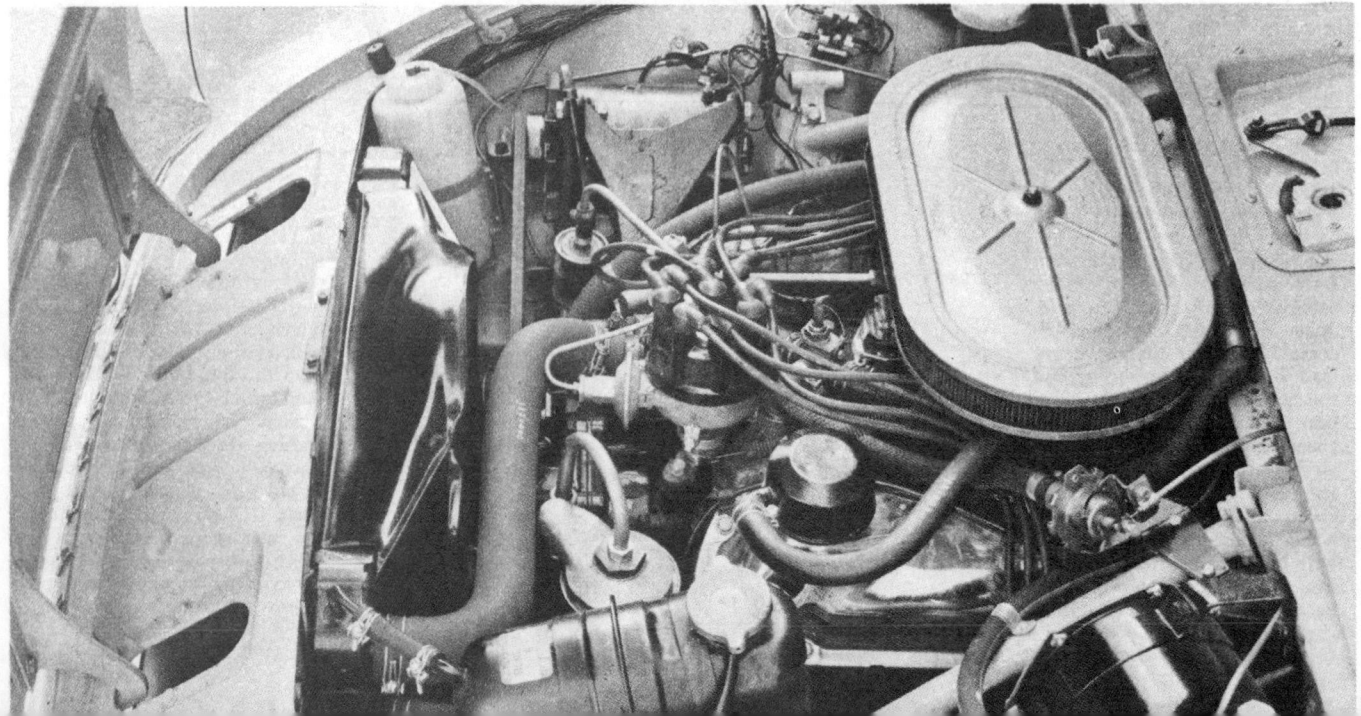

SUNBEAM TIGER II

Latest version offers the 289-cu-in. Ford V-8 engine

BACK IN 1964, life was simpler. Then the Rootes Group in England could mate its latest Sunbeam Alpine with a straightforward mild-tune 164-bhp Ford V-8 engine to make an extremely pleasing sports car and call it the Sunbeam Tiger. Everybody knew where they were and how they stood.

Since then Chrysler Motors Corporation has acquired Rootes (as well as Simca in France) and seems a little embarrassed to find one of its products running a Ford engine. The simple truth is that the parent corporation doesn't have an engine that would fit the package without major re-engineering, so they're stuck with the Ford. We're glad Chrysler chose this route rather than discontinuing the Tiger as they might have done, because it is a fine automotive package without which the world of sports cars would be poorer.

The major feature which distinguishes the Tiger II from the I is that it now has the highly respected 200-bhp, 289-cu-in., single 2-barrel V-8 in place of the 260-cu-in. unit. With the stronger engine come several other related changes, such as a slightly larger clutch (10.4 in. vs. 10.0) and wider

Ford 289 V-8 with single 2-barrel crowds engine compartment.

Comfortable seats are adjustable for both reach and rake.

spaced ratios in the all-synchro 4-speed gearbox (which result in overall ratios of 8.01, 5.56 and 3.92:1 in 1st, 2nd and 3rd compared to 6.68, 4.87 and 3.72:1 with the 260 engine). There's also a bit of rearrangement in the rear suspension, an alternator is fitted instead of a generator and an oil cooler has been added in front of the bottom of the radiator.

There have also been some identity changes, such as full-length stick-on stripes at bumper level, an egg-crate grille (in place of the single chrome bar) and stainless steel trim moldings around the fender cutouts and body sill. And, oh yes, the little crest that used to say "Powered by Ford 260" now says "Sunbeam V-8" and lets it go at that.

There have also been some comfort changes in the passenger compartment since the first Tiger. The seats are better looking and more comfortable, though less deeply bucketed. The steering wheel is marginally higher, which gives a greater amount of useful space for the thighs under the wheel rim. The cockpit ventilation has also been improved by adding vents to bring in raw air from outside.

Stripe is latest Tiger's most prominent identity change.

SUNBEAM TIGER II
ROAD TEST RESULTS

PRICE
List price.................$3797
Price as tested.............3842

ENGINE & DRIVE TRAIN
Engine.............Ford V-8, ohv
Bore x stroke, mm......101.6 x 73
Displacement, cc/cu in...4737/289
Compression ratio............9.3:1
Bhp @ rpm..........200 @ 4400
  Equivalent mph.............106
Torque @ rpm, lb-ft...282 @ 2400
  Equivalent mph..............57
Transmission type....4-spd manual
Gear ratios, 4th (1.00)......2.88:1
  3rd (1.36)................3.92:1
  2nd (1.93)................5.56:1
  1st (2.78)................8.01:1
Synchromesh.............on all 4
Final drive ratio...........2.88:1

GENERAL
Curb weight, lb.............2560
Weight distribution (with driver), front/rear, %....51/49
Wheelbase, in...............86.0
Track, front/rear......51.8/48.6
Overall length..............156.0
  Width....................60.5
  Height...................51.5
Frontal area, sq ft..........17.3
Steering type....rack & pinion
  Turns, lock-to-lock.........3.2
Brake type..discs front/drums rear
Swept area, sq in...........295

ACCOMMODATION
Seating capacity, persons.......2
Seat width................2 x 18
Head room....................39
Seat back adjustment, degrees..30
Driver comfort rating (scale of 100):
  For driver 69 in. tall........90
  For driver 72 in. tall........85
  For driver 75 in. tall........85

PERFORMANCE
Top speed, 4th gear, mph.....122
Acceleration, time to distance, sec:
  0-100 ft...................3.6
  0-250 ft...................5.8
  0-500 ft...................8.8
  0-750 ft..................11.3
  0-1000 ft.................13.8
  0-1320 ft (¼ mi)..........16.0
  Speed at end, mph..........87
Time to speed, sec:
  0-30 mph...................3.1
  0-40 mph...................4.1
  0-50 mph...................5.6
  0-60 mph...................7.5
  0-80 mph..................13.1
  0-100 mph.................22.0

BRAKE TESTS
Panic stop from 80 mph:
  Deceleration rate, % g......68
  Control..................good
Fade test: percent of increase in pedal effort required to maintain 50%-g deceleration rate in six stops from 60 mph..........nil
Overall brake rating........good

SPEEDOMETER ERROR
30 mph indicated.....actual 27.3
40 mph....................36.4
60 mph....................56.3

CALCULATED DATA
Lb/hp (test weight)..........14.3
Cu ft/ton mi.................146
Mph/1000 rpm (high gear)....23.9
Engine revs/mi..............2510
Piston travel, ft/mi........1200
Rpm @ 2500 ft/min..........5215
  Equivalent mph............128
R&T wear index.............30.1
Brake swept area, sq in/ton...205

FUEL
Type fuel required........regular
Fuel tank size, gal..........13.5
Normal consumption, mpg...18–20

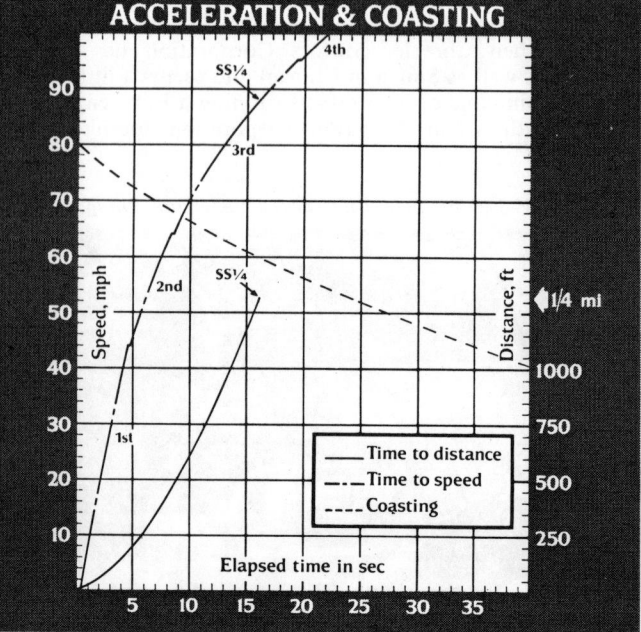

ACCELERATION & COASTING

SUNBEAM TIGER II

We've praised the people compartment of the Alpine and Tiger before and we're happy to do it again. It is well arranged, tastefully styled and the workmanship is above average for a British sports car. It is also big enough for human-size humans, the steering wheel is adjustable for reach, the seats have lean-back control, the heater-demister has a 2-speed blower, the instrumentation is adequate, the switches are labeled and there's a useful, lockable glove box between the seats. It is a very pleasant place from which to operate a very pleasant automobile.

We don't like the top. It's tedious to erect or strike, you can see daylight through places that should seal tight, it isn't sure whether it wants to be inside or outside around the windows and it isn't free of flap except under carefully controlled conditions. The way we like it best is tucked away under the neatly padded boot.

Like the Tiger I, the Tiger II is difficult to fault within the framework of what it is and what it is intended to be. It is a great pleasure to drive a small car that simply has gobs and gobs of power for its size. It makes a nice noise when you twist the key, it burbles confidently along at very moderate revs in 4th gear and it does everything with almost disdainful ease. All this is immensely satisfying to the driver who has felt his TD run out of revs at 14 mph in first gear or experienced the typical high-rev clutch slip necessary to get such things as 1300 Giuliettas away without stumbling. It's gratifying to have an abundance of overlapping power in each gear rather than having to shift at exactly 3217 rpm or lie there, wallowing and hopelessly bogged down while the revs creep back up the torque curve and get you going again.

Though the Alpine lines have begun to look a bit dated (the appearance has undergone only minor changes since it was introduced in 1959), the Tiger II is still a pleasant car to look at. It does seem a bit upright, though, the hood a bit short, the windscreen a bit tall, the hips a bit narrow. It is an efficient package, nevertheless, and within the envelope—which is 19 in. shorter and 9.6 in. narrower than the Sting Ray—there is room to carry two people in comfort, plus a useful parcel area behind the seats, plus a genuinely usable trunk of practical size and shape—a Grand Touring car that is really grand for touring.

As for performance, there's more power available from the 200-bhp V-8 than the Tiger can handle with complete equanimity. There's a multitude of hops and judders in the rear axle if hard starts are attempted (see photo), there's more understeer than we like and when pushed really hard the short wheelbase (86.0 in.) seems to conspire against keeping it in a straight line. The standard tires (5.90-13 Dunlop RS-5s) limit the performance potential in its as-delivered condition, as demonstrated by the fact that our 200-bhp model got through the standing quarter-mile no more quickly than the 164-bhp version and that only a relatively modest 68%-g deceleration rate could be achieved in our panic stop from 80 mph braking test. With more rubber on the road, both these figures should be dramatically improved. Optional 5.5-in. rims are available from the West Coast distributor and if it were our Tiger we'd fit those along with radial ply tires.

The Tiger II doesn't take kindly to being flung around. It's a car with dignity and asks to be driven that way. That doesn't mean slowly, necessarily, but that there's sufficient power on tap to embarrass the incautious. But if you treat it right, respecting it for what it is, the Tiger II can offer driving pleasure of a very high order.

CONTINUED FROM PAGE 71

outfitted with some sort of torque rods at the rear axle. In standard form, it is quite impossible to make a properly fierce start, as the wheels spin furiously for a moment and then the rear axle begins to pound up and down too badly for a prudent driver to hold full throttle; that would be courting a whole raft of broken bits inside the axle casing. Traction bars are to be offered as an option, and we would recommend them to everyone when they become available.

Apart from the fact that the steering feels slightly heavier, the Tiger is in every way a better handling car than the Alpine. Instead of trying to run wide on corners, as we are sure everyone was expecting, the back end can be brought right out by applying plenty of throttle; the added power also makes it easier to hold a drift. The Tiger is a trifle twitchy in a 110 mph drift; but then so would the Alpine be if it were capable of a 110-mile drift.

We would like the car a bit better if it had more rubber on the road, but that is a criticism that can be leveled at most touring-type automobiles, and we found the gear-lever to be a trifle too far forward. However, the Tiger will corner at least as well as its contemporaries, and the lever, even though one must stretch a little for Third, stirs the gears in a most direct and precise fashion. The reverse lock-out did tend to rattle about somewhat, but that seems a niggling gripe to have when all the rest was so good. Oh yes, we should point up the fact that with the Ford transmission, the driver really can shift as fast as his hand can move the lever—which used to be one of those things that was said of Super-Colossal sporting machines that everyone marvelled over and no one really believed. The synchromesh, from First to Fourth, is that good.

All those concerned deserve a big pat on the back for having produced the Tiger—Ford for having made available the necessary engines and hardware in the required quantities, Ian Garrad for having had the vision to see the possibilities in this combination, Lord Rootes for having the strength of character to do something that must run very much against the English grain, and all the people at Rootes for having put an automobile together so well. When all is said and done, fit and finish only come from people who care, and it is evident, from the excellent quality one sees in the Tiger, that Rootes *does* care. **C/D**

Suspension has been reworked slightly particularly in the rear and cornering is great if you don't shove too hard!

Tiger's steering wheel can be adjusted for reach. Dash box is open but there is a locable one between the seats.

SUNBEAM TIGER 2

WHAT'S NEW WITH THE TIGER? JUST A 200 HP FORD V-8 ENGINE WITH ACCELERATION YOU NEVER QUITE EXPECT IN ANY STOCK, STREET MACHINERY!

Sunbeam V-8 appears on rear and prompts truck drivers to ask about the specifications and the overall performance.

The grille is new. Longitudinal stripes and the painted headlight rims are instant identification (see the cover).

■ There have been some very significant modifications made to the Sunbeam Tiger in this new model. Some of them are especially practical and functional for driving the car here in the United States. The addition of an oil cooler to the lower portion of the radiator is vital considering the lack of breathing space up front in the engine compartment. Our test car showed a worrisome tendency to overheat, even with this modification, every time we were caught in heavy traffic. Once out on the highway, however, where you could run fifty or better, the needle came down where it belonged and stayed there.

The car made available to us came equipped with a black hardtop in addition to the usual cloth top which was folded down just in front of the trunk lid. We had the company remove the hardtop and keep it in the garage so that we could "tour" in the open air (Continued on page 162)

161

SUNBEAM TIGER

and shoot the photos we would need. We were forced to raise the top twice during our test period because of sudden showers but it proved easy to erect and fit snugly. We were able to do it fast enough to avoid a good drenching on both occasions.

The seats in the Tiger rate extremely high on our list of good features. They wrap around securely, can be adjusted almost to full reclining and can be moved back and forth enough to satisfy almost any person. Combined with the lap type seat belt they were great in the corners. The locking console/compartment between these seats with the stubby gear shift lever in front of it made long distance driving a real pleasure.

It would have been sheer waste just to drive this automobile around town so we took it for a long weekend out to the middle of Pennsylvania. We used a brand new interstate "freeway" which allowed us to travel for hours at speeds around sixty-five miles per hour. This is where the combination of a 200 horsepower, 289-cu.-in. V-8 engine in an eighty-six ince wheelbase chassis really sells itself! In and around Lewistown, Pa., where we stayed, there are beautiful primeval state forests, with one lane unpaved roads threading themselves up and down mountain sides! We drove through Greenwood Furnace State Park, for example, and recommend it to our readers living or travelling in that area. (It's just west of Lewistown.) Do be careful of the precipices and the rock slides, however.

It was in this area that we proved the excellent steering capabilities of the Sunbeam Tiger. It was as sure-footed as the proverbial mountain goat. We had to do a lot of braking coming down through the area to the main roads and brake fade here would have been disconcerting, to say the least. We drove back to our base in Lewistown with a good healthy respect for this Chrysler import.

On our way back to the New York area, we encountered rain, such as we've not experienced in years. For safety's sake we were forced to pull over to the side of the road until the visibility ahead improved. We had to stop like this twice, yet, with the new road and the excellent performance of the Tiger II, we cut something like an hour from the time it normally takes to make the trip! Ventilation inside the closed car, incidentally, was quite good during this rigorous part of the trip, due in part to the vents which have been added to the car to assure a flow of fresh air from outside.

There is nothing really new about the exterior design of the new Sunbeam Tiger II. It is still basically the Alpine body in general appearance. The white stripes which have been added to the side are most distinctive, however. Painting the headlight rims instead of using chrome tends to lengthen the appearance of the vehicle especially when viewed from the side.

Just recently, some time after we had driven the car, we heard an authoritative rumor that the Tiger II might not be imported into the United States in 1968 because of the difficulty of rigging it to meet the new safety regulations. Certainly, fitting a pollutant reducing device under the hood which is already crammed full with the powerful engine will not be an easy or inexpensive task. Considering the excellent workmanship that has gone into this car plus the fine handling qualities, we would hate to see the Tiger II drop out of the market. A sedate matron could drive this car to church on Sunday while her grandson could burn rubber in it that very afternoon! Its performance range is one of the features buffs tend to deride in big American automobiles but in a sports car like this it is a bit of "having your cake and eating it too."

We had driven the original Tiger I and reported on it a year or two back so this time all the power we had at our command in this compact sports car didn't tempt us to go around emphatically dusting off any of the local citizenry who chose to challenge us at red lights. Perhaps we're getting a little older but just the fact that we could tromp on that accelerator and never run out of revs before we reached 40 miles per hour in first gear if we wanted to was enough to let the wild ones go screeching off from beside us.

This is, of course, a car for the open road. The engine is docile enough to stand tootling back and forth to work every day but if we owned it we would never be satisfied unless we had the engine hood louvered to allow for added heat dissipation. The Tiger II asks to be driven but, as the accompanying action photos show it is safe and stable enough for your wife to raise dust with yet not come home completely shaken when it is time to get supper! We had difficulty getting our better half from behind that wheel. Let's hope Chrysler continues to import this one.

Discover America. It's 3,000 smiles wide.

America is action, ideas and a million surprises.

Isn't this the year to get out and discover it for yourself?

THE BEEFY SUNBEAM TIGER

We drive the only ex-Le Mans racing car to find its way to Australia.

Story and photograph by Ian D. Smith

VERY rarely do we have the opportunity of testing a European sports car in Australia, with such an interesting background as this former Le Mans Sunbeam Tiger.

Life commenced for this beast in 1964 at the Rootes factory in England where three similar cars were prepared for the assault on Le Mans. Basically prototypes, each car was developed for the 24 hour race at a cost of $45,000. After an unsuccessful debut at Le Mans, the Tiger was campaigned in Europe by Bill Chapman, now resident in Sydney. He had moderate success and then in 1966 entered the German Hill Climb Championship.

Hillclimbs in Europe are not the 1000 yard sprints we have here but more like a long four mile climb where you need cubic capacity. Out of 21 events, the Sunbeam Tiger finished third outright at the end of the year, behind a works-entered Porsche and a Ferrari.

The Tiger's V8 power was a 260 cu in. Ford Fairlane extensively worked over by Carrol Shelby and was putting out 270 bhp. At Le Mans it blew a piston after 10 hours when lying in 18th place. It was timed down Mulsanne Straight at 149.7 mph.

Jim Abbott originally imported the Sunbeam to Australia to add to his autosportsman stable, and ran it at a number of local hillclimbs. As well it ran once at Sandown with both Jim and Paul England having a punt.

However, the machine was far too big and awkward for the smaller Australian circuits and was more suited to endurance racing. The motor at this stage was replaced by a Ford 289 cu in. in a mild state of tune. The following owner, Geoff Brown, used the Tiger exclusively for street use where it proved very tractable if not a little 'posey'. Just the thing to take your 'bird' to the drive-in.

Having followed the car's movements in Melbourne town over the years, I finally spotted the 'beast' in a used sports car yard at Doncaster. Lance Dickson of Chequered Flag Motors, a local Datsun dealer, was now the owner.

A test day was arranged and I met Alan Whitely (ex TC Escort pedlar) at Calder Raceway.

At last a close first hand look see; the body is certainly GT 'ish', all hand fabricated and welded aluminium with neer a ripple. Windows, including the windscreen, are Perspex; surprisingly the registered weight tops 22 cwt. The bonnet, held in place with a pair of hood pins, features

Only three racing Tigers were built, for the '64 Le Mans race, at a cost of $45,000 each. The cars were prototypes and barely resemble the road going Sunbeam Alpine versions.

All windows, including the windscreen, are made of Perspex for lightness. Although the body is all-alloy, the car still weighs 22 cwt. The petrol filler is designed to take the Le Mans pressure feeder hoses for quick refuelling.

an air scoop for the carburetion and a wind, stone, rain deflector on the driver's side. Rear end has a slight cam tail with a full fastback roof line. Front side vents feed fresh air to the interior.

Those big mag wheels are fully-cast 15 in. Dunlop, with 8 in. rims all round, carrying Dunlop 5.50-M15 racing rubber. A Borg Warner close ratio T10 gearbox pours the power through the limited slip Salisbury differential. Speaking of pouring, check the size of the filler cap, and I'll tell you that you don't get much change from $20 when you say to the local garage attendant, "Fillerup". The gas tanks hold no fewer than 40 gallons. At eight mpg for our test, a bloke could go broke.

In the early stages of a race, no doubt, this 44-gallon drum in the back seat would put the edge on any brakes, but not the Tiger's. They're 11 in. Girling discs all round with alloy calipers operating on independent systems. These were developed along the lines of the Ford GT 40 which ran in 1964 Le Mans and in fact are very

Off the line, the Tiger burns rubber from the big racing tyres like a dragster. The body has a fast-back design, with just the hint of a spoiler at the rear lines are for aerodynamics not beauty.

The dash is a maze of switches for extra lights etc, and due to lack of space in the engine bay a pair of power boosters is mounted in the glove-box. Just in case you forget you're in a Le Mans car, there's a plate engraved "Le Mans 24 Heures 1964", mounted above the steering column.

Designed for the long European circuits, the car is unsuitable for the tight Australian tracks. But it makes a great "pose" road car.

similar to the present Falcon GT set up.

Interior layout really puts one back on the grid at Le Mans. Tight-fitting bucket seats overlook a mat-black dash, covered in toggle switches, printed name tags and instruments. And if you still don't believe you're in a Le Mans car, then a metal engraved badge, mounted above the steering column reads "Le Mans 24 Heures 1964".

Instruments include oil temp, oil pressure, water temp, amp meter, speedometer and tachometer, redlined at 5200. The mass of switches operate the main fuel tanks, reserve, headlights, side lights (mounted on the doors to show up the racing numbers at night), fresh air, heater, washers and on the right-hand side, two toggle switches for high beam and horn. Mounted in the glove box is a pair of power booster units. The interior shows signs of the car's use over the years.

Back to performance of the beast, which justifies the outward appearance. We averaged a 15.5 for the quarter using only 4800 rpm. The V8 is a basic 289 with a four barrel carburettor, balanced throughout and cleaned up heads to modified exhaust system. A long-needed tune-up would see times below 15.0 seconds. However, after a few quick laps around Calder, times improved greatly, using all four speeds of the close ratio box down the main straight, and third up the back straight.

From 100 mph changing down to third, then second through Repco, the Tiger would decidedly oversteer. You have to treat the machine like a brute and don't spare the kid gloves, throwing it around, then hauling away on the large diameter steering wheel to bring the best results. Body roll was negligible with a very flat and safe ride. The engine easily spins over 5000 rpm and was extremely flexible in all gears.

Nowadays the Sunbeam Tiger is not suited for current local competition, but as a sports enthusiast's street car . . . !

What other machine can grab the looks it gets and still crawl from 10 mph to 140 mph in top gear?

#

165

• **LONG TERM ASSESSMENT**

TALE OF A TIGER TWO
A Versatile Sporting Car with no Successor

Just over two years ago we printed a 12,000-mile test report of a Sunbeam Tiger 260—*Under-rated Tiger* we called it—going on to praise many of its qualities. Since then two things have happened. First, enthusiasts have been taking another look at Tigers in general and good used ones are enjoying renewed popularity; second, Rootes finished developing a much improved Mk II version but reluctantly had to decide not to go into production with it. The reasons are not important now but they were concerned with, among other things, the volume and cost, structural parts in common with the then current Husky, which was to be dropped, Chrysler influence and Ford engines. In fact a small number of Tiger "1½s", called IIs did get through for export and the police. These were up-dated in detail and were fitted with the later and better 4.7-litre, 289 cu. in. Ford V8 engine and matching gearbox.

THIS second tale of a Tiger concerns one of the development Tiger IIs since the time we took it over at 9,000 miles—which is now 16,000 miles ago. This is the full II as originally visualized, which means that, in addition to the American Ford 289 cu. in. engine, with HE HB gearbox, and 2.88 axle ratio, it has five-stud 14 in. wheels and big Girling discs all round with Girling servo. Diameters are 10.7 in. at the front and 9.6 at the rear. There are also some external trim differences as the pictures show; and, because we liked the Techdel Minilite wheels on the previous car, we paid the £85 for a new 14 in. set for this one. Fortunately a special batch was going through for BMWs at the time; this size had only just become available.

We ran on about the nature of Tiger I performance in our full Road Test (30 April, 1965) and in the later long-term appraisal. This time we leave the figures measured at MIRA to speak for themselves. This is probably the first time they have been measured independently and published. The reason for the speedometer's optimism is that the standard speedo had been modified for the Tiger II and we then fitted lower-profile tyres. For some weeks we ran on Firestone Wide Ovals brought over from America. These gave a very nice ride and were directionally true but had insufficient clearance under the wheel arches for rough going or full lock. They also gave rather less adhesion on sticky wet roads. With the Wide Ovals fitted, the speedo was almost accurate and since the engine runs out of safe revs before maximum speed is reached, the car would be fractionally faster on the bigger tyres.

This particular version of the 289 V8 has hydraulic tappets and only modest tune. It runs happily on 4-star petrol or even 3. The rev counter peaks at 5,000 rpm and is red-sectored on to 5,500. What the blow-up point might be we do not know; maybe the engine runs out of breath or valve opening first, but on high speed runs the car was still accelerating when we let-up at a true 129 mph, and maybe 5,700 rpm—the needle

For the cold months there is a snug and roomy hard top (this is Westerham, Kent). The Tiger does not always draw such stony stares

Left: The natural curves of the body front have not dated and are still a credit to the designer of the Alpine of 10 years ago

Top right: Plainly marked instruments and minor controls, together with the after-thought radio and switches are functional but untidy by modern standards

Centre right: A shoe-horn job which is quite acceptable because the engine seldom needs attention. The Speedostat cruise control shows between the alternator and air filter

Right: You can squeeze grown-ups with legs on the back bench seat, but the accommodation is really for 2 + 2 children. The hood is waterproof, noisy and folds away neatly under its cover

166

by Maurice A. Smith, D.F.C.

being a bit unsteady just beyond the red stop. The top speed can be taken as 125 mph at 5,500 for a short burst or 115 mph at 5,000, where the red sector starts, for sustained maximum. It does not help to go much above 5,000 rpm in the intermediate gears.

Acceleration and how you get it are more interesting these days than over-the-ton speeds. The Tiger, *grace de Ford,* has bags of bottom-end torque, and will pull evenly in top from about 12 mph and hard from 20 mph, for example 20-60 mph takes just over 11 seconds. This means in practice that you scarcely need to use the gear box if you are feeling automatic. On the other hand if you get short of time or frustrated by the ruck of traffic, you can use the gear box and take full and safe advantage of gaps and short overtaking stretches. In this case 3.6 sec will take you from 10-40 mph.

Incidentally the 16.0 sec standing-quarter (16.1 mean) was recorded without using brutal methods—after all it's our car! This kick-in-the-back acceleration, and the compactness of the Tiger have been among its many points of practical appeal. Others in the same context are the all-round good view with a commanding sitting position for the driver—as sporting cars go—when the very substantial and weather-tight hard top is fitted. The look out is still good with the alternative folding hood up, but on the negative side, the deep screen and clumsy brow above it give the Tiger rather a dated tall look and help to kick up a fiendish wind noise at speed. Full lock manoeuvring is heavy work and the tyres scrub.

Fuel consumption varies between quite wide limits, dropping to little over 15 mpg in London traffic but rising to over 20 mpg on the open road when you are not hurrying. The 11¾ gal tank needs filling too often. Oil consumption is negligible.

Quite soon after taking the car over, we imported a pair of rear suspension stabilizer bars from International Automobiles in California. They call it a Traction-Master kit and the cost was $52. This kit is rather heavy but effective in two ways: first it has practically eliminated the fierce axle tramp that often developed on a quick get-away; second it relieved the overworked standard rear dampers of much of the pounding. At the moment more expensive Konis are fitted to see if they improve the adhesion and will hold out longer.

The brakes with servo have given no trouble at all, and have always been fully up to the car's performance. In the dry we registered a 1.0g stop for a 100 lb push on the pedal. The hand brake has a warning tell-tale.

When you know a car very well you tend to become blind to its faults, or at least less able to judge and analyse it, so I quote here some impartial notes written for me at the time by an experienced test driver from another manufacturer, who borrowed the car for a weekend. This was before the rear stabilizers were fitted to kill axle tramp, and in theory make the Panhard rod redundant. We mean to take this rod off to see if it eliminates the rear-end steering. The test driver wrote:

"The Tiger is a tremendously satisfying car to drive. The exceptional flexibility and excellent acceleration cannot fail to impress even the most blasé of drivers.

"Handling is much better than I had been led to expect from a Tiger. Understeer is by no means excessive, and can always be nullified by the use of power. The steering is very responsive and has adequate feel without excessive feed-back. The main shortcoming concerning handling is the most marked rear-end steering effect, evident when full throttle acceleration is indulged in. This may well be due to Panhard rod interference, caused by the considerable compression of the rear suspension in such conditions. This is also probably the cause of a gentle yawing and oscillation of the steering wheel sometimes experienced on undulating roads.

"The ride is fairly good, but is not up to, say, E-type standards, neither is traction on slippery roads. If the surface is at all rough, any wheelspin produces violent axle-tramp, and it is essential to lift-off instantly.

"Brakes function very well and seem to be fully up to the car's performance. However, it does suffer from pad "knock-back", which increases the pedal travel significantly during the first application after hard cornering. This problem has been experienced by other users of rear disc brakes on live axles, notably Jaguars and Fiat.

"The body feels much more rigid than I had been led to expect. There is sometimes a trace of scuttle shake, but no more."

Smith's of Cricklewood took a keen interest in this car and of the various items of their special equipment fitted, the electric clock operated by its own hearing-aid-type battery has been a great success. It has been reliable and has kept good time, and of course disconnection of the main battery when the car is serviced does not affect it.

The battery condition indicator has given the correct indications or more correctly has remained in the green sector, except for one occasion when there was in fact a faulty terminal connection giving the impression of a tired battery.

Most useful, have been the electric window motors, accessories so well installed by Smiths that there is no sign of the original winders. Ventilation and heating often need fine adjustments when the hard top is on, and since this car is pre-through-flow ventilation, a crack of window open or closed often provides the right air mixture. The Mark IIs do have extra cold-air vents for the foot wells, and the hard top has extractor rear quarters. To provide more fresh air, or to speak to someone at the kerb-side, would mean shrugging off one's safety harness to reach the window winder. For a driver to lean across to open a passenger side window while driving is dangerous on any car; that window, most of all, should be electrically-operated.

We have already reported on the automatic cruise control, an American "Speedostat" fitted for evaluation by Hepworth and Grandage (AUTOCAR 14 March, 1968). Long term, it has seldom been used as an automatic cruise control but is valuable as a speed limit warning device—it would be particularly so for a driver who had already been "done" twice. There is now a simpler and cheaper Model J to give only speed restraint warning without auto-hold.

Wind noise when the car is driven with the hood up, is considerable, so we went for the best twin-speaker Radiomobile installation. The speakers are buried in the back of the very occasional rear seats and give plenty of undistorted volume. Until you drive an open car in traffic you tend to

167

TALE OF A TIGER TWO...

forget how very noisy commercial vehicles are and how much noise a closed body keeps out.

Since we do much of our own repair and servicing work, we cannot quote representative repair charges, but we can give a list of replacements which is not too daunting for the type of car after its three energetic years and 25,000 miles.

A pair of exhaust systems — quite separate and straight down each side of the car—are used for the two cylinder-banks of the V8. Their silencers are just ahead of the rear axle and the ground clearance is good by sports car standards, the 5 in. only very occasionally running out. We have had to fit only one new pipe and do some repairs to the silencer of the other.

Looking through the job cards, we see in December 1967 the fuel pump packed up and was replaced (£6). At this time also we found that the rear springs had settled and we fitted new ones, supplied free. The straps under the cushion of the driver's seat tore away allowing the stuffing to sag, and the seat was exchanged. The wipers developed a nasty twitch which was put right by adjusting the linkage and fitting new blades. The silencer repair is listed for June 1968, and a new battery followed in October. Earlier this year we replaced brake pads (£4) a wheel bearing (£4 10s 0d). In between-times we twice had to service door latches which would not hold.

On free weekends we do a quick home check-up. Set screws and bolts holding the instrument panel and door fittings often want a half turn, to tighten. The same for the self-tappers holding interior body trim. It is important to keep the scuttle structure tight and the front wheels well balanced, otherwise a touch of the column and panel shake that spoiled early Tigers, comes back. The Techdels help in this respect being lighter and truly round.

The engine scarcely uses any oil or water; and the battery, being in a cool place at the back, evaporates only slowly. Various hinges get stiff and appreciate a drop of oil and there are one or two spots of rust round the hood well but in general the body and brightwork are standing up very well. We still think the centre-lock steering column length adjuster is about the best in the business and we continue to approve the instrument markings, with metric equivalents and the simple brightness adjustment on the panel tell-tales.

This Tiger could well become a classic of its year and kind, most of us continue to like it, so maybe we will keep it running on and on and on. □

Brief Specification Resumé

V8 engine, overhead valves, hydraulic tappets, 4,737 c.c. Bore and stroke 101.6 mm 73 mm (4.0 in. x 2.87 in.). Single twin-choke Ford carburettor; CR 9.3 to 1; 174 bhp (net) at 4,400 rpm; max torque 282 lb. ft. at 2,400 rpm. Four-speed all-synchromesh transmission. Independent front suspension, wishbones, coil springs, telescopic dampers, anti-roll bar; rear, live axle, semi-elliptic springs, telescopic dampers and Panhard rod. Girling disc brakes and servo, 10.7 in. dia. front, 9.6 in. dia. rear.

PERFORMANCE CHECK

Maximum speeds

Gear	mph R/T	mph Staff	kph R/T	kph Staff	rpm R/T	rpm Staff
Top (mean)	117	125	188	201	4,950	5,500
(best)	118	125	188	201	4,960	5,500
3rd	98	90	158	145	5,300	5,500
2nd	74	65	119	105	4,900	5,500
1st	54	48	87	77	5,350	5,500

Standing ¼-mile, R/T: 17.0 sec 79 mph
Staff: 16.1 sec 84 mph
Standing kilometre, R/T:
Staff: 29.8 sec 110 mph

Acceleration,
R/T: 3.2　5.0　6.8　9.5　12.4　17.5　22.4　32.5　45.8
Staff: 3.0　4.2　6.0　7.8　10.7　13.7　18.1　22.6　29.5
Time in seconds 0
True speed mph 30　40　50　60　70　80　90　100　110
Indicated speed MPH
R/T: 31　42　53　64　75　86　97　106　116
Staff: 32　43　53　64　76　87　98　110　121

Speed range, Gear Ratios and Time in seconds

	Top R/T	Top Staff	3rd R/T	3rd Staff	2nd R/T	2nd Staff	1st R/T	1st Staff
	2.88	2.88	3.72	3.92	4.86	5.56	6.68	8.01
10-30	6.6	6.7	5.1	4.8	3.8	3.3	3.0	2.3
20-40	5.8	5.7	4.8	3.8	3.4	2.7	2.7	2.2
30-50	5.8	5.7	4.5	4.0	3.7	3.0	3.2	—
40-60	6.0	5.6	4.6	4.1	4.4	3.4	—	—
50-70	6.8	5.9	5.3	4.5	5.5	—	—	—
60-80	7.7	6.8	6.1	5.9	—	—	—	—
70-90	9.0	7.5	9.8	7.3	—	—	—	—
80-100	11.9	9.8	—	—	—	—	—	—
90-110	19.2	13.8	—	—	—	—	—	—

Fuel Consumption
Overall mpg. R/T: 16.9 mpg (16.7 litres/100km)
Staff: 16.0 mpg (17.7 litres/100km)

NOTE: "R/T" denotes performance figures for Sunbeam Tiger I tested in AUTOCAR of 30 April 1965

COST AND LIFE OF EXPENDABLE ITEMS

Item	Life in Miles	Cost per 10,000 Miles £ s d
One gallon of 4-star fuel, average cost today 6s 6d	16	180 15 9
One pint of top-up oil, average cost today 3s 1d	625	2 6 8
Front disc brake pads (set of 4)	15,000	2 13 0
Rear disc brake pads (set of 4)	15,000	2 13 0
Dunlop SP41 tyres (front pair)	20,000	8 2 0
Dunlop SP41 tyres (rear pair)	18,000	9 4 0
Service (main interval and actual costs incurred)	6,000	74 2 0
Total		279 16 5
Approx. standing charges per year		
Depreciation		280 0 0
Insurance		45 0 0
Tax		25 0 0
Total		629 16 5

Approx. cost per mile = 1s 3d

PRACTICAL CLASSICS **BUYING** FEATURE

Buying an Alpine...
...or perhaps a Tiger!

Attractive sports tourers from the Rootes Group rediscovered by John Williams

Building and selling sportscars did not come naturally to the Rootes Group and this is perhaps reflected by the fact that the original Sunbeam Alpine was really a tuned Sunbeam Talbot 90 saloon provided with an attractive open two seater body. The second Sunbeam Alpine was outwardly rather further removed from its Hillman, Singer and Sunbeam Rapier relations but it was still described as a sports tourer and not as a sportscar.

To some extent the Alpine's lack of exotic flavour, its structural and component links

Growing support amongst classic car enthusiasts should ensure that Alpines receive a new lease of life and the recognition which they always deserved.

with the saloons plus the fact that the Rootes Group and their dealer network were not sportscar orientated set the Alpine off to a bad start from which it never really recovered. In fact there is still a widespread notion that it is not quite the done thing to mention the Sunbeam Alpine in the same breath as the MGs, the Triumph TRs or the Austin Healeys because it is "a woman's car, not a real sportscar."

The truth is that in the early days of the Sunbeam Alpine Rootes had a car that was better built, had more space and comfort and performed quite well considering its weight and engine size when compared to its British

This is the now fairly scarce series I Alpine which shared its tall rear fins with the series II and III cars. The aluminium hardtop was an optional extra on the series II cars as well.

rivals. It also had the advantage of being much more up-to-date in the looks department than any of its mass-produced rivals.

Despite promising showings in competition, particularly winning the Thermal Efficiency Award at Le Mans in 1961, when Austin-Healey, Triumph and particularly MG made their sportscars more civilised the Rootes Group did not pursue performance but went several stages further in making their Alpine even better finished, better equipped and more practical than its rivals. The Rootes approach to the car as a sports tourer rather than as a sports car is best reflected by the early introduction of an optional automatic gearbox and the fact that over a nine year period, whilst the engine capacity rose from 1494cc to 1725cc, performance did not improve accordingly.

After the Alpine was dead and buried and Chrysler had taken the Rootes Group over the same 1725cc engine was developed to give sundry saloons the sort of performance the Alpine could have done with to embarrass
(Continued)

The later styling for the rear fins was introduced with the series IV cars and is seen on this series V model. The luggage rack is not 'correct' for this car but the bootlid was designed to accept the correct accessory.

Continued

MGB owners; but long before that Rootes had been shown Alpines with 4.2-litre Ford V8 power units and were distracted from the Alpine by the promise of the Tiger.

By the early 1960's when the Tiger plot was hatched the Rootes Group was short of money and its financial problems grew steadily worse as time went on so there was little opportunity to make the big-engined car look noticeably different to the Alpine. There is also room to argue that the typical Hillman Minx salesman was perhaps not the best person to sell a car like the Tiger. It might be added that Rootes mechanics probably did not like working in a cramped engine bay or feel at home with American carburation.

Wheels and tyres that were not big enough for the job, weight distribution, braking and cooling that had room for improvement and undergearing sold the Tiger short because it certainly had unusual potential performance which could be used to waft the car from standstill to seventy in top gear without effort, or, if used to the full, terrify the living daylights out of normal people.

Neither the Alpine or the Tiger fitted into the plans of Chrysler who not only chose to forget about them but also hid the evidence of their existence by "running out" of spares — especially body panels — suspiciously quickly.

Series III, IV and V cars could be fitted with a detachable steel hardtop which (unlike its aluminium predecessor) is heavy enough to need two people to carry it.

The steel hardtop also rusts, especially at its lower rear corners and around the side windows. The windows of the hardtop are perspex which ages.

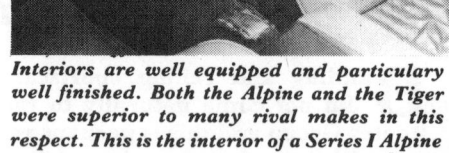

Interiors are well equipped and particularly well finished. Both the Alpine and the Tiger were superior to many rival makes in this respect. This is the interior of a Series I Alpine

Unlike the Tiger the Alpine has room to spare in its engine compartment although the general arrangement is extremely untidy. Various combinations of carburation and manifolding were used. Very few people have a good word to say for the twin choke Solex instrument used at one stage.

Considerable improvements had been made by the time the Series V Alpines appeared in late 1965.

Buying an Alpine...or perhaps a Tiger

The rear seats in Alpines and Tigers hardly offer enough space for one adult passenger but one or two young children could travel in reasonable comfort.

The hood (when fitted) is stored behind the rear seat and under the hinged panels which are prone to ripping the hood. Late cars stowed the hood behind soft covers.

Erecting the hood is a straightforward matter of raising it and connecting the hinged side rails to the windscreen frame before fastening two securing clips at the top of the windscreen and snap fasteners at the sides of the hood. Stowing the hood can be more difficult.

Remember to check the condition of the hood and whether it can be raised and lowered satisfactorily. Replacing a damaged or ill fitting hood could be expensive.

Brief guide to Alpine modifications

Alpine series I: 1494cc ohv engine with twin Zenith carburettors, independent front suspension by coil springs and wishbones, half elliptic springs and telescopic dampers at the rear. Disc brakes at the front, drums at the rear. Available with or without overdrive. Aluminium hardtop an optional extra.

Alpine series II: As above except 1592cc engine.

*Alpine series III: Revised boot layout. Cars available as 'open sports' with folding hood and (optional) steel hardtop or as GT Coupe with removable hardtop but no hood.

*Alpine series IV: Single Solex carburettor. Optional Borg Warner automatic gearbox. From Autumn 1964 an all synchromesh manual box was fitted. Revised rear fins. 'Open' or GT.

*Alpine series V: 1725cc engine with five bearing crankshaft (previously three) and two Stromberg carburettors. No automatic transmission. 'Open' or GT.

*Please note that whether or not you require a hardtop the GT versions of the series III, IV and V cars are to be avoided if you require an Alpine with a folding hood.

A Mk I Tiger shows its paces at our 1981 Goodwood test day. These cars had a 4.2 litre V8 American Ford engine.

Specifications and production

	Alpine I	Alpine II	Alpine III	Alpine IV	Alpine V	Tiger 260	Tiger 289
Production period	Oct '59 -Oct '60	Oct '60 -Feb '63	Mar '63 -Jan '64	Jan '64 -Sep '65	Sep '65 -Jan '68	June '64 -Dec '66	Dec '66 -Jun '67
Production figures	11,904	19,956	5,863	12,406	19,122	6495	571
Bore mm	79	81.5	—	—	—	96.5	101.6
Stroke mm	76.2	—	—	—	82.55	73	73
Capacity cc	1494	1592	—	—	1725	4261	4737
Bhp	78	80	77	82	92.5	164	200
at rpm	5300	5000	—	—	5500	4400	4400
Weight cwt	18¾	—	19	20	—	22	—
0-50 mph secs	10.2	9.9	10.1	10.2	9.8	6.8	6
Maximum speed mph	99	99	95	93	98	117	118
Fuel consumption mpg	31.5	26	25	23.5	25.5	17	16

Buying an Alpine...or perhaps a Tiger!

A very fine Mk II Tiger showing all the original features — the revised grille and headlamp rims, the "decorative" stripes and chrome trimmed wheel arches. The Minilite wheels were not standard but were probably the most suitable type of wider wheel to use, getting away from the under-tyred original specification. A 4.7 litre engine was fitted. The Mk II Tigers are now rare.

The boot on series I and II cars was inadequate . . .

. . . but this area was revised for the series III cars, the spare wheel was moved to a vertical position and single fuel tank (previously in the bottom of the boot) being replaced by twin tanks in the wings.

Check panels around the wheel arches at each side of the engine, these rust quickly but can be easily repaired if tackled early.

What to pay

Relatively few Alpines and even fewer Tigers are advertised for sale and prices vary widely. From the limited information which is available it would be misleading to buyers and sellers alike to attempt an accurate guide to prices. There is some evidence to support the view that an average Alpine with no serious problems can be obtained for about £500-£600, and that a very good example will command a price of around £1500.

Prices asked for the small number of Tigers advertised recently have ranged from £1800 to £3500, and these have all been Mk I cars. It appears that a fairly sound Mk I Tiger can be obtained for not more than £2000 but fully restored cars are expected to fetch up to £2500 more.

Continued

It is now a bit late to discuss why the Alpine, and to a lesser extent the Tiger, were not a popular choice amongst classic car enthusiasts until comparatively recently but a large number have died of neglect and advanced rust and there are still very few Alpine and Tiger specialists. Prices are still low by sportscar standards and provided you buy a sound example and protect it from rust or carry out a proper restoration on a less sound example, both cars offer excellent value. Basically the Alpine shell is very strong and with money, time and determination the majority of the survivors **can** be saved.

What to look for

It is hardly fair to say that Alpines and Tigers are particularly prone to rust but genuinely sound examples are likely to be in a small minority as it is fourteen years since production ended and it was not until recently that owners could obtain a supply of replacement panels. The unitary bodywork is built upon a pair of chassis rails reinforced by cruciform bracing sections, the latter being the last part of the car to become seriously affected by rust. Therefore it is probably as well to check the underside of the car first and if it is seriously rusted you should be ready to reject that particular car. Whilst under the car have a look at the forward hangers for the rear springs and then complete the chassis checks by inspecting the jacking points in turn to ensure that they will not crumble under load. Even when sound they do not inspire confidence.

Next examine the bodywork thoroughly starting with the front valance, and especially under the sidelights where the valance is welded to the wings. The front wings themselves are prone to rust around the

It is alleged that the last of the Alpines was more prone to rust and corrosion than earlier models. Points to check are covered in the text and it is worth looking deeper than the outer panels to establish the extent of structural repairs needed.

A severe case of rust in the scuttle usually caused by blockage of the scuttle air intake drainage channels.

Buying an Alpine...or perhaps a Tiger

Sills and the bottoms of doors rust and door design changed during production limiting the scope for interchangeability (the same applies to bonnets).

Examine the rear wheel arches and the lower rear wings too . . .

. . . and look for rust at the bottom rear corners of the boot. Rust here can damage the rear spring hangers, bumper mountings and jacking points.

With the approval of Rootes, Thomas Harrington Ltd of Hove produced a number of Sunbeam Harringtons based on the Alpine. Back as far as the doors this is an original Alpine but the rest has been restyled and the fixed head coupe roof is in glass fibre. The interior is more luxuriously furnished than in 'ordinary' Alpines and there is more space although rear legroom is still limited. The picture shows a Sunbeam Harrington Le Mans in which mechanical alterations included the addition of a brake servo and some engine tuning which enabled the maximum speed to exceed 100 mph. This company also made the Harrington Alpine which was similar to the Le Mans in appearance but had prominent rear fins. This car in stage III could achieve 110 mph.

headlights and along their top edge adjacent to and below the edges of the bonnet. The rear section of the front wings should be examined too as rust frequently develops along a vertical line behind the wheel arches and in the bottoms of the wings back to the sills. Look under the wings at the panels which form the footwells. These are sealed to the wings (not welded) and there is plenty of scope for rust once the sealing compound ages or falls away. Inside the engine compartment examine the vertical panels on either side between the wheel arches, wings and bulkhead; these are very rust-prone. Sills and their closing panels should be checked and it is worth paying special attention to doors to establish how much repair work will be needed if rust is present. Rear wings rust around the wheel arches and along their lower edges from the wheel arch to the rear valance.

Inside the car carry out further checks on the footwells by looking under the carpets, and look for evidence of leaks between the windscreen frame and the scuttle. It is worth checking the security of the seatbelt anchorages on the rear wheel arches, and handbrakes have been known to pull away from the floor. Make sure that the window winder mechanisms are working (they are prone to failure) and check that the seat mountings are intact and in sound condition.

There are no particular mechanical problems associated with the Alpine but it is obviously sensible to have a test drive and check for any suspicious noises from the engine or transmission. The engines are reputed to leak oil rather than burn it, and if the overdrive (which was fitted to the majority of cars) doesn't work it may well be due to an accumulation of dirt in the vicinity of the solenoid.

Availability of spares

Most mechanical parts of the Alpine were used on other Rootes cars of the period and are still fairly readily available. No body panels were obtainable for these cars for some years but some reproduction panels are now being made again. The parts which are the hardest to replace are the small components which were peculiar to these cars, such items as badges, chrome trim and certain rubber seals. No doubt these can be remanufactured for the owners clubs when there is sufficient demand for them. For the Tiger, mechanical parts are obtainable, the notable exception being the steering rack (Alpines had room for a steering box). □

The writer wishes to thank Trevor Rogers and Kim Faulkner of the Sunbeam Alpine Owners Club for assistance in the preparation of this article.

Clubs

The clubs catering for these cars in the United Kingdom are the Sunbeam Alpine Owners Club, of which the membership secretary is Brenda Harpham, 11 Aspin Gardens, Knaresborough, Yorkshire, and the Sunbeam Tiger Owners Club, membership secretary Carolyn Murray, 25a, The Drive, Ilford, Essex IG1 3EZ. Further information about the clubs can be obtained from their membership secretaries but please enclose a stamped and addressed envelope with your enquiry.

Buying an Alpine...or perhaps a Tiger!

PROFILE

Sunbeam Alpine

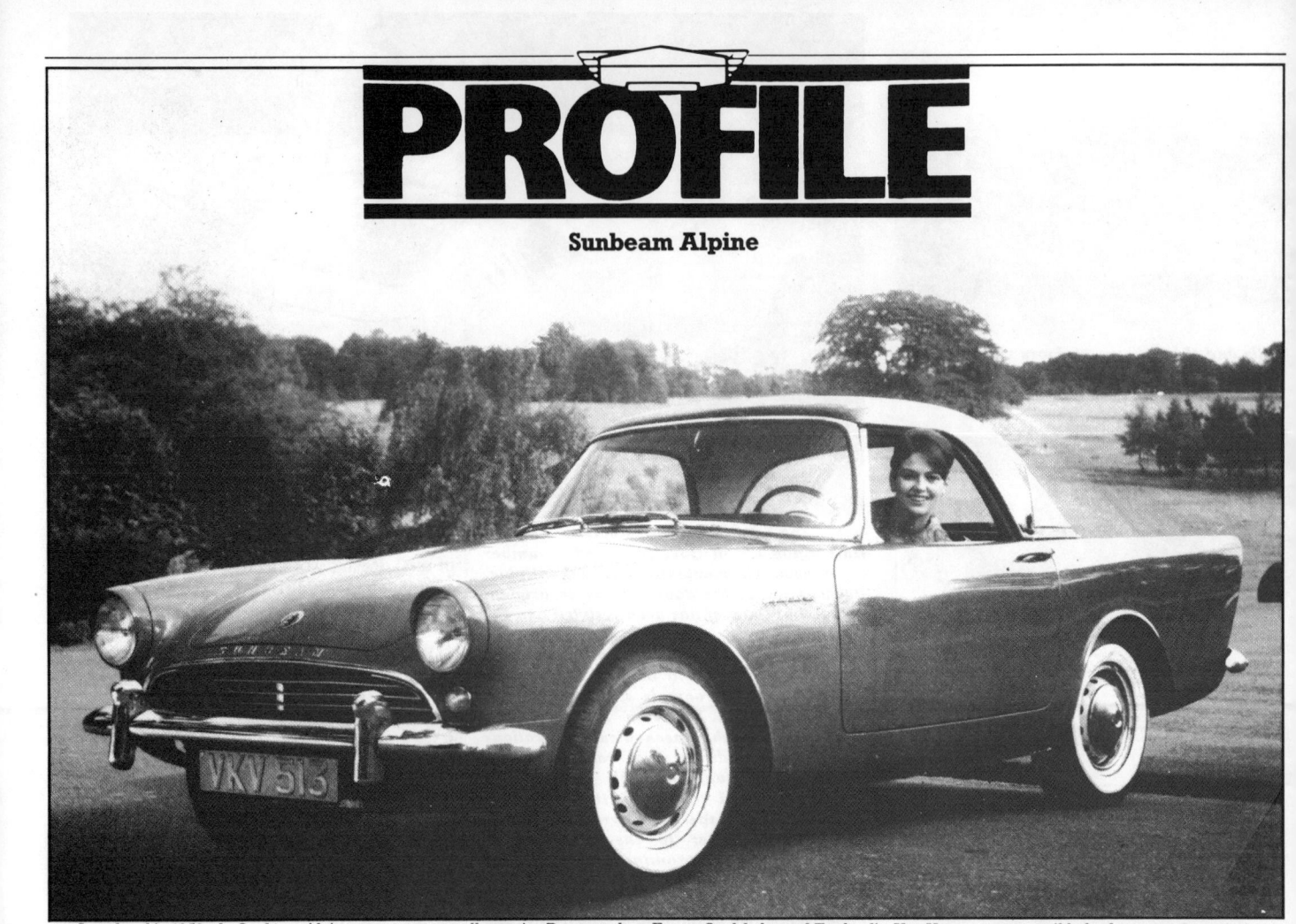

Introduced in 1959, the Sunbeam Alpine was an unexpectedly sporting Rootes product. Former Studebaker and Ford stylist Ken Howes was responsible for the trans-Atlantic looks

SOFT OPTION

Rootes' challenger in the late fifties sports car market was the be-finned Sunbeam Alpine. Has time dealt kindly with it? Mike Taylor tells the history while Richard Sutton investigates buying one today

Sunbeam Alpine's interior was spacious and comfortable

In the fullness of time, motoring historians and classic car enthusiasts may come to look upon the Sunbeam Alpine as a significant model in the evolution of The Rootes Group, that Coventry-based company which had almost as many changes of name as British Leyland. It is also significant that today, neither British Leyland, or rather Austin Rover, nor Talbot (*née* Chrysler, *née* Rootes) offer an inexpensive open sports car, much to many people's lament.

But let's get back to the Alpine (we are covering 1959-68 models for those who remember the earlier Alpine of the mid-fifties). At the time, Rootes was headed up by William 'Billy' Rootes and his brother, Reginald. They were, first and foremost, marketing men, but it is forever to their credit that in the late forties they gave the green light to the setting up of a competitions department, run by a very single-minded and determined man called Norman Garrad. Indeed, such was the success of Garrad's team, driving pretty unexciting machinery on the international rally circuits of the world, that Rootes found itself with a very active competitions department but, alas, no suitable models with which to take full advantage of the unexpected publicity. With interest in sports cars growing on both sides of the Atlantic, the market was moving into high gear. Rootes were determined to get a slice of the action.

A refined sports car

Style, finish and comfort were the hallmarks of Rootes models in the fifties. While companies like Triumph, MG and Austin Healey were manufacturing archetypal wind-in-the-face sports cars, Rootes were convinced that their car needed to be refined — some would say effeminate — by comparison, an image which stayed with the car until its demise.

Ted White, the man in charge of Rootes' styling studios for many years, gave the job of designing the new sports car to his chief appearance designer, Jeff Crompton. The brief was that the styling had to be up-to-the-minute, with elegance, grace and international appeal. Unfortunately, Crompton's proposals fell short of what Rootes management had in mind.

A more radical approach was needed — and this is just what they got when they enlisted the help of Ken Howes, an Englishman who had spent several years in America working for Studebaker and Ford. This experience had proved invaluable, and on joining Rootes, Howes brought fresh ideas to the design team. He was given a free hand to develop his ideas, and after a clay model had been produced the project continued with wind tunnel testing at MIRA. This was then followed up by the construction of a full-size mock-up painted a brilliant red (production colour became Carnival Red).

Swift design work

It was a tribute to the team, and to Howes in particular, that within 12 months or so of Howes taking on the project the finished model was on the viewing turntable in Rootes' styling studios for inspection by the Rootes Board. The Howes design was approved without hesitation . . .

Initial testing of the first prototype seemed to indicate that as a structure the monocoque body lacked integral strength. This was because the car was based on the chassis floorpan pressings of the two-door Hillman Husky estate car. The remedy was to add top-hat section bracing to the underside of the car between the wheelbase, and to fit strengthening stays between the inner wings and bulkhead (this method had proved successful on Rootes' other soft-top cars).

Meanwhile, at board level, another problem was being solved — that of arranging suitable production facilities. At the time, Rootes did not have the assembly space for their new sports car, so it was finally agreed that another Coventry-based company, Bristol Siddeley Engines Limited, should handle production on Rootes' behalf, at least for the time

The full sized mock up — in Carnival Red — as designed by Ken Howes and agreed for production by Rootes management

Underbonnet view of a Series 1 — note twin Zeniths

Harper (left) and Proctor (right) before Le Mans, 1963

being. In return, the Bristol engineers would help the Rootes development staff to produce a facsimile of the Armstrong Siddeley Sapphire engine to power the latest Humber Super Snipe.

Called the Sunbeam Alpine, the new sports car shared many of its mechanical components with the Rapier, although the Alpine's 86ins wheelbase was 10ins shorter. The front suspension incorporated unequal length wishbones with coil springs, anti-roll bar and Armstrong telescopic dampers, while at the rear, a rigid axle was supported on semi-elliptic leaf springs with Armstrong lever dampers fitted. It was not a particularly impressive suspension layout, but Rootes' engineers were aiming to give the car a quality of ride which would be unique among sports cars in this field. As it was, the car's handling was well matched to its performance capabilities.

The braking, too, was well up to the car's speed potential. The Alpine was the first Rootes car to use disc brakes — 9½ins Girling discs were fitted at the front, with 9ins drums at the rear. Considerable testing had been needed to overcome high pad wear, and eventually Girling — much to Lockheed's chagrin — got the Rootes contract.

The first Rootes ohv engine of 1390cc had been introduced in 1954, and then in 1958 it was increased to 1494cc and put in the Rapier. Although the Alpine power unit was identical in capacity to the Rapier's, Rootes' engineers made several basic alterations to give it more power. The cylinder block was new, with reinforcing ribs to give additional strength. The engine had three main bearings, and a crankshaft damper was added to the nose of the crankshaft to help reduce vibration. Also new was the all-alloy cylinder head, with special attention having been paid to the combustion chamber shape and valve angle in order to produce good gas flow. Exhaust gases were passed to single pipes which were brought together in pairs below the carburettors and then into a single pipe by the clutch housing. The compression ratio was set at 9.2:1, with fuel being fed into the cylinder head through twin Zenith carburettors. Power output was rated at 78bhp at 5300rpm, which the Rootes engineers considered would give the Alpine good performance for its 18¾cwt kerb weight.

The gearbox, too, was similar to that used on the Rapier, but with re-spaced ratios (with synchromesh on all but first). To bring the gearshift closer to the driver's hand, a remote extension was fitted. Laycock-de-Normanville overdrive was an optional extra, operated by a switch on the steering column. Where this was fitted, the final drive was reduced from 3.89:1 to 4.22:1. Drive was taken through a single dry plate 8ins clutch.

The Alpine's interior trim was well up on contemporary standards. Wind-up windows and wide-opening doors helped to give the Alpine a feeling of luxury, while a well-equipped dashboard, good seating and roomy interior added to this general air of elegance.

A 100mph car

The Alpine was shown to the motoring press in Cannes in August 1959, and to the public at Earls Court in October. *The Autocar* carried out a full road test in September, and found that performance, roadholding and economy matched those of its competitors. Overdrive top gave a maximum speed of 101mph, while 0-60mph took 14.0secs. It seemed that Rootes had almost achieved the impossible by producing a sports car which was both quick and docile at a price within reach of the average enthusiast. It looked good with the soft-top up or down and even looked right with the hard top in place — few other sports cars could claim that.

Just before the London Motor Show the following year, Rootes announced the Series II Alpine. As part of a development programme embracing all models, the 1½-litre engine was increased in size to 1592cc by boring out to 81.5m. Compression ratio was slightly reduced, torque increased from 89lb ft to 94lb ft and power rose to 80bhp at 5000rpm.

This change seemed modest, but most testers noticed the difference, remarking that the latest Alpine was more pleasant to drive, giving almost identical performance with less apparent stress. It was not possible to reach 100mph in a non-overdrive car. Other modifications included the re-arrangement of the pedals and seating (increasing legroom by 3½ins), wider rear springs and stiffer dampers.

As a cost-cutting measure in 1962, the Alpine's production was moved to Rootes' Ryton-on-Dunsmore plant, but demand remained buoyant, particularly in the United States where the stylish two-seater

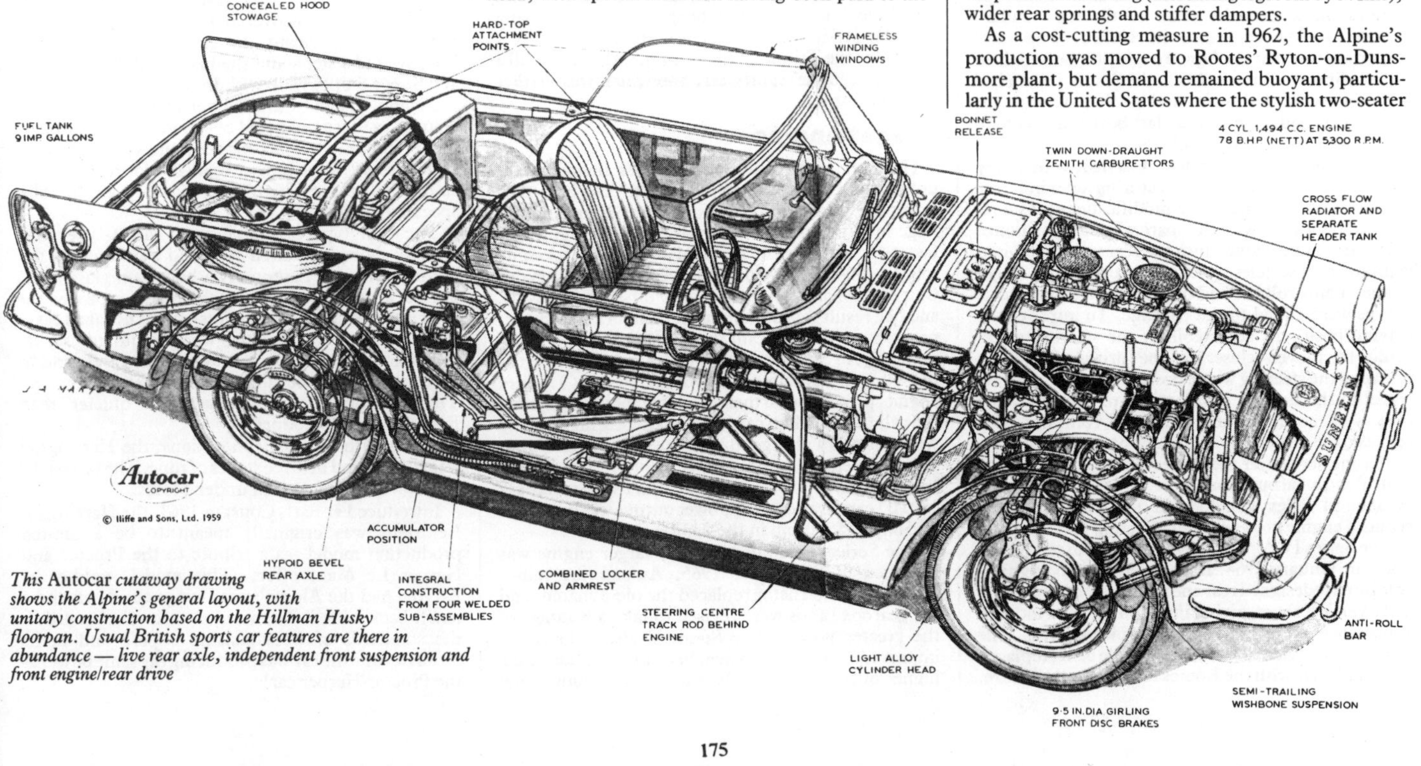

This Autocar cutaway drawing shows the Alpine's general layout, with unitary construction based on the Hillman Husky floorpan. Usual British sports car features are there in abundance — live rear axle, independent front suspension and front engine/rear drive

SUNBEAM ALPINE
Series I
SPECIFICATION
Engine	In-line 'four'
Capacity	1494cc
Bore/stroke	79mm × 76.2mm
Valves	Pushrod ohv
Compression	9.2:1
Power	78bhp @ 5300rpm
Torque	89.5lbft @ 3400rpm
Transmission	Four-speed (overdrive optional)
Final drive	3.89:1 (o/d 3.39:1)
Brakes	Disc front, drum rear
Suspension front	Independent by wishbones and coil springs, telescopic dampers, anti-roll bar
Suspension rear	Live axle. Semi-elliptic leaf springs. Hydraulic lever-arm dampers
Steering	Recirculating ball
Chassis	Unitary construction
Body	Steel, two door, two plus two seats
Tyres	5.60-13

DIMENSIONS
Length	12ft 11.25in
Width	5ft 0.5in
Height	4ft 3.5in
Wheelbase	7ft 2in
Kerb weight	2204lb

PERFORMANCE
Max speed (o/d 4th)	100.6mph
0-60mph	13.6secs
Standing ¼ mile	19.7secs
Fuel consumption	27.4mpg

Series II (where altered)
SPECIFICATION
Capacity	1592cc
Bore/stroke	81.5mm × 76.2mm
Compression	9.1:1
Power	80bhp @ 5000rpm
Torque	94lbft @ 3400rpm

PERFORMANCE
Max speed (o/d 4th)	101.1mph
Fuel consumption	26mpg

Series III
SPECIFICATION
Power	82bhp @ 5200rpm
Torque	93bhp @ 3600rpm
Final drive	3.12:1 (with o/d)
Tyres	5.90-13

DIMENSIONS
Kerb weight	2243lb

PERFORMANCE
Max speed (o/d 4th)	97mph
0-60mph	14.4secs
Standing ¼ mile	19.9secs
Fuel consumption	24.9mpg

Series IV
SPECIFICATION
Compression	9.2:1
Power	80.5bhp @ 5000rpm
Torque	93lbft @ 3500rpm
Final drive	3.39:1 (with o/d)

DIMENSIONS
Length	13ft
Kerb weight	2200lb

PERFORMANCE
Max speed	92.2mph
0-60mph	18secs
Standing ¼ mile	21.8secs
Fuel consumption	24.3mpg

Series V
SPECIFICATION
Capacity	1724cc
Stroke	82.5mm
Power	92.5bhp @ 5500rpm
Torque	103lbft @ 3700rpm
Final drive	3.388:1 (with o/d)
Tyres	6.00-13

PERFORMANCE
Max speed	100mph
0-60mph	12.9secs
Standing ¼ mile	19secs
Fuel consumption	25.5mpg

had won many new friends. Enthusiasts were even competing Alpines on the race tracks and in rallies, often with good results. The highlight came in 1961 when Peter Harper/Peter Proctor won the Index of Thermal Efficiency at Le Mans.

The introduction of the Series III Alpine at the 1963 Geneva Show brought some of the most radical changes to the car since its launch. The most important was that the Alpine could now be bought as either a Sports Tourer or a GT: the Sports Tourer had a PVC covered dashboard and a soft-top, while the dearer GT had a veneered dashboard and colour-keyed hard top — but no soft top.

The Series III hard top was re-styled, with a very much angular shape featuring opening rear quarter light. Among other modifications was a re-vamped boot area, with the spare wheel re-positioned and petrol tanks moved into the rear wings. Revised gearbox ratios, telescopic rear dampers, a larger diameter anti-roll bar and bigger, servo-assisted disc brakes were added to the package. To improve the driving position's adjustability, the steering wheel could be moved closer to the driver simply by releasing the steering wheel boss, moving the steering wheel to the desired position and re-tightening the boss — a novel feature. Microcell reclining seats replaced the earlier versions which had attracted some criticism. Soon after the Series III car appeared, the twin Zenith carburettors were replaced by a single compound Solex which, said the manufacturers, reduced engine noise without affecting performance.

The Series IV Alpine arrived at the Brussels Motor Show in January 1964. It was instantly distinguishable by its redesigned rear end: the fins were lower and had a vertical sheer, giving the Alpine a more modern appearance by making the back look less gross. The front was re-styled, the multi-bar grille being replaced by a single bar with the Rootes emblem in the centre.

The sidelight/indicator cluster was altered to conform with the latest regulations. Later that year, first gear was given synchromesh, and the corners of the doors and bonnet were changed from rounded to square.

By the mid-sixties, the Alpine had established its reputation as a well-finished, fast and refined sports car. True, it never created the same fanatic following that the MGB enjoyed, nor was the performance a match for the Triumph TRs, but the Alpine did fill a need for a 'tame' sports car, one which was neither harsh nor brutal.

Larger engine

However, in the background Rootes' finances were unhealthy. A crippling strike in 1961 had helped to turn their profits into losses the year after, and the huge investment in the Imp — being built at a new factory at Linwood in Scotland — had also taken its toll. In 1964, Rootes joined forces with the Chrysler Corporation as a way of trying to offset these losses, and one result was the announcement of a new model programme which meant the introduction of a whole new range of cars known as the 'Arrow' range. Part of the same programme was to update the 1.6-litre engine, producing virtually a new unit by redesigning the cylinder block to carry five main bearings. Along with this was a change in the stroke size to 82.5mm, giving the engine a cubic capacity of 1725cc. With a compression ratio of 9.21:1 and with twin Stromberg 150 CD carburettors, the power output was quoted as 92.5bhp at 5500rpm in the Alpine form.

The Series V Alpine with this larger engine was launched in September 1965. Among the minor changes, an alternator replaced the old dynamo, and the gearbox ratios were revised to take advantage of the greater power. The Series V also enjoyed an improved hood and stowage, better ventilation and a higher quality of trim. Over the years, though, the Alpine's bulk had slowly increased to the point where the kerb weight was now 20cwt. As a result, despite the increase in engine size and power output, the Series V Alpine's maximum speed remained at just about 100mph.

In January 1967, after several years of financial losses, Chrysler took over majority control of Rootes. Rationalisation meant the Alpine, the Tiger (its V8-powered sister), and the luxury Humber Hawks and Super Snipes were withdrawn.

Finally, a significant chapter of the Alpine story belongs to those produced by Thomas Harrington of Hove, Sussex. The Harrington Alpines were officially approved by Rootes, and took the form of quality coupé bodied cars, highly personalised and usually specially tuned.

The first type of Harrington, the A-type, was initially shown in March 1961 and was based on the Series II Alpine. Essentially a bolted on glass-fibre, fast-back style, hard top which greatly improved the car's interior space, the conversion was not at all easy. Substantial modifications were required inside (including all leather interiors in some cases) and to the chassis, but the results were extremely impressive. The Harrington was stronger and quieter than Rootes' original product.

Along with various trim options, the Harrington was also offered in three stages of tune. The fastest did 110mph and 0-60mph in under 11secs.

Introduced at Earls Court in 1961, the Harrington Le Mans was originally meant to be a limited production model, as a tribute to the Proctor and Harper Le Mans effort. This model, unlike the A-type, had the Alpine's rear wings cut down and a hatch-back added. The results were very beautiful, the standards of workmanship superb and in its ultimate tune the car was producing the same power as the Proctor/Harper car!

Buyer's spot check

The Sunbeam Alpine was a substantially built car. Both its build quality and structural strength were far superior to most volume produced sports cars in the sixties. Unfortunately, this strength is also the car's weakness — the car's complicated structure has water traps, and rust invariably starts from the inside and works its way out. It is for this reason that great care should be taken over pre-purchase inspection.

The first area to examine is the Alpine's chassis. If this, the last area to rust on the car, is 'shot' the car should be left alone. The chassis is made up of two outriggers and a central 'crucifix' cross-member arrangement, and it provides additional torsional stiffness to the unitary box sections. Raise the car by jacking points located at either end of the outriggers. Does the chassis creak? If this is so, treat with considerable suspicion.

Have a look underneath. It is conceivable on poor examples that the front legs of the crucifix may have rusted at the point they join the inner sills. These areas can be repaired, but rust here is a sure sign that the car is structurally risky.

Open the boot and remove the carpet. There are two box sections running fore and aft to the left and right of the boot floor, under which are the outriggers. Check for rust in these sections about 6ins forward of the rear valence. This is the point at which the rear spring hangers are mounted, and they may have rotted around the outriggers. It is a critical area, and is likely to cost around £100-150 per side to repair. Similarly, the front spring hanger points tend to rust through. Lift the interior carpets and examine the small sloping panels behind the front seats near the B posts — this is where the mounts are.

Alpines always seem to rust inside the entire length of the sill box sections and to the bottom of the A and B posts. John Timms, long time restorer of Alpines, always cuts away the outer sills along with the bottom of the front and rear wings on every car he receives for attention, regardless of apparent good condition. He has never known an Alpine to be rust-free in these areas. Naturally there is nothing the would-be buyer can do to ascertain the structural condition of inner box sections (there are three sills) which he cannot see, especially if the outer sills are spotless. Be cautious — if there is any sign of rust on the outer sills, problems with the inners can be guaranteed.

Tug on the handbrake handle and examine the mechanism's interior mountings as it is not unknown for them to pull free. Also check the seat belt mountings for rot.

Before putting the carpets back, close examination of the front footwells is advisable. The panels making up the wells are weather sealed with a *bastik* compound which becomes brittle and falls away, letting in the damp. This is not a difficult area to repair, especially if caught early.

Most reproduction body panels are now available for Alpines, and flat areas can be easily section repaired. From the front of the car working backwards, check the vulnerable front under valence, especially along its join seams. Examine the headlamp areas, the underbonnet edges of the front wings, and the rear of the front wing sides for bubbling. These areas are all easily repairable, so don't be put off too much if they're poor.

Door skins are vulnerable, but again replacements are available. Take off the inner door trim panel and examine the inner door well for signs of pending corrosion. While the panel is off, check the window winder mechanism as it is apt to pack up. The inner and outer rear wings suffer around the arch joins, and bad corrosion can attack the lower contours behind the rear wheel. This is a damp and dirt trap. Replacement is common.

That really covers the usual bodywork problem areas on Alpines. 'If 'your' car is a Series IV or V you may be able to detect scuttle rot problems below the windscreen. This is caused by the addition of an additional reinforcing panel which forms a water trap below the scuttle. Check the corners of the bonnet along the scuttle edge. If they're round, as on Series I, II and III cars, there should be no problem — square cornered bonnets indicate the modification! The factory Series

Harrington Le Mans: rare, beautifully made and desirable

Rootes advertising for the Alpine was hugely ambiguous

I and II hard tops are aluminium and should pose no problems, but the later angular design is steel and rusts behind the quarter lights.

Mechanically, Alpines are immensely rugged and reliable. Engine bays are often filthy as oil leaks are usual around the valve and pushrod inspection cover — don't let that put you off. The engine has no weak spots and reconditioned units are available cheaply should problems arise.

Alpine historian Chris McGovern recommends depressing the clutch while the engine idles at normal running temperature and listening to detect any noticeable drop in revs, or even an engine stall. Such symptoms indicate a worn crank thrust bearing. Most mechanical parts are available and no part of the Alpine's drive train is vulnerable or susceptible to undue wear.

To the best of our knowledge, new splined hubs are not available, so it is advisable to check the condition of these on wire wheeled cars.

An inoperative overdrive can probably be attributed to a dirty actuating solenoid — they are otherwise reliable. Gear changes on both manual and automatic 'boxes should be smooth and precise — whining from the 'box and back axle is a clear sign of wear and pending expenditure.

Clubs, specialists and books

There is only one club in Great Britain catering for the Alpine — the Sunbeam Alpine Owners Club, part of the Association of Rootes Car Clubs.

The SAOC was formed in 1977 by Chris McGovern. Membership quickly grew to 800 in just three years, and has now reached 1000. An excellent bi-monthly magazine, *Alpine Horn*, includes pages on area news, competitions, technical advice, and a classified section. Over 20 area meetings are arranged every month and one major national rally is held annually.

The club has turned its attention recently to spares location. It has arranged for several previously unobtainable chrome, rubber and lighting items to be reproduced, and is presently trying to persuade Girling to remanufacture brake servo units (or repair kits).

Club membership is £9.50 per year and is available from Lynne Goulson, 29 Church Street, Bonfall, Matlock, Derbyshire. Cheques should be made payable to the Sunbeam Alpine Owners Club.

Britain's largest supplier of used spare parts for Alpines is John Hayter, who runs the acclaimed Berkshire Sunbeam Alpine Centre. He deals in everything from new body panels, ball joints and carpets to second hand trim items and engines. He's based in Hermitage, near Newbury, Berks (tel: Hermitage 200368).

Margaret and Barry Farmer run Alpine West Midlands and are suppliers of new and remanufactured parts including rare trim, lighting and rubber items plus over 40 different body panels. They also carry out restoration work to a high standard and even have a purpose-made Alpine chassis jig. Another company with a good reputation, they are based at The Firs, Stratford Road, Hockley Heath, Solihull (tel: 05643 3222).

Danny Noakes specialises in the manufacture and supply of numerous Alpine panels to a very high standard. He is based at Unit 17, Bolney Grange, Hickstead, Sussex (tel: 04446 46055). Radford Panels Company Ltd at 2 Wise Terrace, Leamington Spa, Warwickshire are also manufacturers of replacement panels. They can be contacted on (0926) 313801.

The restorer of Alpines is John Timms, based at Drayton Garage, Barton Stacey near Basingstoke, Hampshire (tel: Long Parish 416). John has an impeccable reputation, having restored numerous Alpines and a fair sprinkling of XK Jaguars and pre-war Bentleys. His cars are often concours winners, his experience very substantial and prices reasonable. Be prepared to join the waiting list for major work.

If it's just mechanical work your Alpine or Tiger requires, Dave Muteham, the 'ex-Tiger Club spares man', is highly recommended. Dave is happy to undertake full blown restorations or just routine servicing and can be reached at DJ Garages (Sunbeam Specialist Services), rear of Flight Path Garage, Effingham Road, Burstow, Surrey (tel: 0342 715925).

Jeff Foss of The Family Repair Service deals in all aspects of Alpine trimming from re-upholstery to new hoods. Jeff is thoroughly recommended by John Timms and is available on (0264) 3144 or at 13 Eastfield Road, Andover, Hants.

The definitive Alpine book is undoubtedly Chris McGovern's *Alpine: The Classic Sunbeam*. This excellent work is a 250-page source book, and every Alpine owner should have a copy. Published by Gentry Books, it costs £9.95.

Richard Langworth's *Tiger, Alpine, Rapier*, published by Osprey, is a good deal less detailed, having to deal with three different Sunbeam models. It nevertheless complements McGovern's book well, including as it does interesting pictures and some finer details McGovern omits. It retails as £9.95, and is a gift for £2.95 as a limited special offer at Chater and Scott booksellers (01-568 9750).

There is also the inevitable Brooklands Book — *Sunbeam Alpine and Tiger 1959-67* — at £5.95 which combines a wide selection of contemporary US and British road test reprints in one volume. There is even a piece on how to race tune your Alpine from the pages of *Car & Driver*.

It must here be mentioned that the Sunbeam Alpine Owners Club also produced a similar style publication in 1984 which reprints just about all the road tests which the Brooklands book omits. It also includes much contemporary advertising. It is very nicely produced and good value at £3.50, but there aren't many copies left. Write now with a cheque made payable to the Sunbeam Alpine Owners Club to Chris Barker, 67 Preston Grove, Yeovil, Somerset.

The final publication of note is Mike Taylor's *Tiger, The Making of a Sports Car*. Although about the Alpine's American muscle engined brother, the book includes significant Alpine history. Priced at £10.95, it is published (now a reprint) by Gentry Books.

All the books detailed are hard-backed with the exception of the Brooklands and SAOC publications.

Rivals when new

Sunbeam effectively found a gap in the British market when they announced the Alpine in 1959. Here was a very pretty and competitively priced open sporting car which had all the creature comforts of an average saloon. No other car could lay claim to all that in one package.

Do you remember the contemporary Alpine advertising? All pretty blonde girls in Arran jumpers and head scarves. Well, when looking for a competitor to the Alpine, at least in its younger days, you would have had to supplement Arran jumpers with leather flying jackets and headscarves with woolly hats. The competitors, notably the MGA and Triumph TR3, were wet, windy, noisy and cold . . .

What pretty blonde girl with any self respect would put up with all that? Of course, they didn't.

Back to the cars! The MGA in MkII 1600 form was just under £50 cheaper than the Alpine at £967, and, while significantly more sporting, it was no quicker. The MGA hadn't the rear seating of the Alpine either, was no more attractive and lacked the Alpine's comfort. That blonde would have been unlikely to sacrifice her hair-do for the sake of a pair of side screens.

The TR3 was even worse. Even more wet, windy, noisy, and cold . . . But the 2-litre Triumph — a 110 mph car, with 100bhp at 5000rpm — was a good deal faster than the Sunbeam, and stopped more quickly than the Alpine too. As a sports car it was vastly superior, but as a civilised touring car it was miserable by comparison. The build quality wasn't up to much either.

By 1961 an Alpine buyer might have considered an Austin-Healey 3000 two plus two, although it was £200 more expensive than the Sunbeam. A very different character of car, it had a different appeal. The Morgan Plus 4 four-seater was competitively priced but lacked the sophistication and comfort of the Alpine.

Unfortunately, some very real competition to the Alpine was never imported into this country. The Fiat 1500/1600 Spiders, the Simca 1200S Cabriolet, the Datsun 1600 convertible and even the Renault Alpine 106 and 108 Cabriolets, are examples.

In Britain, the introduction of the Triumph Vitesse convertible in 1962 was the Sunbeam's first domestic threat in the 'soft' sports car stakes. The six-cylinder 1600cc Vitesse was every bit as civilised as the Alpine with the added bonus of real rear seats, more boot space and more mechanical refinement.

The MGB and Triumph TR4 were undoubtedly the cars to consider in 1963 before rushing to your nearest Rootes dealer, but the TR4 did not handle as well as the Alpine and cost nearly £100 more. The MGB was arguably a better car than the Sunbeam. It combined most of the Alpine's luxuries with the blood and guts of a true sports car. In Series V form the Alpine was nearly on par in performance, but the MG was always much more of a driver's car. In terms of accommodation, running costs and practicality, they were very similar.

The essential difference was that men bought MGBs, girls purchased Sunbeams!

Prices

There is no appreciable difference in value between the standard Alpines, although it should be said that a Harrington Le Mans (probably the most desirable version) will be worth substantially more than a Series IV GT Automatic (probably the least desirable of all the variants).

Series V cars will always be popular on account of their high specification, and similarly the finned Series I, II and III cars will consistently be in demand because of their classic/novelty/rarity value.

Condition is the over-riding factor. An Alpine ripe for restoration can be picked up (in pieces) for £200, while a concours car should reach £3500. If you are after a sound MoT'd car which will provide reliable daily transport and look presentable, be prepared to spend around £1500. The occasional car comes on to the market well above £3500 — witness the £7995 being asked for one at the moment — but that is well above the going rate.

OWNER'S VIEW

Anthony Perrett talks about the concours restoration of his wife's long-serving Alpine

Gill has owned her Series IV Alpine for over 14 years

"I have always been enthusiastic about the Alpine since its introduction in 1959," says Tony Perrett. But in those days a new car was a long way off for the owner of the immaculate red 1964 Series IV GT Automatic pictured in this 'Profile'.

"It was almost in a class of its own," Tony continued, "offering a unique combination of looks, sporting characteristics and refinement. Wind-up windows and removable hard-tops were virtually unheard of on sports cars in those days." He had grown to appreciate the well engineered and rugged construction of Rootes products, having relied first on a 1959 Rapier Series II convertible and then a Series IIIA saloon for everyday transport.

"The convertible was a wonderful car — a real poseur's machine. I clocked up around 10,000 miles in it, but it had to go when the chassis was so rotten the doors wouldn't close! The saloon covered a similar number of miles and, like the convertible, was incredibly reliable. The Alpine, as Rootes' latest product, and rather avant-garde, was a natural choice when my wife, Gill, needed a replacement car in 1970."

And so FMG 459B was bought from its fourth owner, Tony's cousin, for £330. "That wasn't cheap, but at that time the car was in very good condition and handsome on its whitewall tyres and wire wheels."

The Alpine was to lead a well used and unpampered life in Gill's hands. In 1978, with the children substantially bigger and rot well set in, the car was laid up. She lay untouched for about four years during which time Tony made half-hearted attempts to find body panels and a new shell. It was only comparatively recently, as the Alpine had begun to acquire a degree of classic status, that he decided the time had come to rebuild it.

"At the 1982 Stoneleigh Festival of Motoring I saw a prize winning Alpine that had been restored by John Timms of Drayton Garage, Barton Stacey, Hants. This provided me with the stimulus to get started. John agreed to restore the body, which was to be his 20th Alpine, and I spent evenings and weekends for the next five months reducing the car to a completely stripped rolling shell.

"The shell stayed at Drayton Garage for a further five months, and was rebuilt to a stunning standard. I intended to keep the restoration as close to the original specification as possible, and had the underside of the car zinc-primed, stone-chipped, reprimed, undersealed, and coloured red. It took me a little over another year to complete the restoration."

This was not a money-no-object rebuild at all, and much of the work was carried out in Tony's small garage at his home. The first item on the agenda was the front suspension, which was removed and dismantled. All the components were sand-blasted, etch-primed and brush-enamelled or cadmium-plated as appropriate, and the ball joints and wheel bearings were replaced. The rear suspension received similar attention. The brakes followed suit. They were rebuilt with new caliper pistons, pads, shoes and wheel cylinders. The discs Tony machined himself, the master cylinder and servo were reconditioned, and rust-proof brake pipes fitted.

Then came the fuel, electrical and ventilation systems, which received varying degrees of attention. The fuel tanks were sand-blasted and enamelled, and the transfer pipes cadmium-plated. The AC pump was reconditioned and copper fuel pipes fitted. The electrics were in generally sound order, but Tony was keen to replace as many worn items as possible with original factory parts, so a new starter motor, dynamo, battery and control box were fitted. The heater matrix required a rebuild complete with new water valve, and new hoses were fitted throughout the cooling system. The only other mechanical attention the car received was a reconditioned automatic gearbox (unusual in this country but common in the United States), bought as a 'claimed-new' unit for £50.

The wire wheels were stove-enamelled, and fitted with General whitewall tyres. Not unlike the car's original equipment, these were discovered by chance at a local tyre dealers, part of a batch of 10 bought in from the United States.

"Boot hinges and the filler cap were too poor to replate, and I used them as patterns for replacements which were sand cast in bronze. The casting quality wasn't very high, and I spent many hours drilling out pieces of slag, and silver-loading the pits. The end results are excellent."

The original carpets were used as patterns for replacements. Tony also opted to do this job himself, although an experienced carpet trimmer could doubtless have accomplished the same task in a fraction of the time.

Question of originality

"Options are divided on the question of originality of trim items such as seats and door panels. The interior can be completely replaced using non-original material, but difficulties arise in the heat welding. I preferred to use the original vinyl, replacing the backing panels where necessary, accepting that certain correct replacement parts would not be available after 20 years.

"The car is now complete and as original as I could make it. I had intended to use the car as everyday summer transport, but I have spent too much time and money to allow it to deteriorate. I expect I will now use it only under ideal conditions. This is a pity, but, as so many restorers have agreed with me, one must be satisfied that another example of a British sports car survives to be appreciated.

"I cannot impress enough how ideal the Alpine is to a first time restorer. I was continually amazed throughout the job at how easy Alpines are to work on. I have no motor engineer training and have never worked in a garage, but I can't think of a single occasion I ran into trouble. The only time I needed a second pair of hands was when putting the engine back, and that was for convenience rather than necessity.

"Anyone with a degree of common sense and patience can achieve what I have done, and as Alpines in fine condition are quite valuable, the exercise need not be uneconomic. My car, originally very poor, took 18 months to restore, was immediately shown at the IBCAM Motoring Festival in August 1984 and was placed third in class. The project has cost me no more than £3500, and I feel I can now rest assured that it is worth a good deal more than that."

PROFILE

THEY'RE GRRREAT!

With Carroll Shelby's secret formula, did the Sunbeam Tiger eat other performance cars for breakfast? Mick Walsh and Martin Buckley present a classic serial in the making...

'I think that if the figure of speech about the shoehorn ever applied to anything,' Carroll Shelby wrote in his biography *The Cobra Story*, 'it surely applied to the tight squeak in getting that 260 Ford powerplant into the Sunbeam engine compartment. There is a place for everything, but positively not an inch to spare. Still, the Sunbeam Tiger is a lovely road car; well mannered, fast and zippy. Pretty much as in the case of the Cobra, the Tiger allows you to do anything you like, because there's so much power to spare!'

If there is one habit American car culture is obsessed with it is 'mill swapping'. If the standard unit lacks performance, or those elusive mechanical 'innards' have cried enough and replacements can't be found, or are just too darn expensive, you can bet your bottom dollar that, before you can say Bob Bondurant, someone is planning to 'shoehorn' a V8 into that 'little ol' European sports job'.

There was none more respected at this art of mechanical transplants than the tall Texan. Somehow he made the old hot-rod philosophy respectable, and as cynical as discerning Europeans tend to be about Cobras and their brutal engineering methods, no-one can deny how effective they are. And perhaps more importantly, how much fun they are to drive.

It is too easy to forget that the Sunbeam Tiger is essentially the Cobra's cheaper brother, and that the same act of engineering wizardry that turned the AC Ace into a Cobra was performed under the very same roof on the Alpine.

The Tiger tale is well documented, but how many people are aware that it was Ferrari, no less, who were first approached to improve the performance image of the Alpine? Peter Collins even organised an audience for the Rootes competition manager, Norman Garrad, and Brian Rootes to meet the doyen of performance cars, but, not surprisingly, little came of the meeting. Rootes' financial problems in the early sixties meant it was impossible to develop a completely new engine, so the scenario moved to the West Coast where the Cobra was having a profound effect on Californian car culture. Ian Garrad, Norman's son and the sales manager for Rootes, was based in LA, and virtually all it took was an exhilarating ride in a Cobra in the fall of 1962 to inspire the idea of a V8-powered Alpine.

The heart of the Sunbeam Tiger – dressed to kill ...

Without delay, using $10,000 from an advertising and promotional budget, two prototypes were commissioned to be converted by Carroll Shelby and Ken Miles. The latter's conversion, a 'quickie transplant', was finished within weeks of being commissioned, utilising a Ford 260 engine with an automatic gearbox. The handling of this very basic 'trial car' was wicked to say the least, and after Ian Garrad's midnight ride with Ken Miles down the Golden State freeway, he later remarked to have 'furtively looked for the ejector button, and a place to change his underwear!'.

It did, however, convince Garrad of the project's potential. The Shelby American conversion was taken more seriously, and with the bulkhead cut back 4½ins for the new engine, the weight distribution was greatly improved. New rack and pinion steering was needed, borrowed from an MGA! The project took three months and cost just $8700, but Carroll Shelby was later paid a royalty on every Tiger produced.

After some very encouraging testing, the prototype was shipped uncrated to England on a banana boat. The rest is history: Lord Rootes' enthusiastic reception to the Sunbeam 'Thunderbolt' (as it was originally called), the biggest outside purchase of Ford engines (some 4000 initially) in the history of the Ford Motor Company, and the eventual development and production by Jensen.

In 1964, Chrysler acquired Rootes, but the Rootes contract for Ford engines was still in force, which later brought forth the Mk II Tiger, with a larger 289 engine and the original 'Powered by Ford 260' emblems replaced by simple 'Sunbeam V8' logos. Clearly the days of the Tiger were numbered under the new regime. Production eventually ceased in 1967 for several reasons, in particular the impending federal regulations (the very same that sounded the death knell of the Cobra) which would have meant costly modifications, and that would ultimately make the Tiger's price completely uncompetitive. The corporate discomfort between Ford and the new owner, Chrysler, was becoming an embarrassment, and the final sales were dropping fast by 1967. Without question, building 90 Tigers a month was not really Chrysler's cup o' coffee.

Why has classic status eluded the Tiger for so long? Is it the unglamorous heritage associated with the pretty Alpine which even today people seem reluctant to call a real sports car? Is it the bland association with the Rootes saloon cars? Or is it the unfounded reputation the Tiger has developed for lethal handling, which, in the wet, many claim is suicidal? Is it a prejudiced snobbery dismissing the Tiger fan club as custom car cowboys who lack any real sympathy with thoroughbred sports cars or is it simply that the car's rarity in Great Britain has never allowed enough enthusiasts to found their own opinions about the Rootes Rocket?

Is it prejudiced snobbery dismissing the Tiger fan club as custom car cowboys, who lack sympathy with sports cars?

At last it looks like the tide is changing, and a new regard for the Tiger is developing among classic enthusiasts, which to my mind is long overdue. In the *C&S* office, it was the HSCC's Post Historic Road Sports championship which first brought our attention to the merits and charms of this Anglo-American hybrid. The Tiger has always been fairly common in sprints and hillclimbs, but here for the first time was a serious attempt to prove the car against the fastest sporting road cars around, namely Cobras, Tuscans, E-types and the like – all serious market competitors in the sixties. This is no freak modsports championship, but a genuine road sports series which encourages contenders to drive to meetings.

A closer study of contemporary road tests, and driver comments, substantiates this misconception. Admittedly, with 164bhp on tap (200bhp with the 290 engine) in showroom spec and a rather stunted 7ft 2ins wheelbase, one would naturally anticipate very twitchy handling, particularly with a chassis based on the gentle Alpine's. But every road test I have read has nothing but good to say for the Tiger's road manners. In fact, two respected journalists were even moved to acquire Tigers as regular transport; Maurice Smith of *Autocar*, who owned two, and Gregor Grant, Editor of *Autosport*, whose driving style was by no means sober.

Typical comments from those that should know echo *Autocar*: 'The technique of power drifting, even in the dry, is particularly easy to control with the Tiger. One runs into corners on the overrun to a point just short of the apex, then unwinds the lock and stamps on the throttle at the same time. The tail slides out just so far, and then stops on its own as the weight transfers back under power, and adds to the rear wheel grip'. A less aggressive driving style at steady speeds 'produced just a trace of understeer with strong self centring action'.

Other comments were in a similarly enthusiastic

Facing: Tigers at rest. In the middle is Dave Duncanson's ex-Frazer racer, and clockwise from top right are John Arnold's Mk1, Corinne Bryan-Harris' modified 289 car, Don Pither's famous team rally car, David Barraclough's Shelby-style racer, Dave Herning's Mk1 260, Julian Balme's and Steve Burns' Mk1s with 351 Windsor engines. Thanks to all the owners who gave their time for this photograph by John Colley.

180

vein. *Cars & Car Conversions* stated: 'The handling was entirely predictable. In the wet, the car will adopt virtually any attitude you happen to want at the dab of the throttle', and concluded that they 'couldn't think of a more exhilarating way to spend a journey than by doing it by Tiger'. *Motor Sport* confidently stated 'that no combination of an American V8 and a British chassis could be happier', while American journalists were equally unanimous about the merits of the Tiger. 'Rootes are holding a winner by the tail,' claimed *Car & Driver*, whose readers voted it top in the sports car class in their annual poll. Everyone was convinced that Rootes, and Ian Garrad, the mastermind behind the whole Tiger project, had discovered a goldmine. All the road tests concluded that the new car provided 'amazing value for the price' … 'everything you'd expect from a high performance GT or sports car costing twice as much!'

The remarkable similarity of the Tiger's styling with that of the Alpine was surely a grave mistake in marketing the new performance car

The main criticisms were the 'furious kick-back from the front wheels to the steering wheel on bad road surfaces', 'an irritating axle tramp under hard acceleration', and on anything less than average road quality, the unsophisticted suspension really let the Tiger down. George Bishop of *Car* was probably one of the most critical of testers. During a journey to Italy (to visit Modena, incidentally) he found the car completely unsuitable for *Routes Nationales* at speeds over 90mph, which he claimed 'had us bobbing up and down as if in one of Mr Issigonis' older, rubber-sprung midgets, so that the maximum of around 115mph remained just a salesman's ballpoint'. His harsh words continued in his conclusion: 'The Tiger doesn't even come to the starting line. It's engine is as big as that of an E-type yet it is hardly in the same class in the performance and handling stakes'. I'm sure the nearly £600 price differential was quite a consideration to most potential sports car owners in 1967!

The remarkable similarity in almost every respect of the Tiger's styling with that of the Alpine was surely a grave mistake in marketing the new performance car. No-one can deny how pretty Kenneth Howes' original design for the Alpine was, but somehow, with such modest badging and chrome strips, the Roy Axe modifications seemed understated for such a fast machine. How many people, I wonder, simply passed by the new car at the New York and Turin Motor Shows in 1964, presuming it was yet another facelift of an Alpine design which had already been around for five years by then. More than anything, it was the wheel trims that really let the product down. I can understand why Rootes were keen to stay clear of the 'boy racer' image, but for a grand tourer to be graced with disc designs that looked like they had fallen off a Hillman Husky seemed quite incredible.

Facelifts were never a strong point at Rootes, which is clearly proved by the MkII Tiger. The chrome trim which was one of the saving graces of the Tiger's rather stunted lines was removed and replaced by an awful 'stick on' go-faster stripe, but at least the Alpine grille was restyled to give the car a more individual image. Other so-called refinements included rather nasty chrome wheel arch embellishments. The planned restyling for the MkIIA (had Chrysler continued production of the Tiger) was even worse, with heavy chrome sill covers, and tacky tiger motifs on the front wings, while the wheel trims remained identical to the early production cars.

It is not surprising that one of the first modifications owners made to their Tigers was to replace the wheels, in England with the latest Minilites, while on the West Coast with the attactive Los Angeles Tiger (LAT) option.

The associations with the underpowered Alpine cannot have helped the market image of the Tiger in England, although the *Q-car* potential of the Tiger at traffic light grands prix must have been irresistible. But in the car park at Silverstone, or at a country pub, the mistaken identity by the uninitiated must have been very frustrating, much like the proud owner of a new MGC. In America, the novelty value of a European sports car would have overcome the confused market image, I'm sure, not to mention the loyalty of the 'Powered by Ford' enthusiast, no matter how much Chrysler later tried to tone down the connection in all their advertising.

As much as Rootes wanted to avoid the macho aura of the Tiger during the sales programme, promoting the car more as a GT to boost their flagging sales image and to add some glamour to the range, the poor man's Cobra attracted a very different type of enthusiast over the years.

Customising became the order of things, with extended wheel arches, metalflake finishes, and, of course, every variety of mag wheel and fat tyre. Even today, at Tiger Club meets, personalised cars are very much the vogue, with extensive engine and chassis modifications.

Ian Garrad and Carroll Shelby had been quick to anticipate this demand, for there was no shortage of performance options, as they shared much the same origins as the Cobra. Once the enterprising old Texan became aware of just how well the Tiger was selling in the USA (over 5000 in total) he produced a multitude of dress-up and performance goodies from finned aluminium valve covers to glass-fibre air scoops for steel bonnets. In fact, these were all Cobra items with Sunbeam Tiger logos.

On the secondhand market in the seventies, particularly in England, the Tiger image suffered through the hot-rodding fraternity, exploiting and abusing the car's ultimate performance potential. It became a bargain basement sports car which seemed to attract only the brave at heart, and only recently has the Tiger's classic image been restored, with the car's nostalgic charm and Shelby connections becoming reassessed by enthusiasts.

With barely 800 Tigers sold in Britain, and an estimated 200 survivors, too few people have had that pleasure, and even fewer have had the impossible task of changing the plugs, or oil filter, or clutch. Now that's a 'whole different ball game …'

SPECIFICATION — SUNBEAM TIGER Mk1

Engine	V8
Bore/stroke	96.5 × 73mm
Capacity	4261cc
Valves	Pushrod ohv
Compression ratio	8.8:1
Power	164bhp (gross) at 4400rpm
Torque	258lbs ft (gross) at 2200rpm
Transmission	Four-speed manual
Final drive	2.88:1
Suspension front	Ind by coil springs, wishbones telescopic dampers, anti-roll bar
Suspension rear	Live rear axle, half elliptic leaf springs, Panhard rod, telescopic dampers
Steering	Rack and pinion
Brakes	Discs front, drums rear

DIMENSIONS

Length	13ft 2ins
Width	5ft 0.5ins
Wheelbase	7ft 2ins
Height	4ft 3.5ins
Kerb weight	2525lbs

PERFORMANCE

Max speed	117mph
0-60mph	9.5secs
Standing ¼ mile	17secs
Average mpg	17mpg

PRODUCTION HISTORY

Although the Sunbeam Tiger was given its first public airing at the 1964 New York Motor Show in April, production cars didn't begin to emerge from Jensen's West Bromwich factory until late June. For export only to North America and Canada at first, the car sold for $3499 in the USA, the options list consisting of a heater, radio, white-walls and hardtop. The first 57 cars used a Borg-Warner T10 manual gearbox, but this was replaced by a Ford top loader. Right-hand drive British market cars became available in March 1965, for £1446 in open tourer form or £1506 with steel hardtop. In August 1965 the Mk1a Tiger was phased in using different serial numbers, better ventilation, improved hood with storage boot and embossed door trims. The previous cars (which finished at serial number B9473756) were now dubbed Mk1 retrospectively.

The Mk2 Tigers went into production in December 1966, using a bigger 4.7-litre 289 engine – Ford hadn't actually offered the 260 since 1964. The 4.7 used stronger valve springs and threaded rocker arms, an alternator in place of a dynamo, and an oil cooler. It was mated to a wider ratio gearbox (with a bigger clutch), and the rear axle used traction master anti-tramp rods as standard. Cosmetically, the Mk2 featured an egg-crate grille, non-peaked headlamp rims, wheel arch/sill chrome mouldings and silver-painted wheels. The most noticeable additions were the stick-on racing stripes, which some owners removed. Inside, the front seats were shaped and pleated rather differently, and the steering wheel position was raised. The Mk2 Tiger was not officially marketed in Britain, but 17 examples are said to have slipped through the net and six of these became police cars. Production ceased on June 30, 1967. A total of 7066 Tigers were sold to the public, which breaks down into 4669 Mk1s, 1826 Mk1as and just 571 Mk2s.

CLUBS, SPECIALISTS & BOOKS

The Sunbeam Tiger Owners Club has been around since 1975, and membership is essential if you are planning to buy, run or restore one of these rare cars. The annual subscription is £12.50 (£15 for overseas members), and the club currently has about 280 members to whom it sends out a regular magazine called *Cat's Whiskers*. Those members with competition leanings can go racing under the club's 'Team Tiger' banner. More details of the STOC's many other activities can be obtained from Carolyn Murray, 'Oake Cottage', 390 Fencepiece Road, Chigwell, Essex IG7 5DY.

As the popularity of the once unloved Alpine has increased, then so has the Tiger owner's chances of finding the parts and services he needs. As well as body panels, the Berkshire Sunbeam Alpine Centre has new and reconditioned brake, suspension, trim and electrical parts for the Tiger, and can be contacted at Hermitage, nr Newbury, Berkshire RG16 9RD (tel: Hermitage 200368). Sunbeam Specialist Services tackle mechanical and electrical repairs plus bodywork restoration and trimming: call at DJ Garages, Effingham Road, Burstow, Surrey (tel: 0342 715925). Alpine West Midlands is one of the best known specialists in this field and can supply all kinds of body, suspension and trim parts, as well as offering a restoration service. Their address is The Firs, Stratford Road, Hockley Heath, Solihull B94 5NJ (tel: 05643 3222). The Radford Panel Company makes and supplies any panel and can be found at 2 Wise Terrace, Leamington Spa, Warwickshire (tel: 0926 313801). Danny Noakes is also a panel and repair section man, and can be contacted at Unit 17, Bolney Grange, Hickstead, Sussex (tel: 04446 46055). American Autoparts are noted suppliers of Tiger engine components and are located at 132-134 Brigstock Road, Thornton Heath, Surrey (tel: 01 684 7737). Any Tiger work

Mustang 4.7-litre (289) engine as fitted to MkII Tiger

Attractive facia and controls of MkI Sunbeam Tiger

Recent 44-strong gathering at Lanhydrock, Cornwall

Two coupé prototypes were prepared for Le Mans, 1964

Ian Garrad was responsible for creation of Tiger

Only known picture of Tigers being made at Jensen

can be tackled by The Sports Car Clinic, Unit 1, Riverside Industrial Estate, Thames Road, Barking, Essex (tel: 01 594 5868).

Tiger – The Making of a Sports Car by Mike Taylor (£10.95) should be on every Tiger enthusiast's bookshelf as it is easily the most detailed work on the subject. This 219 page volume records the car's prototype, production and competition career and also features a chapter of practical information. The appendices are particularly complete and informative. Despite its title, *Tiger-Alpine-Rapier* by Richard Langworth (£9.95) is really a general overview of the Rootes Group's fortunes during the forties, fifties and sixties, with a certain bias towards the sporting models. Nonetheless, it's quite lively and the author makes no secret of his love for these cars, the Tiger in particular. It runs to 175 black and white pages, 20 of which are devoted to the V8-engined car. Brooklands Books produce an excellent collection of magazine reprints *(Sunbeam Alpine and Tiger 1959-67)* for a reasonable £5.95. Perhaps the best Tiger book, but hard to find, is William Carroll's *Tiger – An Exceptional Motor Car*, published by Auto Book Press. The author introduced Ian Garrad to Shelby, and still owns the original prototype.

BUYER'S SPOT CHECK

Obviously, much of what we said in the Sunbeam Alpine 'Profile' (March 1985) applies here, and although only about 800 Tigers remained in Britain, there are still quite a few waiting to be restored. If you do manage to find a Tiger that needs major work, then it shouldn't cost much more than a humble Alpine to restore, assuming its engine and drive-train are in good order.

First of all, be prepared to get on your hands and knees and have a good look round the Tiger's 'chassis', really just a couple of sturdy rails reinforced by a cruciform bracing section with the unitary bodywork built on top. On really poor cars the front legs of this bracing section rot where they meet the sills, while the cross member in the middle of the car is also susceptible, particularly where it is drilled to allow the exhaust through. Rusted rear spring hangers can be clearly seen under the boot carpet, and the front hangers can be viewed under the carpet behind the rear seats. It is crucial to check that the seat belt anchorages are safe. Water gets into the front footwells from inside the wheel arches (they are sealed rather than welded to the wings), so make sure you have a good look underneath the carpets. Inner sills rot in a big way, so if there's visible rust on the outer section you can assume the worst. Don't forget to check all the jacking points and the Panhard rod mounting.

All these points are expensive to repair (and everything ends up looking twice as bad once you start cutting back), so even if you are searching for a ground-up restoration project, make sure you don't bite off more than you can chew ...

The condition of the outer panels is less critical, and pretty self-evident. The front wings 'go' around the headlights, on the edges inside the engine compartment and at the bottom where they meet the sills. A vertical line of bubbles often develops behind the wheel arches, and the panels on either side of the engine around the inner arches are among the first sections to go, although they are easily repaired. Another point to watch at the front is the valance, which rusts around its seams. Examine the rear wings around the wheel arches and at their lower extremities behind the wheel. Doors are prone to corrosion along the lower edge of their skins and on the well of the inner frame. If the car has a hardtop, check around the quarter lights and corners for rot. Virtually every panel and repair section is available for the Tiger, and they are generally easy to fit.

The Ford small block V8s used in the Tiger are ludicrously understressed, and regular maintenance seems to be the key to a long and trouble-free life. If the oil is not changed fairly frequently (about every 4000 miles), the bearings can fail, although if this should happen then at least the shells can be changed with the engine in the car. Because it is such an awkward task, oil filter replacement is often ignored on these engines and if the unit misfires then an HT lead has probably melted: this is due to the heat the big V8 generates in such a tight engine bay. The carb is a two stage affair by Autolite and is prone to flooding.

There isn't much to say about the rest of the drive-train except that the Salisbury rear axle is reliable but becomes vocal in old age. The Ford top loader gearbox is very strong and well able to cope with the engine's demands. While the front suspension presents no special problems, it is important that the steering rack is not leaking, and speeding wear – this component was specially produced for the Tiger and is no longer available. Also check for wear in the bronze bushes at each end of the rack, and look at the state of the fragile rear leaf springs.

Although the Tiger's interior is basically similar to the Alpine's, it's worth noting that certain instruments are special to the V8-engined car. While examining the interior, make sure that the none-too-reliable window winders are working.

The Tiger lends itself to performance modifications, and a few cars have had engines of 5-litres or more fitted. Obviously, this detracts from the originality, but improves on the already very adequate performance ...

In the seventies, many spares for the Tiger and Alpine were hard or impossible to come by, but today the outlook is much brighter, and improving all the time. The body panels are all shared with the Alpine and – with the exception of the steering rack – virtually all parts that were special to the Tiger are now available. As mentioned earlier, the engines hardly ever go wrong, but if anything should happen then your local American car specialist can supply parts and knowledge.

While a really rough Alpine is probably a waste of time and money, a Tiger in similar condition could be worthwhile, particularly if the asking price is right or the car is an unfinished restoration project with many spares included in the deal. On the other hand, sound cars aren't astronomically expensive, and the Tiger must still rate as one of the most exhilarating open-topped cars for the money.

183

RIVALS WHEN NEW

As the Tiger was created with North American sales very much in mind, one should look at the competition it faced in the USA from the new breed of 'pony cars' being offered by the big three.

It was the ultra-competitive Ford Mustang that started it all, with its strong V8 performance and massive range of options. In stock form it was really no more exciting to drive than the average Yankee barge but it did have price and (arguably) looks on its side. Much the same could be said of the Plymouth Barracuda, even if this 'glassback' car never really matched the Mustang's charisma or sales success. Chevrolet's Corvair Monza Turbo couldn't have been more different from the usual run of 'pony cars', with its rear-mounted air-cooled turbo flat-six and sophisticated, almost European, styling. Once the handling had been tamed it was probably the nearest thing the Americans had to a low cost sports car, even if its actual performance wasn't that sensational. The Corvette? That was an altogether more muscular car, and really in a different price and performance league from the Tiger.

Back in Europe, quite a few cars were making use of American power, but few were true sports cars in the under £2000 price bracket. The V8 Griffith and Tuscan TVRs qualified in this respect, but they went about their business in a much more brutal manner – they also used Ford engines of 4.7-litres. It's hard to think of a car more opposed to the Tiger concept than the Lotus Elan, but its excellent performance and similar price put it in direct contention. Staying with the glass-fibre theme, the Reliant Scimitar coupé was a possible alternative, and with the later V6 engine, its performance wasn't that far behind.

The Austin Healey 3000 was in its declining years by this time, but it was still a worthwhile buy because of its competitive price and wholesome performance. The Volvo P1800 was a costly beast for the performance it offered, but its appearance was distinctive and it was quite well-made. The P1800 actually shared Jensen factory space with the A-H 3000, but made way for the Tiger in 1964. If you could afford the extra outlay then there was always the Jaguar E-type roadster but, like the Corvette, it was really a different sort of car. Had the Daimler SP250 lived beyond 1964 then it would have been a serious Tiger rival, even if it was more of a grand tourer than a road burner.

PERFORMANCE COMPARISON

	Max speed	0-60mph	Price
Sunbeam Tiger Mk1	117mph	9.5secs	£1471
TVR Griffith V8	119mph	7.2secs	£1400
Austin Healey 3000 MkIII	122mph	9.8secs	£1188
Chevrolet Corvair Turbo	114mph	10.2secs	n/a

PRICES

Very few Tigers were sold in Britain, and it is estimated that perhaps 150 remain on British roads today. There are maybe that many again awaiting restoration or some other fate. Happily, although prices have been creeping up over the last few years, they have managed to remain realistic and you can still obtain a Mk1 for hundreds rather than thousands. The handful of Mk2 Tigers that were sold in Britain usually change hands by word of mouth for a considerable price premium.

A car under £1000 is obviously going to be poor in just about every area, but with such a good spares situation these days it is possible to restore cars like this, given enough time and money. £1500, give or take a couple of hundred either way, seems to be the going rate for less dilapidated Tigers needing major chassis work before they can even get a sniff of an MoT. If you want to get straight down to the business of using your Tiger, then sound cars come in at around £3000 to £3500, but you can go as high as £5750 for a really excellent car.

OWNER'S VIEW

Corinne Bryan-Harris has already owned two Tigers, and before that she had a horse …!

Corinne Bryan-Harris regularly upstages the 'macho-men' of the Tiger Owners Club in her 'personalised' 289 Sunbeam Tiger

Corinne Bryan-Harris was an irresistible choice for our Tiger owner's view. As if the novelty of a female Tiger tamer was not tempting enough to investigate, Corinne has a reputation of being one of the fastest drivers in the Tiger Owners Club.

The sight of the 'Flying Flea', as her personalised (the term customised offends her) metallic sky blue 290 Tiger is known, at Curborough charging into the first bend, over the rise and into a wild spin has been the talk of the Club's barbeques all summer.

"I've always had a competitive nature, first athletics at school and then horse gymkhanas. I've simply swapped one horsepower for 200! It's not an easy car to sprint, but that moment at the start is brilliant. My throat tightens, and I get a tingling sensation at the finger tips on the steering wheel.

"None of the lads in the club seem to mind when I'm quicker, besides, they encouraged me to have a go in the first place. They look after me really well, although the tactical advice about corners isn't so forthcoming now. Mum, however, never asks what I get up to – I think she's frightened to death by the whole scene. It's a great shame Dad's not around (he died six years ago) to witness my competition with Tigers as I'm sure he'd have loved it. He was a mechanic, and loved cars. He was the proud owner of a Stag so V8s seem to run in the family!

"I think my interest stemmed from him, although I've always loved speed. The big dipper at Blackpool was always an addictive thrill when I was a kid, and I'd always played with Dinky Toys and mechanical toys rather than dolls! My passion for Tigers began about nine years ago when a friend came round with a really scruffy 260.

"I just had to get more involved, so I put an ad in *Exchange & Mart* under the Sunbeam section: 'Anyone interested in Tigers, please contact …'. There was no reference to my sex, but within a day, a Midland member was on the doorstep. He even let me have a drive, the trusting fool, down the motorway and from that moment on, the Tiger bug had well and truly bitten."

The 'Flying Flea', so-called because of its registration number FLE 517C, is in fact Corinne's third Tiger.

"The first, a very standard Mk1 with a 260 engine, was in 1979. It was midnight blue and a good, straight car. I had a lot of fun with it, but just craved for something a little faster and more jazzy. It's an irresistible temptation when you own a Tiger to personalise your car a little.

"My second Tiger was another 260 in carnival red. It was mechanically very sound and had led a much easier life … until then! It looked really great with Wolfrace wheels, and a custom interior. The car was very reliable, and I began doing Tiger Club trials, driving tests, and treasure hunts. I've fond memories of that car but it seems to have disappeared from the scene now.

"The latest is the best so far. I'd always fancied one with a 289 engine, and this one's very individual. All Tigers should be I think. We resprayed it metallic blue and re-upholstered it in grey leather. We've also widened the wheel arches and fitted a bonnet scoop just to make the car look even meaner.

Last year Corinne and her fiancé Neil, thankfully another Tiger fan, took the 'Flying Flea' on a 3000 mile trip to Switzerland to an International Tiger meet. "It was the best holiday I've had. All those mountain bends and Alpine passes, and everywhere we went the Tiger caused a great deal of attention – a little more than usual probably because it was driven by a woman!

"We had no overheating problems (it was midsummer), although it must be said we fitted a high efficiency core into the radiator. The Tiger's only complaint was a smoking clutch on the Alps, and we averaged about 21mpg on the whole trip. Even when sprinting, it only drops to about 18mpg. I must confess Neil does most of the maintenance work. My lack of strength prevents me getting more involved." Neil, however, was quick to point out that Corinne has a sharp mechanical sympathy, and can tell what's wrong with the car before most men.

What is the biggest attraction of Tigers for Corinne? "Well, it has to be their brute force. The beast is always a real challenge to drive fast, and I'm still learning in sprints. But I think more than anything, it's the temptation to burn up lads in Escort XR3s. You can hear them at traffic lights – 'look at the little girl in the nice little sports car'. They all think it's an Alpine."